War, Peace and Social Change in Twentieth-Century Europe

This reader is one part of an Open University integrated teaching system and the selection is therefore related to other material available to students. It is designed to evoke the critical understanding of students. Opinions expressed in it are not necessarily those of the course team or of the University.

War, Peace and Social Change in Twentieth-Century Europe

edited by
Clive Emsley, Arthur Marwick and Wendy Simpson at the Open University

Open University Press
Milton Keynes · Philadelphia

Open University Press
12 Cofferidge Close
Stony Stratford
Milton Keynes MK11 1BY

and
1900 Frost Road, Suite 101
Bristol, PA 19007, USA

First published 1989

British Library Cataloguing in Publication Data

War, peace and social change in the twentieth-century
    Europe: a reader
    1. Europe. Social change. Influence of World War 1 &
    World War 2
    I. Emsley, Clive   II. Marwick, Arthur, *1936–*   III.
    Simpson, Wendy
    940.5

    ISBN 0-335-09291-8
    ISBN 0-335-09290-X (pbk)

Library of Congress Cataloging-in-Publication Data

War, peace, and social change in twentieth-century Europe/edited by
    Clive Emsley, Arthur Marwick, and Wendy Simpson.
        p.   cm.
    Includes bibliographical references.
    ISBN 0-335-09291-8   ISBN 0-335-09290-X (pbk.)
    1. World War, 1914–1918—Causes.   2. World War, 1914–1918
—Influence.   3. World War, 1939–1945—Causes.   4. World War,
1939–1945—Influence.   5. Europe—Social conditions—20th century.
6. Social change.   I. Emsley, Clive.   II. Marwick, Arthur, 1936–
III. Simpson, Wendy, 1941–   .
    D521.W34   1989
    940.53′11—dc20   89-38919 CIP

Printed in Great Britain by
St Edmundsbury Press Limited, Bury St Edmunds, Suffolk

Contents

Acknowledgements

Open University Press would like to make grateful acknowledgement for permission to reproduce the following material.

1   Ian F.W. Beckett, 'Total War', *Warfare in the Twentieth Century: Theory and Practice* edited by Colin MacInnes and Y.D. Sheffield, pp. 1–23, London, Unwin Hyman.
2   Arno J. Mayer (1981). *The Persistence of the Old Regime*, pp. 1–15, 17–23, 77–8, 79–88, 135–7, 186–7, 189–91 and 322–3, Beckenham, Croom Helm.
3   G.D. Josipovici (1970). 'The Birth of the Modern: 1885–1914', *French Literature and its Background* edited by John Cruickshank, Vol. 6, pp. 1–20, The Twentieth Century, Oxford, Oxford University Press.
4   Micheal R. Gordon (1974). 'Domestic Conflict and the Origins of the First World War: The British and the German Cases', *Journal of Modern History*, No. 46, June, pp. 191–226.
5   Anna Bravo (1982). 'Italian Peasant Women and the First World War', *Our Common History: The Transformation of Europe* edited by Paul Thompson and N. Burcharat, pp. 157–170, London, Pluto Press.
6   Gerald D. Feldman (1966). *Army, Industry and Labor in Germany, 1914–1918*, pp. 519–41, Princetown, Princetown University Press.
7   Charles S. Maier, (1975). *Recasting Bourgecis Europe: Stabilization in France, Germany and Italy in the Decade after World War I*, pp. 3–15 and 579–93, Princetown, Princetown University Press.
8   MacGregor Knox (1984). 'Conquest, Foreign and Domestic in Fascist Italy and Nazi Germany', *Journal of Modern History*, No. 56, pp. 1, 4–6 and 43–57, Chicago, The University of Chicago Press.

9   Norman Rich (1986). 'Hitler's Foreign Policy', *The Origins of the Second World War Reconsidered* edited by G. Martell, pp. 119–39, London, Unwin Hyman.

10 R.J. Overy (1982) 'Hitler's War and the German Economy: A Reinterpretation' *Economic History Review*, 2nd Series, Vol. XXXV, No. 2, pp. 272–91.

11 Stanley Hoffman (1961). 'The Effect of World War II on French Society and Politics' *French Historical Studies*, Vol. 2(1), pp. 28–63.

12 Penny Summerfield (1986). 'The Levelling of Class', *War and Social Change, British Society in the Second World War* edited by Harold L. Smith, pp. 179–207, Manchester, Manchester University Press.

13 Edward Bubis and Blair A. Ruble 'The Impact of World War II on Leningrad', *The Impact of World War II in the Soviet Union* edited by Susan J. Ling, pp. 189–206, New Jersey, Rowman & Littlefield.

14 Mark Roseman (1988). 'World War II and the Social Change in Germany', *Total War and Social Change* edited by Arthur Marwick, pp. 58–78, London, Macmillan.

Introduction

Arthur Marwick and Clive Emsley

What do we mean by social change? Some historians conceive the answer in quite broad terms, in terms, indeed, of shifting patterns of dominance, of changing structures of power, of groups and classes overthrowing or replacing or reaching accommodations with each other, of, perhaps, a bourgeois class replacing a landed class and then, say, of the bourgeois class skilfully fending off the claims of a 'rising' working class. The Introduction to the Open University course, *War, Peace and Social Change*, in conjunction with which this Reader has been designed, suggests a different approach which, rather than dealing with broad shifts in power relationships, tries to get at the detail of social change by defining ten overlapping areas: social geography (including basic population statistics, distribution of urban and rural populations, etc.); economic and technological change; social structure (including questions of 'class' etc.); national cohesion (questions of ethnic composition, etc.); social reform and welfare policies; material conditions; customs and behaviour; women and the family (however, this grouping is not to be taken as implying that the role and status of women cannot be discussed independently from the family); high and popular culture; political institutions and values.[1]

What do we mean by total war? How is total war distinguished from other kinds of war? It is common practice to refer to both 'the Great War' of 1914–18 and the 'Second World War' of 1939–45 as total wars, and to see the former as the first total war in history. Questions then arise about how true the second generalization is, and about how far there were critical differences between these two wars. What is the relationship, if any, between the Great War and the revolutions which broke out in various countries towards the end of it? Between that war and the rise of Fascism and of Nazism? What are the differences, and what the links, between total war, other international wars, revolutions, civil war and 'internal war'?

How do wars come about? As total wars, did the two major wars of the twentieth century have essentially similar origins? Were they perhaps just two instalments of one massive conflict? Or were the assumptions and conditions obtaining in 1914 very different from those of 1939? Can we make a distinction between long-term 'structural' and 'ideological' forces making for war, and more immediate political and military decisions? What are the possibilities, if any, of a negotiated peace during the course of a total war?

In the popular mind, the two world wars loom large: to many in the 1920s, the world of 1914 and before seemed very remote; people in the 1940s, too, had the feeling of having lived through cataclysmic change. What exactly is the relationship, if any, between these wars and social change? To give a rigorous answer it is not good enough simply to list changes that took place during or after the wars. It is first of all vital to identify the other forces which, entirely independently of war, were making for social change. And, if we are to get an accurate assessment of the effects of war, we have to be absolutely clear what the various European countries were like in 1914, and again in 1939, *before* each war. Whether the wars did have significant consequences within any, or all, of the ten areas of social change already identified, and, if so, how much, is a matter for careful exploration. So too is the question, if the wars did have social consequences, *why* exactly was this so? Can it be possible that wars (which, after all, are in their very nature immensely destructive and negative) touch off processes which do actually bring about social change? Social change apart, obviously the wars have had important geopolitical consequences: the First World War, for example, greatly reduced the power of Russia in Europe; the Second World War greatly increased it. All over Europe, at the end of each war, boundaries were redrawn.

In effect, these opening paragraphs have identified four themes (each containing further sub-themes): the nature of social change and the form it takes in different countries; the nature of total war, other kinds of war, war's relationship to revolution, etc; the causes of war; the consequences of war. In this Introduction we shall be attempting to indicate the ways in which each of the essays which follows contributes to one or more of these themes. But there is something else. Right at the start it was suggested that there are two rather different ways of looking at the question of social change. Now, it is the case that historians often do bring different approaches to bear on the sorts of issue with which this book is concerned. One hallowed way (it goes back to the late nineteenth century) of defining the way approaches differ is to say that some historians adopt a *nomothetic* approach (one which, rather in the manner of the natural sciences, seeks to advance and refine theory and tends to make use of broad explanatory categories), while others prefer the *idiographic* approach (one which stresses the uniqueness of historical events and developments and tends to stress precise detail). The division is not a hard-and-fast one; most historians recognize that their subject does differ significantly from any of the natural sciences, while, at the same time, most of those who avoid general theories do recognize the need for generalization and the exploration of structural interrelationships: many historians, it could be said, incorporate elements from both approaches. Thus, a simpler and less rigid way of identifying differences of approach might be to speak, on the one hand, of historians who are 'more-theoretical', and, on the other, of historians who are 'less-theoretical'. Still another way would be to distinguish between historians who are *strongly* influenced by the ideas of Karl Marx, or the ideas of Max Weber, or perhaps by elements from both, and historians who, while probably recognizing the important intellectual contributions made by both Marx and Weber, do not give any special weighting to their theories about social change or structures of power, preferring to follow where their primary sources lead them. (Thus this latter approach might also be described as 'source-based', save that most Marxist historians would claim, very reasonably, that they too place great emphasis on the primary sources; as a further alternative to 'less-theoretical' or 'source-based', there is the label 'liberal humanist', usually used by critics of this approach.) This elaborate discussion has been necessary because although differences of approach are widely recognized to exist, there is no agreement on how they are best defined, *nomothetic* and *idiographic* being at best very crude labels. Yet it can be absolutely crucial to know what kind of approach a particular historian is following, since the approach may very well determine the assumptions attaching to such terms as 'class conflict' or 'corporatism', or, for example, influence what conclusions are presented about the significance, or otherwise, of war. A historian who gives greatest weight to long-term structural change may well play down such 'short-term' influences as those brought about by a particular war. However one defines the differences, there can be no denying that the distinguished authors of the essays that make up this book do differ in their approaches to historical study. 'Know your historian' is always good advice to any student of history. Thus for the purposes of this Introduction we have a fifth theme, the 'historiographical' one, the question of the different approaches followed by the different authors. In following up this theme, we hope to bring out particular points of originality or utility in the essays which might otherwise be missed, and, as relevant, to indicate where issue may be taken with their authors.

The first essay in this volume, 'Total War', is by a military historian. However, Ian Beckett's concerns are not those of the traditional military historian; battles, campaigns and generalship are replaced here by a broad introduction to current debates among historians about the nature of 'total war' and its effect on social change. This puts the focus of the essay directly on the second and the fourth of our themes. Beckett begins by charting the way in which the study of war has changed over the last thirty years; before the 1960s war was generally conceived as having a negative or retarding impact on social development. It might be noted as illustrative of this point how many history courses, and how many history books, used peace treaties as their opening paragraphs and wars as their full stops. But increasingly from the 1960s, war, in Beckett's words, has been perceived 'as a determinant of major social change'. It is flattering to see the prominence given to the History Department of the Open University here, and particularly to one of the editors of this book, but perhaps we should not be too bashful and seek to hide our lights under a bushel.[2] Of course there is a difference between accepting that war can produce major social change and agreeing with each and every analysis of the kind of social change brought about by war; controversy and debate are central to the practice of history. Having described the way in which historical thinking has focused on war, Beckett goes on, in the meat of his essay, to discuss some of the new areas of research and some of the current controversies. He suggests that, while the scale and impact of twentieth-century total wars are new, yet these wars are, in many respects, a natural progression from earlier conflicts. What is central to the new studies of war and society is the insistence that war, however appalling, cannot be considered purely in terms of disaster. Beckett notes some of the research which indicates that, in some places, war led to increased living standards and decreases in infant and maternal mortality. The demands of twentieth-century wartime economies have produced changes within the labour forces of the combatant states: often more women have been employed; trade unions have increased their bargaining powers; but, at the same time, skilled labour has found itself diluted. All of these are issues which are touched on again in some of the essays that follow in this volume. Finally, Beckett provides a word of warning about some of the shibboleths which have emerged from the two world wars: the 'war generation' and the 'people's war' are both evocative terms utilized by politicians and adopted, at times rather uncritically, by historians, but what do they really mean when analysed?

The second reading in the volume is extracted from Professor Arno Mayer's challenging monograph *The Persistence of the Old Regime*, a work conceived as 'a Marxist history from the top down . . . with the focus on the upper rather than the lower classes'.[3] The extracts included here touch on almost all of our themes, but primarily we have included it for the way that it addresses the nature of social change in Europe before World War I, and thus lays the bases for an assessment of the effects of the war. Mayer believes that the two World Wars of 1914–18 and 1939–45 are best understood as 'The Thirty Years' War of the general crisis of the twentieth century' (p. 45); it was only as a result of these wars that the old order reconstituted itself in 1918. This is asserted rather than discussed in relation to the evidence, and a later chapter in this collection takes a very different interpretation. Central to the argument of this book is Mayer's insistence that historians have concentrated too much on the modernizing elements within European society before 1914 and have consistently ignored the strength of the pre-industrial, pre-bourgeois order which constitutes his 'old regime'. While considerable historical research has concentrated on tracing industrialization in nine-teenth-century Europe and on charting the growth of an industrial and financial bourgeoisie, Mayer points out that the European economies of 1914 were grounded in petty commerce, consumer manufacture and, above all, in labour-intensive agriculture. Moreover it was landowner-ship which provided most of the wealth, and landowners, drawn pre-dominantly from old-regime families, who dominated society and the organs of government. Far from challenging the cohesive and self-confident old regimes, the rising bourgeoisies were divided among themselves and the most successful individuals among them generally sought to emulate their social superiors or to worm their way into their ranks. Of course there were national differences: France had abolished her monarchy; and Britain was exceptional in not having the largest proportion of her labour force engaged in the agricultural sector of the economy. There were also regional differences, with varieties of consti-tutional monarchy in Britain and Italy contrasting with the rigid, absolutist monarchies of eastern and central Europe. Yet the underlying structures, Mayer insists, were the same; even in the realms of art, the avant-garde and various modernist movements 'were effectively bridled and isolated' by the cultural establishments which both leaned on and propped up the old regime.

Mayer's work falls within the *nomothetic* approach which we outlined above, and he believes that 'no comprehensive historical vision is possible without recourse to organizing generalizations and principles'.[4] The inclusion of these extracts thus relates as much to the fifth as to the first of our themes, while the concluding pages address directly the causes of war – our third theme. It is a pity that Mayer chose to eschew footnotes and references in the book, yet to employ so many apparent quotations; nevertheless, he writes with considerable rhetorical power and he deploys formidable knowledge in describing both Europe on the eve of World War I and the forces operating within it both for and against social change. Yet even the most brilliant works of history, however good at setting a scene and persuasive in argument, need to be approached with caution. The view that Mayer puts forward about the persistence of the old regime has already been proposed by others, though generally within the context of a single national experience and without his authoritative and comparative sweep of the whole continent including Britain[5] – and as an Englishman and a Scot we feel duty bound to criticize his use of 'England' in place of 'Britain'. The principal prob-lem with the book is that, writing a 'Marxist history', Mayer understands classes as essentially factors of production, and while this is a perfectly respectable stance both within, and outside of, a Marxian tradition, it leads him to persist in describing aristocracy and bourgeoisie as inherently separate classes, even when discussing the interpenetration between them, as for example on p. 52 and especially on p. 64. It also leads him, from time to time, to address what the European bourgeoisies ought to have done in fulfilling some predestined historical role, as, for example on p. 53, where he writes of their impairing 'their own class formation and class consciousness', and again on p. 63 where he implies that the leaders of the class should have done something other than line up with the nobility. Similarly, towards the end of the extracts, he seems to be addressing culture as something linked directly to class, a view which is challenged in the third chapter here.

The third essay, 'The Birth of the Modern: 1885–1914' by G.D. Josipovici, may seem an eccentric choice in at least two respects. First, with regard to the period covered: while, as the title makes clear, the essay delves far back into the nineteenth century, it terminates in 1914 and thus does not even touch upon either of the two world wars. Second, since it is exclusively concerned with trends in high art (in particular, poetry, music and painting), it may seem very remote from the central concerns of the student of history. There is possibly a third oddity in that the essay is reprinted from a collection entitled *French Literature and its Background*. Let us take these three points in reverse order. First of all, although Josipovici was providing background for a book on French literature, in fact he covers the whole of Europe. The arts are international: even if one were to be so parochial as to wish to study only British high culture, one would still have to discuss the Europe-wide antecedents of modernism. This is exactly what Josipovici does. On the second point, the riposte is simple: if we are to have a full understanding of the development of Europe in the twentieth century, we must have a grasp of the main lines of cultural change. There are various ways in which one evaluates a society, or a continent: by its political institutions, by its economic achievements, for instance; but not least is the evaluation of its products in the realms of high art. If we are to assess the significance of the two world wars, we must make an assessment of their effects on culture. This takes me back to the first point. If we are to assess the influences of war, we must, as has already been said, have a clear understanding of the base-line. In the textbooks you will find all kinds of sweeping statements about war poets, war novelists, Nielsen's 'Inextinguishable' Symphony, Elgar's Cello Concerto, Britten's 'War Requiem', German Expressionism as it developed immediately after the First World War, and so on; but we cannot pin down the influences of war (if any) until we know how the arts were developing in the period before the war. In a nutshell, modernism, the key movement in the arts in the twentieth century, was not initiated by the First World War. This, with rigour and clarity, is explained by Josipovici. That is why his contribution is so important to the study of war, peace and social change. It is, let this be admitted frankly, only a preliminary to the studies with which we are concerned: but angels get the preliminaries sorted out first, while fools rush in regardless.

The central sentence with regard to our concerns (in this case, the fourth theme, the consequences of war) occurs on the second page of Josipovici's chapter (p. 73):

> Although the First World War effectively marks the break between the world of the nineteenth century and our own – both in the minds of those who lived through it and of those of us who read about it in the history books – the modern revolution in the arts did not take place during the war or immediately after it, but a decade or so before it.

But that is not the end of it. Historical writing should be a dialogue between reader and historian. Josipovici makes his case most efficiently. Unlike many writers, he sets up a clear question (in his second sentence, devoting the rest of the essay to answering it):

> What are the specific features of the [modern] movement, and how are we to account for its emergence?

We as readers may well feel bound to accept Josipovici's account, but while it would be difficult to argue that the modern movement in the arts was created by the First World War, that does not mean that, within the framework set by modernism, it is not possible to tease out specific developments affected by the war. To do this, of course, we would have to turn both to primary sources (artistic works and contextual documents relating to them) and to secondary authorities dealing with the effects of the war. Many such secondary authorities have indeed suggested that the First World War was so catastrophic, so disillusioning for human- itarian liberals believing in the inevitability of human progress, that it had a 'scorching' effect on intellectuals and artists; the American literary critic Paul Fussel has stressed how the tragic irony of the First World War entered into literary consciousness.[6] All this needs further study far beyond the scope of this collection; but – and this is the point – any such study needs to be conceived within an analysis of modernism such as that provided by Josipovici.

Josipovici's analysis, readers will surely not be surprised to learn, is far from uncontroversial. Josipovici does not fall into the *nomothetic*, more theoretical, or, to look the matter in the eye, the Marxist tradition. What he does do is exemplify certain methodological points which readers, whatever tradition they favour, should grasp to their bosoms. Ponder over Josipovici's second paragraph: he fully admits that there is no specific thing called 'modernity', yet through setting up a 'frame of reference' it is possible to identify something important which quite appropriately can be called 'modernism', even if it is something as much

reacted against as accepted (third paragraph), even if individual exponents of modernism loathed, or ignored, or never knew, each other
(p. 72). When Josipovici speaks of being wary 'of too facile an identification of art with the culture and society out of which it springs', the
implicit criticism is of certain Marxist writers: he emphasizes the un-
changing *forms* of art – very important again if we are to make a genuine
assessment of the influences of war on the arts.

The importance of Chapter 3 in this collection, then, is that it provides
a basic understanding of the nature of modernism in the arts against
which one can assess the influences of the two world wars, and also that
it offers some general reflections on the relationship between the arts
and society, helpful also for this particular endeavour. It is in the context
of these two points that, first, some comments on Josipovici's text will be
made; the discussion will be concluded with some further general points
on the relationship between total war and the arts. Essentially what
Josipovici is arguing is that modernism is both a *development* of Romanticism, and a *reaction against* certain aspects of latter-day, or decadent,
Romanticism. Thus, of course, he has to say quite a deal about Romanticism, and particularly its later forms. To develop his arguments about
late Romanticism he, very properly, quotes in the original French from
some key primary sources: you may not find the translations we have
inserted particularly clear, but, read on – the confused expression of
these utterances is exactly the point Josipovici is about to make. As a
reaction against Romanticism (p. 72), and indeed a reaction against
four centuries of western artistic tradition (p. 81) modernism stresses
the *limitations* of the arts. In summary:

1 Art is simply itself, not a key to the universe – brush-strokes on a
  canvas, notes played in certain combinations, etc. (p. 79).
2 Art is 'a pair of spectacles' helping us to see things in a different way
  from the lazy, unthinking, habitual way in which we see them – it
  'makes the spectator work' (p. 80).
3 Art no longer claims to be 'magical', but simply represents itself as a
  'game' with its own rules (p. 83).
4 While art is recognized as being supremely important, it is recognized
  that it is helpless to change the world – this is all part of a 'modest'
  retreat from the exaggerated claims for art made by the Romantics
  (p. 84).

Furthermore:

5 Modern art breaks with a long tradition in which art had simply
  attempted imitation (or, to use a posh word, *mimesis* – a most important point taken up by Paul Fussel in his study of literature and World
  War I). Thus there tends to be a break with the anecdotal tradition.

Some of the later Romantics believed that music somehow had a
freedom which language did not have. Josipovici makes a valuable point

on p. 77 when he remarks that 'music is nearly as conventional as speech': when discussing the relationship between society, wars, revolutions, etc. and the arts, it is always important to consider the particular 'languages' of the different arts. Josipovici brings out the long-term significance of modernism (which extends far beyond the chronological framework of our own studies) when he says it is 'first and foremost a rethinking of the whole field of aesthetics as it had been seen in the West since the time of Plato and Aristotle' (p. 86). If that seems a little removed from the concerns of the student of history, consider what Josipovici says on p. 79 where he speaks of 'the connection between decadent Romanticism and the rise of totalitarianism'. Josipovici is referring to Stalin's Russia, Hitler's Germany, and Mussolini's Italy. A later chapter (by MacGregor Knox) raises questions about the connections between the latter two and total war (our second theme). Josipovici is pointing to another element; certainly it is true that the 'totalitarian' regimes were very hostile to modernism. One cannot refrain from commenting that Josipovici is grossly unfair to Wagner: however it remains a legitimate question whether there is a link between Romantic mysticism, the exploration of ancient folk legends, central to many of the operas of Wagner, and the mystique of Hitler's Nazi philosophy.

On p. 79 there is a highly quotable, though fictional, phrase which captures the essence of the decadent, and rather arrogant Romanticism of some elements in upper-crust society at the end of the nineteenth century – 'as for living [as distinct from experiencing art], our servants can do that for us'. Could such an attitude persist after the First World War? After the Second World War? On p. 86 Josipovici refers to the pessimism of the twentieth-century artist (however much he may hark back to the wit of the eighteenth century). A major question which Josipovici doesn't go into is whether, in so far as artists show a sensitivity to horror, violence, and evil, this is a reaction to general developments in the twentieth century, rather than just to war: a question that has to be asked is whether artists respond directly to the evil of war, or whether they simply see war as part of a wider evil characteristic of the twentieth century as a whole. Perhaps the greatest literary parable of German history in the twentieth century is Günther Grass's *The Tin Drum* (1959). Is the Second World War central, or is it simply a facet of the whole nightmare of twentieth-century German history? If one is to analyse the relationship between war, peace, and social change, that is the sort of issue one must pin down. Although, as noted, the dates appended to Josipovici's title confine the essay to the period before the First World War, he does in fact refer to later writers: Joyce and Proust, whose great works straddled the First World War, Virginia Woolf, whose main works came in the aftermath of the First World War, Robbe-Grillet, one of the pioneers of the 'new novel' of the 1950s and 1960s, Picasso, at work all through the horrors of the twentieth century, and Francis Bacon, whose international successes as a British artist came only after World War Two. (Can it be, perhaps, that while wars do not affect artistic styles, they may help to make 'modern' styles acceptable to a wider audience? Is it true that World War Two – the 'people's war' – brought a reaction away from modernism towards realism?) Josipovici also refers on his first page to Stravinsky, and on his last to the Russian Ballet: reminders again that modernism in music had hit Paris some years before the First World War broke out. At the end of the essay, Josipovici identifies Paris as a uniquely important cultural centre, different, it would seem, from London, or Berlin, or Vienna, or Rome (a later essay discusses the significance of Leningrad). Occupied Paris in World War Two was the setting for the very close interpenetration between war and culture represented in the poems of Louis Aragon and the short novel by 'Vercors', *Le Silence de la mer* [*The Silence of the Sea*].[7] Cultural studies, indeed, keep bringing us back to historical 'reality' as more conventionally understood.

The origins and immediate causes of World War I have long exercised a fascination for historians, both those who relish the detailed scrutiny of diplomatic and military decision-making, and those who, like Arno Mayer, analyse long-term structural trends. The fourth essay is extracted from a much longer conceptual article (based on an analysis of the writings of others, not on primary sources) by a political scientist, Michael Gordon, and relates above all to our third theme. Like most recent analysts of the war's origins, Gordon takes as his starting-point the seminal books of the German scholar Fritz Fischer, *Griff nach der Weltmacht* and *Krieg der Illusionen*, translated into English respectively as *Germany's Aims in the First World War* and *War of Illusions*.[8] Fischer's first book was a lengthy study of German war aims which argued that the Wilhelmine Empire, a new nation with a burgeoning economy, was prepared to risk war in order to establish herself as a world power on a par with much older established powers like Britain and France; thus far Fischer was dealing essentially with structural issues. But the book also included a detailed study of the 'July Crisis' which followed the assassination of Archduke Franz Ferdinand, and this analysis placed the blame for the outbreak of World War I squarely on the Kaiser and his advisers; they encouraged the Austro-Hungarian government to take a strong line against Serbia, fully conscious of the fact that this could lead to war, and, as the crisis escalated, so they failed to take any steps to calm the situation even though they were probably best placed so to do. Indeed, Fischer maintained, rather than easing the situation they attempted to impede last-minute mediation. Gordon describes the blow delivered by Fischer's work to a traditional explanation of why wars begin, which was rooted in diplomatic history and which suggested that historical conclusions could be reached by a detailed analysis of diplomatic documents and an assumption that decisions respecting peace or war were made based on considerations of state power and prestige compartmentalized by the decision-makers as 'foreign affairs' and separated from 'domestic politics'. It is, however, probably fair to say that Gordon rather overstresses the novelty of his argument here; after all it was as long ago as 1933 that Eckhard Kehr published *Der Primat der Innenpolitik* (literally 'the primacy of internal politics'), a book to which Fischer has acknowledged a debt. Gordon is critical of Fischer's work in as much as it singled out Germany as a culprit and focused on the policies of Kaiser Wilhelm's government; and this is a criticism which could be levelled at most of those who have concentrated on the 'primacy of internal politics' in seeking the origins of World War I, since nearly all of this work has concentrated on the German experience. All of the great powers of Europe went to war in the summer of 1914; they had all experienced strikes and social unrest in the years before the conflict, but is it really conceivable that their leaders simultaneously all resolved to, in the words of Shakespeare's Henry IV, 'busy giddy minds with foreign broils'? Gordon does not take the line that all can be explained with reference to internal politics. Rather he compares and contrasts the influence of Germany in the run-up to the war, and during the crisis of July 1914 particularly. He finds similarities between the internal problems of the two states during the period, notably economic dislocation, social strife and developing constitutional crisis. These problems, he suggests, played a significant role in the way that the two governments approached the crisis, yet the outcomes were different. In Britain domestic issues tended to reinforce defensiveness in foreign policy; in Germany, in contrast, where domestic conflict seemed more latent, the repercussion was an aggressive diplomacy.

Chapter 5, 'Italian Peasant Women and the First World War' by Anna Bravo, fits firmly into our fourth theme, the consequences of war. Indeed, the argument over whether or not twentieth-century wars have, or have not, resulted in improvements in the conditions and status of women is one of the most intense in the whole area of war and society studies. With regard to our fifth, historiographical, theme, Bravo's essay is also important as an example of the feminist influence on historical writing (in her very first paragraph she announces a general theme, 'the relationship between women's conditions and external historical moments – between women's history and "great" history') and, also very important, as an example of a very effective use of 'oral history'. If you turn to the notes, you will see that apart from the very few references to secondary sources, this essay is entirely based on the oral accounts of women interviewed by the author and her collaborator; the account given in note 1 should be read carefully. At first sight it seems almost astonishing that this method could be employed for events as remote as the First World War and, of course, from the dates of birth given in the notes we can see that the women interviewed were very old. It is a fact encountered in research of this type that elderly women tend to be much more coherent in recounting their memories than men of similar age. Certainly the quotations cited in the text seem very clear and offer convincing testimony to the value of the oral approach. The fundamental consideration is that for this particular sort of topic – dealing with the poor, who leave few written sources – very little other evidence exists.

In general (though, of course, the complete picture is more complex and nuanced than that) feminist writers have tended to contest the thesis that wars bring opportunities and gains for women: overall, understandably enough, feminist writers have been concerned to stress the continuing subjugation of women, to argue that the main trend in wartime was the further exploitation of women in the interest of the war effort, that hard manual work for women was nothing new, and that even if there were some changes during the war, these were always short lived. Where women have made gains, these are usually attributed by feminists to the activities of politically conscious women's movements (the suffragettes, for instance) or to longer-term economic and technological changes which were in any case drawing women into new forms of employment. As is often the case with carefully argued and well-documented pieces of historical writing, Anna Bravo's essay does not point conclusively in one direction or the other. She speaks boldly in the opening paragraphs of 'the transformation of women's social conditions in the countryside during the First World War' and of the war appearing 'as a moment of primary importance', and she certainly demonstrates conclusively that women did take on new tasks and new responsibilities. With regard to long-term effects she seems to be indicating that while many changes were temporary, some were permanent, while there were perhaps also losses. Bravo speaks of a growth in 'self-realization' and here fixes on a point which other writers, both feminist and non-feminist, have agreed to be important, the change in 'mentalities', the way in which women gained in self-confidence because of their war experience. The answer Bravo seems to be giving is that outside of their community, in dealing with state officials in particular, the role of women did expand permanently, but that within the community they were 'forced back into traditional peasant silence'. Read the article very carefully, try to let the evidence of the women themselves speak directly to you, and decide which side of this equation presented by Bravo carries the greater weight. You will need, of course, to set this study within the wider context where, for instance, Italian women, unlike those in many other European countries, did not gain the vote at the end of the war. You might wish to ask how far the forces of traditional Catholicism served in Italy to hold back progress which women elsewhere were beginning to make.

Chapter 6, 'Epilogue to *Army, Industry and Labor in Germany, 1914–1918*', unlike Chapters 3, 4 and 5, is not a self-standing, self-contained essay, but like Chapter 2 has been taken from a substantial book, in this case Gerald Feldman's famous and thoroughly documented study of *Army, Industry and Labor in Germany 1914–1918*, published in 1966 but still a standard authority. What we have printed is in effect the Conclusion, and we have also decided to include the Appendix, which in the original follows immediately, and which consists of one of the key documents in this study, the Auxiliary Law of December 1916. This Reader, of course, is intended as a collection of secondary sources, but the opportunity of presenting an important primary source which is redolent of the changes in relationships between workers, unions, employers and government brought about by the experience of total war seemed too good to miss. This chapter relates both to the fourth theme, the question of the social consequences of the war, and to the second theme, the question of the relationship of the war to revolution and, within that, the nature of the revolution as it actually took shape in Germany. The phrasing of Feldman's title is in itself significant: he is concerned with the relationships between three broad 'factors', or 'agents', or, as he puts it once or twice in the Epilogue, 'interest groups'

army, industry and labour. Feldman, then, is one of those American historians (he is a Professor at the University of California at Berkeley) strongly influenced by the German sociological tradition in historical writing (less obviously so than Charles Maier, author of the next chapter; and Feldman is in no way a Marxist in the style of Arno J. Mayer).

Explicitly in the Epilogue, Feldman is concerned with why changes taking place during the war were so limited, why the revolution at the end of the war did not accomplish much more, and with the connections between the war and post-war period and the advent of Hitler (the main body of the book has concentrated very meticulously on the war period itself). The basic theme, one might say, is that the war experience brought a good deal less social change than it might have done, and that the revolution was a most unsatisfactory one. Yet, if one changes the focus, and concentrates less on the might-have-beens, or ought-to-have-beens of revolution, and more on what, as compared with the pre-war situation, did actually change, one may glean some positive points from Feldman's scrupulous and delicately balanced account. If one wished to give credence to notions of war as test, and war as involving participation (concepts mentioned by Beckett in Chapter 1) then some of Feldman's comments might be cited in support. In approaching the chapter it is most important to see that above all it is about relationships between the three broad categories of army, industry and labour – by which Feldman means organized labour, the unions and the official Social Democratic party, it being one of his most important points that these organizations often failed to represent the real interests of the workers. The leading figures who feature in the Epilogue, are Groener (representing the army), Stinnes (representing industry), and Legien (representing labour).

In common with a number of other leading historians (including Charles Maier, author of Chapter 7) Feldman makes much use of the concept of 'corporatism', a process in which government, industry and labour leaders deal directly with each other in making major decisions, thus bypassing the constitutional organs of representative government. Feldman argues that corporatism (or, in his alternative phrasing, 'the effort to make the interest-group alliance the center of the socioeconomic decision-making process') formed the basis of the war economy and was continued in the post-war years. (Mussolini openly boasted of establishing a corporatist system in Italy; undoubtedly there were strong elements of corporatism in Weimar Germany; how appropriately the term can be applied to Britain and France is a matter of some contention.) Feldman leans even further towards a social science approach in speaking (in his opening sentence and first footnote) of 'substantial rationality' and 'functional rationality'. In essence, his argument is that the different interest groups he is concerned with followed their own immediate short-term interests ('functional rationality'), while completely failing to consider the wider interests of the country as a whole ('substantial rationality'). Feldman is particularly critical of the union leaders (this is partly because Feldman, almost unconsciously, accepts what is fundamentally a Marxist premise, that there *ought* to have been a full working-class revolution – 'their task, if anything, was to legitimize the Revolution by giving it their full support'). In a very central sentence, he says of the union leaders:

> Unhappily, they were so opportunistic, so habituated to the struggle for the attainment of immediate goals within the existing socio-political framework, and so fearful of disorder, they were willing to settle for an immediate and illusionary success.

Later he pins down how 'functional rationality' bound the different interest groups together:

> As the Stinnes–Legien Agreement bound the industrialists to recognise the union in return for union protection of employer interests, so the Ebert–Groener alliance bound the army to support the Republic in return for the Republic's support of order.

Feldman, then, while using broader 'sociological' categories, is, as is appropriate to one of the world's leading authorities on Germany in this period, concerned specifically with developments in Germany linking the war, the revolution, the Weimar Republic, and the advent of Hitler to power; he is not concerned with generalizations about relationships between total war and social change. He is concerned with the way in which arrangements established during the war and continued afterwards set severe limits on the nature of the German Revolution. His first paragraph, nevertheless, could be seen as making quite a powerful statement about the 'test' effects of the war, which 'led to the final disintegration of the Bismarckian state', exposing the inadequacies of the Emperor, the bureaucracy, the army, and the Reichstag, and the destructive characteristics of the existing class structure. In the next few paragraphs Feldman is concerned to show that the labour leaders threw away the opportunities offered to them by their necessary *participation* in the war effort; he does recognize the fact of this participation, the securing of the Auxiliary Service Law, and the movement towards co-operation with labour on the part of many industrialists. What Feldman brings out well is that there were both gains and losses for labour. The notion of the 'leaving certificate' (without which a worker during the war could not change his job) was fiercely resisted in other countries (particularly Britain) where it was introduced: yet a scrutiny of Paragraph 9 of the Auxiliary Service Law, and of other paragraphs, does show that in terms of status as a negotiating power with the authorities, labour had gained enormously over its pre-war situation. However, Feldman's conclusion is that the agreements labour leaders entered into did 'much to prevent the thoroughgoing political and social reconstruction required by the failure of the old regime'.

Feldman insists that full agreement between the industrialists and the organized workers came only at the end of the war (when the strength of the latter was clearly apparent), not during the war: at that moment (this is very relevant to the second theme, and the nature of the Revolution) 'the bankers and leading industrialists were among the first to demand the abdication of Emperor William II'. The containment of the Revolution Feldman attributes to the permanent social partnership established between employers and trade union leaders. He is cynical about the attitude of the latter towards the implementation of a socialist programme. But perhaps the fear of chaos was not quite such a disreputable motive as Feldman seems to assume; and no assessment of the social significance of the war (as distinct from the question of the success of the Revolution) would be complete without a discussion of the social and political reforms which *were* enacted at the end of the war.[9] On p. 122 Feldman exposes the real attitudes of the big employers: however, there is an interesting piece of unwitting testimony to the genuine significance of the Auxiliary Service Law when we learn that it was achieved against the opposition of leading industrialists. In explaining the fear of the rank-and-file felt by the union leaders, Feldman incidentally brings out the fact of the growth of industrial unionism during the war. However, Feldman's final indictment is a powerful one: in going for collaboration with the employers, rather than exploiting the situation brought about by the war (a 'failure of leadership', he calls it) the major trade union and Social Democratic Party figures not only destroyed the Revolution but also weakened the potential of the Weimar Republic to defend itself against the forces of Nazism. Much of relevance to the fourth theme can be gleaned from Feldman although, in fact, he is not so much writing about the consequences of the war, as about the way in which the main interest groups responded to the problems of the war and its aftermath.

Like Arno Mayer, Professor Charles Maier (Chapter 7) believes that the social hierarchies of twentieth-century Europe have proved to be remarkably tenacious. But Maier is concerned with a 'twentieth-century capitalist order' which is very different from the old order based on landholding discussed by Mayer. Maier defines the conservatives who wrested security from disorder in the aftermath of World War I as 'bourgeois', and, again in contrast to Mayer, he stresses how, during the nineteenth century, these bourgeois had achieved social rights and a close association with the old elite. European society in 1914 was, according to Maier, essentially bourgeois – and he gives a careful discussion of the relevance and meaning of the word. In the aftermath of the war this bourgeois society was not restored, as some had hoped, but recast in a mould which owed much to the pressures of war. Like Mayer, Maier deploys and advances a broad conceptual framework, but while Arno Mayer claims to be writing a form of Marxist history, Charles Maier's angle of vision might best be labelled as Weberian. The focus of Maier's *Recasting Bourgeois Europe* – a book based on enormous and highly original pioneering work in primary archives – is on France, Germany and Italy; the extracts printed here, drawn from the introduction and the conclusion, range more widely, taking in Britain and the USA, chiefly with reference to the reorganization of the world economic order necessitated by the war. For our purpose, the extracts included here are of particular relevance to the fourth theme, the consequences of war, yet Maier's conception also raises issues about the general pattern of social change and broad historical conceptualization, our first and fifth themes. Maier argues that the pressures of war in Europe led to an integration of organized labour into state-supervised bargaining systems and to an erosion of the distinction between the private and the public sectors. This is similar to the corporatism described by Gerald Feldman in Chapter 6 as emerging in Germany during World War I, though curiously Maier makes no reference to Feldman's use of the term. The idea of corporatism has also been deployed by Keith Middlemas with reference to the development of twentieth-century British society; according to Middlemas, as a result of the First World War 'what had been merely interest groups [trade unions and employer associations] crossed the political threshold and became part of the extended state'.[10] Maier's new corporatism, similarly, did not come to an end with the war but continued to develop after it; as a consequence, he argues, during the 1920s, parliaments declined in power and authority and the nature of representative government altered. In the first half of the decade the prime object of Maier's bourgeois forces was to keep the socialists out of power; at the same time they transformed the principles of class division, making social consensus more possible. Two kinds of tension imperilled the emergent equilibrium: as economies, both national and international, sought to restructure in the aftermath of the war, there was conflict between the needs of international economy and those of the different domestic situations; and inflation, beginning in the war but continuing until the mid-1920s, brought big business and strong trade unions together in a wage spiral at the expense of the middle strata of society. Ultimately these tensions undermined the equilibrium, most notably in Germany where they contributed to the rise of Nazism, and in Italy where they worked in favour of the Fascists. Nazism and Fascism, in Maier's view, were the responses of extreme radicals of the right to the corporatist collaboration of industry and the organized labour; but the forms of these responses differed in Germany and Italy as a result of their different social and economic structures. France escaped a similar fate partly because she had a less developed corporate structure and thus experienced a less serious challenge from the radical right.

Again, as with Arno Mayer's book, we are confronted by a text written with tremendous force and erudition, but which contains certain basic assumptions that are not universally accepted. Most notably, the whole of Maier's analysis is based on a Weberian conception of 'emerging structures of power', and he uses the word 'corporatism' explicitly in the Weberian style of an 'ideal type' against which events in France, Germany and Italy can be assessed, rather than as an actual description. Even though the word has been used by Feldman and Middlemas in similar contexts, this is not the only way to approach interrelationships between the state and interest groups such as trade unions and employers' associations in the period of the First World War and its aftermath. Moreover, while Maier believes that corporatism was less advanced in France than in Germany and Italy, many historians would challenge the extent of 'a decay of parliamentary influence' in post-war France, and even more in post-war Britain. Might not Maier's 'relative backwardness in terms of corporate organization' be another man's effective pluralism? Might not the more empirical historian replace Maier's notions of rescuing bourgeois Europe through recasting with the simple recognition that societies had to be reorganized for peace after five years of total war? Going back to 1914 was impossible; the empiricist, searching in vain for monolithic social classes, might argue that pragmatism and the various pressures on different governments and administrations meant simply that some wartime practices were kept and others discarded.

The ideologies of Fascism and Nazism, which Maier portrays as responses to elements within his recast Europe, are central to MacGregor Knox's essay 'Conquest, Foreign and Domestic, in Fascist Italy and Nazi Germany', which touches intriguingly on the second theme (in particular relations between World War I and the revolutions of Mussolini and Hitler) and the fourth theme (consequences of war). Knox begins by addressing the problem of defining 'fascism' in a manner that takes account of the different manifestations in Germany and Italy; his solution is to opt for a broadly empirical analysis comparing the intellectual development of the 'fascist' leaders Mussolini and Hitler, based on what they wrote and said. He is keen to rebut 'pat social interpretations' especially that which roots the origins of fascism in the First World War, and the essentially Marxist insistence that the fundamental cause of fascism was economic; in this way his essay, as a fine example of the *idiographic* approach (which does not, of course, exclude middle-level generalizations), is explicitly relevant to our fifth theme. Mussolini's assumptions, Knox suggests, are more difficult to pin down since, unlike Hitler, he was not a doctrinaire. Mussolini appears to have had a world view (similar, incidentally, to that of the Futurists) resting first on the assumption that life was a struggle, and second on myths about national mission and the inevitability of revolution. The First World War fused these ideas in Mussolini's mind, shaping his conception of the destiny of the Italian nation and of the place of new Rome in the world. Hitler, in contrast, had a genuine philosophy of history which, Knox argues, was 'at least as systematic as [that] of Marx'; for Hitler all history was the history of race struggle. Knox argues that while the basic idea of Nazism did not originate in World War One, it was reinforced by Hitler's reading of what had happened after the war. While the world views of Hitler and Mussolini differed, the events of 1914–19 contributed to their evolution; moreover, when it came to the working out of their respective political programmes, the results were strikingly similar. Mussolini advocated imperial expansion to demonstrate that Italy was truly a great power; Hitler wanted living space for the Aryan people in the east – both aims meant conquest. Both men intended the destruction of the old societies in the countries which they ruled; they wanted to create new societies out of international war and domestic revolution. Knox's essay thus brings us back to our third theme of the causes of war, the interrelation between foreign and domestic policies and the danger, noted by Gordon, of too rigid historical compartmentalization; it also pitches us specifically into the controversy over the origins of World War Two in Europe.

In passing, Knox is critical of historians like A.J.P Taylor who have denied that Hitler had any ideas relevant to the foreign policy which he pursued. In the ninth essay, Norman Rich begins with a devastating attack on Taylor's *The Origins of the Second World War* for precisely the same reasons. Taylor's book was first published in 1961,[11] the same year as Fischer's *Griff nach der Weltmacht*, and it created something of a similar furore. Taylor insisted that the war was not brought about by megalomania on Hitler's part; Hitler was an opportunist politician simply following the traditional line of foreign policy pursued by German statesmen, and in 1939 he miscalculated the response of the British and French to his Polish adventure. The work of Fischer and Taylor suggests a continuity in German expansionist foreign policy within Europe, and they have both been criticized for this. But Taylor's book was largely a reworking of well-known sources rather than a study based on the kind of detailed archival research undertaken by Fischer, and while Taylor had, in an earlier book,[12] traced a pattern in a united Germany that was dangerous for European peace he did not detail any precise links between Hitler, Bismarck, Kaiser Wilhelm and his advisers in *The Origins*. Rich is especially critical of Taylor's description of Hitler as both a typical German politician in his foreign policy and an opportunist. While it is wrong to think that Hitler had a blueprint and a precise timetable for his actions, and while it is right to emphasize the accidental and improvised nature of the execution of Nazi foreign policy, neither of these mean that Hitler had no policies and no intentions. In the second half of the essay, Rich provides a concise survey of the main interpretations and debates over Hitler's foreign policy, ranging from those who argue over the extent to which this policy was rooted in the German historical experience, to those who debate the role of domestic problems in formulating Nazi policy abroad – the latter has been especially popular with Marxist historians who have seen the causes of war as fundamentally economic even if the economic aspects enter the picture in a mediated form. In conclusion Rich draws on the work of the German historian Eberhard Jäckel, to portray Hitler as a man who had a very precise list of objectives and priorities in foreign affairs; but Rich parts company with Jäckel where the latter implies that Hitler was continuing a long-standing tendency in German history, on the grounds that this effectively denies the significance of both individuals and accidents.

Richard Overy's essay, 'Hitler's War and the German Economy: A Reinterpretation' (Chapter 10), focuses on Nazi preparations for war from an economic perspective; and perhaps it should be stressed at the outset that this is, of course, very different from seeing the fundamental cause of the war as economic.[13] Ian Beckett stresses that control of the economy 'lies at the heart of the concept of total war' and he notes the controversy over when, and the extent to which, the economy of Nazi Germany was organized for war. The essay by Overy is his first re-appraisal of the notion of the *Blitzkrieg* economy developed by economic historians who have suggested that, until 1942, Germany was organized only for *Blitzkrieg* wars, having built up armaments in breadth rather than in depth. Like most historians challenging an orthodoxy Overy does tend to make his target appear rather less substantial than it was: Alan Milward's original research in this area was both pioneering and persuasive;[14] moreover it should be noted that Mark Roseman's essay later in this volume largely accepts the *Blitzkrieg* thesis. Overy confronts the thesis with a detailed analysis of German economic life between 1936 and 1942. Along with the other critics of Taylor, Overy considers that Hitler was planning a large-scale war of conquest, and while the Führer may have had only a weak grasp of the facts of economic life, nevertheless both he and his subordinates were contemplating a war which would last a long while and which would require a massive economic effort directed by the state – from the beginning they were thinking in terms of 'total war', and they had a model in the experience of World War One. Overy shows that Germany was spending enormous sums on armaments before 1941, that the work-force employed on military projects increased from 20 per cent of the total in 1939 to 60 per cent in 1941, and that as early as 1937–8 a large state-owned and state-operated industrial structure was being built up. There were problems in all of this: Goering was incapable of the task of supervising the organization for war, and civilian and military economic leaders disliked having to work under him, and went out of their way to avoid his jurisdiction; much of the expenditure had to be used for rebuilding the military infrastructure; there was conservatism among both workers and employers militating against necessary changes; and the German military insisted on the highest quality of equipment when something cheaper, quicker and easier to produce would probably have served. But perhaps most significantly, the economic preparations for war were out of step with the events of foreign policy: Hitler was planning his big war for some time in the 1940s; he did not expect that his adventure in Poland would be the cause of war against Britain and France.

The title of Chapter 11, 'The Effects of World War II on French Society and Politics' by Stanley Hoffmann, firmly places it in the fourth theme. In fact, since the article both discusses the nature of French society as it had developed by the 1930s, what Hoffmann calls the 'Republican synthesis', and looks in detail at developments between 1934 and 1940, it also belongs to our first theme of general social change. All in all, Hoffmann's piece is a good example of the methodological principle which argues that you cannot properly assess the effects of a war on a particular society without first defining the nature of that society and the processes of change already at work in it, before the war. Many academics, including quite a proportion of those who deny any connection between war and social change, stress the influence of politics: at its simplest, a left-wing government will introduce social change, a conservative one will tend to resist it. Hoffmann's paper, delivered as long ago as April 1960, was genuinely casting new light on events in France when, instead of making a rigid distinction between the right-wing Vichy regime installed in France by the Germans between 1940 and 1944, and the Liberation regime which came into power in the final stages of the war, and to which, traditionally, all the major social changes associated with the war were attributed, Hoffmann suggested some continuity as between the two regimes. Thus, though this was not his deliberate intention, he was directing attention away from guided political action, and focusing on war itself as a complex experience which tends to bring about social change whatever the deliberate intentions of politicians. Hoffmann (an American, like so many of our authors) was a political scientist as well as an historian much interested in developments in contemporary French politics, particularly at a time when the Fifth Republic under De Gaulle had just come into existence (in this reprint of his paper some of the detailed political material has been omitted).

The paper is not based on detailed historical research, though Hoffmann was able to draw upon his own considerable expertise as well as on the mainly secondary sources cited in the footnotes: his paper, as he says at the beginning, consists of 'a number of hypotheses' which 'need further study and qualification'. The article, then, presents many generalizations, sometimes in the form of quite striking metaphors. Yet it does not reflect the sociological or nomothetic tradition in the way that, say, Maier does: Hoffmann explicitly disavows attributing a 'revolutionary tradition' to the French workers, preferring what he calls the clumsy but more accurate expression, a 'tradition of non-cooperation'. Unlike, for example, Feldman, Hoffmann makes few value judgements, and clearly does not see the advance of the working class as something which 'ought' to happen; he simply records, as he sees them, the consequences, often unintended, of the actions of politicians of different persuasions.

In the first numbered section of the chapter (p. 234) Hoffmann provides a very useful summary of what he terms the Republican synthesis. The first paragraph contains a good brief explanation of the nature of class in France (and one which could well also be applied to Britain at this time). While one could at times challenge the way in which Hoffmann summarizes quite complex material, he does give a persuasive view of how France, with the working class effectively excluded from the mainstream of French life, was both a contented and a 'stalemate' society (the main influence of World War One, he suggests, had been to foster complacency). The second section discusses the 'destruction of the Republican synthesis' in the period 1934–40. Now, almost certainly, Hoffmann makes too rigid a break at 1934; he also underestimates the amount of economic progress which, recent research has shown, was being made in France during both the 1920s and the 1930s. It may be that he exaggerates the forces of change in the 1930s, and thus overall underestimates the significance of the Second World War; or it may be that in underestimating developments throughout the inter-war period he actually ends up exaggerating the effects of World War Two. These are propositions that could be evaluated only in the light of a good deal of further reading. Here what it is important to concentrate on is the way in which Hoffmann brings out how developments under Vichy (which many in the past had considered purely regressive, and 'corporatist' – here is that concept again, though Hoffmann only once refers to 'Vichy corporatism') formed the basis for social advances under the Liberation. The interconnections are often complex, and it is worth spending time working carefully through Hoffmann's arguments; one does, it could be maintained, get quite a strong impression of the various accidents and necessities of war being more important than the deliberate decisions of politicians. The general conclusion Hoffmann presents is of a France more dynamic and more united after the Second World War than it had been previously, though he does not really go into much detail. In assessing society at the end of the war, Hoffmann speaks of 'both major innovations and a few sharp limits'; he spends some time going into these limits, particularly the, as he sees it, continuing isolation of the French working class. That an independent French working class has continued to exist has been demonstrated in many social surveys; but arguably Hoffmann, perhaps because he happened to be writing in the aftermath of De Gaulle's 1959 victory, exaggerates the isolation of the working class and its distance from the rest of French society. Two critical points that really do have to be made about post-war France: are the granting, for the first time, of votes for women, and the development of advanced social insurance, medical and other welfare services.[15]

In contrast to the sweeping hypotheses of Hoffmann's article, Penny Summerfield in Chapter 12, 'The "Levelling of Class"', builds up a meticulous analysis from detailed statistical sources. Summerfield's article, indeed, is a model example of the rigorous and relentless development of historical arguments, carefully considering at each stage the cases which have been put forward in support of there having been changes in the condition of the British working class brought about by the war, then with clarity and thoroughness exposing the weaknesses in these cases. This chapter, then, is firmly related to the fourth theme, the social consequences of war, and, with respect to the particular instance of the position of the working class in Britain, is very strongly arguing against the thesis that war helps to bring about social change. It may be noted that the phrase 'levelling' is an unsatisfactory one, often used in a vague way. Summerfield is certainly right that classes were not levelled, which would imply class distinctions being removed altogether (this did not happen anywhere, apart from the countries that fell under Russian Communist influence, and even what happened there is open to some debate). The debate with regard to class in Britain (and indeed in France, Italy and Germany) centres on whether or not, given that the basic framework of the class structure remained the same, there were significant changes in the relationships between classes and attitudes about class. Although Summerfield's article is basically an empirical study without anything in the way of sociological theorizing, her basic definitions of class are essentially the economic ones derived from Marxism. As with most studies in that tradition, she is concerned solely with the relations between working class and middle class and does not consider the possibility of there being a significant distinction between a middle class on one side, and an upper class on the other. In fact, she finds herself in contention with the view of class which attempts to integrate the perceptions and images of class which people hold with the realities of differing life-styles and of economic and political inequality, though she dismisses that view somewhat cursorily. Summerfield's article is also distinguished by the great attention she gives to both the earnings of women and the conditions under which they had to support their families during the war: this is a most important dimension which gives a tremendous sense of practical reality to the article, and is entirely in keeping with the fact that Summerfield is one of the leading younger feminist historians in Britain. Overall, it can be said of the article that it is a most effective antidote to those who have romanticized about the war having transformed the British class structure and transformed the position of the working class within it. But it is not by any means the last word on this subject.

Clearly, Chapter 13, 'The Impact of World War II on Leningrad' by Edward Bubis and Blair Ruble (both Americans), also falls firmly into the fourth theme. Like the Summerfield article, it shows itself to be very much a part of the most recent developments in historical methodology in that it is heavily based on statistical sources, immediately distinguishing itself, indeed, by the large number of statistical tables which are incorporated directly into the text. It also, of course, draws most impressively on a range of Russian printed sources, both secondary and primary. To a considerable degree this is an exercise in economic history; however, it also draws interestingly upon a concept drawn from social anthropology, that of certain cities serving as 'charismatic active centers', cities where 'a society's leading actors, ideas, and institutions come together' (the adjective 'charismatic', more usually applied to political leaders, originates with Weber).

Apart from the peculiarly tragic instance of Poland, the Russian experience in the Second World War, as is widely recognized in the historical literature, was the classic case of war at its most catastrophically destructive. Some historians have argued that the disasters of war can result in reconstructive, regenerative impulses, leading to ambitious, and perhaps even enlightened, rebuilding. Assessment of the long-term effects of war can then often take the form of trying to balance out the undoubtedly negative destructive effects from any positive ones. The heroism of the siege of Leningrad and the composing by Shostakovich of his 'Leningrad Symphony' are parts of the mythology of the Second World War. However, the straight and unremitting message of the Bubis and Ruble article is that the destructive effects on Leningrad were permanent and serious, unredeemed by revival and reconstruction. In making one of their major points, Leningrad's loss of its charismatic status, the authors do recognize that this was part of a longer-term process deliberately fostered from Moscow, and was not attributable to the war alone. Actually it may emerge that the authors' conscientious presentation of the facts does not always totally support their general conclusions. One sentence, and its phrasing, is especially worthy of note: '*Remarkably* [our italics], the city's overall industrial output managed to surpass pre-war levels as early as 1950.' Of course, if one were trying to support the alternative thesis that destruction can lead to the release of energy and a spirit of reconstruction, then one would not require the '*remarkably*'. Whatever the rights and wrongs of that, the social experiences of Russia must be prominent in any study of 'War, Peace and

Social Change', the events at Leningrad are among the most emotive in the history of the war, and this article has a number of particularly valuable aspects, not least the way in which it introduces quantifiable evidence to substantiate its arguments about changes in Leningrad's scientific base.

The final chapter in the book, 'World War II and Social Change in Germany' by Mark Roseman, concludes this clutch of articles devoted to the controversial question of the social consequences of war. Roseman is a young British historian, and his article is the only one to be reprinted here from the collection of papers delivered in January 1987 to the Open University Conference on 'Total War and Social Change'. It is in many respects a perfect example of how to go about answering the question presented to the contributors to that conference: 'What if any, social change is brought about by war?' Roseman points out that most of the relevant historical writing concentrates on the Nazi period as a whole, rather than singling out the experience of war. In his pioneering study he points out, first, that great weight must be given to the transformations already carried out by the Nazis in the period (which he wittily defines as one of 'total peace') *before* the war, and to the fact that with German military defeat the shaping of German society was very much influenced by the nature and policies of the occupying powers – Roseman is dealing essentially with West Germany and the influence of the Americans. This actually takes us to one of the major debates within the whole question of the effects of war. Is it perhaps the case that rather than social change developing out of the war experience itself, its character is essentially determined by the geopolitical situation obtaining at the end of the war?

This is the position taken, in particular, by many latter-day Marxists who, conceiving of social change in the very broad manner indicated in the opening sentences of this Introduction, see social structure and social life in one half of Europe as being dominated by Russian Communism, while that in the other half is dominated by Americanization. It may be, indeed, that Roseman's article lends some support to this thesis. However, it is also of great significance for the painstaking way in which it does tease out a number of changes attributed to the war experience itself, of which the new self-confidence engendered in the working class is perhaps the most important.

This Introduction has simply sought to show where the essays which make up this book fit into the broad themes associated with the topic 'War, Peace and Social Change'. The essays themselves have been chosen for the major contributions they make on these themes, and for the variety of methodological approaches and broad 'philosophies' (Marxist, non-Marxist, feminist, etc.) they present. The complex topic of 'War, Peace and Social Change' serves to raise some of the most important problems and debates in the study of twentieth-century European history. Together, the essays which follow offer no simple conclusions, save that of the outstanding importance of the subject itself. These essays must now be left to speak for themselves, the reader always bearing in mind that in reading the work of an historian it does pay to know just a little bit about the attitudes and approaches of that historian. Readers should also remember that the best historians often make important points which may actually fall outside the basic theses which they were intending to present in their writing.

Notes

1 See Arthur Marwick, 'Introducing the course', in A. Marwick, C. Emsley and I. Donnachie, *Europe in 1914*, Book 1 of *War, Peace and Social Change*, Milton Keynes, 1990.

2 Perhaps it should be noted here that Arthur Marwick does not speak of a 'model' or 'four dimensions of war' in *The Deluge*, London, 1965, as Beckett maintains. This was a later formulation used in Arthur Marwick, *War and Social Change in the Twentieth Century*, London, 1974, and in the Open University Course, A301, *War and Society*, Milton Keynes, 1973. The most up-to-date statement of Marwick's thinking is to be found in his Introduction to *Total War and Social Change*, London, 1988.

3 Arno J. Mayer, *The Persistence of the Old Regime: Europe and the Great War*, London, 1981, p. x.

4 Ibid.

5 See for example, for England, F.M.L. Thompson, *English Landed Society in the Nineteenth Century*, London, 1963; and for France, Maurice Halbwachs, *Les Classes Sociales*, Paris, 1937.

6 Paul Fussel, *The Great War and Modern Memory* (1975). See also Barry Cadwallader, *Crisis of the European Mind* (1981) and John Cruickshank, *Variations on Catastrophe* (1982).

7 See Arthur Marwick, 'The debate over the impact of World War II: high and popular culture', in C. Emsley, A. Marwick, W. Purdue and A. Aldgate, *World War II*, Book 4 of *War, Peace and Social Change*, Milton Keynes, 1990.

8 Fritz Fischer, *Germany's Aims in the First World War*, London, 1966; Fischer, *War of Illusions: German Policies from 1911 to 1914*, London, 1975.

9 See Arthur Marwick, 'The debate over the impact of World War I: social reform and welfare policies', in H. Cowper, A. Marwick, W. Purdue, C. Emsley and D. Englander, *World War I*, Book 2 of *War, Peace and Social Change*, Milton Keynes, 1990.

10 Keith Middlemas, *Politics in Industrial Society: The Experience of the British System since 1911*, London, 1979, p. 373.

11 A.J.P. Taylor, *The Origins of the Second World War*, London, 1961.

12 A.J.P. Taylor, *The Course of German History*, London, 1945.

13 Indeed Overy has subsequently debated vigorously with one of the leading Marxist historians of Nazi Germany over the economic origins of the war. R.J. Overy and T.W. Mason, 'Debate', *Past and Present*, 1989.

14 See especially Alan Milward, *The German Economy at War*, London, 1965.

15 *War, Peace and Social Change: Europe 1900–1955*, Book 4, Units 22–5, Milton Keynes, 1989.

1
Total War

Ian F.W. Beckett

The historiography of total war

In the last twenty years, historians have come increasingly to recognize the often pivotal role played by war and conflict in historical developments. In the process, the interpretation and understanding of the impact of war upon states, societies and individuals have been transformed. In particular, the concept of 'total war', as applied to the two world wars of the twentieth century, has become a familiar one and a matter for modern historiographical debate. Generally, the term 'total war' is used by historians not only to describe the nature of the world wars but also to differentiate such wars from other conflicts. The study of total war within the context of war studies or studies of war and society is largely a product of the 1960s, but the term itself is older. Ludendorff appears to have used the term first in his memoirs, published in 1919, but it was also employed in a ritualistic fashion during the Second World War. Josef Goebbels, for example, threatened the Western Allies with 'total war' in a celebrated speech in February 1943 and was himself appointed Reich Plenipotentiary for the Mobilization of Total War in July 1944; Winston Churchill also used the phrase in an address to the United States Congress in May 1943. Now, the term has become almost synonymous with the concept of war as a catalyst of far-reaching social change, and it is in precisely that sense that total war is a subject of continuing historical debate.

The American scholar, J.U. Nef, whose *War and Human Progress* was published in 1950,[1] may stand perhaps as representative of an earlier period of historiography, when war was regarded as having a purely negative impact, in so far as it was at all relevant to historical development. However, there were other scholars in the 1950s whose work was suggestive of the future approach to the question of war and social change. Richard Titmuss made a connection in 1950 between the two in his volume, *Problems of Social Policy*, for the British official history of the Second World War[2] while Stanislas Andrzejewski offered the 'military participation ratio' in 1954,[3] which postulated a firm correlation between the extent of wartime participation by society in the war effort and the amount of subsequent levelling of social inequalities. The English historian, G.N. Clark, also produced during the 1950s a pioneering study of war and society in the seventeenth century,[4] but the real broadening of historical perspectives with regard to what became known as war studies came in the following decade. A comparison of Michael Howard's classic military history of the Franco-Prussian War, published in 1961,[5] with his *War in European History*[6] fifteen years later may serve to indicate the profound historiographical change that occurred.

In the forefront of that change was Arthur Marwick, whose study of British society in the First World War, *The Deluge*,[7] published in 1965, was followed by *Britain in the Century of Total War* in 1968 and *War and Social Change in the Twentieth Century* in 1974.[8] Marwick was not the only historian in the field and the titles of Gordon Wright's *The Ordeal of Total War* in 1968 and Peter Calvocoressi's and Guy Wint's *Total War* in 1972 were also indicative of the new approach.[9] However, it was largely Marwick who established the framework for the study of total war. Four 'modes' put forward in *Britain in the Century of Total War* had become a 'four-tier model' in *War and Social Change in the Twentieth Century*, by which the changes effected by total war might be gauged and compared between different states. Thus, for Marwick, total war implied disruption and destruction on a vast and unprecedented scale; the testing of the existing social and political structures of states and societies; the participation, in the context of the total mobilization of a state's resources, of previously disadvantaged groups in the war effort; and, lastly, a 'colossal psychological experience'. The cumulative effect would be real and enduring social change. The model became familiar to a wide readership through the 'War and Society' course introduced by Marwick and his colleagues at the Open University in the 1970s.[10]

To be fair to Marwick, the model was offered only as a 'rough tool', but it is undeniable that the idea of war as a determinant of major change has had a profound impact during the past decade. Indeed, this concept has been described recently by Michael Bentley as one of the most common 'misapprehensions' in the perception of modern British social history.[11] From the beginning, too, some historians were far more cautious than Marwick in their appraisal of the impact of total war upon society. Examples are Angus Calder's *The People's War*[12] – a title itself derived from a British propaganda slogan in the Second World War and echoed in a 1986 television series and accompanying book on Britain at war[13] – which was published in 1969, and Henry Pelling's *Britain in the Second World War*, published two years later.[14] More recently, Brian

Bond has described total war as being as great a myth as the idea of total victory or total defeat[15] and, while the debate has continued to be waged within the context of parameters laid down by Marwick, recent and current research has done much to suggest that the social impact of total war in the twentieth century should not be overstated.

The emergence of total war

A preliminary consideration is that the acceptance of the periods between 1914 and 1918 and between 1939 and 1945 as those of total war implies that conflicts prior to the twentieth century were more limited. Traditionally, historians have described the late eighteenth century as a classic era of 'limited war', in which armies were relatively small in size and would manoeuvre with the intention of avoiding rather than engaging in battle. Campaigns would be designed to exhaust an opponent's economy by occupation, in search of strictly limited political and dynastic aims. Societies as a whole would hardly be touched by the impact of war and, indeed, a prevailing bourgeois assumption that military activity was not the destiny of mankind ensured that trade flourished between states at war. Examples usually cited of the normality of social intercourse include Laurence Sterne's visit to Paris during the Seven Years' War (1756–63) and the continuance of the Dover to Calais packet service for a year after France in 1778 had joined the United States in the American War of Independence (1774–83). Closer analysis, however, reveals that war between 1648 and 1789 was limited, in the words of John Childs, 'only when it was compared with the holocaust that had gone before and the new totality of the Napoleonic wars'.[16] As surely as the Thirty Years' War (1618–48) had devastated Germany, reducing its urban population by 33 per cent and its rural population by 45 per cent, so incipient warfare during the next 120 years laid waste much of central Europe and the Low Countries at regular intervals. Conventions applied by armies in relation to each other did not extend to civilian populations, as the French army's ravages in the Palatinate in 1688 and 1689 or both the Russian and Swedish armies' depredations in the Great Northern War (1700–21) well illustrate. In any case, for all their balletic appearance, battles were murderous affairs, the 'butcher's bill' at Malplaquet in 1709 of an estimated 36,000 casualties not being surpassed until the Battle of Borodino in 1812. Borodino itself was then exceeded by the 127,000 casualties at the four-day 'Battle of the Nations' at Leipzig in 1813. The cumulative effect of such conflict upon areas that were fought over was considerable. Equally, participation in five major wars between 1689 and 1783 was a major stimulus for English industry and trade at a crucial early stage in the world's first industrial revolution.

None the less, warfare was to become increasingly more total in its impact during the course of the nineteenth century, which can be taken as representing an extended transitional period. During the French

Revolutionary and Napoleonic wars (1792–1815), the motive forces of nationalism and democracy combined to create a mass French citizen army through the introduction of universal male conscription. The success of this 'nation in arms' or 'armed horde' resulted in the example being emulated elsewhere, notably in Prussia. Although the concept of the nation in arms came under sustained attack after 1815 from monarchs and restored monarchs, who distrusted its social and political implications, the actual system of short-service conscription survived in Prussia. The military victories then won by Prussia in the German wars of unification of 1864, 1866 and 1870 and the ability of short-service conscription to produce large numbers of trained reserves upon mobilization encouraged European states – with the exception of Britain – to reintroduce Prussian-style conscription. Although the forms of universal service adopted were necessarily selective in practice, states were rapidly accepting the national birthrate as an index of military power. Moreover, the transformation wrought by the technological innovations of the industrial age, particularly the development of the railway, ensured that ever larger armies could be mobilized theoretically more quickly than hitherto and sustained in the field for far longer.

At the same time, industrialization dramatically increased the destructive capacity of armies by providing them with weapons of enhanced range, accuracy and rate of fire. By 1870, a firefight between opposing infantry, which might have been conducted at 60 yards' range seventy years before, had now stretched to a possible 1,600 yards and a breech-loading rifle such as the Prussian Dreyse now fired seven rounds for every one from a smoothbore musket of the Napoleonic era. By the 1880s and 1890s magazine rifles, quick-firing artillery and machine guns had all entered service with major European armies. Just before the First World War, most armies were also experimenting with aircraft, even if it appeared to require a considerable feat of imagination to conceive that airmen could offer any valuable intelligence while flying over the ground at speeds approaching 30 mph. At sea, too, wood, sail and round shot had given way to iron and steel, steam and screw propellor, and shell, while mines, submarines and torpedoes all threatened the traditional supremacy of the capital ship.

Through the innate conservatism of European military and naval officer corps, the significance of much of the change that had taken place during the nineteenth century was misinterpreted. Contrary to popular belief, soldiers did recognize the problems inherent in crossing the so-called 'empty battlefield' in the face of modern firepower, but they believed mistakenly that they could solve the difficulty simply by closing with an enemy more rapidly. Moreover, the use of bayonet, lance and sabre implicit in this 'offensive spirit' ideally complemented traditional military ideals of honour and glory, which some feared devalued by the unwelcome intrusion of technology and professionalism into an overwhelmingly aristocratic occupation. While soldiers conspired to discount the more uncomfortable evidence of such conflicts as the American Civil War (1861–5), Franco-Prussian War (1870–1) and Russo-Japanese War (1904–5), civilians were equally seduced by the general trend in the later nineteenth century towards popular nationalism, imperialism, militarism and crude social Darwinism into a more ready acceptance of war and conflict as an appropriate test of nationhood and national virility. There were pacifists but, in 1914, it was nationalism and not internationalism that triumphed across Europe. Similarly, a succession of international conferences, such as those at St Petersburg in 1868 or at the Hague in 1899 and 1907, failed to find a universal readiness among nation states to compromise their future freedom of manoeuvre by accepting meaningful limitations on the actual conduct of war.

Wars between 1789 and 1914, while such developments were occurring, were hardly devoid of impact upon those societies that waged them. In the case of Britain, for example, the manpower problems experienced during the Crimean War (1854–6) were very similar to those encountered in the First World War, and losses sustained in the twenty years of almost continuous warfare between 1793 and 1815 were almost certainly proportionately higher in terms of men under arms than in the First World War.[17] Military participation in Britain was also probably greater in proportion to the male population between 1793 and 1815, and it is at least arguable that the resulting social, economic and political upheaval in the immediate post-war period was of more significance for the future pattern of British society and democracy than developments in the aftermath of either of the world wars. Of course, the wars of German and Italian unification were of very limited duration, but they still had profound political consequences for Europe.

There was once a tendency to view the American Civil War largely in terms of its military developments and to focus upon such innovations as armoured trains, the first clash of armoured warships, the first loss of ships to mines and submarine torpedoes, the first extensive use of the telegraph, and so on. In fact, the largely amateur armies fought the war on the battlefield as if it were the last Napoleonic encounter rather than the 'first modern war' but it is now recognized widely that the war was truly modern in terms of its impact upon society. Both the northern states of the Union and the southern states of the Confederacy deployed large numbers of men in the field but, for the predominantly agricultural Confederacy, war also demanded efforts to create an industrial economy to challenge the far greater manufacturing potential of the North. It had become essential to outproduce as well as to outfit an opponent. Despite its efforts at industrialization, the mobilization of 75 per cent of its white male population, and unprecedented participation by white women and blacks in industry and agriculture, the Confederacy was doomed to defeat by the superiority of the North's numbers and resources. The inescapable logic of the attempt to create a war economy was the recognition that a society that sustained a war became as much a legitimate target for military action as an army that waged war on its behalf. Thus, in the autumn of 1864, Sheridan's Union forces swept down the southern 'bread basket' of the Shenandoah valley while Sherman's armies wrought equal destruction in cutting a swathe from Atlanta to the sea in November and December 1864 and through the Carolinas in the following months in a determination to expose the Confederacy to the 'hard hand of war'.[18]

The world wars

Thus, there are sufficient examples of the way in which the impact of war upon society was increasing through the nineteenth century to suggest that the world wars should be regarded as a natural progression from earlier conflicts rather than as unique. But, of course, this is not to suggest that the impact of world war was not greater than that of earlier wars through the sheer scale of conflict enhancing the effect. Quite obviously, both world wars were global in scope, although both began as European conflicts. In the First World War, the Central Powers comprised Imperial Germany, Austria-Hungary, Ottoman Turkey (from October 1914) and Bulgaria (from October 1915), but the Allies eventually embraced twenty-two states including the major European powers of Britain, France, Imperial Russia and Italy (from May 1915) and their colonies and dependencies, and also Japan, the United States (from March 1917), Liberia (from August 1917) and Brazil (from October 1917). Similarly, the Second World War widened with the aggression of Germany, Italy (from June 1940 to September 1943) and Japan (from December 1941) bringing in the Soviet Union (from June 1941) and the United States (from December 1941), although the Soviet Union did not join in the war against Japan until August 1945. Successive German and Soviet occupation contributed to a bewildering proliferation of contradictory declarations of war by many eastern European states during the war, while, between February and March 1945, no less than ten states ranging from Peru to Saudi Arabia declared war on both Germany and Japan and a further two on Japan alone.

Total war therefore implies a far wider global conflict than previous wars and, while limited war suggests a degree of constraint, self-imposed or otherwise, total war implies a lack of constraint. In practice, total war was still a relative concept in both world wars since, as an absolute, it was unrealizable through a lack of instantaneously destructive weapons. Nevertheless, belligerents could not be accused of failing to attempt the absolute even if they were unable to mobilize all their resources at the same time and at the same point. In effect, they employed all the weapons they felt appropriate rather than all the weapons available in every case. The array and potential of weapons increased dramatically over previous wars. For example, in eight days before the opening of the British offensive on the Somme on the Western Front on 1 July 1916,

British artillery fired 1.7 million shells at German positions. In fourteen days preceding the opening of the Passchendaele offensive on 31 July 1917, the British fired 4.2 million shells. In addition to the weight of shell, horrendous new weapons were introduced in search of an elusive breakthrough. Gas was first used on the Western Front at Langemarck near Ypres on 22 April 1915, although it had previously been used by the Germans at Bolimov on the Eastern Front, and, in July 1915, flame-throwers were used effectively for the first time by the Germans at Hooge near Ypres. In all, over 150,000 tons of varying gases were produced during the First World War and caused an estimated 1.2 million casualties, of which more than 91,000 proved fatal. Tanks were also introduced for the first time by the British on the Somme on 15 September 1916.

Although gas was not used in the Second World War other than in the context of Nazi genocide, its military use was pressed by a powerful military–industrial lobby in Germany. There were also considerable technological advances that further enhanced the destructive power of the belligerents. Paradoxically, the speed of the early German *Blitzkriegs* actually made these operations less costly in terms of casualties than trench warfare during the First World War but, equally, there was the development in the capacity to bring aerial destruction to civilian populations. Ultimately, Germany utilized its V1 and V2 rockets and the Allies, of course, dropped the first atomic weapons on Japan.

The conscious abandonment of most if not all restraints was paralleled by the wider war aims adopted by belligerents in total war. Limited dynastic aims had given way to sweeping territorial aggrandisement and the total destruction of states and of peoples. It could be argued in this respect that the necessary manipulation of the population of democratic states through propaganda and other means, in so far as this proved possible, in order to sustain the war effort, introduced as great a push towards total war aims as the attempt by authoritarian or totalitarian states to impose their ideologies on others. Thus, on the one hand, the Germans pursued total domination in the Second World War, while Britain and the United States adopted a declaration of the need for the unconditional surrender of Germany at the Casablanca conference in January 1943. At Cairo in November and December 1943, Britain, the United States and nationalist China also agreed to strip Japan of all those overseas possessions taken by her forces since 1894.

Quite clearly, the participation of many states and their willingness to use extreme means to achieve wide aims resulted in destruction of life and property on an unprecedented scale compared with previous wars. In all, the First World War is thought to have resulted in 10 million dead and 20 million maimed or seriously wounded, leaving 5 million women widows and 9 million children orphans. The Second World War may have cost 30 million dead in Europe, although other estimates put Soviet losses alone at well over 20 million dead. Although figures for the First

World War usually exclude an estimated 1.5 million Armenians exterminated by the Turks in 1915, those for the Second World War do include an estimated 5.9 million Jewish victims of Nazi genocide. Moreover, as many as 26 million people may have become displaced from their country of origin during the Second World War through forced transportation or other reasons: in Britain alone, which did not suffer such displacement, there were still 60 million changes of address during the Second World War. Compared with previous wars, also, civilians had become subject to sustained and deliberate attack to an unprecedented degree. During the First World War, some 1,413 British civilians were killed by aerial attack, but, between 1939 and 1945, German bombers and rockets accounted for 51,509 civilian deaths in Britain. Hamburg suffered approximately 50,000 dead in a week in July and August 1943, and calculations of the loss of life at Dresden on a single night in February 1945 range from 35,000 to 135,000. In all, total German civilian losses to aerial bombardment may have been 593,000 during the Second World War. USAAF 'fire raids' on Japan caused an estimated 100,000 deaths in Tokyo on one night in March 1945, or approximately the same number of immediate deaths at both Hiroshima and Nagasaki combined in August 1945.

The loss of life in individual states could be grave, but total war was not necessarily a cause of demographic loss overall. In France, the loss of life during the First World War did cast a long shadow, at least in political terms, and draconian laws were introduced against birth control and abortion in the inter-war period. Yet, it would appear that more men and women married than might otherwise have been the case. In Britain, as Jay Winter has pointed out, the war was dysgenic in that some sectors of society volunteered for war service in larger numbers than others and many of the working class were physically unfit for service through pre-war deprivation. Hence, the idea of a 'lost generation' current in Britain in the 1920s and 1930s had some basis in fact. But, as Jay Winter has also demonstrated, infant mortality declined through the improvement in the nutrition of mothers and children with the redistribution of food and increased family income consequent upon wartime changes in public health policy. These, paradoxically healthier, standards of living were not eroded by the depression years.[19] Similarly, J.J. Becker has concluded that standards of living were not materially diminished in France during the First World War.[20] Unexpectedly, too, there was a close correlation during the Second World War between Britain, which suffered little real violence and deprivation, and most other European countries in terms of more and earlier marriages, increased fertility, and decreased infant and maternal mortality. Such demographic gains were achieved despite the estimated 27 million deaths worldwide from the Spanish influenza pandemic of 1918 and 1919. The latter in itself was once attributed to war-related conditions of less resistance to infection and easier transmission of disease through armies but, in fact, it hit neutrals as hard if not worse than belligerents and the highest mortality rates were recorded in the United States and India. Advances in medicine were of considerable account in preventing disease during and after the Second World War. It must also be borne in mind that total war is a stimulus to medical development and, even in the First World War, soldiers were far more likely to survive serious wounds than any of their predecessors on countless battlefields in the past.

The reduction of suffering and much else to statistics is unfortunate but unavoidable in conveying the totality of the world wars. Similar repetitive statistics are available to compute the undoubted losses of property and of manufacturing and agricultural production as a result either of direct attack or of occupation. Certainly, the cost of waging war had increased spectacularly. In 1870, for example, it has been suggested that the Franco–Prussian War cost Prussia and the other German states some 7 million marks a day, whereas the First World War cost Imperial Germany an estimated 146 million marks a day in 1918. Just 18 months' participation in the First World War cost the United States $112 billion, but the Second World War cost the United States some $664 billion. In fact, such exact calculations of the direct and indirect costs of war are notoriously difficult to make and quantitative evaluations may not in themselves be particularly helpful in suggesting the impact of war upon the economy. Structural changes are far more significant and, in this regard, both world wars were of unquestionable importance as economic events. As a result of the First World War, there was not only a global depreciation in the value of currencies, which had repercussions in terms of currency instability in the inter-war years, but also a decentralization of the international economy. Europe's share of world production and trade fell through the stimulus afforded non-European competitors. Much the same effect was reproduced during and after the Second World War with the growth of manufacturing capacity outside Europe and a legacy of post-war economic planning very different from the policies followed prior to the war.[21]

The primary beneficiary of the stimulus to non-European economies in both world wars was the United States, which moved from being an international debtor before 1914 to an international creditor on a large scale. In the process, the United States also emerged as a global power, even if subsequently choosing isolation for another twenty years. The First World War also destroyed four empires – those of Imperial Germany, Austria-Hungary, Tsarist Russia and Ottoman Turkey. It left a legacy of new states in eastern Europe, such as Poland, Czechoslovakia, Hungary and Yugoslavia, with significant racial minorities. It directly fostered the growth of nationalism among subject peoples in those empires that did survive. The British, whose empire reached its greatest extent in 1919 with the acquisition of former German colonies and custody of new Middle Eastern territories, encountered nationalism in such areas as

Palestine, India and Ireland. Later, the Second World War made a significant contribution to the further decline of western Europe *vis-à-vis* the United States and the Soviet Union. Moreover, the occupation of much of South-East Asia by the Japanese struck severely at the hold of the remaining European colonial powers. Nationalism was fostered both through the establishment by the Japanese of puppet governments and quasi-nationalist organizations and also through the emergence of anti-Japanese opposition movements, such as the Viet Minh in French Indochina and the Malayan Peoples' Anti-Japanese Army (MPAJA) in Malaya, which proved equally opposed to the return of former colonial administrations once the Japanese had been defeated. It would be difficult to argue that such global changes in the balance of power would not have occurred but for the world wars. Both wars also saw some attempt at a new internationalism in the shape of institutional mechanisms for world order – the League of Nations and the United Nations – although such ideals were not entirely novel.

The growth of state control

The collapse of some states and the post-war political challenges to others suggests that Marwick is perfectly correct in postulating total war as a testing experience for the institutions of state. Certainly, the world wars did promote far greater state control in its broadest sense as a response to wartime challenges. In 1914 a spate of emergency legislation, such as the revived Prussian Law of Siege of 1851 in Imperial Germany and the Defence of the Realm Act (DORA) in Britain, enabled the state to assume wide powers. In all cases the railways were swiftly nationalized and, in Britain and France, this was followed by state control of mines and the shipbuilding industry. Precisely the same pattern occurred in the United States in 1917 and key areas such as munitions, food and manpower policies were submitted to intervention and control by new governmental agencies. In Britain, the Ministry of Munitions was created in May 1915 with an accompanying Munitions of War Act extending state control to munitions factories to prevent strikes, suspend trade union activities and to prevent free movement of labour. More new creations followed Lloyd George's appointment as prime minister in December 1916 (such as the Ministry of Labour and Ministry of Food), although often with ill-defined responsibilities. Canada created an Imperial Munitions Board; Austria-Hungary, a Joint Food Committee; the United States, a War Industries Board and a Fuel and Food Administration; Imperial Germany's new agencies included the War Wheat Corporation, the War Food Office and the splendidly named Imperial Potato Office. In the Second World War, Britain established new ministries of supply, home security, economic warfare, information, food and shipping, and aircraft production. New executive agencies wielding wide powers in areas previously untouched by the state appeared in the United States as well, the number of government employees there increasing from 1 million in 1940 to 3.8 million by 1946. Even the Vichy regime in France experienced the growth of organization committees in the supervision of the wartime economy.

In essence, it is this control of the economy that lies at the heart of the concept of total war, because it is assumed that a state is required to mobilize all its resources in order to survive. However, it has become increasingly apparent that many of the wartime creations did not necessarily alter the pre-war structure. Much of the dramatic change once attributed to Lloyd George's premiership in Britain during the latter stages of the First World War is now seen more in terms of administrative continuities with that of his predecessor, Asquith.[22] The new centralized War Cabinet was not the administrative revolution Lloyd George claimed, many of its functions being hived off to *ad hoc* subcommittees in the manner of the War Committee it replaced. In terms of manpower policy at least, co-ordinated manipulation and distribution of mobilized resources was not effected until late 1917[23] and, in many respects, similar effective control of food production and distribution was achieved only in July 1918. Businessmen were introduced to government by Lloyd George and they also featured in the United States, where Wall Street broker Bernard Baruch headed the War Industries Board, and even in Imperial Germany, where Moellendorf and Rathenau of the electrical giant, AEG, were early appointees to the raw materials section of the war ministry. However, businessmen in government and the failure of the British Treasury to secure wartime control of the new ministerial creations were but temporary phenomena, with wartime controls speedily divested in Britain after the armistice.

In the case of Nazi Germany, there has been a lively debate on the extent to which Germany was already or became a total war economy during the Second World War. An earlier interpretation associated with Alan Milward postulated an economy designed for swift and lightning *Blitzkrieg*, which was then required to be converted into a total war economy from 1942 onwards under the guiding hand of Albert Speer. By contrast, Richard Overy has argued that fewer changes were required early in the war because the logic of Goering's Four-Year Plan Office of 1936 was the creation of a total war economy, and that what Milward has seen as rhetoric prior to 1942 was rhetoric applied. This should be seen within the context of competing agencies and interests that promoted gross inefficiency rather than effective preparation for war, and also in the context of German miscalculations as to the likely starting date for that war. Thus, Speer's efforts should be regarded as an attempt to improve the performance of an economy already geared for total war rather than to initiate the process in the first place.[24]

Undoubtedly, however, total war did result in increased state control over the individual. Some state systems already involved a degree of coercion, citizens of Nazi Germany and Soviet Russia having relatively little choice as to the degree of their participation in the war effort. But increased state control was equally a feature of democracies. During the First World War, both British and United States citizens were exposed to military conscription for the first time in many generations. The restrictions of DORA in 1914 were easily exceeded by the theoretical powers of the British government under the Emergency Powers (Defence) Act of 1939 and its revised version in May 1940. However, there were few compulsory labour directions in Britain and, although Britain also went further than any other belligerent in taking powers for the conscription of women, the legislation was again used sparingly. But there was compulsory direction of men to serve in the mining industry – the so-called Bevin Boys – in 1943 and, following a spate of unofficial strikes, it became an indictable offence in April 1944 to instigate or incite industrial stoppages in essential war work. Canada compulsorily transferred 127,000 workers from low to high priority employment under its National Service Civilian Regulations of January 1943 and, in the United States, the War Labor Disputes Act of the same year enabled government to conscript strikers. In the First World War, both British and American governments had contemplated conscripting striking Midlands engineering employees and copper miners respectively. At a lower level, too, government impinged on everyday life in new ways, although in the United States the population tended to fight the wars, to use J.M. Blum's words, 'in imagination only'.[25] Bread was rationed in Imperial Germany in the First World War as early as January 1915, and meat rationing was introduced in Britain in February 1918. In the Second World War commodities such as butter, bacon, sugar, meat, tea, cooking fats and margarine were all rationed in Britain before July 1940. Both wars saw the imposition of a blackout in Britain and the licensing laws and summer time of modern Britain remain legacies of the First World War.

War and social change

Military and industrial conscription also reflected the greater demands made upon manpower in total war. Just as pre-war soldiers in 1914 had not anticipated the kind of warfare that was to be waged on the Western Front, few politicians or soldiers had estimated correctly the extent of the demands which would be made upon industry. Britain, France and Imperial Russia all suffered 'shell shortages' in 1915, as did Germany in the following year. Part of the problem derived from the way in which skilled workers had been either conscripted or allowed to volunteer for war service in 1914 but, in any case, industries such as munitions expanded to such an extent that there was a massive growth in the labour force. In Italy, for example, those involved in war industries increased from 20 to 64 per cent of the industrial working force during the First World War, and in Imperial Russia there was a staggering increase from 24 to 76 per cent of the working force. Precisely the same happened in the Second World War. The shipbuilding industry in Canada, for example, alone increased its work-force from 4,000 in 1939 to 126,000 in 1943 and the United States labour force as a whole increased from 54 million to 64 million. Such increased demands provided new opportunities, not only for unskilled male labour, but for groups previously under-represented in the industrial labour force. In Imperial Germany, the number of women employed in industry increased from 1.4 million in 1914 to 2.1 million by 1918, and there were 800,000 more women in British industry in 1918 than in 1914 and two and a half times the number of women in United States industry in 1918 than a year previously. In the Second World War, there were 3 million more women in full or part-time employment in Britain in 1943 than in 1939 and 4.5 million more in the United States in 1945 than in 1940. In the United States, a parallel can be drawn with Negro employment in both world wars, the number employed in industry increasing from 2.9 million in 1940 to 3.2 million in 1944, for instance.

Particular attention has been devoted by historians to the condition of labour and to the question of the employment of women in total war. Total war invariably effected a stimulus for those sectors of the economy considered especially vital to war production: heavy industries such as coal, shipping and heavy metals, but also newer lighter industries such as chemicals, electrical goods and motors. In the United States, there was a boom in synthetic rubber manufacture during the Second World War owing to the loss of South-East Asian sources. As a result of such trends, unemployment declined rapidly and the position of labour generally was liable to be improved. One manifestation was the increase in trade union membership. In the United States this rose from 2 million in 1917 to 3.25 million in 1918 and from 10.5 million in 1941 to 14.75 million in 1945. In Britain, the increase was from 4 million to 8 million between 1914 and 1918 and by one-third – to 8 million – during the Second World War. Through enhanced union strength, continued militancy on the shopfloor and the need of government to ensure a better relationship with labour, total war would then generally result in lower working hours and higher wages in real terms. In Britain, it is estimated that average working hours fell from 50 hours to 48 hours a week between 1914 and 1918 and, although they increased from 48 hours in 1939 to 54.1 hours for men and between 44.2 and 46.9 hours for women by 1943, they declined to an average 44–5 hours in 1945.

However, average figures do not always reflect reality. In British industry during the First World War, for example, much of the earlier interpretation of the effect of dilution of trade and the narrowing of differentials within and between differing sectors of industry was based on the experience of engineering. Further research has indicated that the experience of labour employed in other sectors such as shipbuilding was very different. Calculations were also made in terms of differences between wage rates and earnings, a presumption being made that skilled men paid by the hour would not benefit to the same extent as unskilled men paid by piecework rates, but this ignored the widespread official and unofficial bonuses and incentives provided for skilled labour during the First World War. In any case, there was no substantial reorganization of British industry in either of the world wars, pre-war differentials being restored in 1918 so that, if labour could be said to have gained generally, most groups moved up together in broadly the same relationship as previously. In Britain, too, trade union membership declined rapidly in the 1920s and 1930s. In the Second World War, industrial wage differentials in Britain widened to such an extent that there was official concern at the level of wages in Midlands engineering and aircraft factories.

Another factor to be taken into account is wartime inflation: while, on average, wages in real terms kept ahead of inflation in Britain in both world wars, this was far from true in other states such as Imperial Germany. There, real wages fell and, although it can be said that the working class did relatively well, with unions forging a new partnership with employers in 1918, it did so only in the context of losing less than other social groups, which were affected even more in a society impoverished by wartime inflation. Similarly, although wages kept ahead of inflation in the United States in the Second World War, this was not the case in France. Generalization, therefore, is exceptionally hazardous and wide differences must be expected between and within varying social groups, not all of which might be in the position to benefit from the opportunities afforded by wartime participation in the labour market. Much remains to be done on the experience of social and occupational groups other than the working class and the unskilled – to give but one example, some of the most profound social changes in Britain in both wars took place not in industry but in the agricultural sector.

The judgement of the impact of total war upon the position of women is equally beset with difficulties of interpretation. As already indicated, there were measurable increases in female employment in most belligerents in both wars, Nazi Germany being the most notable exception. In many cases, however, it is the increase of women in areas such as transport or white-collar employment that is more significant than increases in the numbers in manufacturing industry, because the former employment was more likely to endure after the end of hostilities. The degree of female dilution in the munitions industry in both Britain and France in the First World War has been exaggerated, because most women were employed for specific functions and did not supplant skilled male labour. Equally, during the Second World War, British trade unions negotiated dilution agreements that protected male jobs. In many cases, many women may not have perceived wartime employment either as permanent or as an expression of long-term emancipation, and it can be argued that there was a significant revival of domesticity in

Britain in 1945. Some trends can be perceived in Britain in terms of the increase in part-time female employment during the Second World War and the greater employment of married women and older women, although the proportion of married women within the female labour force as a whole was still relatively small. Clearly, however, wartime employment neither implied equality of pay nor an erosion of the sexual divisions of labour. It is also arguable how far the extension of the suffrage in Britain after the First World War reflected an appreciation of female participation in the war effort. The enfranchisement of women aged over 30 in 1918 compensated for that of the 40 per cent of the adult male population, mostly working class, who had not been able to vote prior to the war. Moreover, in France, although the Chamber of Deputies voted for female suffrage in 1919, the Senate repeatedly rejected it. It has been argued that the final conceding of the principle of female suffrage in France in 1944 reflected the role of women in the resistance movement, but, in fact, the leftward turn in the indirectly elected Senate – especially among radicals, who had previously opposed the vote for women – guaranteed such an outcome anyway. Yet, if the world wars did not improve the status of women, they did perhaps offer some women wider opportunities and freedoms. Again, generalization about the perceptions or expectations of women is no easy task.[26]

It is also largely in terms of perception that social change as a result of total war must be gauged. Of course, the tendency of the modern state to collect statistics ensures that there are some measurable social trends. In both world wars, there were likely to be more marriages, more divorces and more illegitimate births. In Britain, attendance at the cinema rose in both world wars and, in the Second World War, 'eating out' increased with the 79 million meals per week of May 1941 increasing to 170 million meals a week by December 1944. Crime rose also in both world wars, although this included offences against wartime regulations. In the United States and Britain, for example, juvenile delinquency increased in both wars. There was also enhanced urbanization. In Imperial Russia, the urban proletariat grew from 22 million in 1914 to 28 million by 1916, one-third of the increase taking place in St Petersburg, with particular repercussions when the widespread failure of the transportation system contributed to the hunger and unrest in the cities in 1917. In the United States, the First World War saw the beginnings of a large-scale migration of the Negro population from the rural south to the industrial north, and this continued both through the interwar period and the Second World War. The Willow Run township in Detroit increased its population by 32,000 during the Second World War owing to the location of production of B-24 bombers there, and Detroit as a whole increased by 500,000 inhabitants, of whom 12 per cent were blacks. Changes in occupation can also be measured, such as the permanent decline in the number of domestic servants in Britain during and after the First World War and, in Britain, it is also possible to measure the changes in the numbers paying income tax. In the First World War, this increased from 1.5 million in 1914 to 7.75 million in 1918 and from 1 million to 7 million among manual workers between 1939 and 1944.

The measurement of quantifiable trends contributes to some extent to an understanding of those that cannot be so calculated, such as the degree to which total war resulted in greater social homogeneity and the breakdown of class distinctions through participation. Two commonly expressed vestiges of this are the concepts of a 'war generation', emerging from the shared experiences of the trenches in the First World War, and the idea of a 'people's war' during the Second World War. In terms of the former, it appears doubtful that shared experience between officers and men in the front line brought a greater understanding between different classes in the post-war period, not least because of the considerable distinctions that were preserved in the relationship of officer and man. Richard Bessel and David Englander have concluded from a survey of the literature in this field that the war generation lasted 'only as long as it remained under fire'.[27]

The identification of a 'people's war' by contemporary socialist, and invariably middle-class, intellectuals in Britain during the Second World War has tended to disguise the persistence of class differences. A significant change was the post-war bargaining power of labour through trade unions, but this occurred within the existing structure of social consciousness and the structure of the trade union movement itself was also unchanged. The image of the happy communion of the London underground shelters during the Blitz and much else in popular mythology does not bear close investigation.[28] Much was made by Titmuss, for example, of the wartime reformist consensus that was said to have emerged as a result of the compulsory wartime evacuation of 1.75 million persons, mainly women and children, from inner cities and coastal towns in Britain in 1939. In fact, it would appear that most hosts were as working class as the evacuees themselves and the experience merely reinforced existing pre-war analyses among middle-class observers of the nature of the working class. In any case, the great majority of the evacuees had returned to the cities by 1940.[29] In general, therefore, although there may have been some changes in social stratification during wartime, a temporary equalizing effect upon income had little impact upon class differences or the ownership of property. Nevertheless, total war does imply at least a temporary throwing together of different social groups, and it would be hazardous to deny altogether the impact of evacuation upon individuals or, for example, the presence in Britain during the Second World War of some 1.5 million foreign servicemen.

At the same time, although states did not go to war to transform their societies, total war did produce the ideals if not the reality of post-war social change and guided reconstruction. In the United States, the housing shortages resulting from the growth in urban population during the First World War and the attendant social problems did establish a precedent for federal intervention, which foreshadowed the programmes of the 1930s. Britain also experienced the intention for reconstruction through such measures as the Ministry of Health Act and the Housing and Town Planning Act of 1919. Economic depression left such promise unfulfilled but, during and after the Second World War, an apparent wartime consensus on guided change bore fruit in such measures as the Town and Country Planning Act, the Education Act, Keynesian declarations of full employment and the establishment of a welfare state along the lines of the Beveridge report of December 1942. Again, however, care must be exercised in interpreting post-war changes as novel. A broad consensus on such matters as family allowance provision and the principle of a National Health Service had existed before the war, and the 1944 Education Act did not materially affect the pre-war status quo. Full employment rested upon the assumption that a condition already arrived at in wartime would be maintained, and the war generally created a false impression that emergency apparatus would also be maintained to ensure the preservation of social solidarity and the un-challenged consensus on a welfare state. Some changes resulted from the electoral success of the Labour party in 1945, itself arguably a result of the unguided change in popular expectation through enforced egali-tarianism and creeping collectivization. But the Labour party had mod-erated during the war through participation in coalition government; in the United States, there was actually a shift to the right rather than the political left despite equal measures of guided social change. Though not rivalling the far-reaching provisions of Canada's Marsh report of March 1943, both Negroes and ex-servicemen were the theoretical beneficiaries of social measures in the United States. In reality, of course, discrimina-tion against blacks continued, irrespective of presidential executive orders to the contrary, although the US Servicemen's Readjustment Act of 1944 – the 'GI Bill' – illustrated the ability of veterans' organizations to achieve far more through the power of pressure-group lobbies in the American system than through comparable veterans' organizations elsewhere.

In effect, wartime changes may not mean much in practical terms thereafter and the lack of success of British veterans' organizations merely illustrates how far change depended upon the political system of the state waging total war. Clearly, too, changes were potentially greater where a state collapsed under the strain of war, as in Imperial Russia in 1917, or suffered total defeat as in Germany and Japan in 1945. Generally, however, it would appear that institutional mechanisms are more liable to change than social structures, although here, too, the example of the British army as an institution in the First World War is instructive. In theory, it ought to provide clear evidence of the impact of total war, since a small pre-war regular cadre of 250,000 officers and men expanded to almost 6 million in the course of the war, becoming theoretically more representative of society than ever before. In fact, the army remained unrepresentative of British society through the unequable distribution of war service and, in the long term, there was little or no change in its social structure or ethos owing to the survival of the pre-war officer corps. Even the impact of service life may be challenged, since the popular image of men such as Robert Graves or Siegfried Sassoon as representative of the thousands who served in the army is hardly compatible with the reality.[30] In short, armies as institutions do not seem to change to the same extent as society is said to change as the result of total war.

Furthermore, it is also necessary to place wartime change and development within the context of long-term social trends, which often suggest evolutionary rather than revolutionary change during the course of the longer period. This would suggest, for example, that female suffrage would have come to Britain irrespective of the impact of the First World War, although that experience may have accelerated changes already taking place. Total war could not fail to generate some change through its sheer scale, but it is important to judge how far changes survived the immediate postwar situation that generated them and, indeed, how far such changes would have occurred in any case. In conclusion, therefore, it might be suggested that total war is an important and largely instructive concept, provided that its limitations are kept in mind.

Notes

1 J.U. Nef, *War and Human Progress*, London, Routledge & Kegan Paul, 1950.
2 R. Titmuss, *Problems of Social Policy*, London, HMSO and Longman, 1950.
3 S. Andrzejewski, *Military Organisation and Society*, London, Routledge & Kegan Paul, 1954.
4 G.N. Clark, *War and Society in the Seventeenth Century*, London, Cambridge University Press, 1958.
5 M.E. Howard, *The Franco-Prussian War*, London, Hart-Davis, 1961.
6 M.E. Howard, *War in European History*, Oxford, Oxford University Press, 1976.
7 A. Marwick, *The Deluge*, London, Bodley Head, 1965.
8 A. Marwick, *Britain in the Century of Total War*, London, Bodley Head, 1968; Marwick, *War and Social Change in the Twentieth Century*, London, Macmillan, 1971.
9 G. Wright, *The Ordeal of Total War*, New York, Harper Torchbooks, 1968; P. Calvocoressi and G. Wint, *Total War*, London, Allen Lane, 1972.
10 Open University, A301 *War and Society*, Milton Keynes, Open University Press, 1973.
11 M. Bentley, 'Social change: appearance and reality', in C. Haigh (ed.) *The Cambridge Historical Encyclopedia of Great Britain and Ireland*, Cambridge University Press, 1985, p. 327.
12 A. Calder, *The People's War*, London, Cape, 1969.

13 P. Lewis, *A People's War*, London, Thames Methuen, 1986.
14 H. Pelling, *Britain in the Second World War*, London, Collins/Fontana, 1971.
15 B. Bond, *War and Society in Europe, 1870–1970*, London, Fontana, 1984, p. 168.
16 J. Childs, *Armies and Warfare in Europe, 1648–1789*, Manchester, Manchester University Press, 1982, p. 2.
17 C. Emsley, *British Society and the French Wars 1793–1815*, London, Macmillan, 1979, p. 169.
18 P.J. Parish, *The American Civil War*, London, Eyre Methuen, 1975.
19 J.M. Winter, *The Great War and the British People*, London, Macmillan, 1986.
20 J.J. Becker, *The Great War and the French People*, Leamington Spa, Berg, 1985.
21 G. Hardach, *The First World War, 1914–1918*, London, Allen Lane, 1977; A.S. Milward, *War, Economy and Society, 1939–1945*, London, Allen Lane, 1977; A.S. Milward, *The Economic Effects of the Two World Wars on Britain*, 2nd edn, London, Macmillan, 1984.
22 K. Burk (ed.) *War and the State: The Transformation of British Government, 1914–1918*, London, Allen & Unwin, 1982.
23 K.R. Grieves, *The Politics of Manpower, 1914–1918*, Manchester, Manchester University Press, 1988.
24 A.S. Milward, *The German Economy at War*, London, Athlone Press, 1965; R.J. Overy, *The Air War, 1939–1945*, London, Europa, 1980; R.J. Overy, *Goering: The Iron Man*, London, Routledge & Kegan Paul, 1984.
25 J.M. Blum, *V was for Victory*, New York, Harcourt Brace Jovanovich, 1976.
26 P. Summerfield, *Women Workers in the Second World War*, London, Croom Helm, 1984; G. Braybon, *Women Workers in the First World War*, London, Croom Helm, 1981; A Marwick, *Women at War, 1914–1918*, London, Croom Helm, 1977.
27 R. Bessel and D. Englander, 'Up from the trenches: some recent writing on the soldiers of the Great War', *European Studies Review*, vol. 1, no. 3, 1981, pp. 387–95.
28 T. Harrisson, *Living through the Blitz*, London, Collins, 1976.
29 T.C. Crosby, *The Impact of Civilian Evacuation in the Second World War*, London, Croom Helm, 1986; B.S. Johnson, *The Evacuees*, London, Gollancz, 1968.
30 I.F.W. Beckett and K. Simpson (eds) *A Nation in Arms: A Social Study of the British Army in the First World War*, Manchester, Manchester University Press, 1985.

2

The Persistence of the Old Regime

Arno J. Mayer

Introduction

Even with the passage of time the first half of the twentieth century stands out for having witnessed an unprecedented cataclysm and a major watershed in the history of Europe. Growing temporal and psychological distance is not likely to significantly lessen or normalize the enormity of the Great War and the Verdun Ossuary, the *outrance* [ultimate success] of the Second World War and Auschwitz. But because of the fixed infamy and atrocity of this self-immolation and holocaust – including Hiroshima – historians will forever continue to probe their underlying causes. They will also keep trying to penetrate the agony and ferocity of the Bolshevik revolution and regime, which were the main ray of hope during one of Europe's darkest nights. Russia was fatally caught up in this colossal turbulence, sacrificing more blood and patrimony than any other nation. Paradoxically, though peripheral to Western civilization, Russia was nevertheless among its greatest de-stabilizers and ultimate saviors.

[*The Persistence of the Old Regime*] is intended as a contribution to the discussion of the *causa causans* [ultimate cause] and inner nature of Europe's recent 'sea of troubles'. It starts with the premise that the World War of 1939–45 was umbilically tied to the Great War of 1914–18, and that these two conflicts were nothing less than the Thirty Years' War of the general crisis of the twentieth century.

The second premise is that the Great War of 1914, or the first and protogenic phase of this general crisis, was an outgrowth of the latter-day remobilization of Europe's *anciens régimes*. Though losing ground to the forces of industrial capitalism, the forces of the old order were still sufficiently willful and powerful to resist and slow down the course of history, if necessary by recourse to violence. The Great War was an expression of the decline and fall of the old order fighting to prolong its life rather than of the explosive rise of industrial capitalism bent on imposing its primacy. Throughout Europe the strains of protracted warfare finally, as of 1917, shook and cracked the foundations of the embattled old order, which had been its incubator. Even so, except in Russia, where the most unreconstructed of the old regimes came crashing down, after 1918–19 the forces of perseverance recovered sufficiently to aggravate Europe's general crisis, sponsor fascism, and contribute to the resumption of total war in 1939.

The third and major premise of [this] book is that Europe's old order was thoroughly preindustrial and prebourgeois. For too long historians have focused excessively on the advance of science and technology, of industrial and world capitalism, of the bourgeoisie and professional middle class, of liberal civil society, of democratic political society, and of cultural modernism. They have been far more preoccupied with these forces of innovation and the making of the new society than with the forces of inertia and resistance that slowed the waning of the old order. Although on one level Western historians and social scientists have repudiated the idea of progress, on another they continue to believe in it, albeit in qualified terms. This abiding and tacit faith in progress is coupled with an intense aversion to historical stasis and regression. There has been, then, a marked tendency to neglect or underplay, and to disvalue, the endurance of old forces and ideas and their cunning genius for assimilating, delaying, neutralizing, and subduing capitalist modernization, even including industrialization. The result is a partial and distorted view of the nineteenth and early twentieth centuries. To achieve a more balanced perspective, historians will have to view not only the high drama of progressive change but also the relentless tragedy of historical perseverance, and to explore the dialectic interaction between them.

But [the] book does not offer a balanced interpretation of Europe between 1848 and 1914. To counteract the chronic overstatement of the unfolding and ultimate triumph of modernity – even the general crisis itself, including fascism, is being credited with serving this universal design and outcome – it [. . .] concentrates on the persistence of the old order. The conventional wisdom is still that Europe broke out of its *ancien régime* and approached or crossed the threshold of modernity well before 1914. Scholars of all ideological persuasions have downgraded the importance of preindustrial economic interests, prebourgeois elites, predemocratic authority systems, premodernist artistic idioms, and 'archaic' mentalities. They have done so by treating them as expiring remnants, not to say relics, in rapidly modernizing civil and political societies. They have vastly overdrawn the decline of land, noble, and peasant; the contraction of traditional manufacture and trade, provincial burghers, and artisanal workers; the derogation of kings, public service nobilities, and upper chambers; the weakening of organized religion; and the atrophy of classical high culture. To the extent that economic, social and political historians accord any vitality to these vestiges of a dying past, they present them as using or misusing that vitality to delay, derange, and complicate the ultimately inevitable growth of capitalist industrialization, social leveling, and political liberalization. In this same teleological spirit, cultural historians have pored over the accomplishments of the artistic avant-garde while curtly dismissing academic cultures for being exhausted and for obstructing the preordained march to modernism.

In order to reconstruct the historical matrix in which the general crisis and Thirty Years' War of the twentieth century originated, it may be necessary to reconceive and perhaps even totally reverse this picture of a modern world commanding a recessive and crumbling old order. At any rate, it is the thesis of [the] book that the 'premodern' elements were not the decaying and fragile remnants of an all but vanished past but the very essence of Europe's incumbent civil and political societies. This is not to deny the growing importance of the modern forces that undermined and challenged the old order. But it is to argue that until 1914 the forces of inertia and resistance contained and curbed this dynamic and expansive new society within the *anciens régimes* that dominated Europe's historical landscape.

There are no value-free categories with which to address this reality. On the one hand, to speak of the Europe of the time as saliently premodern, preindustrial and prebourgeois is to endorse the view, at least implicitly, that the forces of progress were on the verge of inheriting the earth. On the other hand, to refer to Europe as an *ancien régime* or a quasifeudal society is to ratify the presumption that the forces and institutions of perseverance were on the point of collapse. Obviously, such labels and images have a retrospective inference, and the choice of one set over another is in itself an historical judgment. A book, however, which proposes to explore and reassess the dimensions of 'oldness' in Europe between 1848 and 1914 cannot avoid applying and refining such notions as *ancien régime* and feudality.

Europe's old regimes were civil and political societies with distinct powers, traditions, customs and conventions. Precisely because they were such integral and coherent social, economic, and cultural systems, they were exceptionally resilient. Even in France, where the *ancien régime* was pronounced legally dead between 1789 and 1793, it kept resurfacing violently and lived on in many ways for more than a century. Of course, Europe was not a single entity. There were vast national and regional variations of economy, social structure, legal tradition and mental outlook, and these historical singularities cannot be ignored or minimized. Nonetheless, in its prime as well as in its perdurable extension into modern times, the *ancien régime* was a distinctly pan-European phenomenon.

The old order's civil society was first and foremost a peasant economy and rural society dominated by hereditary and privileged nobilities. Except for a few bankers, merchants and shipowners, the large fortunes and incomes were based in land. Across Europe the landed nobilities occupied first place not only in economic, social and cultural terms but also politically.

In fact, political society was the linchpin of this agrarian society of orders. Everywhere it took the form of absolutist authority systems of different degrees of enlightenment and headed by hereditary monarchs. The crowns reigned and governed with the support of extended royal families and court parties as well as compliant ministers, generals, and bureaucrats.

The Church was another vital constituent and pillar of the *ancien régime*. Closely tied to both the crown and the nobility, it was, like them, rooted in land, which was its principal source of revenue. The upper clergy was of distinguished social provenance, exercised far-reaching influence, and enjoyed important fiscal and legal exemptions. As a great corporate institution the Church exerted considerable sway through its quasi-monopoly of education and social services and its exclusive control of the sacred rites of birth, marriage and death.

The entire regime was suffused with the legacy of feudalism that presumably expired with the Middle Ages and finally was declared 'totally abolished' in France in August 1789. Since the term 'feudality' remains controversial in discussions of medieval and early modern history, it is bound to be even more disputed in the study of modern and contemporary history. According to Marc Bloch,[1] no region in Europe ever had a 'complete' feudal society, and different parts of Europe were feudalized to varying degrees and at differing speeds. But Bloch also stressed that notwithstanding great diversities in form, intensity, space and time Europe's feudal societies shared important common features: the fractioning of the central state into fiefs; the ties of personal dependence, protection, and heredity implanted in the ownership and exploitation of land; the 'honorable obligation to bear arms' reserved to the upper orders or vassals; and the extreme social and political inequality favorable to a small oligarchy of landed proprietors, warriors and churchmen. Predecessor to the *ancien régime*, the feudal regime was characterized by a particular form of property, frequently by serfdom, and always by the payment of feudal and seignorial dues. This system of production that relied on the legal subjection and economic exploitation of a vast underclass was embedded in a complex structure of social and political institutions.

With the rebirth of the territorial state and the development of the idea of political sovereignty, monarchial authority put an end to political and military feudalism. Claiming the monopoly of coercion, the dynasties presided over expanded standing armies and centralized bureaucracies loyal to the crown. They also secured the fiscal independence needed to pay for this large and growing state apparatus without excessively bending to the nobility.

To the extent that political, legal and military power was closely associated with landownership, the former declined much more rapidly and extensively than the latter. The enduring seignorial system left a deep imprint on the old regime by perpetuating the privileged noblemen who exalted and arrogated the ethos of personal loyalty, the exercise of martial virtues, and the duty of public service. To be sure this nobility was politically diminished by the loss of direct and exclusive legal and administrative authority over land and labor and by changes in military organization and technique. Even so, since they were not shorn of their stake in the landed property, agriculture, and processing of primary products that dominated economic life down to 1914, the nobles retained their wealth and status. Moreover, while working out a *modus vivendi* with the crown, the nobility of the sword infused the entire public service nobility, both civil and military, with its time-honored precepts. In fact, the kings themselves became imbued with this noble conceit. Seeing their own thrones tied to the hierarchical society of orders, they bolstered this civil society economically and socially. At the same time, though the absolute monarchs deprived noblemen and seigneurs of their sovereign political and military authority, they assimilated them into their state apparatus. The result was that by permeating the state apparatus, and in particular its officials of non-noble birth, with their own precepts, and by occupying key positions in the new armies and bureaucracies, the nobles compensated for their loss of private political power. The nobility also benefitted from close connections with the Church, whose top personnel was of high birth and whose wealth, like the nobles' own, continued to be overwhelmingly landed.

Clearly, then, feudalism endowed Europe's old order with much more than a mere integument of upper-class traditions, customs and mentalities. It penetrated the *anciens régimes* through nobilities positioned to monopolize strategic economic, military, bureaucratic and cultural stations. These postfeudal noblemen adjusted their ties of dependence, heredity and ennoblement to reflect and enhance their privileged place in the ruling and governing classes of the new territorial states. Of course, the configuration and repressiveness of this prolongation of feudality differed by country and region. The dissimilarities between Europe east and west of the Elbe became most striking. In Russia and Prussia in particular, but also in Hungary and southern Italy, labor service and legal servitude actually intensified before they gradually disappeared. Throughout most of the rest of Europe, the landed nobles became postfeudal in economic terms as they adopted capitalist methods of agricultural production and land exploitation. But notwithstanding this growth of capitalism on the land, the nobility continued to suffuse high society, high culture and high politics with its feudalistic spirit.

The European economies provided the material underpinning for this continuing pre-eminence of the landed and public service nobilities. Land remained the ruling and governing classes' principal form of wealth and revenue until 1914. No less significant, consumer manufacture continued to outweigh capital goods production in its share of national wealth, product, and employment. This was true even in England, where agriculture was radically reduced in economic importance, and in Germany, which experienced a spectacular spurt of industrial development between 1871 and 1914. Across Europe small and medium-sized firms that were family owned, financed, and managed dominated the manufacturing and commercial sectors of the national economies. This entrepreneurial capitalism spawned a bourgeoisie that was at best protonational. As a class this bourgeoisie shared economic interests, but it had only limited social and political cohesion. This manufactural and mercantile bourgeoisie could not measure itself with the landed nobility in terms of class, status or power. To be sure, in the last third of the nineteenth century the growth of capital-intensive producer-goods industries gave birth to an industrial bourgeoisie. But quite apart from remaining of limited economic importance until 1914, these magnates of industry and their associates in corporate banking and the liberal professions were more disposed to collaborate with the agrarians and the established governing classes than with the older bourgeoisie of manufacturers, merchants, and bankers.

Just as there was no complete or model feudal society, so there was no archetypal postfeudal or preindustrial *ancien régime*. England was only one of its variants. Although England's economy was dominated by manufactural and merchant capitalism, the aristocracy continued to be paramount. This was so because land remained the chief source of wealth and income despite the radical contraction of British agriculture in the course of the nineteenth century. In other words, the monarchy and landed elite tamed the industrialization of England without succumbing to it.

There is no denying that British agriculture was eliminated 'as a major social activity' and that the power of the land-based nobility was transformed. But even after taking these steps along the democratic route to modernity, England never became a 'bourgeois order' run by a 'conquering' or 'triumphant' bourgeoisie. Of course, the House of Commons, elected by an expanding male franchise, controlled the executive, and regional and local bourgeois interests were represented in it. But there was no movement to remove the crown, the royal court, the House of Lords, and the ascriptive public service nobility. Despite the decline of agriculture and despite insular security, which obviated the need for a strong military caste, the landed classes managed to perpetuate this 'archaic' political order and culture.

The major Continental powers, except for France, had none of Britain's advantages: the landed elites were intact, agriculture remained a major social activity, and insecure frontiers justified the military presumption of kings and nobles. This explains, in part, why Russia, Austria-Hungary and Germany persisted as absolutist monarchies.

France alone among the major powers finally became a republic in 1875. But except for no longer having a king and for now being governed by a *petit bourgeois* political class, France stayed in tune with the rest of the Continent, its economy dominated by agriculture and traditional manufacture. Ironically, an excess of agrarian and political democracy impeded French industrialization, notably after the onset of the second industrial revolution in the late nineteenth century. If France became 'a half-hearted republic in continual crisis', it was because its bourgeoisie was too weak and divided to steady it.

In any case, neither England nor France had become industrial-capitalist and bourgeois civil and political societies by 1914. Their polities were as 'obviously outdated' and 'stubbornly concerned with their longevity' as the polities of the other four big powers. All alike were *anciens régimes* grounded in the continued predominance of landed elites, agriculture, or both.

As Joseph Schumpeter saw so clearly,[2] except in France the kings remained the divinely ordained 'centerpieces' of Europe's authority systems. Their position was feudal in both 'the historical and the sociological sense', not least because 'the human material of feudal society' continued to 'fill the offices of state, officer the army, and devise policies'. Although capitalist processes, both national and international, generated ever larger shares of government revenue – for the 'tax-collecting state' – the feudal element remained a *'classe dirigente'* [directing class] that behaved 'according to precapitalist patterns'. While the entrenched upper classes took account of 'bourgeois interests' and availed themselves of the 'economic possibilities offered by capitalism', they were careful 'to distance themselves from the bourgeoisie'. This arrangement was not an 'atavism ... but an *active symbiosis* of two social strata' in which the old elites retained their political, social and cultural primacy. In exchange they let the bourgeoisie make money and pay taxes. In Schumpeter's judgment, even in England 'the aristocratic element continued to rule the roost *right to the end of the period of intact and vital capitalism'*.

By controlling what Schumpeter called the 'steel frame' or 'political engine' of the *ancien régime*, the feudal elements were in a position to set the terms for the implantation of manufactural and industrial capitalism, thereby making it serve their own purposes. They forced industry to fit itself into pre-existing social, class and ideological structures. Admittedly, industrial capitalism distorted and strained these structures in the process, but not beyond recognition or to the breaking point. The old governing class was both resilient and flexible. It had the support of the landed nobilities and interests, which quite rightly considered the steel frame of the *ancien régime* to be the protective armor for their privileged but exposed positions. In addition, the managers of the state won the loyalty of the bourgeoisie by furthering or safeguarding their economic interests with government contracts, protective tariffs and colonial preferments.

If the feudal elements in both political and civil society perpetuated their dominance so effectively, it was largely because they knew how to adapt and renew themselves. The public service nobilities, both civil and military, took in qualified and ambitious scions of business and the liberal professions, though they were careful to regulate closely this infusion of new blood and talent. Newcomers had to pass through elite schools, ingest the corporate ethos, and demonstrate fealty to the old order as a precondition for advancement. Besides, the highest ranks of the state bureaucracy and military services continued to be reserved for men of high birth and proven assimilation.

The landed magnates were no less effective in adjusting to changing times. Above all, they absorbed and practiced the principles of capitalism and interest politics without, however, derogating their aristocratic world-view, bearing and connections. Some noble proprietors became improving landlords. Others combined the rationalized exploitation of the soil and agrarian labor with large-scale milling, distilling, brewing and dairying. Still others turned to extracting timber, coal and minerals from their lands and invested in industrial ventures. Moreover, all learned alike to resort to lobbying and log-rolling as well as pressure and partisan politics to protect or promote their interests. Increasingly, the landed estate assumed the attributes of class and class consciousness, and acted accordingly.

This extensive and many-sided adaptation is usually considered evidence for the de-noblement and de-aristocratization of the old order, for the inevitable if gradual *embourgeoisement*, or bourgeoisification, of Europe's ruling and governing classes. But there is another way of viewing this accommodation. Just as industrialization was grafted on to pre-established societal and political structures, so the feudal elements reconciled their rationalized bureaucratic and economic behavior with their pre-existent social and cultural praxis and mind-set. In other words, the old elites excelled at selectively ingesting, adapting and assimilating new ideas and practices without seriously endangering their traditional status, temperament and outlook. Whatever the dilution and cheapening of nobility, it was gradual and benign.

This prudential and circumscribed adjustment was facilitated by the bourgeoisie's rage for co-optation and ennoblement. Whereas the nobility was skilled at adaptation, the bourgeoisie excelled at emulation. Throughout the nineteenth and early twentieth centuries the *grands bourgeois* kept denying themselves by imitating and appropriating the ways of the nobility in the hope of climbing into it. The grandees of business and finance bought landed estates, built country houses, sent their sons to elite higher schools, and assumed aristocratic poses and life-styles. They also strained to break into aristocratic and court circles and to marry into the titled nobility. Last but not least, they solicited decorations and, above all, patents of nobility. These aristocratizing barons of industry and commerce were not simply supercilious parvenus or arrivistes who bowed and scraped for fatuous honors from the parasitic leisure class of a decaying old order. On the contrary, their obsequiousness was highly practical and consequential. The bourgeois sought social advancement for reasons of material benefit, social status and psychic income. In addition, and no less important, by disavowing themselves in order to court membership in the old establishment, the aristocratizing bourgeois impaired their own class formation and class consciousness and accepted and prolonged their subordinate place in the 'active symbiosis of the two social strata'.

But there was another result as well. As part of their effort to scale the social pyramid and to demonstrate their political loyalty, the bourgeois embraced the historicist high culture and patronized the hegemonic institutions that were dominated by the old elites. The result was that they strengthened classical and academic idioms, conventions, and symbols in the arts and letters instead of encouraging modernist impulses. The bourgeois allowed themselves to be ensnared in a cultural and educational system that bolstered and reproduced the *ancien régime*. In the process they sapped their own potential to inspire the conception of a new aesthetic and intellection.

Indeed, the self-abnegating bourgeois were among the most enthusiastic champions of traditional architecture, statuary, painting and performing arts. This high classical culture had formidable state support. Academies, conservatories and museums provided training, access to careers and official prizes. The governments financed most of these institutions, awarded commissions, and sponsored individual and collective artistic activities. The churches and universities were part of this towering hegemonic edifice.

But to say that the conventions and idioms of high culture remained traditional and classical is not to say that they were archaic and lifeless. To the extent that Europe was an old order, its official high culture was congruent with it. It might even be said that some of Europe's finest cultural achievements were and continued to be 'inseparable from the milieu of absolutism, of extreme social injustice, even of gross violence, in which they flourished'. No doubt, judging by the tendency to formalist replication, overdecoration, and monumentalization, some of the arts were becoming sclerotic and trailed behind their times. But cultural productions were no less effective for being turgid and specious. Certainly the official cultures were not about to be subverted or toppled by the modernist avant-garde, which kept being assimilated, defused and turned back.

The mentalities of Europe's elites probably trailed even further behind economic developments than their social and cultural life. In any case, their mind-set changed very slowly and was perhaps most revealing of their continuing implantation in and allegiance to the old regime. The governing classes, in which the feudal element remained particularly conspicuous, were thoroughly imbued with nobilitarian values and attitudes. Their world-view was consonant with an imperious and hierarchical rather than a liberal and democratic society.

In the 1780s an aristocratic reaction in defense of fiscal, social and bureaucratic privilege had become an important, possibly a decisive, underlying and immediate cause for the French Revolution, the first act of the breakup of Europe's *ancien régime*. At that time the lay and clerical nobilities resisted any further loss of control in political society, which had become an ever more essential shield for their privileged status. Similarly, between 1905 and 1914 the old elites proceeded to reaffirm and tighten their political hold in order to bolster their material, social and cultural pre-eminence. In the process they intensified the domestic and international tensions which produced the Great War that started the final act of the dissolution of Europe's old regime.

The economies: *the endurance of land, agriculture, manufacture*

Down to 1914 Europe was pre-eminently preindustrial and prebourgeois, its civil societies being deeply grounded in economies of labor-intensive agriculture, consumer manufacture, and petty commerce. Admittedly, industrial capitalism and its class formations, notably the bourgeoisie and the factory proletariat, made vast strides, especially after 1890. But they were in no position to challenge or supplant the tenacious economic and class structures of the pre-existent capitalism.

Even in Western and Central Europe the economy was still dominated by merchant and manufactural capitalism, while monopoly, finance or organized industrial capitalism was only in its first growing phase. This meant that cosmopolitan merchants and bankers, along with local manufacturers, continued to carry more weight than the owners and managers of big industry and corporate banking.

While progress in production techniques was prodigious and continuous, the process and rhythm of economic growth were spasmodic and uneven. The first industrial revolution reached its technological and economic climacteric in parts of Western and Central Europe in the late nineteenth century, when the second industrial revolution entered its infant stage. But this does not mean that by then merchant and manufactural capitalism was stagnating or disintegrating – nationally, regionally or locally. Although some of its branches experienced a decline in production and in profit rates, other branches continued either to hold their own or to expand. On balance, the capitalism of the first industrial revolution not only remained robust during the transition to the new capitalism of the second, but also furthered this transition and gained from it.

The protracted but far from general economic crisis that lasted from the mid-1870s, to the mid-1890s was not so much a watershed between the old and the new capitalisms as the costly catalysis of their early interpenetration. Nor did this crisis inaugurate an era of 'sharpening conflicts between the growth of productive power and business profitability'. While the new capitalism established itself as semi-autonomous growth centers within the existing economic structures and helped put an end to the persistent economic crisis, it was in no position to take command of Europe's political economy. During the quarter-century between 1890 and 1914 even the German economy did not fall under the control of its large and interwoven industrial and financial corporations. Indeed, it would appear that by 1914 monopoly and finance capitalism was in its first rather than its highest or last stage. To be sure, there was substantial and rapid industrial growth and concentration. Even so, the new capitalism did not 'supersede' the old with the start of the twentieth century, nor was capitalism 'transformed' into an imperialism driven by capital exports rather than the export of merchandise.

Not only the growth of industrial capitalism but also the contraction of 'premodern' economic sectors proceeded very gradually. The result was that agriculture and consumer manufacture continued to outweigh the capital goods sector, in large measure because key landed and manufacturing interests excelled at adapting new production techniques and at enlisting state support to cushion their relative economic decline. Despite dramatic advances by the new capitalism, agriculture, urban real estate, and consumer manufacture continued to provide the essential material foundations for Europe's *anciens régimes* between 1848 and 1914.

Except in the United Kingdom, the agricultural sector claimed a larger share of the labor force and also generated a larger proportion of the gross national product than any other single sector. Moreover, except in France – and particularly in England – vast property holdings occupied a paramount place either as estate agriculture or as land let out for cash rent or crop sharing. In addition, in all countries landed property was still without exception the principal form of personal wealth and the main source of private income, also because of rising real estate values in the cities. It is true that although agriculture and land remained first in absolute terms, they were losing relative ground to industry and movable capital. But this is not to say that the landed estate and the postfeudal seigneur were about to crumble. The large magnates in particular more than held their own. While in some areas they bought the lands of the faltering small gentry at advantageous prices, in others they benefitted disproportionately from rising land values. Furthermore, numerous big proprietors became improving landlords. They rationalized land management, went into food processing and lumbering, and diversified their capital by investing in urban real estate and business ventures. Last but not least, particularly during times of economic adversity, the big agrarians managed to secure favorable tariffs, interest rates, subsidies and taxes because of their close ties with the feudal element in government. More often than not they obtained these government benefits by collaborating with spokesmen for traditional consumer manufactory and infant heavy industry that also clamored for state aid.

On every major score the manufacturing sector came right after agriculture, except in Britain, where it had stood first since midcentury. This sector consisted mainly of four branches of consumer goods production: textiles and apparel, food processing, leather (including shoes) and wood (especially furniture). The technology of consumer manufacture was that of the first industrial revolution, notably the application of coal and steam as well as the ready availability of iron and steel and of rail transport. This sprawling economic sector comprised, above all, single-unit enterprises of labor-intensive small workshops and medium-sized plants (below factory level) staffed by artisans and unskilled hands using simple, low-energy machinery. Because of their relatively small capitalization most manufacturing firms were family owned, financed and managed. As for the class formations of this precorporate entrepreneurial capitalism, the owners of small workshops were the backbone of the independent lower middle class. In turn the proprietors of medium-sized as well as large plants, especially in textiles and food processing, constituted a bourgeoisie that was predominantly local and provincial rather than national and cosmopolitan. This bourgeoisie, including commercial and private bankers, acted less as a social class with a comprehensive political and cultural project than as an interest and pressure group in pursuit of economic goals.

For its part, the capital goods sector was like an archipelago surrounded by vast oceans of agriculture and traditional manufacture. Paradoxically this sector had its real beginnings during the protracted recession of 1873 to 1896, and it was still of only limited scope in 1914. These four decades saw the launching of the second industrial revolution with its organic chemistry and synthetics, electric power, turbines, internal combustion engines, nonferrous metals, special alloys and streamlined iron-ore processing. These innovations in technique, energy sources and materials went hand in hand with the growth of giant firms, some of which established their own research laboratories.

This dynamic lead sector of producer goods industry was centered in the now stupendous iron and steel industry as well as in metallurgy and machine-making, vehicle construction, and chemicals. These four branches saw the greatest concentration of multi-unit companies operating large factories with specialized and high-energy machinery manned by a work-force of factory artisans and proletarians. The capital-intensive production that furthered labor's marginal efficiency called for a scale of investment that exceeded the financial capacities of family entrepreneurship. Even family-controlled enterprises became outposts of corporate and managerial capitalism that spawned a business bourgeoisie with a national perspective and with growing ties with both investment banks and government. Because of their high capitalization, the mining and railroad industries ought to count as part of the corporate capitalist complex that spurred the second industrial revolution.

Curiously enough, the ascending national bourgeoisie of industrial capitalism was even less a social class 'for itself', with its own interests and objectives, than the local and parochial bourgeoisie of traditional manufacture. Throughout Europe the magnates and 'robber barons' of industry, and their (subordinate) associates in the professional middle class, solicited indispensable state aid from governments that continued to be dominated by preindustrial and prebourgeois governing classes. According to Joseph Schumpeter there was a systematic trade-off: in exchange for economic benefits the bourgeoisie supported the 'feudal elements . . . [that] filled the offices of state, officered the army, [and] devised policies'. The new national bourgeoisie, for its part, secured advantageous tariffs, legal codes and labor policies. In turn, the old governing class counted on industrialists and bankers to help modernize in particular the war-related branches of the *ancien régime*'s economy without claiming an independent say in politics and culture.

For Thorstein Veblen[3] this amalgamation of 'the latest mechanistic science and . . . machine industry' with the feudal elements in and out of government was the quintessential characteristic of the second German empire. Veblen quite rightly insisted that Germany's old regime succeeded in assimilating capitalist science and industry only because it was so 'securely lodged in the interests and traditional ideals of the dynastic rulers and privileged classes'. In fact, it was these ancestral elements that 'extended the dominion and improved the efficiency' of the old order by facilitating the 'technical advance' essential to large-scale industry and trade as well as to the 'larger and more expensive equipment and strategy of war'.

Admittedly, Meiji Japan was the only other country with a governing oligarchy as adept at harnessing the industrial arts for an *ancien régime* as Imperial Germany's inveterate margraves. But the traditional governing classes of the other European nations, including England, also grafted industrial capitalism into inherited social and cultural structures. They did so with methods and consequences that were different in degree rather than kind.

The tertiary sector, for its part, was one of small finance, commerce and trade. To be sure, there were a few large banks, trading firms, and shipping and insurance companies. Having long since become dependent on international trade, Britain was the uncontested leader in this sector, the City of London being a conspicuous outpost and symbol of this supremacy. Nonetheless, even England continued to be a nation of small shopkeepers, along with all the other European nations. The retail and service trades especially were dominated by petty operatives. In terms of turnover, floor space and personnel, the department and chain stores of the major cities were of only marginal importance. Smallness was also the rule rather than the exception in the wholesale, import and export trades. Similarly, in finance the terrain was occupied by modest banking houses, though the capital needs of heavy industries stimulated the growth of a few large joint-stock investment banks.

In sum, even as late as 1914 the civil societies of Europe's old regimes were far from being industrial-capitalist and *grand bourgeois*. In what were mixed or dual economies, gradually contracting landlord agriculture, consumer manufacture and petty commerce remained substantially ahead of conspicuously but slowly expanding capital goods production, investment banking, and large-scale merchandising. To treat Europe's dominant economic sectors as obsolete residues is to distort reality, for these survivals were as massive as they were vigorous. Although they gradually yielded and lost economic ground to the new corporate capitalism, the landed and public service nobilities maintained their social and cultural hegemony in the capitals and countryside while the merchant bourgeoisie claimed codetermination in the manufacturing and port cities. In turn, this continuing social and cultural dominance sustained the old elites' hold on the state that helped them slow down their long-term economic decline and soften the blows of the business cycle.

Despite its contraction as a contributor to national employment, income and wealth, as late as 1914 agriculture still remained the principal sector in most European economies. Admittedly, by then agriculture accounted for only 12 per cent of the active labor force, 9 per cent of national income, and 15 per cent of national wealth in the United Kingdom. On the continent, however, it occupied an altogether more vital place. In the Tsarist empire easily 66 per cent of all employment was in agriculture and well over 80 per cent of the population lived in rural areas. Moreover, agriculture contributed 35 per cent of Russia's national income, 45 per cent of its national wealth, and over 70 per cent of its exports – Russia being the world's leading grain exporter. In France, the land claimed between 40 and 45 per cent of the active population and generated between 30 and 35 per cent of national income, or about 40 per cent of the total national product. But even in the German Empire, which was in the forefront of industrialization and urbanization, 40 per cent of the population in 1907 still lived in villages and towns of fewer than 10,000, and 40 per cent of the labor force worked the land to produce 20 per cent of the national income.

[. . .] In the early twentieth century, Europe, except for England, was still predominantly rural and agrarian rather than urban and industrial. Moreover, all over the Continent as well as in England consumer manufacture and shopkeeping significantly outclassed capital goods production, mining and rail transport in every major respect. Even Europe's predatory economic relations with the colonial and semicolonial world were anchored in manufactural and mercantile rather than industrial and finance capitalism. As we have seen, agriculture, consumer goods manufacture, traditional commerce and local banking were not mere remnants in Europe's political economies. In fact, these supposedly declining modes of capitalist production, distribution and credit continued to be dominant and to define class relations and status structures.

That most economic sectors recurrently needed and received state support to lessen the damage of cyclical downswings and foreign competition is not to say that without such assistance they would have been ruined overnight. In particular agriculture, the understructure of these essentially preindustrial but not precapitalist economies, periodically managed to secure government aid, not least because the landed nobilities – in France, commercialized agriculture – continued to command vast political power. But postfeudal nobilities and landed elites generally survived into the twentieth century not simply or primarily because of their privileged political, social and cultural positions but also because of their still massive, if slowly decreasing, economic weight. Even in England and Germany the wealthiest men and families still came from the landed estate, bolstered by the rising value of urban properties and mineral-rich domains. Not only were the great landowners numerically important but also their fortunes far exceeded those of businessmen, though the latter's wealth was now growing more rapidly.

Moreover traditional manufacture, banking and commerce remained economically vigorous, both individually and collectively. Banking and trading dynasties still claimed the largest fortunes in the nonagrarian sectors, ahead of the magnates of manufacture and industry, while small shopkeeping provided large segments of the independent *petite bourgeoisie* with an adequate income. Accordingly, the interest and class formations dating from before the second industrial revolution were not just relics of archaic production relations that incongruously lingered on within the capitalist societies of nineteenth-century Europe. Of course, each national economy was a mixture of different forms and relations of capitalist production and finance. But in Europe's mixed economies large-scale capital goods production and corporate finance remained a subordinate element in civil society. They were more a portent of the future than an accomplished reality of the early twentieth century. Much the same was true of mechanized assembly production and mass consumption. The motorcar was still being handcrafted for the very rich, many of whom had personal chauffeurs, while department stores catered to a clientele that was only slightly less prosperous.

The ruling classes: *the bourgeoisie defers*

The rising business and professional classes were in no position to challenge the landed and public service elites for parity or first place in

Europe's ruling classes, let alone in its governing classes. Quite apart from their numerical and economic disadvantage, the rising bourgeoisies were weakened by internal cleavages between heavy industry and large-scale consumer manufacture and their respective banking associates. They were also estranged from petty manufacture and commerce, which left them without much of a popular base. But most important, the new-fledged industrial and financial bourgeoisies as well as the subaltern free professions lacked a coherent and firm social and cultural footing of their own. Unsure of themselves, they remained obsequious in their relations with the venerable notables of land and office.

The nobilities were not only larger than the rising bourgeoisies but also more cohesive and self-confident. Of course, there is no denying the defeudalization of Europe's nobilities, in that they were being divested of their legal and prescriptive military, administrative and judicial prerogatives and responsibilities. But this is not to say that during the course of the nineteenth century they were reduced to archaic and impotent leisure classes trapped in virtually bourgeois societies. In fact, it was the rising national bourgeoisies that were obliged to adapt themselves to the nobilities, just as advancing industrial and financial capitalism was forced to insert itself into preindustrial civil and political societies. The nobilities comprised not only the largest landed proprietors, including many driving agrarian capitalists, but also the high and highest civil and military servants of the state. Whereas the former were rooted in slowly shrinking agrarian sectors, the latter, except in France, were thoroughly anchored in fast-expanding government structures.

These landed and public service nobilities were not identical with the aristocracies, though they were closely interwoven with them. The aristocracies were altogether more exclusive and restricted. Composed of only a few large families bound by kinship and wealth, they claimed superior birth, breeding and status. In addition to commanding precedence at grand public rituals and social functions, also on the pan-European stage, the blue-bloods considered the top posts in the public service theirs by entitlement. Although aristocrats earned their living in these nonhereditary positions, they did not man them for the sake of money. Indeed, they relied on their lands to provide the (unearned) income and wealth that underwrote their presumptive, not to say presumptuous, ethos, comportment and world-view.

The royal families outranked both the nobilities and the aristocracies. But in postfeudal times the nobilities were peculiarly dependent on crowned heads, who could make nobles but not aristocrats. Kings, emperors and tsars were the fountainheads of new titles and honors that, along with provident marriages, revitalized the nobilities by infusing them with fresh wealth and talent. By absorbing outstanding members of the fledgling counter-elites of the third estate – notably of the *grande bourgeoisie*, bureaucracy and professions – the nobilities preserved not only themselves but also the aristocracies. The titled society owed its longevity as much to its remarkable absorbency as to its inherited landholdings and ascriptive positions and privileges. Nothing ever really interfered with this reproductive process which assimilated notables of movable wealth and public office into the nobility.

Like the rising bourgeoisie, the nobility was far from homogeneous. It was marked by fine but telling gradations of status and influence due to differences in birth, wealth, residence, office and talent. The nobility cemented its unity, however, with ancient but living collective representations and traditions, shared social and cultural presumptions, and common political predilections. In addition, while the business magnates remained essentially solitary, the landed notables were able to use their prestige and mastery to tie much of the poor gentry and deferential peasantry to themselves.

Evidently the old nobility of the land and the new magnates of capital never really embarked on a collision course. At most they jostled each other as they maneuvered for position in ruling classes in which the bourgeoisie remained liegelike suitors and claimants. Inveterate nobles firmly occupied and controlled access to the high social, cultural and political terrain to which the bourgeoisie aspired. With characteristic flexibility and adaptability, and capitalizing on the bourgeois element's craving for social status and advancement, the grand notables admitted individual postulants from business and the professions into their midst. Rather than yield institutional ground, they opted for this selective co-optation, confident of their ability to contain and defuse its attendant ideological and cultural contamination. This strategy or gamble paid off, for the fusion of the two strata remained manifestly asymmetrical: the aristocratization or nobilization of the obeisant bourgeoisie was far more pervasive than the bourgeoisification of the imperious nobility.

Except in France, anointed dynasts and royal courts were the apex and fulcrum of Europe's stratified nobilities. Kings, emperors and tsars alone could legally confer new and higher titles, and throughout Europe landed estates provided the required nimbus. In descending order the noble estate comprised, on the Continent this side of Russia, dukes, princes, marquises, counts, viscounts, barons and knights; across the Channel in England, dukes, marquesses, earls, viscounts and barons. Although the various ranks no longer reflected distinctions in wealth and status as accurately as in the past, they nevertheless remained an approximate index of grandeur and influence. The high aristocracy combined blue blood with enormous wealth in land, including urban real estate, and with considerable political influence or power. These peerless peers, many of them courtiers, had privileged relations with the royal families, who shared their concern for not diluting the status of their rarefied caste with needless ennoblements. Moreover, the extended royal and aristocratic families shared a pan-European predilection for the French language, the English hunt and the Prussian monocle, which they displayed at the Continent's fashionable resorts. Yet while Europe may be said to have had a single aristocracy, it had as many nobilities as there were nations.

The intermediate nobilities were of more modest and recent descent, landed wealth and overall position. They also served as receptacles for the newest recruits from big business, the grand professions, and the high public service. There were, in addition, those distended layers of mere nobility. They kept being replenished by automatic or quasi-automatic ennoblement for civil and military service, by the purchase of ennobling patents, and by the aristocratization of family names. Super-ambitious Englishmen fancied the use of *sir* or *lord* before their names, Frenchmen the particle *de*, and Germans and Austrians the prefix *von*. The Italians, for their part, had a penchant for tripling or quadrupling their surnames by adding the names of their mothers and grandmothers, thereby making them longer and more noble-sounding. Precisely because Russian nobles, high and low, had surnames without title and prefix, they were uniquely punctilious about the uniform and the form of address that were prescribed for each of the numerous grades reaching back to Peter the Great.

Even with all the genuine and counterfeit newcomers to its ranks, the venerable elite continued to be small in both relative and absolute numbers. Ennoblement was used sparingly and inconstantly. In order to feed the aristocratizing ambition honors were kept rare and valuable, and the criteria for awarding them remained shrouded in mystery tempered by presumed merit. The entire system was at one and the same time open and closed, the barriers being adjustable to enable desirable postulants to clear them. The press for admission fostered the elemental solidarity of the multi-tiered nobility at the same time that it pitted rigid exclusionists against flexible absorptionists. Whereas hide-bound purists spurned bourgeois upstarts for polluting the aristocracy's blood, social code and life-style, pliant integrationists had no such fears. Confident of their superior wealth and gravitational pull, they deemed the individual and subordinate assimilation of fresh blood, wealth and talent, as well as the appropriation of new ideas, to be a measure of the nobility's continuing vitality. But even this intramural dissension was functional in that the disdain of the purists quickened the parvenus' rage for social acceptance at the same time that it gave the integrationists a deceptively open image.

Although ennoblement, above all elevation into a hereditary rank, was the most coveted recognition, commoners were also encouraged to value such lesser badges of distinction as decorations, titles and honorific orders of different grades. Some of these were in the nature of prere-quisites and tryouts for ennoblement. In Russia the higher degrees of the orders of Saint Anna and Saint Stanislav actually conferred personal nobility. In addition, the crowned heads invited aspiring wealthy and famed commoners to court while eminent families received them in their city mansions and country houses. Simultaneously, their sons were admitted to exclusive schools as well as to honorable bureaucratic and military careers. And then, of course, members of the old society accepted or pursued the progeny of suitable commoners as marriage partners, substantial dowries or fortunes being *de rigueur*.

By encouraging and implementing so many contacts and associations the nobility diluted its own stock and invited permeation from below. To be sure, the bourgeois aspirants steadfastly courted and invested in this assimilation, as they sedulously emulated and cultivated those they considered their superiors. But in the process they also left their imprint on the amaranthine world that indulged their ambitions. While the nobility encouraged aspirants to social promotion to imitate its ways, it did not remain immune to new influences itself. Imitation was reciprocal between noble and bourgeois, though the balance remained weighted in favor of the stately elite. The result was not so much a profound debasement of the old society as a surface change that left its vitals intact. Even the ingrown aristocracy never became particularly degenerate, dissolute or worn.

While the traditional and heavily landed elite was inordinately absorbent and resilient, the bourgeoisie was singularly impressionable and flaccid. The magnates of capital and the professions never coalesced sufficiently to seriously contest the social, cultural and ideological preeminence of the old ruling class, only in part because the nobility kept co-opting some of the wealthiest and most talented among them. Above all, because of his sycophancy the bourgeois, bent on social climbing and yearning for ennoblement, eagerly denied himself. His supreme ambition was not to besiege or overturn the seignorial establishment but to break into it. For the socially and psychologically insecure business, financial and professional grandees the upper bourgeoisie 'was but an antechamber to the nobility', and their 'highest aspiration was first to gain admission to the nobility and then to rise within it'. At the same time that these magnates sought acceptance by high society, or in exchange for it, they reconciled themselves to their continuing political subordination, not to say vassalage. Except in England, the bourgeoisie cannot be said ever to have abandoned or departed from economic and above all political liberalism, never having embraced it to begin with.

There is no disputing the sempiternal *rise* of the bourgeoisie. Instead, what remains problematical is the congenital inability of the grandees of business and the professions to fuse into a cohesive estate or class of more than local dimension. As Schumpeter noted, although 'the bourgeoisie produced individuals who made a success at political leadership upon entering a political class of nonbourgeois origin, it did not produce a successful political stratum of its own'. Through the centuries rich and wealth-accumulating commoners of the cities and of the nonagrarian economic sectors were bent upon rising out of their 'bourgeois' stations into the nobility that was their archetypal model.

[...]

On this score England was typical of much of Europe. Until the early twentieth century the new magnate of money who did not invest in a landed estate with a country house was the exception. Because of the limited supply of old and sought-after country houses in prestigious locations, would-be nobles had architects build new ones, invariably in traditional styles. To be sure, country houses with time expressed social status stripped of political pretension, and therefore came to be less stately. Even so, by purchasing or building country houses girded by extensive lands, England's merchants, bankers and industrialists struck an aristocratic rather than a bourgeois pose as they steered their sons away from the world of business.

On both sides of the Channel new wealth-holders climbed the irregularly spaced steps of the social ladder to ever higher noble stations. Once there, many of the novices became snobbish purists, leaving it to more poised and accomplished – and perhaps also wealthier – social transvestites and their patrons to admit new men and ideas into the time-honored establishment. Down to 1914 even the most zealous and brazen social climbers were rarely satirized as vainglorious fools, there being few Figaros to taunt and trick counterfeit nobles without falling prey to their wiles.

Of course not all nonlanded magnates aspired to pass, there being men of great new fortunes who proudly spurned the aristocratic embrace. Immune to the lures of high society, they declined official honors and ennoblement. But quite apart from being rare exceptions, even these self-conscious and self-willed recusants were more nobiliar than bourgeois in mentality and demeanor. Besides, since their children were educated and socialized in elite schools and cultural institutions, many of these resistant families could not help but drift into the orbit of the old establishment, a movement that more often than not was intergenerational. Perhaps it should be added that the mounting need for economic preferment from the state made the bourgeois element that much more disposed to pay homage to the noble element which dominated civil and political society.

[. . .]

It would appear, then, that down to 1914 the interwoven landed and service nobilities throughout Europe continued to be dominant in the ruling classes. Except in England and France, they also maintained their primacy in political society. Their position was solid and awesome, not precarious and quaint, precisely because their immense capital was not only cultural and symbolic but also economic. To be sure, their time-tested and resilient material base was being impaired because of the relative decline of the agrarian sector. But the nobilities, especially the magnates among them, bolstered their failing economic fortunes by securing government supports, by investing in the non-agrarian sector, and by adopting clever marriage strategies.

The ascendant and claimant *grands bourgeois* had little beyond their economic capital with which to challenge this comprehensive, coherent and formidable upper establishment. They were at a disadvantage in every major respect: social, cultural and political. The future was acknowledged to be theirs, but the nobilities, for the present, blocked their path. Doubting their own legitimacy and in no position to subvert or conquer the old ruling classes, the new big businessmen and professionals decided to imitate, cajole and join them.

[. . .]

Political society and the governing classes

In 1914 the kings were still 'the centerpiece' of civil and political society 'by the grace of God, and the root of [their] position was feudal, not only in the historical but also in the sociological sense'. Certainly there is no denying that following the preventive 'regicide' at Sarajevo the sovereigns of the Hohenzollern, Habsburg and Romanov empires – William II, Francis Joseph I, Nicholas II – played a crucial role in pushing Europe over the brink of war. As autocratic rulers all three commanded ministers and advisers who were nobles of one sort or another and who were creatures not of party, parliament, or movable capital but of the inveterate public service estate. As for George V of England and Victor Emmanuel III of Italy, they were more than reigning figureheads, although their prerogatives and powers were rigorously and constitutionally limited. Neither of them exerted himself to dampen the fires of war. Of course, being a republic, France had no king, though the incumbent president, Raymond Poincaré, increasingly acted like one. Abetted by aristocratized *notables*, he adopted a military and bellicose posture considerably ahead of the Chamber of Deputies and the cabinet.

But between 1848 and 1914, whatever the differences in their powers and prerogatives, all the kings exercised grave and impressive ceremonial and representational functions which heavily benefitted the hereditary leisure class, including the dynasties themselves. King, emperor and tsar remained the focus of dazzling and minutely choreographed public rituals that rekindled deep-seated royalist sentiments while simultaneously exalting and relegitimating the old order as a whole. The coronation was the most solemn and resplendent of these studied spectacles of power, and it was saturated with historical and religious symbolism. Although the relationship of throne and altar was left studiedly ambiguous in this supreme ceremony, a high priest – appointed or approved by the sovereign – solemnly administered the oath of office and consecrated the initiate's crown, scepter, and sword. At the same time, this elaborate inaugural pageant, though centered on the king, displayed and ratified the latest ranking of status and influence in civil and political society at large. There were, of course, other rites of passage and rededication of comparable pomp, display and mystery: the christenings, weddings, funerals and jubilees of the ruling houses. At all these punctiliously staged sociodramas the grand, costumed and rankordered nobles of blood, land, office and church totally eclipsed even the most prominent un-uniformed commoners. Foreign royalty and nobility which invested these occasions with a cosmic aura and sanction also overshadowed them.

Nor did the kings hesitate to appropriate the highest religious and national holidays for the benefit of the feudalistic elements in the *anciens régimes*. In addition, as the incarnation of the warrior tradition, they flaunted their martial powers at infantry and naval maneuvers, military parades and the changing of elite guards. Last but not least, the crowned heads dominated the social scene with their grand receptions, soirées and hunts.

All these civil and social rituals invigorated the monarchy, cemented the discordant nobilities, and heralded the latest changes in the order of precedence. This ceremonial rearticulation of calibrated cohesion in the upper class was as significant as the institutional enaction of laws and forewarnings to control counter-elites and underclasses. The populace, high and low, was to be awed rather than cowed by the effulgent uniforms, vestments and decorations that intensified the magic and mystery of rites in which the kings lorded over the fusion of the scepter, the altar, the sword and the national flag. Furthermore, the kings embodied and sustained this conflated potence during the state visits they paid one another.

These king-centered ceremonial rounds may appear stilted and contrived because of the ebbing of public ritual in recent decades. At the time, however, they were still very much alive and genuine. If anything, the use of old-world attire, transport and splendor intensified the spell of meticulously staged pageants in tradition-soaked societies. Except in France, the royal family and the nobiliar notables dominated the nation's ceremonial calendar, which remained linked to high rather than low culture. The succession of spectacular civic rites reinforced hegemonic ideas, values and feelings that braced the prebourgeois elites. This political ritual also integrated the lower orders by catering to their craving for dazzling spectacles, which was the counterpart of the passion for strict hierarchy among the upper orders.

[...]

Down to 1914 the 'steel frame' of Europe's political societies continued to be heavily feudal and nobilitarian. In spite of vast national and constitutional variations, there were significant family resemblances among all the regimes. Perhaps this affinity was rooted first and foremost in the enduring importance of landed interests and of rural society throughout Europe. While in England land was more a source of social status and political ascendancy than of economic and financial power, in France it provided the principal material understructure of the Third Republic, and most notably of its ruling and governing class. Although the Revolution of 1789–94 had swept away the monarchy, it had reinvigorated the agricultural estate: quite apart from leaving many of the landed notables as well as the praedial Catholic Church in place, it expanded and strengthened small and medium peasant holdings. Throughout Europe upper houses, legislatures, bureaucracies and armies drew their life-blood from land-enveloped villages, towns and provinces rather than from industrializing cities or regions. Moreover, except in France, king and court, like the nobilities, were inconceivable without the wealth, income and nimbus generated by large landed proprietorship.

To the extent that this landed society was in relative economic decline, political society was there to brace it. King and court served an overall agglutinating function in the politics of economic, social and cultural defense, France being the exception that proved the rule. By virtue of ancient custom or constitutional convention, or both, the strength of the old ruling class was magnified not only in local and provincial councils but above all in central government. The two houses of parliament and the public service nobilities worked to preserve or reinforce the pre-industrial civil society. They passed protective tariffs for uncompetitive agriculture and manufacture everywhere except in England and provided prestigious government positions for embattled nobles and aspiring commoners. No less important, they blocked tax, suffrage, educational and social reforms that threatened to hasten the erosion of the old order.

Official high cultures and the avant-garde

Europe's official cultures conspicuously mirrored the tenacious persev-erance of preindustrial civil and political societies. In form, content and style the artifacts of high culture continued to be anchored and swathed in conventions that relayed and celebrated traditions supportive of the old order. The eclectic revival and reproduction of time-honored and venerable styles dominated not only in architecture and statuary but also in painting, sculpture and the performing arts. Museums, aca-demies, churches and universities actively promoted this congruent academic historicism, and so did the state, which enlisted historicism to articulate national and regional purposes. Overall, the hegemonic arts and institutions maintained sufficient inner vitality and synoptic coher-ence to invigorate the *anciens régimes.*

Of course, between 1848 and 1914 Europe's official cultures exper-ienced discordant modernist movements in the arts as well as in the churches and higher schools. But these defections were easily contained, above all because they were no match for the reigning cultural centers. Admittedly, most defectors were young, spirited and aggressive experi-mentalists and innovators, and many of them eventually won recogni-tion. Even so, successive waves of the avant-garde hit against the official cultures, which, like breakwaters, survived intact. In the long run the victory of the modernists may have been inevitable. In the short run, however, the modernists were effectively bridled and isolated, if need be with legal and administrative controls. Despite or because of relentless challenges and gibes from the avant-garde, the producers and guardians of official academic traditions remained at once imperious and adaptive. Like kings and nobles, they learned to defuse ascending rivals through calibrated assimilation and co-optation. And just as outworn economic interests made the most of their political leverage to secure protective tariffs and fiscal preferments, so eminent artists used their influence in key hegemonic institutions – academies, salons, museums, ministries of culture – to rally support for their timeworn idioms.

Compared to the vanguard, the cultural establishment and its rear guard were above all protective. But even though the historicist legacy for and with which they did battle was aesthetically impoverished, it was far from spent. Historicism was not an archaic, lifeless and inert accretion that trailed far behind the economic and social developments of the nineteenth century. In fact, between 1848 and 1914 historic academicism declined no further than the rest of preindustrial civil society. To be sure, it lost in vitality as fixed form prevailed over idea, imitation over authenticity, ornateness over artlessness, and pomp over sobriety. But historicism was no less useful and effective for being turgid and specious.

The major historical styles – classical, medieval, Renaissance, Baroque, rococo – were part of the storehouse of symbols and images that served to thwart, dignify and disguise the present. Historicism provided critics of modernity with an inexhaustible reservoir of representations with which not only to glorify and reinvigorate their own privileged though beleaguered world but also to censure and traduce the rival new society. Landed and service nobilities, political catonists and Arcadian social critics each had their own reasons for harking back to time-honored metaphors and emblems.

But the makers and bards of modernity also had recourse to ancient tropes as they set out to justify their project and make it fathomable. While capitalist entrepreneurs excelled at creative destruction in the economic sphere, they took care not to tear the inherited cultural fabric. Indeed, in their quest for divine sanction and social recognition they enveloped their exploits and themselves with historical screens. This use of and solicitude for historical culture substantially mitigated and disguised the stress of fitting modernity into pre-existing civil and political society.

For the political classes high culture was an important ideological instrument. Not only public buildings, statues and spaces but also the pictorial, plastic and performing arts were expected to exalt the old regimes and revalidate their moral claims. The ruling classes took an equally functional view of the arts. Whereas new men enlisted them to display their wealth, taste and aspiration, well-established families used them to reaffirm their fortune and status. For the two factions the consumption of high art and culture was both badge and sacrament of achieved or coveted positions of class, prestige and influence in what remained distinctly traditional societies. Having assigned art such practical functions, the governing and ruling classes were disinclined to sponsor vanguards that balked at ratifying and extolling the *anciens régimes* and their elites in the accustomed ways.

In an age in which the declining old order easily held down the rising new society, traditional conventions, tastes and styles only gradually yielded to breakaway visions and representations. [. . .]

World view

The upper classes of Europe were prepared to take their peoples into a catastrophe from which they hoped against hope to draw benefits for themselves. In other words, though unprecedented, the catastrophe was not expected to be total. To be sure, there might be millions of victims, massive devastation and severe unsettlement. Even so, a general war would not turn out to be 'the end of history', though it would overload the circuits of military planning and control. Certainly the politicians and generals of the aristocratic reaction were accomplices rather than adversaries or rivals in the march to the brink. This is not to deny that there were strains between civil and military leaders and that the military plans, including their operational provisions, limited the freedom of action of politicians and diplomats. But these civil-military tensions were embedded in factional battles over means, not ends, within conservatism and the governing classes. Once the ultraconservative resurgence lifted the soldiers into the highest levels of government, the generals militarized the civilians no more than the civilians politicized the warriors. The latter left their mark not because of their expertise but because the civilians were in search of military solutions to political problems. What tied them together, quite apart from shared social and political attitudes, interests and objectives, was a common commitment to struggle against political democracy, social leveling, industrial development and cultural modernism. These *idées-forces* [key ideas], wrapped in pugnacious patriotism, significantly influenced the making of strategic and tactical plans. To be sure, these required the expertise of generals. But military know-how alone did not dictate the stress on mass assault *à outrance* in pursuit of a swift battlefield victory, regardless of human cost. Besides, that know-how was obsolete. The generals meant to re-enact the lightning campaign of 1870, in which the first Moltke had overwhelmed France with his pioneering speed and concentration of infantry divisions, having over-looked the fact that since then Moltke's formula had been assimilated by all the general staffs. Furthermore, they deceived themselves into thinking that by using the railroads they were appropriating the latest technology for their own purposes, when as a military technique the rails for troop trains, immovably fixed in space, were nearly as much a legacy of the first industrial revolution as the officers were of feudalism.

At any rate, the civilian governors were not disposed to scrutinize the military's strategic and operational schemes. Not that they lacked the intelligence and knowledge to do so. But the statesmen were locked into the same impetuous worldview and political project as the generals. Accordingly, they screened out other options, such as defensive strategies which would have reduced the pressures of timetables and mutual fear. Clearly, the rigidity of diplomatic and military master plans was 'as much in the mind as it was in the railway timetables'. In addition, Europe's politician-statesmen refrained from questioning the wisdom of the quick and massive strike because of their gnawing realization that the *anciens régimes* were too fragile to support the burdens of a protracted war of attrition. In sum, their position was highly paradoxical, and more than likely they knew it.

Eventually, in July–August 1914 the governors of the major powers, all but a few of them thoroughly nobilitarian, marched over the precipice of war with their eyes wide open, with calculating heads, and exempt from mass pressures. Along the way not a single major actor panicked or was motivated by narrow personal, bureaucratic and partisan concerns. Among the switchmen of war there were no petty improvisers, no romantic dilettantes, no reckless adventurers. Whatever the profile of their populist helpers or harassers, they were men of high social standing, education and wealth, determined to maintain or recapture an idealized world of yesterday. But these politician-statesmen and generals also knew that to achieve their project they would have to resort to force and violence. Under the aegis of the scepter and the miter, the old elites, unrestrained by the bourgeoisie, systematically prepared their drive for retrogression, to be executed with what they considered irresistible armies. They, the horsemen of the apocalypse, were ready to crash into the past not only with swords and cavalry charges but also with the artillery and railroads of the modern world that besieged them.

For its own reasons and interests the capitalist bourgeoisie, symbiotically linked to the old elites, was ready and willing, if not eager, to serve as quartermaster for this perilous enterprise. The magnates of movable wealth calculated that the requisites of warfare would intensify the *ancien régime*'s need for the 'economic services of capitalism'. Like their senior partners, the bourgeois did not shy away from what they too knew would be absolute war, confident that it would be a forcing house for the expansion of industry, finance and commerce and an improvement of their status and power. As for the industrial workers, they were too weak and too well integrated into nation and society to resist impressment, though theirs was the only class in which there was any marked disposition to do so.

[. . .]

Notes

1 Marc Bloch: the distinguished French historian and co-founder of the *Annales* school.
2 Joseph Schumpeter: economist and economic historian, born in Austria-Hungary, moving to the USA in the 1930s.
3 Thorstein Veblen: American economist and sociologist.

3

The Birth of the Modern: 1885–1914

G.D. Josipovici

The problem to be dealt with in this chapter can be formulated quite simply: the years 1885–1914 saw the birth of the modern movement in the arts.[1] What are the specific features of the movement, and how are we to account for its emergence?

Three points have to be made before we start. First of all we must be clear that from one point of view our inquiry is nonsensical. There is no specific thing called 'modernity' which we can extract from the variety of individual works of art and hold up for inspection. Every modern artist worth his salt is good precisely because he has found his own individual voice and because this voice is distinct from that of his fellows. And yet it cannot be denied that something did happen to art, to all the arts, some time around the turn of the century, and that Proust, Joyce, Picasso, Klee, Schoenberg and Stravinsky, for all their manifest individuality, do have something in common. Before we plunge into a study of individual artists and works it may be useful to have a frame of reference, a set of common assumptions, which will stop us asking the wrong kinds of questions or looking for the wrong sorts of answers.

This leads to the second point, which is that such an inquiry is far more than an academic exercise, the reconstruction of the past for its own sake. Although more than half a century has passed since those decisive years, the majority of people who are interested in the arts have still not come to terms with what happened then. The indiscriminate abuse of Picasso and Schoenberg may have ceased, but it has merely given way to equally indiscriminate praise. Great artists create their own posterity, said Proust; but though it may be fashionable to enthuse over the latest avant-garde music and painting, there is everywhere – among professional reviewers as well as academic critics – a real failure to understand the premises upon which the great artists of the turn of the century based their works. And until such an understanding has been arrived at, the serious artists of today, who are their heirs, are bound to be misjudged – though not necessarily to go unrecognized. It is thus of paramount importance for us today that we should make sense of the great change that came over the arts at the turn of the century.

The third point is merely a reminder of a historical fact which, if rightly interpreted, should serve as a guide and a warning throughout this investigation. Although the First World War effectively marks the break between the world of the nineteenth century and our own – both in the minds of those who lived through it and of those of us who read about it in the history books – the modern revolution in the arts did not take place during the war or immediately after it, but a decade or so before it. This should make us wary of too facile an identification of art with the culture and society out of which it springs. For, paradoxically, while artists have always been ahead of their times, art has always fulfilled the same basic needs, and men have not fundamentally altered since the days of Homer. It is with the changing *forms* of art and not with what one might call the furniture of art – the props and backdrops which it borrows from the world around it – that we will be concerned in the pages that follow.

The modern movement in the arts cannot be understood in isolation. It must be seen as a reaction to the decadent Romanticism that was prevalent in Europe at the turn of the century. Some of the theoreticians of modernism, such as T.E. Hulme in England, tried to argue that it was nothing other than a wholesale rejection of Romanticism and all it stood for, and a return to a new classicism. Looking back at those pre-war decades from our vantage-point in the mid-century, however, we can see that the matter was considerably more complex than Hulme suggests; that it was more a question of redefining Romanticism, of stressing some of those aspects of it which the nineteenth century had neglected and discarding some of those it had most strongly emphasized, than of rejecting it outright. If we are to understand what the founders of modern art were doing it will be necessary to grasp the premises and implications of Romanticism itself.

Romanticism was first and foremost a movement of liberation – liberation from religious tradition, political absolutism, an hierarchical social system, and a universe conceived on the model of the exact sciences. Reason and scientific laws, the Romantics felt, might allow man to control his environment, but they formed a sieve through which the living, breathing individual slipped, and which retained only the dead matter of generality. What man had in common with other men, what this landscape had in common with other landscapes, was the least important thing about them. What was important was the uniqueness of men and the uniqueness of everything in the world around us, be it a leaf, a sparrow or a mountain range. There were moments, they felt, when man was far from the distractions of the city and of society, and when the reasoning, conceptualizing mind was still, when life seemed suddenly to reveal itself in all its beauty, mystery and terror. In such moments man felt himself restored to his true self, able to grasp the meaning of life and of his own existence. It is to experience and express such moments, both in our lives and in our art, that we should strive, for these are the moments when we throw off the shackles of generality and are restored to our unique selves.

The function of art thus becomes that of digging deep down into those areas of the mind and the world which lie beyond the confines of rational thought and ordinary consciousness; and the hero of Romantic art becomes none other than the artist himself, who is both the explorer of this unknown realm and the priestly mediator between it and his audience. Something of this is suggested by August Wilhelm Schlegel, who is most probably responsible for introducing the term 'Romantic' as a description of the age:

> Ancient poetry and art is rhythmical *nomos*, a harmonious promulgation of the eternal legislation of a beautifully ordered world mirroring the eternal Ideas of things. Romantic poetry, on the other hand, is the expression of a secret longing for the chaos . . . which lies hidden in the very womb of orderly creation . . . [Greek art] is simpler, cleaner, more like nature in the independent perfection of its separate works: [Romantic art], in spite of its fragmentary appearance, is nearer to the mystery of the universe.

Schlegel, it is true, is not here talking only of the nineteenth century; he is contrasting the whole 'modern' or Christian era with the Classical age of Greece and Rome. But his stress on the transcending impulse of Romanticism, on the aspiration towards the mystery of the universe, is taken up by Baudelaire nearly half a century later, in a discussion of the 'Salon' of 1846: 'Qui dit romantisme dit art moderne, – c'est-à-dire intimité, spiritualité, couleur, aspiration vers l'infini, exprimées par tous les moyens que contiennent les arts' [He who speaks of Romanticism speaks of modern art – that is to say intimacy, spirituality, colour, aspiration towards the infinite, expressed by every means at the disposal of the arts].

But here a curious contradiction begins to emerge, a contradiction that lies at the heart of the whole Romantic endeavour, and on that was to determine its future course. One final quotation, from the theologian Schleiermacher, will bring it out into the open:

> I am lying in the bosom of the infinite universe, I am at this moment its soul, because I feel all its force and its infinite life as my own. It is at this moment my own body, because I penetrate all its limbs as if they were my own, and its innermost nerves move like my own. . . . Try out of love for the universe to give up your own life. Strive already here to destroy your own individuality and to live in the One and in the All . . . fused with the Universe.

Romanticism had begun as a movement of rebellion against the arbitrary authorities of the eighteenth century and its abstract laws, a rebellion undertaken in the name of the freedom of the individual. But this freedom, which, as we saw, involves the suppression of the tyrannical intellect, now appears to be synonymous with the loss of individuality as most men conceive it; thus the ultimate freedom, according to the Romantic logic, is death.

Where consciousness itself is felt to be an imprisoning factor, keeping man from his true self, freedom must lie in transcending it. Yet the only times we escape from consciousness for more than a brief moment are in sleep, under the influence of alcohol and drugs, or in madness, while the only total escape is death; hence the key place accorded by Romanticism to dreams, to various forms of addiction, to madness, and to the death-wish. In all these cases the result is, of course, extremely ambiguous. The freedom from consciousness and from social convention does often result in deeper insight, but it results also in the destruction of the individual. Hence the general tone of Romantic art and literature is one of melancholy gloom, for there seems to be no way of resolving the contradiction.

This pull between freedom and annihilation is even easier to discern in the sphere of art itself. The task of the poet, as the Romantics saw it, was to communicate those moments of visionary intensity which only he could experience, moments in which the meaning and value of life were revealed to him. But the poet's only means of expression is language, and language belongs almost by definition to the realm of consciousness and of social intercourse. For language, as Plato had already noted, only exists at a certain degree of abstraction and universality; it takes for granted that there is some sort of social agreement as to the referents of words: we can use the word 'tree' or 'man' only because we all agree roughly what these two words stand for. But if we feel that what is important is the individuality, the 'instress' as Hopkins called it, of this tree or this man – what essentially differentiates it from all other trees or men – then clearly words are going to be a hindrance rather than a help. How then are we to express this insight? The Romantic poet finds himself struggling to express by means of language precisely that which it lies beyond the power of language to express. He is a man desperately trying to get away from his own shadow.

Only one poet in the nineteenth century was fully aware of the implications of the Romantic endeavour, and was prepared to accept and try to overcome them. In Rimbaud's famous letter to Paul Demeny of 15 May 1871, we can see that he had fully understood the problem and had decided on a radical solution:

Donc le poète est vraiment voleur de feu.

Il est chargé de l'humanité, des *animaux* même; il devra faire sentir, palper, écouter ses inventions; si ce qu'il rapporte de *là-bas* a forme, il donne forme; si c'est informe, il donne de l'informe.

Trouver une langue; – du reste, toute parole étant idée, le temps
d'un langage universel viendra! Il faut être académicien – plus mort
qu'un fossile – pour parfaire un dictionnaire, de quelque langue que
ce soit. Des faibles se mettraient à *penser* sur la première lettre de
l'alphabet, qui pourraient vite ruer dans la folie!

Cette langue sera de l'âme pour l'âme, résumant tout, parfums,
sons, couleurs, de la pensée accrochant la pensée et tirant. Le poète
définirait la quantité d'inconnu s'éveillant en son temps dans l'âme
universelle: il donnerait plus – que la formule de sa pensée, que
l'annotation *de sa marche au Progrès*! Énormité devenant norme,
absorbée par tous, il serait vraiment *un multiplicateur de progrès*!
[Thus the poet is truly a plunderer of fire.

He is responsible for humanity, for the *animals* even; he must
produce creations which can be felt, touched, heard; if what he
brings back from *beyond* has a shape, he gives it shape; if it is
shapeless, he gives it shapelessness. He must find a voice – so all
speech being idea, the era of universal language will come! One
needs to be an academician – deader than a dodo – to fuss over a
dictionary confined to a single national tongue. The feeble-minded
apply themselves to *pondering* the first letter of the alphabet, quickly
ending up in foolery!

That voice will come from the soul for the soul, embracing everything, scents, sounds, colours, and from thought linking and drawing upon thought. The poet will explain the great awakening in his
own time of the unknown in the universal spirit: he will provide
more – more than the expression of his thought, more than the
account *of his march towards Progress*! As infinitude becomes
commonplace, imbibed by all, he would truly be *a multiplicator of
progress*!]

The failure of this ideal can be traced through the poems themselves,
and forms the explicit content of *Une Saison en enfer*. And, indeed, how
could he succeed? What he desires is not communication but communion, the direct and total contact of one person with another through a
language so charged that it will act without needing to pass by way of
the mind at all. Such a language can never be more than a Utopian
dream, for to give words the meaning we want them to have, regardless
of the socially accepted meaning they already have, is tantamount to
abolishing language altogether. When Rimbaud recognized this, with
admirable logic, he gave up writing poetry.

But just because he was so ready to push the premises of Romanticism to their ultimate conclusion, Rimbaud remains one of the key
figures of the nineteenth century, marking for ever one of the two poles
within which modern art is to move. His contemporaries (Mallarmé
excepted – but see below), both in England and in France, chose a
somewhat less arduous and therefore less interesting path. They tried

to solve the problem by making their verse approximate as closely as possible to their own conception of music – which had, naturally enough, become for the Romantics the artistic language *par excellence*, since it appeared to have none of the disadvantages of speech. To this end they made their verse as mellifluous as possible, stressing its incantatory qualities, smoothing out all harshness of diction, minimizing its referential content, and rigidly excluding all forms of wit and humour for fear these would break their fragile spell. The result was aptly described by T.S. Eliot in a famous essay on Swinburne:

> Language in a healthy state presents the object, is so close to the object that the two are identified. They are identified in the verse of Swinburne only because the object has ceased to exist, because the meaning is merely the hallucination of meaning, because language, uprooted, has adapted itself to an independent life of atmospheric nourishment.

So, as with Rimbaud, we see the normal function of language being denied and words taking on an independent meaning. But here the meaning is not just independent of general usage, but of the poet's own will into the bargain. The result is not insight into the mystery of the universe but empty cliché, not the articulation of what lies beyond the confines of rationality, but simple reflex, the verbal equivalent of the canine dribble. For language has a way of getting its own back on those who try to step over it in this manner, and just as the Romantic dreamer found that he escaped from the bonds of his intellect at the cost of his life, so the Romantic poet, trying to escape from the bonds of language, found himself its prisoner, uttering platitudes in the voice of prophet.

But if the poets dreamt of living in a world freed from the stifling restrictions of language, and looked with envy to the composers, these, had the poets but known it, were no freer than themselves. For if language is not natural, that is if words are not inherently expressive, as Rimbaud had thought, the same is true of music. Although Hoffmann wrote enthusiastically about the inherent qualities of a chord of A flat minor, the truth of the matter is that music is nearly as conventional as speech. We find it difficult to grasp music which is distant from us in space or time (Indian or Japanese music, or Gregorian chant, for instance); to know when it is 'cheerful', when 'sad'. Musical instruments, too, have different and highly specialized functions in other societies, and so are associated with different things than they are for us. It is only through frequent hearing, through a familiarization with its 'language', that we can come to appreciate Indian music; the composer, no less than the poet, works in a language which is largely the product of convention, and according to rules to which he voluntarily submits in order to master the world of sounds. Thus, when the initial impetus of Romanticism starts to peter out, we find a development in music parallel to that we traced in poetry – a slackening of formal control, a loosening of the harmonic texture, and the emergence of a soulful, cliché-ridden style that strives to lull the listener into a trance as the music struggles to express the world of the infinite which Baudelaire had urged the artist to seek with every means at his disposal. Naturally enough the piano, instrument of the half-echo, the indefinite, the suggestive, becomes the favourite of artist and public alike. And in music, as in poetry, the attempt to express everything, the totality of experience, unfettered by the rules and limitations of convention or consciousness, leads to its own destruction. More than any of the other arts Romantic music is imbued with the melancholy which stems from the knowledge that to achieve its goal is to expire.

The apotheosis of Romantic art, as all his contemporaries recognized, is to be found in the operas of Richard Wagner. These vast music-dramas seemed to be the perfect answer to Baudelaire's plea for a work of art that would make use of all the arts, thus finally lifting the spectator into the realm of the infinite, the very heart of the mystery of the universe. And we are fortunate in possessing a critique of Wagner by one of the few men who was really aware of the implications of Romanticism because he was so much of a Romantic himself: Friedrich Nietzsche. Nietzsche's analysis of the 'decadent' style sums up some of the points already made:

> What is common to both Wagner and 'the others' consists in this: the decline of all organizing power; the abuse of traditional means, without the capacity or the aim that would justify this; the counter-feit imitation of grand forms . . . ; excessive vitality in small details; passion at all costs; refinement as an expression of impoverished life, ever more nerves in the place of muscle.

But Nietzsche is not content with a simple catalogue of Wagner's characteristics: he wants to understand what lies behind this, and to try to account for Wagner's enormous popularity. He sees first of all that for Wagner music is only a means to an end: 'As a matter of fact his whole life long he did nothing but repeat one proposition: that his music did not mean music alone. But something more! Something immeasurably more! . . . "Not music alone" – no musician would speak in this way.' And he explains what this 'more' is: 'Wagner pondered over nothing so deeply as over salvation: his opera is the opera of salvation.' And this, thinks Nietzsche, is the source of Wagner's power, that what he offered was nothing less than the hope of personal salvation to a Europe – and especially a Germany – bewildered by the rapid social and technological changes of the previous forty or so years: 'How intimately related must Wagner be to the entire decadence of Europe for her not to have felt that he was decadent!' And again: 'People actually kiss that which plunges them more quickly into the abyss.' We remember that Schlegel had already talked about a 'secret longing for the chaos . . . which lies hidden in the very womb of orderly creation', and that this longing was nothing other than the Romantic desire for a total and absolute freedom. Nietzsche's suggestion that with Wagner this longing spills out of the realm of art into that of politics and society allows us to glimpse the connection between decadent Romanticism and the rise of totalitarianism. The cataclysmic events of the first half of the present century would have occasioned him little surprise.

What Nietzsche particularly objects to in Wagner is precisely the fact that by trying to turn his music into a religion he debases both music and religion; by trying to turn the entire world into a music-drama, drawing the audience up into the music until they shed their dull everyday lives and come into contact with the heart of the mystery, he dangerously distorts both the life of every day and the nature of art; by blurring the outlines between life and art he turns art into a tool and life into an aesthetic phenomenon, that is, into something which is to be judged entirely by aesthetic criteria and where the rules of morality no longer apply. In so doing Wagner is typical of decadent Romanticism in general, of Huysmans and Swinburne and all those who took to heart Axël's dictum that, as for living, our servants can do that for us.[2] The end of the nineteenth century is the great era of the *poète maudit* [accursed poet], of the dandy, of the Romantic agony. It marks the final bankruptcy of the Romantic revolt.

But even as Wagnerism swept through Europe and Nietzsche sank into his final madness the reaction to Romantic decadence had already begun. This did not take the form of a movement in the sense that surrealism, say, was a movement, with polemical manifestos and self-appointed leaders and spokesmen. If was not even a movement of like-minded men holding the same beliefs about human liberty and the function of the artist in society, as Romanticism, in its early phases, had been. Proust and Joyce met once and barely spoke to one another; Schoenberg loathed Stravinsky; Eliot was more interested in Laforgue than in Mallarmé or Valéry; and Kafka ignored them all. Yet it is easy for us today to see that all these artists were united by one common attitude, albeit a negative one: they all insisted on the *limitations* of the sphere of art. More than that, they all stressed, in the art itself, that what they had created was only art and nothing more: that a painting was nothing except a series of brush-strokes on a flat canvas; that music was nothing except certain notes played by certain combinations of instruments; that poetry was nothing except a grouping of words on the page; that prose fiction was fiction and not reality.

Since the Romantics had regarded art as simply a means to a transcendental end, they naturally tended to see all the arts as more or less interchangeable – it doesn't matter what train you take since they're all going to the same place. The insistence on the part of the moderns that their work was art and not something else, their stress on the particular *medium* in which they were working, was not meant to be a denial of art but rather a reassertion of its crucial function. Art, they argued, was not a means of piercing the sensible veil of the universe, of getting at the 'unknown', as Rimbaud and others had claimed, for there was nothing beyond the world that lay all round us. The whole mystery was there, right in front of us, where everybody could see it – except for the fact that normally men are too blind or lazy to do so. What most of us tend to do in front of the world, of ourselves, of works of art, is to neutralize what is before us by reducing it to something we know already. Thus we are for ever shut up inside our preconceived notions, reacting only to that which makes no demands that we should really see. As Giacometti put it:

> Où y a-t-il plus de monde? Devant le 'Sacre de Napoléon'. Pourquoi les gens regardent-ils justement ce tableau? Parce qu'ils imaginent d'abord assister à la scène, y participer. Ils deviennent des 'petits Napoléons'. En même temps le spectacle devient l'équivalent de la lecture d'un roman.
> [Where is the biggest crowd to be found? In front of the 'coronation of Napoleon'. Why exactly do people look at this painting? Because, first of all they imagine that they are present at the scene, are taking part in it, they become 'little Napoleons'. Simultaneously, the viewing becomes the equivalent of reading a novel.]

Like the library novel, it becomes an excuse for daydreaming. The modern artist, on the other hand, holds that the work of art is meaningful precisely because it reveals to us the 'otherness' of the world – it shocks us out of our natural sloth and the force of habit, making us 'see' for the first time what we have looked at a hundred times but never really noticed. Art is not a key to the universe but a pair of spectacles, as Valéry, echoing Proust's Elstir, points out:

> Nous devinons ou prévoyons, en général, plus que nous ne voyons, et les impressions de l'œil sont pour nous des signes, et non des *présences singulières*, antérieures à tous les arrangements, les résumés, les raccourcis, les substitutions immédiates, que l'éducation première nous a inculqués.
> Comme le penseur essaie de se défendre contre les *mots* et les expressions toutes prêtes qui dispensent les esprits de s'étonner de tout et rendent possible la vie pratique, ainsi l'artiste peut, par l'étude des choses informes,[3] c'est-à-dire de forme *singulière*, essayer de retrouver sa propre singularité . . .
> [In general, we guess or imagine rather than see, and the impressions our eyes take in are signs, not *unique presences* with a real existence prior to all the instant arrangements, summaries, foreshortenings, and representations instilled in us by previous education.
> Just as the thinker tries to avoid the sayings and ready-made expressions which destroy the possibilities of surprise but may

make everyday life possible, so the artist may, by studying disordered items, that is to say of *unique* form, try to rediscover his own
uniqueness . . .].

Art, then, does not feed us information, nor does it give us a glimpse of
a world beyond or above this one. What it does is to open our eyes by
removing the film of habit which we normally carry around with us. It
does this by shocking us into awareness through its insistence on itself
as an object in its own right, irreducible to anything we could see or
think in the normal course of affairs. The cubist picture, for instance,
teases the eye as we follow shape after shape on the canvas, always on
the verge of understanding it, yet never quite allowed to do so. And
because we cannot step back and say: 'Ah, yes, a mandolin, a glass of
wine, a table', etc., we go on looking at the canvas and in time learn to
accept its own reality instead of reducing it to our own preconceived
idea of what a mandolin or a glass of wine looks like. Thus Braque can
say: 'le tableau est fini quand l'idée a disparu' [the painting is complete
when the idea has vanished], and Valéry, elsewhere in the essay on
Degas quoted earlier: 'Regarder, c'est-à-dire oublier les noms des choses
que l'on voit' [to look is to forget the names of the things one is looking
at]. Proust's whole novel can be seen as an attempt to substitute the
object for the name, to render the uniqueness of the feeling by recreating
it rather than simply by naming it.

An art of this kind clearly makes the spectator work. It does not, like
Wagnerian opera, claim to provide a passport to salvation, nor, like the
'Sacre de Napoléon', allow each of us to indulge his daydreams. What it
does claim to do is to recreate within the willing reader or spectator the
liberating experience of the artist himself. When Picasso said, of his
famous sculpture of the bull's head made out of the seat and handlebars
of a bicycle, that the whole point would be lost if the viewer, through
excessive familiarity with it, were to see *only* a bull's head, he neatly
illustrated this aspect of modern art. What is important is not the
finished product, but the *process*. Picasso wants us to be aware of the fact
that what is in front of us is not a bull's head but a man-made object. The
product is not there to be contemplated for its own sake but to stimulate
the viewer's own perception and to allow him to relive the act of creative
discovery for himself. In the same way Proust's novel does not so much
tell a story as create within the reader the potentiality for telling the
story Marcel is about to set down as the work ends. Thus, paradoxically
again, the artist's very acceptance of limitation, his open acknowledgement of the medium in which he is working, leads beyond art to alter
the very life of the reader or viewer.

We have been looking at the modern revolution in the arts as a
reaction to decadent Romanticism, but if we look at it in a larger perspective it becomes clear that this reaction entailed a radical break with
four centuries of the Western artistic tradition. Shifts in taste and forms

of expression had occurred at regular intervals in those four centuries, of course, but these were really modifications within a fixed framework. Romanticism, by trying to give full expression to the individual, burst this framework and so made it possible for the moderns to step out of it and see that the frame enclosed not the whole universe but only a restricted area of it. Perhaps a more accurate way of describing the change would be to say that what the artists of the previous four centuries had taken to be the limits of the universe were now discovered to be only the limitations imposed by spectacles they had not realized they were wearing. It is not by chance that the birth of the modern coincides with the discovery or rediscovery of Japanese art, African sculpture, Romanesque painting, the musical instruments of the Far East, and the poetry of the troubadours. This was no simple widening of the cultural horizons; it was the momentous discovery that what had been taken as *the* way of seeing was really only one way among many; that perspective and harmony, far from being in each case a datum of experience, were almost as conventional as the sonnet form and, unlike the latter, were the product of certain metaphysical assumptions which began to emerge in the West at the time of the Renaissance.

All art, since the Renaissance, had been based on the twin concepts of expression and imitation. In an earlier chapter,[4] I suggested why these two should always go hand in hand, and why they should have emerged as the primary criteria of art at the time when medieval notions of analogy could no longer be accepted. It seems appropriate to conclude this brief analysis of modernity by looking at it from the point of view of each of these concepts in turn.

The artist expresses himself and he imitates external reality. For three centuries there was an uneasy compromise between these two notions, until the Romantics, by stressing the first of these aspects to the exclusion of the second, brought the hidden assumptions of both out into the open and showed how unsatisfactory they both were. Writing again about the 'Salon' of 1846, Baudelaire quotes at some length from the German Romantic writer, E.T.A. Hoffmann. The passage, as will readily be seen, is central not only to Baudelaire's whole aesthetic, but to that of Romanticism in general:

> Ce n'est pas seulement en rêve, et dans le lèger délire qui précède le sommeil, c'est encore éveillé, lorsque j'entends de la musique, que je trouve une analogie et une réunion intime entre les couleurs, les sons et les parfums. Il me semble que toutes ces choses ont été engendrées par un même rayon de lumière, et qu'elles doivent se réunir dans un merveilleux concert. L'odeur des soucis bruns et rouges produit surtout un effet magique sur ma personne. Elle me fait tomber dans une profonde rêverie, et j'entends alors comme dans le lointain les sons graves et profonds du hautbois.
> [It is not only while dreaming, nor in the gentle delirium which precedes sleep, it is also evoked when I listen to music, in which I

find an analogy and an intimate conjunction of colours, sounds and scents. It seems to me that all of these things have been engendered by the same ray of light, and that they have to come together in marvellous concert. The scent of brown and red marigolds above all has a magical effect on me. It makes me fall into a deep reverie, and then I hear as if in the distance the dark and solemn tones of the oboe.]

The implicit belief behind this passage is that individual sights, sounds, smells and tastes touch each one of us in the same way and are themselves interchangeable. In other words, that each speaks a natural language. In a similar way the poet has simply to reach down into himself and pour out what he feels, while the reader allows this to enter into his own soul. We have seen how this grossly oversimplified view of the poetic process led to the breakdown of art into a series of utterances so individual that they no longer made sense, or else turned into the banal expression not of vision but of cliché. This failure showed the moderns that the work of art is not simply the expression of some inner feeling, but the creation of a structure which will 'hold' this feeling for the poet as well as for the reader. Hence the insistence on the impersonality of the poet, the radical distinction between the artist and the man made by Proust and Rilke and Eliot. For the artist *qua* man is no different from the reader; the difference lies in the fact that he is a craftsman who can 'catch' the fleeting sensation and make it communicable in the form of a poem or a painting. The work of art, to use a famous phrase of Archibald MacLeish, no longer says, but is.

This is really only another way of making the point discussed earlier about the modern artist's emphasis on the limitations of his medium. To draw these two together it may be useful to look at the change from Romanticism to modernity from a slightly different point of view, that of the change from a view of art as magic to a view of art as game.

The Romantic artist, as we saw, be he Rimbaud or Wagner, claimed, in some way, to be a magician. He claimed, that is, that words and sounds hide within themselves certain magical properties over which the artist alone has power. Through this power that artist can confer salvation upon the rest of mankind. The reader or listener has simply to submit to the words or sounds in order to shed the pains and frustrations of daily living and to emerge reborn. The consequences of such a view were quickly seen by Nietzsche in connection with Wagner, and his description of the Wagnerian style can be paralleled in all the other arts: there is everywhere a solemnity, a pompousness, the stifling feeling of a magical ritual no longer quite under control. In contrast to this view, the moderns sought to instil the notion of art as a game. The work of art does not offer permanent salvation, its function is to increase the reader's own powers of imagination. This requires his active participation and he can, if he wishes, withdraw from the game – no one is forcing him to take part. If he agrees to go on, however, he must abide by the rules laid down by the artist. Again it is not a matter of what the work is saying, but rather of what it is doing. This notion of art as game, moreover, lays stress on the essential modesty of the modern artist, and his awareness that though art has a supremely important place in life, it is helpless to change the world. The rediscovery of the hieratic and stylized arts of other periods and cultures, we must remember, went hand in hand with the rediscovery of genres and forms of art which had not been considered serious enough to form part of the mainstream of European art: the puppet-play, the shadow-play, children's games of all sorts, used to such good effect by Jarry and a little later by Stravinsky, Picasso, Satie, and Debussy. The latter's *Jeux*, a ballet performed by the Diaghilev company in Paris in 1913, and one of the most subtle and inventive works of the period, is 'about' nothing other than a game of tennis!

If all art is a game with its own rules – something that happens between the author and the reader, viewer, or listener – then what is important is the mastery of convention, not the accuracy with which either external reality or the author's own emotions are depicted. And this leads us to the final and most obvious aspect of the modernist revolution: its break with four centuries of mimesis.

Because all Western art since the Renaissance had been essentially an imitation of reality, it was necessarily anecdotal. Paintings have been concerned with subjects such as coronations, battles, weddings, landscapes, and so on. Novels have told stories, and so have all but the shortest lyrical poems. But, as the Romantics realized, to tell one story, to describe one scene, is at once to cut out the possibility of telling a lot of other stories, of describing quite other scenes. Why should the artist paint this rather than that? Why should the novelist tell this story rather than that, put in this incident rather than another? It is not enough to say: 'Because he feels like it', since this feeling is itself in need of justification – why does he feel like it? Since everything is possible, everything is equally arbitrary, as the hero of Kafka's *The Castle* recognizes:

> It seemed to K. as if at last those people had broken off all relations with him, and as if now in reality he were freer than he had ever been, and at liberty to wait here in this place usually forbidden to him as long as he desired, and had won a freedom such as hardly anybody else had ever succeeded in winning, and as if nobody could dare to touch him or drive him away, or even speak to him; but – this conviction was at least equally strong – as if at the same time there was nothing more senseless, nothing more hopeless, than this freedom, this waiting, this inviolability.

The problem already haunted the Romantics, and we find its echoes everywhere in their poetry. But so long as they held to any expressive theory of art they could never solve it, however hard they tried to blur the outlines of their fictions, their music, their painting, until it merged with the surrounding world. The paintings of Cézanne mark the decisive break, and his phrase 'Je pars neutre' [I set out neutral] is the key one for this aspect of modernist aesthetics. What he meant was that he tried to paint, eliminating the inevitable personal slant in both subject and object, seeking instead to discover the general laws of light and space in the scene before him, rather than reproducing that particular scene on his canvas. Proust, whose design is similar, makes the point again and again in *Le Temps retrouvé* [Time rediscovered]: he is not interested in imitating a flat reality but in drawing out the general laws inherent in love, in perception, in speech. And thinking perhaps of a Cézanne and of one of those society portraits even more popular then than now, he says:

> Si l'un dans le domaine de la peinture, met en évidence certaines vérités relatives au volume, à la lumière, au mouvement, cela fait-il qu'il soit nécessairement inférieur à tel portrait ne lui ressemblant aucunement de la même personne, dans lequel mille détails qui sont omis dans le premier seront minutieusement relatés, deuxième portrait d'où l'on pourra conclure que le modèle était ravissant tandis qu'on l'eût cru laid dans le premier, ce qui peut avoir une importance documentaire et même historique mais n'est pas nécessairement une vérité d'art.
>
> [If one example in the domain of painting demonstrated certain truths relative to volume, to light, to movement, it would not necessarily be inferior to a totally different portrait of the same person in which a thousand details omitted in the first painting are meticulously rendered, this second portrait allowing one to conclude that the model was ravishing while one would, on the basis of the first one, have believed her to be ugly, this being a matter of documentary or even historical importance, but not necessarily an artistic truth.]

In other words the work of art does not convey a fixed meaning from the artist to the reader or viewer: rather, it creates an object which did not exist before in either the one or the other, an object which both gives joy and uncovers a truth about the world hitherto hidden. The work of art becomes necessary rather than arbitrary because it is, rather than simply tells. The words in a novel by Joyce, Virginia Woolf, Proust, Robbe-Grillet, Claude Simon, do not enclose a content which the reader simply takes in as he takes in a telephone message, they live and function within the whole work asking the reader to reactivate them within himself as he reads. Ultimately we cannot extract a meaning from the painting or poem or novel, the meaning is the work itself, to be re-experienced every time the reader or viewer wishes to renew the experience.

It might be thought that the search for an art of total potentiality, an art of laws rather than things, would lead to a complete abstraction. Certainly the danger is there and one could say that, if Rimbaud forms one of the poles within which modern art moves, Mallarmé forms the other; for both took to their limits the implications of the Romantic revolt. To go too far in the direction of one or the other is to burst the bonds of art; it leads to either total noise or total silence, either total randomness or total organization. The artist then either plunges in and relies on the honesty of his gesture, on the spontaneity of his response to the paint he handles or the words or notes he puts down, or he organizes his work so rigidly that it might as well be – and often is – produced by a machine. Both points of view are prevalent in so-called avant-garde circles today, and both would have been anathema to the great modern revolutionaries, since both do away with the artist's most precious possession, his individual freedom of choice. As we have seen, this is a limited freedom, and to imagine that it is total is to lose what little there is. But it is essential to maintain it if art is going to survive.

Two quotations from painters would seem to sum up admirably the central features of the modernist movement. The first is from Picasso, who, it will be remembered, broke away from the strict cubism of his early period when he felt he had subjected himself sufficiently to its discipline. Talking to his friend, the photographer Brassai, he said:

> I always aim at the resemblance. An artist should observe nature but never confuse it with painting. It is only translatable into painting by signs . . . . But such signs are not invented. To arrive at the sign you have to concentrate hard on the resemblance. To me surreality is nothing and never has been anything but this profound resemblance, something deeper than the forms and colours in which objects present themselves.

The second is from the English painter, Francis Bacon:

> Art is a method of opening up areas of feeling rather than merely an illustration of an object . . . . A picture should be a re-creation of an event rather than an illustration of an object; but there is no tension in the picture unless there is the struggle with the object.

The preceding pages are an attempt to sketch out some of the characteristics and implications of the modernist revolution and to account for its sudden outbreak at the turn of the present century. Inevitably we have been involved in a discussion which has moved backwards and forwards from the sphere of history to that of aesthetics – inevitably because modernism is first and foremost a rethinking of the whole field of aesthetics as it had been seen in the West since the time of Plato and Aristotle. But this is not to say that this was a mere revolution in the theory of art, for, if the moderns have grown more modest than the Romantics in their view of the function of the artist, they are even more firmly convinced of the crucial place of art in human life.

It has also been necessary, as a matter of strategy, to make the division between the Romantics and the moderns sharper than it really is. For however much the modernist movement is a reaction to a decadent Romanticism, its basic assumptions are still the Romantic ones; a refusal to rely on any external system of values, moral or epistemological, the attempt to discover and communicate the uniqueness of the individual and of each object. If the modern artist frequently harks back to the wit, irony and sophistication of the eighteenth century, it is always a wit tinged with anguish, an irony that is mainly self-protective, a sophistication that has in it the stoic desire for evil to destroy itself mixed with the gnawing certainty that it is far more likely to destroy the good.

Finally, this chapter has deliberately not been confined to French artists because the modern movement was above all an international one. More specifically, and again in implicit reaction to Romanticism, it was an urban movement, one whose exponents are to be found in all great cosmopolitan centres of Europe: Vienna, Munich, Prague, and especially Paris. It was to Paris that the painters and sculptors who formed the backbone of the movement came; in Paris that Proust, Valéry and Joyce published their work; in Paris that Diaghilev's Russian Ballet burst upon the world as the modernist answer to the Wagnerian *Gesamtkunstwerk*. For this reason the modernist revolution has affected the cultural life of France more than that of any other country. In England and Germany the public remembers the leaders of the movement much as they remember all their classical writers – distant and embalmed, standard editions and dreary hours in the classroom. Only in France are they still the mentors of every aspiring artist, the source of all that is most alive in the intellectual life of the country. The history of French literature in the twentieth century is the history of the fortune of one or other of the modernist discoveries. And such was the richness and importance of these discoveries that we are only now beginning to realize their full implications.

Notes

1 The best introduction to 'modernism' is to be found in certain major modern novels, particularly those of Proust and Thomas Mann, but also those of Joyce, Virginia Woolf, Musil, Broch, etc. Other key texts are: T.S. Eliot, *The Sacred Wood* (1920), Valéry's essay 'Poésie et pensée abstraite' (a lecture delivered in Oxford in 1939 and reprinted in *Variété V* (1944)), and Hofmannsthal's 'The Letter of Lord Chandos' (first publ. as 'Ein Brief' in 1902; transl. in Hugo von Hofmannsthal, *Selected Prose*, publ. in the Bollingen Series XXXIII in 1952). A selection of views by modern painters on their art is to be found in G. Charbonnier, *Le Monologue du peintre* (1959), and R.L. Herbert (ed.) *Modern Artists on Art* (1964). To these should be added Brassai, *Conversations avec Picasso* (1964), and Françoise Gilot and Carleton Lake, *Vivre avec Picasso* (1965). Important views by modern composers on music will be found in Schoenberg, *Letters* (1964), and the conversations between Stravinsky and Robert Craft:

Stravinsky in Conversation with Robert Craft (a Pelican book of 1962 containing *Conversations with Igor Stravinsky* (1958) and *Memoirs and Commentaries* (1959)), *Expositions and Developments* (1962), and *Dialogues and a Diary* (1968). A varied selection of texts on 'modernism' by writers, painters, and musicians will be found in H.M. Block and H. Salinger, *The Creative Vision: Modern European Writers on their Art* (1960); R. Ellmann and C. Feidelson, *The Modern Tradition* (1965); J. Cruickshank, *Aspects of the Modern European Mind* (1969).

Criticism. Even a selective bibliography of interesting secondary works would quickly reach enormous proportions. The following books are in the nature of a few tentative suggestions:

R. Barthes, *Le Degré zéro de l'écriture* (1953);

M. Blanchot, *L'Espace littéraire* (1955) and *Le Livre à venir* (1959);

M. Butor, *Répertoire* (to date 3 vols.: 1960, 1964, 1968);

G. Hartman, *The Unmediated Vision: an Interpretation of Wordsworth, Hopkins, Rilke and Valéry* (1966);

F. Kermode, *Romantic Image* (1957);

W. Mellers, *Caliban Reborn: Renewal in Twentieth-Century Music* (1968);

D. Mitchell, *The Language of Modern Music* (1963; paperback 1966);

Marthe Robert, *L'Ancien et le nouveau: de Don Quichotte à Franz Kafka* (1963).

2 Axël: fictional character in the drama *Axël* (1890) by the French symbolist writer Villiers de l'Isle-Adam.

3 A lump of coal, a handkerchief thrown anyhow on to a table.

4 'From analogy to scepticism', Chapter 1 in *French Literature and its Background: 1, The Sixteenth Century.*

4

Domestic Conflict and the Origins of the First World War: the British and the German Cases

Michael R. Gordon

For those interested in the First World War, two recent debates loom especially large. The first, inspired by Fritz Fischer, concerns the degree of German responsibility for the war's outbreak and course. The second, which has in part been thrashed out in [the *Journal of Modern History*] between Arno Mayer and Peter Loewenberg, concerns the proper way to study international conflict – wars in particular. The present paper joins both debates and tries to show how they interrelate.

I

More than thirteen years have gone by since Fischer first startled the German historical profession with *Griff nach der Weltmacht*, and just about five since his follow-up work, *Krieg der Illusionen*.[1] Of his numerous challenges to orthodoxy, not the least provocative lies in the books' methodology. Both, but especially the second, have broken cleanly with the traditional explanatory model (or logic) of diplomatic history.

Briefly, the key assumption underlying this model is about the 'primacy of foreign policy'. From it three or four postulates follow. The model distinguishes rigorously between domestic and foreign politics; it tends to treat the state as a unified, monolithic actor operating within an external environment of competition and imperatives: and it lays down that these actors are primarily motivated by rational power considerations – by the cold rules of statecraft. The controlling concepts for describing these rules are national interest and national security, power, prestige, and perhaps reasons of state. The explanatory power of the model derives from a pattern of inferences about the relationship between specific situations and the state's adherence to these rules: the state – as a rational, unitary decision-maker uninfluenced by domestic politics – will presumably choose the one alternative in the situation that best promises to maximize its security, its power, its prestige, and other interests. The state may turn out to have miscalculated, of course; nevertheless, the grounds for its actions are largely reducible to these considerations. It follows that the crucial evidence for a foreign-policy move will be located in the 'minutes of bilateral or multilateral negotiations or the texts of foreign office dispatches'; and for the scholarly investigator, the problem is then to reconstruct the motives and other causes behind the move through careful textual analysis.[2]

In the renewed debate over the origins of the First World War, this traditional model has proved diminishingly fruitful. Even some of Fischer's most hostile critics have come to scrap it.[3] Its main drawback is its inability to explain why the same foreign office document can serve to underpin two totally opposed interpretations.[4] Such ambiguity can be overcome, or at any rate delimited, only if the traditional postulates are dropped or relaxed in favor of a wider perspective. On the Fischer side of the debate, for instance, he and his sympathizers have tried to uncover the degree to which German foreign policy was prompted by the logic of domestic bargaining maneuvers – by concern for the social status quo, for the prestige of the imperial regime, for the needs of the economic elites. In Fischer's second book, this domestic impact even becomes decisive. Its argument – stripped to the bone – amounts to a thesis of aggressive war, launched by the principal German policy-makers in 1914 to preserve an expansionary future in the belief that expansion alone could preserve the threatened status quo at home. Not for nothing has a younger generation of German historians come to turn Ranke on his head and to speak of the 'primacy of domestic policy'.[5]

All this is extremely thoughtful and stimulating, a major scholarly accomplishment. None the less, two important problems remain.

First, for all his clearing away of old and unfruitful assumptions. Fischer has not been so explicit about the methods and assumptions that he has put in their place. As things stand now, he has clearly effected a productive shift in perspective: whether this perspective adds up to a consistent and realistic pattern of explanatory logic is, however, not too clear. His second book, for instance, uses a mixture of categories and concepts from Marxist theories of imperialism, from elitist theorists like Robert Michels, from standard liberal critiques of German militarism and equally standard conservative critiques of mass society; and therefore, although the resulting argument is massively documented and his findings possibly sound, the criteria governing his choice of materials remain ambiguous – and so does the logical status of his inferences. It is hard to be categorical here, and I wish to stress my uncertainty. But that is also precisely the problem; a greater degree of explicitness seems desirable.[6] And second, as well as being insufficiently explicit, Fischer's work is also inadequately comparative. As a result, he has left himself exposed to the charge that he and his sympathizers have unfairly singled out Germany as the culprit in the war controversy.

It is at this point that the second debate between Mayer and Loewenberg joins the first. Like Fischer, both have broken with the traditional model and argued for an alternative framework of analysis. Mayer, in a series of theoretically bold writings, has developed a completely explicit and comparative model of domestic violence, counter-revolutionary reaction, and precautionary or diversionary war.[7] To Loewenberg, Mayer's model is too structural and macroscopic; he believes that a more psychological approach – especially depth-psychological – would be better.[8] But for reasons that will emerge later. I take exception to both alternatives. Loewenberg seems wrong in regarding psychological and structural explanations as incompatible: handled properly, the two are complementary to one another, not contradictory. As for Mayer, his model – theoretically provocative though it is – strikes me as one-sided and to apply, at most, to one of the two nations under study here.

The model used here is taken from theories of economic development and political modernization. Intended to uncover more of the 'why' of things in the Fischer debate, it compares the domestic impact on foreign policy in Britain as well as Germany before and during the July crisis, 1914. [. . .]

II

The first task is briefly to describe British and German foreign policies before 1914.

As far as German policy is concerned, its readiness to risk war for its own ends – either a local Balkan war fought by its ally in Vienna or a larger, continental-sized war in which it, France and Russia participated – now seems unshakably established.[9] Albertini, Schmitt, Renouvin and Taylor had already argued this point persuasively before 1961, and the debate sparked by Fischer has underpinned it with different sources of evidence and methods of argument. By either one of these two wars the German government thought its interests would be served: at a minimum, a successful localized war – kept limited by Russia's backing off in fear – would in the German view probably break up the Franco-Russian alliance, shore up the tottering Austro-Hungarian empire, and clear the way in Central Europe for an eventual German breakthrough to successful *Weltpolitik*. On a more ambitious level, the German government was convinced it could also secure these aims even more emphatically in a triumphant continental war. As for the world war that happened, German leaders did not consciously aim at it, not at any rate in 1914, and for that matter not even Fischer has claimed this. What they hoped was that Britain would remain neutral or at least a nonbelligerent at the outset. None the less, the possibility of British intervention was appreciated at the very outset, even by Bethmann himself: and by risking its occurrence, the German government bore the responsibility for the ensuing worldwide struggle in at least the sense of conditional intent.[10] To this extent the work of Fischer and his sympathizers seems to be unchallengeable. Fischer himself is probably justified, therefore, when he claims that the debate has now moved irretrievably away from any thesis of coequal responsibility or international anarchy, let alone of German innocence, and toward convergence on a thesis of 'preventive war'.[11]

What remains controversial is the precise meaning of a 'preventive German war policy' and especially the motives behind it. Fischer started out in his first book with an argument that the motives were coolheaded, deliberate instances of outright expansionist goals. Some of his pupils, however, came to lay less emphasis on such goals and more on 'the German mood of 1914, that strange mixture of ideological despair, political bankruptcy and overwhelming economic and military power' as the propellant behind the plunge into war.[12] Most scholars of the subject, it is fair to say, hew closer to the latter interpretation – without, however, necessarily buying the argument that the motives were therefore 'defensive'. Fischer himself, though willing in his latest book to allow for an explosive bundle of German ambitions and complexes, has persisted in imparting to the motives as 'aggressive' a cast as possible. This article will itself have something to say later on about these motives.

As for British foreign policy, it was something quite different in the period before and right through the July crisis. Except for prevailing opinion in inter-war Germany and some revisionist historians elsewhere, nobody has made a charge of bellicosity stick. On the contrary, if any charge can be levelled at Sir Edward Grey, the foreign secretary, it is that he did not pursue as effective and energetic a policy as he might have during the crisis – that, instead, he wavered between two inconsistent courses, backing France and, to a lesser extent, Russia in order to deter Germany on the one hand, and on the other hand playing the role of the disinterested mediator; that, in addition, he never clarified his policy one way or another until the very end, by which point German policy-makers had already decided to risk even a world war; and that, consequently, British influence during the crisis fell far short of what British power in the international system warranted at the time.[13]

Judged strictly in terms of the traditional model – that is, from the viewpoint of external pressures and national interests – the ineffectuality of British policy remains an impenetrable puzzle. After all, neither Grey nor Asquith, the prime minister, had overlooked the multitudinous danger signs hinting at German aims over the years. Just the reverse; the major premise of Grey's diplomacy ever since coming to office, in 1906, had been to avoid a situation in which Britain might face a German menace without any allies.[14] Hence the ententes with France and Russia; hence, too, the reinforcement of ties, especially to France, including recurring staff talks since late 1905 and the important naval arrangements of 1912.[15] These were weighty moves, which nudged Britain away from isolation and toward alliance relationships. Why, accordingly, did the Liberal government not pursue more rigorously the logic behind the effort to reorient British policy? Why settle for a dangerous half-way adjustment, which went far enough to entail uncertain commitments and so a limitation on British freedom, but which stopped short of a full-fledged alliance that might have created both an effective control over French policy and an effective deterrent to German belligerence?[16]

The answer is to be found, of course, in places outside the scope of the traditional model – in domestic politics, especially the resistance to a reoriented policy on the part of the radical wing within the Liberal party and Cabinet. A courageous campaign of re-education might have reduced the ranks of the resisters; the Foreign Office, for one, had long thought so and advised accordingly.[17] Yet Grey and Asquith, far from undertaking to lead such a campaign, shied away from spelling out the implications of their new policy to even the Cabinet. It was largely for this reason that British diplomacy remained stuck, when the July crisis erupted, with an 'unsatisfactory compromise' as a guide – with a 'policy of partisan and unforeseen commitment'.[18] The result was widespread confusion on the Cabinet level, and also no little self-delusion.[19]

As this last line of argument suggests, British policy cannot be fully accounted for in terms of the traditional model.[20] The same can be said (and will be argued) about German policy. Those scholars who work with a traditional explanatory logic balk at recognizing this: they persist in trying to explain German and British behavior by reference to unified decision-makers, objective and perceived threats, and the rules of statecraft.[21] The fact is, however, that the international situations of the two countries did not differ enough to justify such contradictory responses to the July crisis – British policy hesitant and wavering, German policy rash and aggressive. If anything, Germany's future prospects in the international system looked brighter by far than Britain's. In industrial productivity, economic growth, and foreign commerce – in literate population, technology, and military weight – Germany had a decisive advantage not only over Britain but over all its European rivals.[22] It is true that Germany's ability to achieve a breakthrough in *Weltpolitik* seemed temporarily hemmed in by several factors in 1914. But it is equally true that Britain's pre-eminent position was under assault, both from within and from without, at almost every point on the globe.[23] Moreover, these strains soon colored British psychology in several quarters. A spiral of apprehension shook British life in repeated waves after 1900: invasion scares, scares about imperial disintegration, scares even about the quality of the British 'race', abounded.[24] Nor were fears about encirclement a German monopoly. Recurringly, after 1880, British policy-makers were haunted by the specter of a hostile coalition.[25]

Given these trends, might not the traditional logic of statecraft point to a reversal of policies? Should it not have been British policy-makers who were rash and desperate, determined to stave off decline in a bold showdown struggle, and German policy-makers who were increasingly buoyant, increasingly confident that their nation was riding a glorious wave of history?

III

If, then, the gap between British and German foreign policy is too great to be explained fully by their international situations, the next task is to inquire whether their domestic situations differed enough to account for it.

At first glance this does not seem a promising undertaking. What immediately strikes one is the apparent parallel between the two domestic scenes before 1914. Each nation experienced an alarming wave of unsettling events, resulting in social strife, economic dislocation, and left-right polarization. In both a constitutional crisis was emerging and with it the prospect of large-scale violence.

In Germany, the situation heated up in proportion as the enemies of the existing system (*Reichsfeinde* [enemies of the state] as Bismarck had branded them) advanced in numbers and organizational strength. At one time the Catholic center figured among these enemies; by the turn of the century the term referred almost exclusively to Social Democrats (SPD) and the trade unions. Their advance seemed irresistible. In fact, the more the nation industrialized and modernized, the more the social structure that underpinned the Reich at its founding, in 1871, inevitably altered in their favor. The SPD's revisionism did little to assuage the fears of the *staatserhaltende Kraefte* – the forces of order. On the contrary, the most moderate proposals for electoral and fiscal reforms were denounced as though tantamount to revolution. And, indeed, in a sense they were: for the Bismarckian system, fabricated for a traditional social order, could hardly accommodate strong bourgeois participation – let alone that of the working class.[26] Following the SPD advances in the 1912 Reichstag elections, a precarious situation, latent for years, was thus pushing to the surface. The more the forces of change pressed for reforms, the more the forces of order took fright. Hence the alarming wave of fanatical chauvinism, mass demagogy, and crude racism that enveloped the nation from the right in the years before the war.[27] Hence, too, the revised interest in *coup d'état* schemes.[28] The whole interrelated but untenable system of power and privilege was moving toward crisis and probably breakdown.[29]

As for Britain, classic home of political stability, it too was undergoing a cycle of internal unrest and tensions. Class conflict was spiraling, unions were growing militant, women suffragettes resorted to violence. Worse, with segments of the army dabbling in mutiny and the Conservative-Unionist party toying with sedition, the prospect of civil war loomed ever likelier in Ireland.[30] Culturally, a jittery mood of unease and dislocation pervaded much of Edwardian England; 'decay, decline, fall, and decadence were the language of the time and not of party'.[31] Neither inherited political habits nor tested mechanisms of adjustment could readily cope with the sudden upsurge in strife. The English Constitution was based largely on tacit gentlemanly agreements – implicit rules of the game. On the Tory side, however, these rules were no longer being observed. In fact they were being openly flouted, as the ancient props of patrician Britain (land, paternalism, the House of Lords, the Church) came under repeated blows.[32] Even Liberals suffered from the distempers of the time. Divided between Whigs and Radicals over domestic affairs, and between Imperialists and Internationalists over foreign policy – faced also with an emerging Labour party on its left – the Liberal party could not spawn a coherent vision of a new society to replace the one currently under attack. Amidst these circumstances, the Cabinet itself tended more and more to postpone and to wobble – Asquith, indeed, was something of a master at inaction. By July 1914 a sense of national disaster lurked in the air.

In many respects, then, the German and the British situations overlapped. But the parallel between them goes only so far. Dig deeper, and certain crucial differences are found that still separated the two nations – not least, in the strength (or really lack thereof) of the British extreme right as compared with its German counterpart. The fact is that the social base for powerful reactionary or counter-revolutionary mass movements was built into the very structures of Imperial Germany; in Britain, by contrast, it was almost wholly lacking. Again, a strong state but a weak regime reinforced the prospects for such extremist activity in Germany; in Britain no such state apparatus existed. The importance of this contrast cannot be overestimated. Because of it, the quality of politics in the two nations diverged in essential ways.

For decades, and not just after 1912, the elites in Wilhelmine Germany lived in an ambivalent and anxiety-ridden condition regarding modernism. On the one hand the inexorable industrial advance was welcomed by them as a means to national aggrandizement, a step toward successful *Weltpolitik*. On the other hand, few were optimistic about the future of an industrial society, and the social and political changes it created.[33] At the same time the existing ruling groups lacked a political system with built-in mechanisms of political adjustment – indeed, they steadfastly opposed changes that might create such mechanisms; even a moderate like Bethmann Hollweg was no major exception.[34] Finally, Germany was still, for all its advanced industry, predominantly pre-industrial in social structure; this meant that millions of threatened peasants in the countryside and more millions of old *Mittelstaende* [middle class] within the cities were available for political mobilization from extremists on the right against the working class or the pitifully small progressive middle class.[35] Edwardian England, by contrast, was simply not fertile ground for right-wing extremism of a mass sort, any more than was depression-laden England in the 1930s. By then there were no peasants to mobilize, and no militaristic aristocrats to lead them.[36] By then, too, the commercial and industrial middle classes were numerous, articulate, and independent minded, putting a liberal stamp on British politics. As for the lower-middle classes, they were, it is true, growing in number, but unlike those caught up in the turmoil of Germany's rapid industrialization, they had long been assimilated to modern life and took it for granted.[37] Moreover, there was no standing army, no powerful state bureaucracy, no large state role in the economy – in fact, despite recent changes, hardly a state in any modern sense at all.[38] Least of all was there, for all the jitters of the time, a potent antimodernist tradition on which an embattled right could draw in order to rally mass support. The contrary was the case: thus, whereas Bethmann was a fatalist and full of forebodings for the future, Asquith remained certain that something good would turn up even over Ireland.[39] For all these reasons, accordingly, even to speak of an extreme right-wing movement is to speak at best of what might have happened, and not what did in fact happen, as a noted left-wing historian concedes.[40] Indeed, Unionist flirtation with extraconstitutional methods, far from mobilizing mass enthusiasm, did not even command widespread support within the Unionist party itself.[41]

The reasons for these contrasting situations remain to be set forth. What is important to note here, before leaving this section, is the hook-up with foreign policy. Owing to the divergent political conditions, not only were the domestic crises in the two nations approached in contrary ways by the British and the German governments, but so, too, were the problems of foreign policy that faced each. German political elites (as will be seen) had an overwhelming incentive to use foreign policy as a method of domestic control: in fact, they had been doing so for years. No similar temptation offered itself to British elites, nor is there evidence that they ever used foreign policy to that end. It follows that any effort to explain British and German decisions to wage war in equivalent terms, as comparable cases of diversionary war, seems misplaced.[42] [...]

V

If the various strings of the argument are now drawn together, the following conclusion emerges.

Domestic conflict had a contrary impact in the two nations. In Britain, for all the turmoil that erupted before 1914, foreign policy remained moderate and largely defensive; and this was so even though the nation's world position was itself on the decline and under challenge at almost every point on the globe. None the less, internal conflict did take its toll.

It added to the defensiveness of Britain's posture, indeed its increasing reactiveness, by inhibiting Grey's efforts to reorient foreign policy and leaving the nation stuck, therefore, at a dangerous point halfway between isolation and full-fledged alliances. The result was the ambivalent policy 'of partial and unforeseen commitment' with which the Liberal Cabinet approached the July Crisis, uncertain whether it should try to act as a mediator in the old 'free hand' sense of Salisbury's days or to act as an ally of France and Russia so as to deter Berlin. In the event, Grey's cautious zigzagging as the crisis unfolded only 'reinforced the German hope that England would stand aside'.[43]

Grey's advisers at the Foreign Office saw that his policy revisions added up to an unsatisfactory compromise, with consequent confusion both at home and abroad. Again and again, accordingly, they pressed him to clarify his actions and carry his campaign for reorientation through to its logical end; yet again and again Grey balked, well knowing that the Liberal party, and hence the Cabinet itself, was too divided to permit such clarification. 'I do not know', Arthur Nicolson, the permanent under-secretary, wrote in April 1914, 'how much longer we shall be able to follow our present policy of dancing on a high rope and not be compelled to take up some definite line or other'.[44] But the high-rope act went on; what else could Grey do in view of the political situation? Mayer argues that he and Asquith could move toward the right, toward the hawkish Unionist party – that, in fact, they did precisely this during the July Crisis, overcoming the waverers and the non-interventionists in the Cabinet with a threat to create a Liberal-Unionist coalition.[45] There are some scattered indications that Asquith toyed with such a threat.[46] Yet it does not appear to have had nearly the effect that Mayer maintains it did.[47] On the contrary, Asquith himself thoroughly feared the reactionary consequences that would follow from any such coalition.[48] In short, as before 1914, so throughout the July Crisis itself: partisan conflict and internal Liberal discord continued to obstruct a clarification of foreign policy one way or another.[49]

In Germany, even though domestic conflict appeared to be more latent than in Britain, it was in fact even more politically far-reaching, and its repercussions on foreign policy were pronouncedly of an aggressive sort. Three such repercussions have been distinguished here. First of all, quite apart from deliberate foreign-policy decisions, there was a set of spillovers that arose from the very national situation of the Reich in 1871 and after. Among the most prominent of these were the unsolved problem of national identity, doubts about the viability of the Reich's borders, and the unforeseen consequences of tariff policies that arose out of the bargains struck between industrialists and Junkers. There was a second set of spillovers, on the other hand, that did derive directly from calculated political maneuvers. These maneuvers aimed at trying to control an increasingly impossible domestic situation by ever-greater efforts of social imperialism, mass propaganda, *Weltpolitik*, armaments programs, and diversionary quests for prestige of the quickest and cheapest sorts – in short, the whole complex of foreign adventures and aggressive diplomacy that embittered relations with other great powers and created diplomatic isolation. Finally, somewhere in between there was a third pattern of repercussions, a psychological pattern, by which the fears and grudges that German elites nurtured in domestic politics were turned outward and led them to detect international specters all over Europe. Bismarck, who had unified the nation, had spoken ominously of his 'nightmare of hostile coalitions'. By 1914 the whole nation, at any rate to the right of the Social Democrats, was tormented by such nightmares, even if they were overwhelmingly self-induced. The upshot of all three kinds of repercussion was the calculated gamble in favor of war that was taken in July 1914. With one sudden desperate charge, the Reich's leadership hoped to achieve that ultimate breakthrough in *Weltpolitik* that would safeguard the nation's expansionist future and its conservative order at home. By 1917, to take a date that was uppermost in German thinking at the time, it would be too late. By then, Russian and French military reforms would be completed and the chances of a successful breakthrough, therefore, that much less.

Bethmann Hollweg himself, it has been argued, had doubts that a war would actually strengthen the conservative order.[50] He seemed in fact to fear that it might hasten its decline and lead through mass mobilization to democratic concessions or worse. But one should not make too much of these qualms. For one thing, as Fischer notes, Bethmann's warnings in this respect 'only confirm how widespread the contrary view was'.[51] For another thing, he clearly embraced the 'curious blend of contradictory beliefs – social Darwinism, misunderstood romanticism, and cultural pessimism – all pointing to German expansion as the only alternative to stagnation'.[52] In this respect, as Stern also hastens to add, there was really no fundamental divergence of political aims between Bethmann and the other leaders of Imperial Germany; 'the general consensus about Germany's national destiny was too broad and the Kaiser's tolerance for dissent too narrow' to permit anyone who dissented too much from continuing in office.[53] For a third thing, finally – as Riezler's diary makes clear – he unequivocally hoped that 'if war comes and the veils fall, the whole nation will follow, driven by necessity and peril'.[54]

Notes

1 Fritz Fischer, *Griff nach der Weltmacht: Die Kriegszielpolitik des kaiserlichen Deutschland 1914/1948*, Dusseldorf, 1961; *Krieg der Illusionen: Die deutsche Polltik von 1911 bis 1914*, Dusseldorf, 1969.
2 Arno J. Mayer, 'Internal causes and purposes of war in Europe, 1870–1956: a research assignment', *Journal of Modern History*, 41, September 1969, 302. Admittedly, owing to the brevity of formulation, a pretty sharp and simpli-

fied picture of the traditional model has been sketched in. None the less, I do not think that it is a caricature. On the contrary, even though many diplomatic historians had come to modify the key postulates long before Fischer was heard of, most have probably continued to use a variant of the traditional model until quite recently.

3 For instance, Egmont Zechlin, 'Bethmann Hollweg. Kriegsrisiko und SPD' and 'Motive und Taktik der Reichsleitung 1914', in *Erster Weltkrieg: Ursachen, Entstehung und Kriegsziele*, Wolfgang Schieder (ed.) Cologne and Berlin, 1969, pp. 165–204.

4 James Joll, *1914: The Unspoken Assumptions*, London, 1968, p. 7.

5 See Hans-Ulrich Wehler. 'Einleitung', in Eckart Kehr, *Der Primat der Innenpolitik*, Hans-Ulrich Wehler (ed.) Berlin, 1970, pp. 1–30; Michael Stuermer (ed.) *Das kaiserliche Deutschland: Politik und Gesellschaft 1870–1918* Dusseldorf, 1970.

6 In other words, to paraphrase a general argument of Richard Hofstadter: Fischer's analysis does a better job of accounting for 'what' happened and 'how' it happened than 'why' it did so: yet until the 'why' of things emerges more clearly, one cannot be fully confident about the 'what' and the 'how' (see 'History and Sociology in the United States', in *Sociology and History: Methods*, Seymour Martin Lipset and Richard Hofstadter (eds) New York, 1968, pp. 8–18.

7 In addition to the article in no. 2 above, see Arno J. Mayer. 'Domestic causes of the First World War', in *The Responsibility of Power: Historical Essays in Honor of Hajo Holborn*, Leonard Krieger and Fritz Stern (eds), New York, 1967, pp. 286–300; *Dynamics of Counterrevolution in Europe, 1870–1956: An Analytic Framework*, New York, 1971.

8 Peter Loewenberg, 'Arno Mayer's "Internal Causes and Purposes of War in Europe, 1870–1956" – an inadequate model of human behavior, national conflict and historical changes', *Journal of Modern History*, 42, December 1970: 628–36.

9 Fischer, *Krieg der Illusionen*, pp. 663–82; Konrad H. Jarausch, 'The illusion of limited war: Chancellor Bethmann Hollweg's calculated risk, July 1914'. *Central European History* 2 March 1969, 48–77; Fritz Stern, 'Bethmann Hollweg and the war: the limits of responsibility', in *The Responsibility of Power*, p. 268.

10 See Hermann Kantorowicz (ed) *Gutachten zur Kriegsschuldfrage 1914: Aus dem Nachlass*, Frankfurt, 1967, Imanuel Geiss, for the meaning of the term.

11 Fischer, *Krieg der Illusionen*, pp. 663–4.

12 Imanuel Geiss (ed.) *July 1914: The Outbreak of the First World War: Selected Documents*, New York, 1967, pp.367–8.

13 Herbert Butterfield, 'Sir Edward Grey in July 1914'. *Historical Studies*, 5, 1965, 20.

14 George Monger, *The End of Isolation: British Foreign Policy 1900–1907*, London, 1963, pp. 329–31.

15 Samuel R. Williamson, Jr., *The Politics of Grand Strategy: Britain and France Prepare for War, 1900–1914*, Cambridge, Mass., 1969, especially pp. 284–5.

16 Pierre Renouvin, 'Britain and the Continent: the lessons of history', *Foreign Affairs*, 17, October, 1938, 111–27.

17 A. J. P. Taylor, *The Struggle for Mastery in Europe, 1848–1918*, London, 1954. pp. 525–6; Zara S. Steiner, *The Foreign Office and Foreign Policy 1898–1914*, Cambridge, 1969, pp. 131–9.

18 J. A. S. Grenville, *Lord Salisbury and Foreign Policy; The Close of the Nineteenth Century*, London, 1964, p. 436.

19 Monger, p. 330.

20 Cameron Hazlehurst, *Politicians at War: July 1914-May 1915*, New York, 1971, pp. 88–91.

21 See, for instance, Joachim Remak, '1914 – the Third Balkan War: origins reconsidered', *Journal of Modern History*, 43, September 1971, 353–66.

22 Derek H. Aldcroft and Harry W. Richardson, *The British Economy 1870–1939* London, 1969, pp. 101–68; David Landes, *The Unbound Prometheus*, London, 1969, pp. 326–58. More generally, Ross Hoffman, *Great Britain and the German Trade Rivalry*, New York, 1964.

23 Ronald Robinson and John Gallagher, *Africa and the Victorians: The Climax of Imperialism*, New York, 1968, pp. 287–9: Max Beloff, *Imperial Sunset*, London, 1969, pp. 5–24.

24 Samuel Hynes, *The Edwardian Turn of Mind*, Princeton, NJ, 1968, pp. 15–54.

25 Lord William Strang, *Britain in World Affairs*, New York, 1961, p. 222.

26 Guenther Roth, *The Social Democrats in Imperial Germany: A Study in Working-Class Isolation and National Integration*, Totowa, 1963, p. 59.

27 Fischer, *Krieg der Illusionen*, pp. 117–45; Dirk Stegmann, *Die Erben Bismarcks: Parteien und Verbaende in der Spaetphase des Wilhelminischen Deutschlands: Sammlungspolitik 1897–1918*, Cologne and Berlin, 1970, pp. 262–3; Klaus Wernecke, *Der Wille zur Weltgeltung: Aussenpolitik und Oeffentlichkeit in Kaiserreich am Vorabend des Ersten Weltkrieges*, Dusseldorf, 1970, pp. 288–314.

28 Hartmut Pogge-v. Strandmann, 'Staatsstreichplaene, Alldeutsche und Bethmann Hollweg', in *Die Erforderlichkeit des Unmoeglichen*, Hartmut Pogge- v. Strandmann and Imanuel Geiss (eds), Frankfurt, 1965, pp. 11–45.

29 Hans-Juergen Puhle, 'Parlament, Parteien und Interessenverbaende 1890–1914', in *Das kaiserliche Deutschland*, pp. 361–4.

30 The classic study is George Dangerfield, *The Strange Death of Liberal England*, New York, 1961.

31 Hynes, *The Edwardian Turn of Mind*, p. 45.

32 Robert Blake, *The Conservative Party from Peel to Churchill*, New York, 1970, p. 190.

33 Kenneth D. Barkin, *The Controversy over German Industrialization 1890–1902*, Chicago, 1970, pp. 1–15, 131–2; Ralf Dahrendorf, *Society and Democracy in Germany*, New York, 1967, pp. 9–10; Fritz Stern, *The Politics of Cultural Despair: A Study in the Rise of the German Ideology*, Berkeley, Calif., 1961.

34 See Klaus Hildebrand, *Bethmann Hollweg, der Kanzler ohne Eigenschaften? Urteile der Geschichtsschreibung: Eine kritische Bibliographie*, Dusseldorf, 1970, pp. 50–64.

35 As late as 1895, more than half of the German work-force was still employed in preindustrial occupations – 36 per cent in agriculture alone (see Juergen Kocka, 'Vorindustrielle Faktoren in der deutschen Industrialisierung. Industriebuerokratie und 'neuer Mittelstand', in *Das kaiserliche Deutschland*, pp. 279–80).

36 In 1911, only 8.6 per cent of the British work-force was still on the land, and only an additional 6.0 per cent still in other preindustrial occupations (see Aldcroft and Richardson, *The British Economy*, p. 14; also F. M. L. Thompson, *English Landed Society in the Nineteenth Century*, London 1963, pp. 9–24, 269–70).

37 S. G. Checkland, *The Rise of Industrial Society in England 1815–1885*, London, 1964, pp. 301–14.

38 A. J. P. Taylor, *English History 1914–1945*, New York, 1965, p. 1.

39 Stern, 'Bethmann Hollweg' p. 262; R. C. K. Ensor, *England 1870–1914*, London, 1960, p. 452.

40 E. J. Hobsbawm, *Industry and Empire*, New York, 1968, p. 163.

41 Alfred Gollin, *Proconsul in Politics: A Study of Lord Milner in Opposition and in Power*, London, 1964, pp. 220–1; Blake, *The Conservative Party*, p. 192.

42 It is precisely for this reason that Mayer's thesis of counterrevolution – diversionary war – illuminating though it is in the German case, goes astray in the British.

43 Williamson, *Politics of Grand Strategy*, p. 345.

44 Quoted in Steiner, *The Foreign Office and Foreign Policy*, p. 138.

45 Mayer, 'Domestic causes of the First World War', pp. 288–9, 298–300.

46 Hazlehurst, *Politicians at War*, pp. 103, 112–13.

47 Williamson, *Politics of Grand Strategy*, pp. 345–60; Steiner, *Foreign Office and Foreign Policy*, pp. 153–64.

48 Hazlehurst, *Politicians at War*, p. 136.

49 Taylor, *Struggle for Mastery in Europe*, p. 525.

50 Jarausch, 'The illusion of a limited war', p. 58; Stern, 'Bethmann Hollweg and the war', p. 263.

51 Fischer, *Krieg der Illusionen*, pp. 13, 693.

52 Stern, 'Bethmann Hollweg and the War', p. 257.

53 Ibid., pp. 259–60; see, too, Fischer, *Krieg der Illusionen*, p. 158; Imanuel Geiss, *July 1914*, p. 47.

54 Quoted in Jarausch, 'Illusion of Limited War', p. 58.

5

Italian Peasant Women and the First World War

Anna Bravo

The topic of this paper – part of a larger research project on the role and identity of peasant and working class women[1] – is the transformation of women's social conditions in the countryside during the First World War. At the same time I shall be looking at the processes of adaptation and the elements of conflict present in the way in which women experienced these changes. In this way we shall be examining a specific example of the broader problem of the relationship between women's conditions and external historical moments – between women's history and 'great' history.

Among the various significant events which have affected Italian peasant society, the First World War appears as a moment of primary importance. Indeed, the war's importance as representing one of the central elements of popular memory has recently been re-emphasized in Nuto Revelli's great collection of life stories from the countryside around Cuneo, south of Turin, *Il Mondo dei vinti*. However, until now research has been primarily focused on the figure of the peasant soldier and the conflictual relationship between resignation and dissent which characterize his behaviour.[2] Much less attention has been given to analysing the impact of the war on the rural communities themselves, whose life was thrown into disorder by the massive call-to-arms, by material difficulties, and by the increased interference of state authorities in the fabric of daily life.

As for women, while some attention has been given to female workers in their role as labour power, which was of primary importance in this period, and as the subjects of a significant process of social activation, peasant women have been considered only as silent victims of poverty or as protagonists of sporadic and spontaneous outbursts of struggle against the war.[3]

Between these two extremes, which represent the two sides of an existence of radical oppression and exclusion, there is nothing: these women have a past, but not a history.

In a similar way, the researcher whose interest is women's social conditions, faces a central problem: the risk of oscillating between a narrowly specialized and 'ghettoized' understanding, and an understanding that results in a subsidiary inclusion of women with a larger predetermined framework of interpretation. We do not want to create a separate history which makes no sense of history as a whole, nor do we wish to see ourselves relegated to a small women's section – no more important than many other sub-sections – in 'great' history.

The current interest in the use of oral sources – linked to a growing attention now being given to the methodological and analytical categories of social science disciplines like anthropology, sociology and psychoanalysis – can bring a significant contribution to the redefinition of this problem. New areas of research, new keys to interpretation, different measures of social changes and continuities are now all suggested to the historian. Furthermore, the political and cultural presence of feminism has contributed to a better understanding of the theoretical and methodological complexities of research, and has made clear the inadequacy of some of the conceptual systems now used in social science: for example, the inadequacy of concepts of the social division of labour which deny the social and ideological relevance of the condition of women, or of a history seen as the development of Reason, which entails a radical exclusion of women, identified as irrational, subjective, 'different'.

To overcome this exclusion, it is necessary to reaffirm the specific centrality of women in any attempt to reach an understanding of social structures and social and political processes. Thus, the analysis of the workings of mature capitalist societies remains not only incomplete, but also profoundly falsified, if the importance of the economic and social role and the cultural significance of women's condition is not considered. But even this approach still risks establishing the centrality of women simply in their old role as symbols of the particular cultural level reached by society – as the passive 'stepping stones' which mark the stages of historical development: restored to the centre of attention, but of a broadened, all-encompassing 'great' history, rather than a history of women.

Although we still lack the fully developed theory and concepts which such a true history of women demands, we can at least attempt to penetrate behind the fixed image of women's 'nature' which culture has produced and history documented. We can try to see how at different times this 'nature' of women is socially constructed, by examining the connections between women's roles and ideology, the elements of consciousness and false consciousness, the non-rational aspects and subconscious impulses. In other words, we can interpret consciousness and subjectivity as a historically determined reality – but with stages of development and causal processes of its own.[4]

Within this perspective, oral sources become essential, precisely for the very specific richness they offer for an understanding, not only of daily experience, but also of processes of adaptation and resistance to social and structural transformations. In other words, oral sources can contribute to a project of women's history which lays the foundation for the recovery of different times and spaces, of different and hidden historical facts.

The territory which we have been studying, the Langhe, is a hilly region of extremely poor countryside to the south of Turin, with a great predominance of small, or extremely small, family-run farms. Only marginally influenced by industrialization, these communities have been marked by a sense of exclusion and a close-knit defensiveness towards the outside world. Inside the communities, life has been dominated by the struggle for survival, by the hunger for land and the conflict to possess it. Land is what unites but can also divide the community and the family.[5]

The women work both in the house and in the fields. Their existence is characterized, on the one hand, by the centrality of their family and work roles which makes their presence indispensable, and, on the other hand, by the delimited nature of their recognized rights.

The hereditary system excludes them from land ownership; the dowry consists exclusively of items of clothes and furniture. Therefore, women have value, in the matrimonial market and the social life of the community alike, only as labour power and reproductive power; and, along with this, to fulfil the demand for a psychological and moral force which guarantees the cohesion of the family. The space for women's social life is severely restricted both by the characteristics of their role and by the moral rigidity of the community. Sexual alienation is generalized and brutal. Their identity is marked by the contradiction between the image of strength and indispensability which they hold of themselves, and their acceptance of the weakness of their social conditions.[6]

The intervention of the war made its mark, first, on the women's relationship to both agricultural and domestic work. The delicate balance between consumers and producers upon which the peasant family is based was disrupted by the disappearance of the most active section of the male labour force. The women found their work cycle expanded even more: small baby girls and old women now had to work; the work day grew longer; and the variety of their tasks increased until it included all of those formerly held by men.

This meant the end of the traditional division of labour in which the men performed the heavier and, in some ways, more exacting jobs, such as manoeuvring the threshing machines. All of the oral accounts insist on this point:

> I had to do all the tasks the men used to do. I even had to unload the wheat, spread the wheatsheaves, help to thresh when the machine came around. And then, I was always looking after the animals. We even took the hoes and weeded the corn, the beans, everything.[7]

> They didn't give me any easy jobs just because I was a girl. I hoed, watered the vines, cleaned the stalls, looked after the animals.[8]

The marks that this excessive exertion left on the women's bodies are emphasized, and so is the women's capacity to resist and adapt:

> I had to do everything that a man does. My brothers were in the war. We watered the fields barefoot. It was bad for our health. We ate badly, but we would have eaten anything ... I got married when I was twenty; no doctor had ever touched me.[9]

> The hired boy was in front watering the vines. I came behind spreading the sulphur. When I came home in the evening my eyes were burning. I washed and washed. But when I went to bed I didn't even want to sleep any more because if I closed my eyes they watered all night long ... I weighed only 45 kilograms.[9] [My brother] always said: 'You look like the living death' ... Well, I'm still here: I've always been healthy.[10]

When this redistribution of work was not sufficient to ensure the family's survival and the continued possession of the land, the women returned temporarily to the nearby factories or to some other type of work outside the family, including, in some cases, semi-clandestine seasonal emigration to France. This migratory work even involved married women with children, and thus disrupted the tradition whereby such experiences ended at marriage.

Beyond these cases of forced absence, there was also a reorganization of family life and domestic activity. Mothers devoted themselves almost entirely to work in the fields, while the weight of the house and the care of the children fell on the daughters who were often only slightly older. In some cases a daughter looked after the childen from several families, so that the other girls could work in the factories or as servants. In any case, daily household tasks – cleaning, cooking – were reduced to a minimum. There was a parallel growth in the time devoted to the tasks which external changes imposed, in particular to those imposed by rationing and by intensified forms of immediate family consumption of production:

> We made oil by crushing the nuts and sunflower seeds in the wine press.[11]

We dealt with the problems ourselves. We milked the cows to make butter because what they gave out for the rations was meagre and awful. We made our own bread.[12]

We had rationing cards, but we made a type of bread mixed with potatoes.[13]

In spite of the quantity of these efforts, the situation of certain families became so desperate that some were forced to eat animal feed and others even to stealing. Two women openly admit it:

We stole . . . Well, if you wanted to eat . . .[14]

My mother, your grandmother Antonietta, Carolina, eight or ten women altogether, you know what they did? They stole at night; potatoes, onions; they stole firewood together. They did all these things just to keep going.[15]

These women justify these small-scale thefts and other illegal activities by their families' need to survive. But the unambiguous social and cultural rejection of these women by others is a stark confirmation of community disapproval:

The wife would take a large apron, roll it up, and walk around the streets. In one place, potatoes, in another, beans. She stole a little here, a little there, and came home with the apron full. That woman was looked down on.[16]

In all oral accounts, the women's acceptance of such a vast array of responsibilities appears both as out of the ordinary and also as a duty almost as if it were natural for women to make themselves responsible for exceptional tasks, tasks which were accepted as the utmost expansion of a multiform and never-ending role.

This attitude seems accurately to reflect the meaning of matrimonial exchange in the community, and the conditions which had to be endured in order to be accepted in the new family. The man brought the land, which was a quantifiable good, always equal to itself; the woman brought a subjective capacity to work which was indeterminate. This capacity of hers had to be adapted to the family's life cycle and needs. The woman realized that she was accepted – and could feel her own value – only through her own capability and this willingness to adapt. Hence, there were no special compensations envisaged for her efforts. The few attempts to rebalance the family relationship in her favour tended primarily to improve her own condition only within the traditional family structure. The situation was perhaps slightly different for unmarried girls who worked within their original families, where the promise of some small rewards in exchange for longer and heavier work[17] was not merely a sign of consideration for their youth as such, but also an indication that their obligation to show unconditional willingness to work was less institutionalized and less general.

In the life of these communities, the war manifested itself above all through an increase in the presence and power of the state; in inspections, requisitions, forced hoarding, rationing; and the introduction of difficult procedures for obtaining benefits, exemptions from the draft, and military leave. This new relationship with authority fell on the women, as the only remaining young section of the population. But the new responsibility was also asked of them by their husbands at the warfront.[18] The women's lives, previously restricted to the house and community, were now filled with new tasks; going to government offices, discussing with local administrators and officials, travelling as far as provincial capitals to follow through these extended chores. Thus greater contact was established with the outside world, with new places, with a new environment of different experiences, with the public sphere of life. The women now had a direct relationship with the activities of a state authority which they also identified as responsible for the war. When the oral accounts deal with these themes, they are given great emphasis:

> When my husband was a soldier, they sent a letter to my mother-in-law saying that she had to pay a certain amount because he was unfit for war duty. The poor old woman paid, and then wanted me to pay her back. 'I'm not paying. He may be unfit for war, but he sure isn't at home, he's off in the army.' I said it to the police too. I went to talk to the city officer. Other notices of payment due arrived. They told me to go to the tax office here in Caraglio. There they told me to pay and then to sue to get back my mother-in-law's and my money. 'Thanks, I have my money in my pocket and I'm keeping it. My mother-in-law paid her own money. I don't want it.'[19]

> I was in bed with the six-year-old baby, and I caught the Spanish 'flu too. One day the marshal comes; I was in bed. He wanted me to give some hay to the government. I told him: 'Doesn't it seem disgraceful to you that they ask me for hay; me, here in bed, with my husband a soldier, and young as he is they've never given him an hour's leave; and I'm here in bed with nobody to help me. Aren't you ashamed?' Finally they sent my husband a telegram and gave him a ten-day leave.[20]

Attitudes of this type were an integral part of a more general estrangement from the state and of peasant society's opposition to the war. Furthermore, the encounter with the state occurred with the woman acting as representative and defender of the family, and this role appeared as a necessary extension of her function as guardian of the common interests. There are, however, other elements which suggest additional interpretative keys. It would be reasonable to expect that these women's behaviour would be marked by a combination of both insecurity and aggressiveness. The oral account, however, emphasizes only the latter aspect, often presenting a kind of drama in which the woman actively sets herself against arrogance and arbitrariness. This strong element of self-affirmation suggests the hypothesis that we are also dealing with the dynamics of a more general conflict with authority. Repressed and forbidden expression inside the family, these dynamics of conflict were shifted outside against a socially shared enemy, against an authority experienced as pure abuse of power, against an authority which could not, therefore, kindle processes of identification and complicity.

Furthermore, if we examine the special emphasis given in the oral accounts to other war-imposed encounters with the external world – the purchase of a pair of oxen, buying and selling at the market in the husband's absence – we discover that each of these episodes, beyond the particularities of the conflict with authority, is also experienced as a moment of self-realization, of individualization in the social world and the public sphere. The women seem only partially conscious of this stimulus, but as they tell their stories, one senses resonances of emotional involvement, not only in the goal they had in each encounter, but also of a hidden ability and quiescent desire which they had at last found acceptable ways of realizing.

The war affected relations between the sexes in contradictory ways. It opened – as we shall see – spaces for a less restricted and less orthodox sexuality. However, given that the peasant models of morality and the power relationships did not undergo any change, the position of women, already structurally fragile, appears to have been further weakened. In this society the women were not only productive and reproductive power, but were also sexual objects to be used as freely and brutally as the weakness of their social and personal position permitted. Their only defence was the family's control or protection. When this was lacking – something which coincided with extreme poverty or internal disintegration – violence, incest, the cheap sale of children and child prostitution, and persecution endured as farm hands and servants, were not uncommon.

The departure of husbands and brothers left the women weaker and more exposed. Furthermore, with the war women had increased contact with the external world; they needed masculine help for certain agricultural operations; local officials and police entered their houses to identify animals and goods to be requisitioned; deserters and draft-dodgers sought refuge in their barns. Certain oral accounts – only a few, probably because of a form of self-censure – document the spread of a threatening and predatory attitude. The man takes it for granted that the woman is suffering from male absence and aggressively proposes himself. The accounts speak of cases of rape and murder.[21]

In most of the accounts it appears that the women experienced this situation by a strong denial of their own sexuality: those accounts that deal with the problem do so only in order to reject its existence, and, at the same time, to re-confirm their own adherence to the model of wife and mother:

> My head was filled with other things. I swear that I never even thought about 'that' because I had so many other worries. I thought about him off in the war, and the children, the animals, the land, everything, and the debts to pay.[22]

Male sexual proposals were experienced without gratification, and the only emotional agitation was in the expression of harsh disapproval for an initiative considered 'shameful'. The women's refusals never betray an effort to control themselves, never show anything like the rejection of 'temptation'. The episodes take on the character of simply dealing successfully with a difficult moment, with a dangerous or socially embarrassing situation. Only the male has sexual impulses – and those that chase women are *lurdun* – good-for-nothings and pigs – because women have more important things to do.

Only through the women's references to deviants – from whom they rigidly distinguish themselves – do they let us see that the war had introduced specific kinds of disturbance in their sexual behaviour:

> There was one . . . The marshal always went to see her . . . I wasn't one of those that they could go to bed with.[23]

> There are women who had a hard life. And there were those who used their husband's absence, but you certainly had to have a lot of courage![24]

> The woman wanted to enjoy herself, and neglected the house, or else gave up the land and everything, and when the husband came back he didn't find anything.[25]

Certainly, this subject is influenced by the demands of social and self-respect and the need to reaffirm the values of their own past against the greater permissiveness attributed to the present. However, when evaluating this model of behaviour it is necessary to keep in mind that the acceptance of a subordinate and restricted sexuality in marriage is a 'natural' fact of these women's experience, and is closely linked to the other aspects of their roles. It is not a coincidence that sexual transgression is associated with the spectre of the loss of the land and the ruin of the household. Since the husband's absence created new material problems of solidarity and respect, the women had an even stronger stimulus to hold on to the models they had been socialized to accept. This stimulus was further strengthened both by the intensified control or protection exercised by the community and neighbourhood, and by the woman's understanding of the weakness of her social position, a weakness based on her exclusion from landownership. This under-standing makes the risk of destroying the marriage unthinkable.

In this situation – in which the stimulus to maintain the established order went hand in hand with increased opportunities to violate it – the traditionally marginal dimension of sexuality in women's lives and self-identity presumably favoured the mechanism of self-repression and, beyond that, of total denial, which controlled the women's sexual behaviour and judgment.

The changes that the war created in social life are seen with particular prominence in the social life of women which was, until then, tied to very rigidly traditional and limited relationships. The time and space for the old forms of social life became even more restricted with the war:

> Life changed a lot during the war . . . To think that I hardly learned how to dance. Before the war people often danced during the festivals. But we didn't dance very much. People were worried. We still spent the evenings together in the barns, but we laughed and joked a lot less.[26]

In this exceptional situation, new, infrequent and 'unorthodox' parallel forms of social life began to develop. Many were directly linked both to the reorganization of agricultural and domestic work, and to the new solidarity created among the peasants:

> In Rivera, I remember, we were all women who threshed the wheat. There were a few machinists . . . but we did everything else ourselves: some of us spread the sheaves, others cut the wheat. We were all young girls and we enjoyed ourselves. There was a steam engine we called the 'black locomotive' because it seemed like the old train locomotives you had to feed with coal.[27]

> In Albaretto, everyone who lives in that farmhouse there is still called 'oilman', 'cause we all used to take our walnuts up there to be pressed.[28]

> In the evening we would help the women who had small babies. We did some of their work for them . . . One of them had her husband off in the war. She wasn't very quick, so we went and did her sewing and knitting. She made us a plate of fritters, and we ate![29]

New relationships were also formed as a result of those created at the warfront:

> I had all the addresses of his companions: one from Mondovi, another from Garessio, and many more. Afterwards, they all came by to see me and bring me the war news.[30]

But the most significant element for understanding the transformation of both the women's daily social life and their subjective attitudes is the presence of small bands of deserters and draft-dodgers who moved from one hillside to another. This extremely important development was dependent on a conspiracy of silence and on the solidarity of the peasants.[31]

The subject is often discussed in the oral accounts. This presence of so many unknown young men, who lived clandestinely and suddenly appeared – perhaps in the middle of the night – in the barns or court-yards of a farmhouse, became a part of daily life, and enlivened it. For women, stuck to the old-established system of relationships, it was an entirely new experience:

> They wandered around at night and came to ask for something to eat . . . then others came on Sunday. They slept wherever they could, in hay-lofts, under the porch. Sometimes we'd see one come down from the loft, and we hadn't even realized he was up there. Once I got frightened: my father sent me to throw down some hay from the loft, and I uncovered one who was half asleep.[32]

In this extremely closed and suspicious society, the new situation was experienced with a tolerance and sympathy that cannot be fully ex-plained, either by the fact that some of the deserters came from the villages under discussion, or by the generally exceptional situation. The young men helped the women with their field chores, and, although their lives were semi-clandestine, in some cases they became so inte-grated into the peasant family's life that they were allowed to organize football matches, festivals, and barn dances:

> They said to my father: 'Bastiano, let us dance a little.' He replied: 'Oh sure! If I let you dance, the police will arrive tomorrow!' Mean-while, one of them began to play the accordion, and we started dancing.[33]

> Sometimes they sent around trying to find a house they could dance in, and then invited everybody. They always did the organizing. I remember that there were some who could really dance!![34]

The opinion of the women is explicitly positive, and contains none of the rumours of rape and other forms of violence which are present in some of the men's oral accounts.[35] On the contrary, the women's opin-ion emphasizes that the deserters were good people, who worked, who moved from one hillside to another in order not to weigh too heavily on the peasants, who never did anyone any wrong, and with whom it was perhaps even pleasant to talk and dance.

This evaluation is clearly influenced by the implicit comparison with the partisans of 1943–5 who are remembered in this region in a more conflictual manner.[36] However, the approval and emotional involve-

ment are too strong to be tied only to this negative comparison: the
personalities, the nicknames – one is found in a number of different
accounts – are recalled with precision; the dangers faced to give them
hospitality are emphasized; their courage is exalted:

> They sure were courageous! They weren't scared of anything;
> played football in San Sabastiano village. One always kept guard in
> case someone arrived. We helped them, but if the police found us
> with deserters in the house, we were in for a lot of trouble. But the
> police weren't in any hurry to come to this region, because there
> were a lot of deserters, even if they weren't armed. I never saw
> them armed.[37]

The accounts emphasize the continuous cycle of escapes and arrests in
the life of the deserters. They are recalled as the protagonists of an
unfought war with the 'carabinieri' which in reality was probably less
intense than this would suggest. The regret that some relative who died
in the war did not follow their example is present in almost all of the oral
accounts.

The role of positive hero given to the deserter springs above all from
the tradition of peasant estrangement from the state and opposition to
the war already mentioned. The deserter incarnates the most explicit
opposition to the war which was achieved within this culture. But for
the women there were probably additional aspects to the question: not
so much elements of specific sexual and emotional tension – hinted at
in the male accounts – which would have set off conflictual dynamics
among the women; but rather, the presence of a desire for a less restricted social life, for a way out of daily routine, for affection. This gives
the entire experience more complex emotional content and significance.

The deserter became a part of daily life and brought with him new,
less 'orthodox' relationships; at the same time, however, he did not
violently disrupt this existence. It was a parenthesis that was, at any
rate, destined to end. It was danger, adventure, disorder, but it was also
the denial of a rule imposed by the outside world. It was a transgression
which could be identified with, a symbol of a conflict of values in which
everybody was involved. The deserter was a young man, courageous
but needing protection, afraid of nothing, but evoking pity.

The relationship was at the same time both completely internal to the
experience and culture of these women, and completely external, suspended in a temporary time-slot and in imaginary spaces. In the oral
accounts, the relationship crops up as a central element of the war
experience and as a subject for many recollections; it is on the one hand
escape, on the other a confirmation of the women's own existence.

It is no coincidence that only at this point do the women's oral accounts
reveal a recuperation and recollection of the war. In all other parts of the
accounts this is entirely absent. While in the men's accounts, the experience of the war-front is revisited 'with a certain level of immediate iden-

tification, and often even with a reserved form of pride and nostalgia',[38] the women's accounts express a total rejection. Forced to endure the entire weight of the war, yet at the same time excluded from those 'heroic' aspects worth re-evoking, the women respond by denying them:

> I tell him: 'Drop it: you're boring, by now we are all tired of hearing the same stories over and over again.' But him? Never. Onward with Monte Grappa, the Neapolitans, the Germans, his colonels. I've heard about the war so many times it comes in one ear and goes out the other.[39]

And the women counter the four-year war with one that lasts a lifetime: with the fact that 'the war was out there, but here we had to eat every day'.[40]

For when the war was over and the men had come back home, apart from a few wives whose husbands returned seriously disabled, or went off abroad for work, the women had to retreat to their earlier confines, and forget most of the wider responsibility they had briefly borne. A venthole had been opened, which could not be wholly closed; and a good many wives continued to exercise their new-found expertise in dealing with state officials, now on behalf of their husbands. But, within the community, old roles were resumed, and the women forced back into traditional peasant silence, leaving the men to monopolize the claim to war honours. Yet the fight to feed the family had to continue without respite in the new circumstances. And the weight of that still fell primarily on the women: a seemingly timeless, immutable labour – a fate without history – moulding their consciousness of both past and present.

Notes

1 This is a research project on which I am working together with Lucetta Scaraffia. We are using the biographies of Piedmontese peasant women, born around the turn of the century, all married with children, and all from the same social stratum, and the biographies of Turinese working-class women. Altogether, we have carried out forty interviews.

  The peasant witnesses all belong to families of small or very small farmers. Some of them had short experiences as domestic servants in the city before marrying; a very few of them worked for some time in small industries; and others migrated as young girls to France for seasonal work. All of them married farmers and spent most of their lifetime in the country, where some of them still work, although now very old. On the whole their response to being interviewed was positive, as was their interest in a research project on women's conditions in the past. In fact, several of them told us that they saw this as a chance to re-evaluate their own life experience and communicate it to the outside world.

2 N. Revelli, *Il Mondo dei vinti*, Turin, 1977; E. Forcella and A. Monticone,

Plotone di esecuzione: i processi della prima guerra mondiale, Bari, 1968.

3 See R. De Felice, 'Ordine pubblico e orientamento delle masse populari italiane nella prima meta del 1917', in *Rivista storica del socialismo*, VI, 20, 1963.

4 Among contributions to the study of consciousness and psychology, see especially, A Besançon, *Storia e psicanalisi*, Naples, 1975; and for women's consciousness, U. Prokop, *Realtà e desiderio L'ambivalenza femminile*, Milan, 1978.

5 Revelli, *Il mondo dei vinti*.

6 See A. Bravo and L. Scaraffia, 'Ruolo femminile e identità nelle contadine delle Langhe: un'ipotesi di storia orale', in *Rivista di storia contemporanea*, 1, 1979.

7 Oral account of Nina Rinaldi (b. 1893).

8   "   "   Luisa Nebbia (b.1901).

9   "   "   Maria Civalleri (b.1900).

10   "   "   Nina Rinaldi.

11   "   "   Maria Chiavarino (b.1894).

12   "   "   Nina Rinaldi.

13   "   "   Domenica Bertaina (b.1901)

14   "   "   Maria Bernardino (b.1893).

15   "   "   Rita (b. 1902). In 1917, the worsening of living conditions in the region was such that there was a protest demonstration with insults, rocks, and vegetables thrown against the 'carabinieri', with the workers hidden in a tannery, the railroad station, and the grain warehouse: see Forcella and Monticone, *Plotone di esecuzione*, op. cit., pp. 124–6. This event does not often appear in the oral acounts, perhaps because it occurred in a nearby village and not in that of the women interviewed.

16 Oral account of Spirita Arneodo (b. 1891).

17 Oral account of Maria Bonetti (b. 1903).

18 See the correspondence of the soldier Sabino Traversa with his wife in A. Bandand 'Problemi e aspetti della participazione dei contadini delle Langhe alla prima guerra mondiale', University of Turin, 1979, unpublished dissertation supervised by Anna Bravo.

19 Oral account of Spirita Arneodo.

20   "   "   Spirita Arneodo.

21   "   "   Maria Domini (b. 1896).

22   "   "   Spirita Arneodo.

23   "   "   Spirita Arneodo.

24   "   "   Lucia Cravero (b. 1892).

25   "   "   Carolina Arneodo (b. 1902).

26   "   "   Angiolina Boschis (b. 1893).

27   "   "   Maria Cagnasso (b. 1893).

28   "   "   Maria Chiavarino.

29   "   "   Lucia Cravero.

30   "   "   Nina Rinaldi.

31 On the phenomenon of desertion, see Revelli, *Il mondo dei vinti*, II, Le Langhe and Introduction.

32 Oral account of Nina Rinaldi.

33   "   "   Maria Domini.

34   "   "   Nina Rinaldi.

35 See Revelli, *Il Mondo dei vinti*, II, Le Langhe.

36 ibid; and N. Gallerano, '*Il Mondo dei vinti*', in *Rivista di storia contemporanea*, 4, 1978.
37 Oral acount of Nina Rinaldi.
38 M. Isnenghi, 'Valori populari e valori "ufficiali" nella mentalità del soldato fra le due guerre mondiali', in *Quaderni storici*, 38, 1978, 704.
39 Oral account of Luisa Nebbia.
40 Oral account of Angiolina Boschis.

6

Epilogue to *Army, Industry and Labor in Germany, 1914–1918*

Gerald D. Feldman

The conduct of the German war effort during the First World War was marked by a complete breakdown of 'substantial rationality', of 'intelligent insight into the inter-relations of events in a given situation'.[1] Germany's war aims were an unattainable conglomeration of the aspirations of industrialist and agrarian interest groups, bureaucratic *Machtpolitiker*, militarists, and Pan-German dreamers. It was hoped that the realization of these imperialist goals would strengthen the old authoritarian system and the special interests it served. Instead, the prolonged war led to the final disintegration of the Bismarckian state. The Emperor virtually went into seclusion; the bureaucracy surrendered to the army; the army led the nation to disaster and then abdicated power itself. Neither the bureaucracy nor the army was capable of giving the nation the direction it needed, and the Reichstag failed to fill the gap. At the same time the class basis of the Bismarckian state, and its destructive tendencies, were revealed in the crassest manner. The Junkers continuously sabotaged the government's food supply and ruthlessly undermined the regime's prestige in their attack on its foreign and domestic policies. The industrialists joined in this assault and engaged in an underhand feud with the War Ministry and the War Office. Only when the army was willing to grant high profits and suppress labor did it receive the full support of the industrialists.

No less depressing was the manner in which organized labor had been absorbed into this system of political and economic opportunism. Because the war effort could not succeed without the help of organized labor, the bureaucracy and the army sought to come to terms with it at the cheapest possible price. The labor leaders found themselves living in two worlds. As semi-official agents of the government, they encouraged their followers to support a war whose success would have strengthened the hand of their opponents. As representatives of the workers, they took advantage of their newly won power to extract concessions from the government. Pressed from below and bribed from above, they were compelled to disappoint everyone. They denounced strike agitators to the army and then defended and even joined the strikes they officially deplored. Their greatest success, the Auxiliary Service Law, was attainable only through the abrogation of the worker's fundamental right to change his job, and this intensified the dissatisfaction of the workers. At the same time their insistence upon Paragraph 9 led to conflict with the authorities. Such was the price which the labor leaders paid for their attempt to come to terms with a bankrupt system. Here, too, functional rationality had triumphed.

If the competing groups within German society pursued their special interests to the disregard of the fundamental problems of their society, however, they were also compelled to recognize that their survival was endangered by the mismanagement of Germany's affairs and the growing threat of revolution. Thus the interest groups and the army continuously demanded the creation of new and more efficient forms of executive authority in the form of an economic dictator, a War Office, or a political dictator. At the same time they insisted on the right to regulate their own affairs and to play a decisive role in the policies of executive agencies through advisory councils. What they wanted, in short, was a dictator or a powerful agency which scrupulously adhered to their policies. The effort to find a man or an agency that would be 'above politics' was always determined by special political purposes. This pattern of political behavior, the two chief components of which were the tendency to reduce politics to a series of tactical alliances among competing interest groups and the tendency to search for some new authority to correct the disorder created by the system, is of exceptional importance. It lies at the very heart of the agreements between industry and labor and between the army and labor which did so much to prevent the thoroughgoing political and social reconstruction required by the failure of the old regime.

After the conclusion of their 'social partnership' in November 1918, the industrialists and the union leaders tried to propagate the myth that the industrialists' acceptance of the social partnership was not the product of the Revolution but rather the outcome of a long series of negotiations which had begun in 1917. This interpretation totally neglected the fact that until October 1918 the leaders of heavy industry were, with few exceptions, adamant in their refusal to accept collective bargaining. Although willing to collaborate with the unions in the demobilization, they were unwilling to offer the unions the kind of concessions that would have made such collaboration possible. Even in July 1918, when Ludendorff's great offensives had failed and a farsighted official of the electrotechnical industry, Hans von Raumer, sought to resume negotiations to establish 'an organic collaboration with the unions . . . before the flood of events overcame us all', the leaders of heavy industry continued to remain aloof.[2]

There was, however, an important grain of truth in the claim that industrialist resistance to cooperation with the unions was weakened in the course of the war. On the one hand, heavy industry's old allies, the Junkers, the bureaucracy and the army, had failed to withstand the rising power of organized labor. Indeed, the bureaucracy and the army had compelled heavy industry to accept the onerous Auxiliary Service Law, had given *de facto* recognition to the unions, and had treated wage movements and strikes with unpardonable lassitude. On the other hand, industry was irritated by the severe restrictions of the war economy and the continuous interference of the bureaucrats and the Reichstag in its affairs. The attempt to use the War Office for its special purposes had also failed. If industry was to attain the self-government it desired, it needed freedom from bureaucratic and parliamentary restrictions. Yet how could industry free itself from such hindrances without the help of organized labor? The attempt to fight the government and labor at once would only have served to unite these forces. The unions, like the industrialists, were irritated by the clumsy bureaucratic machinery of the old regime. The union leaders shared the industrialists' fear of the growing revolutionary sentiment among the workers. Finally, both groups shared the tendency to think in purely bread and butter terms and to dislike the combination of doctrinaire verbiage and thoughtless log-rolling which typified the Reichstag. The significance of the secret negotiations between industrialists and union leaders during the war was not that the former were ready to accept collective bargaining, but rather that the employers were already toying with the idea of using the unions against the bureaucracy, against the Reichstag, and against the workers, and that the unions were predisposed to cooperate with the employers. These negotiations anticipated the character of the final arrangements made in the fall of 1918.

Until October the employers expected to get the best of all possible worlds. A German military victory would, they hoped, strengthen the authoritarian regime and, as a consequence, their position *vis-à-vis* the unions. Union cooperation could thus have been bought at a minimal price. Ludendorff's failure terminated their dilatory tactics. They knew that the days of the old order were numbered, and they were among the first to abandon it. On 9 October the leading iron industrialists met at Düsseldorf to discuss ways and means of warding off revolution and socialization. They correctly surmised that the Max von Baden regime would last no more than four or five weeks, and they considered the German middle class too weak to act as a satisfactory ally for the protection of industry's interests. One possibility remained open to them:

> Only the organized workers seemed to have an overwhelming influence. From this fact one drew the conclusion that, in the midst

of the failing power of the state and the government, industry can only find strong allies in the camp of the workers, and they are the unions.[3]

Hugo Stinnes was empowered to negotiate with the trade union leaders. The general significance of this step cannot be underestimated. Faced with economic chaos and a potential threat to their property, the industrialists were, in effect, abandoning their long-standing alliance with the Junkers and the authoritarian state for an alliance with organized labor. It was completely in keeping with this attitude that the bankers and leading industrialists were among the first to demand the abdication of Emperor William II.[4]

Following the meeting of 9 October, labor–management negotiations were held in Düsseldorf, Berlin and elsewhere. The employers agreed to recognize the unions as the representatives of labor, establish factory workers committees, and organize labor exchanges and mediation agencies on the basis of parity between labor and management. They refused, however, to terminate their support of yellow unions, to establish collective wage agreements throughout industry, or to introduce the eight-hour day in all industries. Despite the defeat of such major portions of their program, the unions agreed to industry's terms.

Having made as few unpleasant concessions as possible, Stinnes and his colleagues turned to the immediate problem of securing union support against the bureaucracy and the Reichstag in the demobilization. On 2 November the two interest groups decided to demand that the government establish a demobilization office with 'extensive executive powers'. At its head was to be a state secretary, 'a Ludendorff for the tasks of the demobilization',[5] who would be advised by representatives from the employer and union organizations. The new agency was to have complete control over the employment of the returning troops, the distribution of contracts, the supply of raw materials to the factories, and the general transformation from a wartime to a peacetime economy. Thus the interest-group program was composed of the same combination of authoritarian and corporatist strands which had typified the efforts to organize the war economy. It was of dubious constitutionality in that it excluded the federal states from participation in the decision-making process. At the same time it pushed aside the legally constituted agency that had been established for the demobilization, the Imperial Economic Office. In short, the interest groups wanted an economic dictator who would implement their program without the interference of either the duly constituted legislative or executive bodies.

The government of Prince Max von Baden, feeble as it was, turned a 'cold shoulder' toward this plan to exclude it from the determination of economic policy. On 5 November, however, the representatives of labor and management informed Prince Max that, in the words of Legien, 'if the government does not create the institutions which we consider necessary, . . . then it will have to carry out the demobilization without the help of the labor and employer organizations'.[6] This blackmail worked, and on 7 November Colonel Koeth was appointed State Secretary of the new Demobilization Office. Koeth had the confidence of both labor and heavy industry. He had ruthlessly cut off the coal supply of non-essential plants and had protected the profits of heavy industry. He was an ardent advocate of centralization and could be counted on to distribute coal and food in the manner desired by the interest groups. At the same time he had always been diplomatic in his dealings with the trade unions. Koeth's first demand was that the unions and the employer organizations create a central organization, a 'social partnership', in order to work with the new Demobilization Office more effectively. This need had already been anticipated and work had been begun.

The outbreak of the Revolution on 9 November 1918 caused the trade union leaders to express reservations concerning the advisability of entering into a permanent social partnership with the employers. It is possible that some of them felt that this would commit them to oppose socialization. It is more likely that they wished to avoid creating this impression. Whatever the case, they were extremely anxious to reach an agreement with the employers and finally accepted the employers' request for a permanent social partnership. Legien told Stinnes that he was of the view that Socialism was 'to be sure, the final goal, but that it would be many decades before it was carried out'.[7] Legien's greatest fear was chaos, which would destroy the economy and ruin his organizations. He needed the employers because he was convinced that only they had the skills necessary to keep the economy going. He also feared the radicals in his own camp, particularly the soldiers' and workers' councils. When the latter began interfering with union functions, they were warned that the unions would simply cease their activity and then there would be an 'employer strike with all its terrible consequences'. Finally, Legien had little faith in compulsory measures undertaken by the revolutionary government. As Stinnes reported:

> The unions correctly say that that which is now introduced by compulsion by the government and which actually has no real legitimation cannot have the same significance as a voluntary agreement between the unions and the industries. The latter will remain; the former is something that can be abrogated again.

It is difficult to fathom the logic behind this remark. If the uncertainty of the times made a voluntary agreement between labor and management desirable, the very novelty of the situation militated against the expectation that it would last. Most important, the 'significance' of labor's triumph would ultimately depend upon the success of the Revolution. For the trade unions to question the legitimacy of the revolutionary regime's actions at this point was not merely inappropriate, it was also destructive. Their task, if anything, was to legitimize the Revolution by giving it their full support. Unhappily, they were so opportunistic, so habituated to the struggle for the attainment of immediate goals within the existing sociopolitical framework, and so fearful of disorder, that they were willing to settle for an immediate and illusionary success.

Thus the unions concluded an aggreement whose terms were prejudicial to the further development of the Revolution. It was drawn up on 12 November, the very same day on which the Council of People's Commissars abrogated the Auxiliary Service Law, with the exception of its provisions for the mediation and arbitration of labor disputes, and committed itself to the realization of a Socialist program. The industrialists naturally were forced to make some new concessions, but Stinnes skillfully gave them an ambiguous character. The employers agreed to discontinue all financial support of the yellow unions. The latter were to continue to exist if they could survive without employer support. Furthermore, Legien secretly promised to permit them to take part in labor–management negotiations when things calmed down. Legien undoubtedly did not think this concession particularly significant since the survival of the yellow unions without employer support was very doubtful, but it is quite astonishing that Legien could bring himself to make such a concession. The eight-hour day was to apply to all industries, but overtime work was permissible. Even more important, a secret protocol was drawn up making this part of the agreement valid only if the other countries would agree to introduce the eight-hour day. Germany's perilous economic situation unquestionably made rigid schematization undesirable, but the secret protocol did commit the unions to vitiate their support of the eight-hour day at the very moment when the revolutionary regime declared it in force as of 1 January 1919. With their usual care for the wording of the agreement, the employers also accepted the general introduction of collective wage agreements, but 'in accordance with the conditions of the affected industry'. Stinnes succeeded in warding off all attempts to give the workers the right to interfere in the operation of the plants or oversee business affairs. The functions of the workers committees were strictly limited to matters pertaining to the projected collective wage agreements. Finally, the agreement provided for the establishment of a permanent Central Committee for all of industry and suborganizations for the various industries to implement the agreement and to act for the interests of both parties in the demobilization and the 'maintenance of economic life'. Thus the effort to make the interest-group alliance the center of the socioeconomic decision-making process continued despite the fact that the regime had changed and despite the demands for socialization or greater worker control over the factories.

The industrialists were fully conscious of the advantages which their alliance with labor had brought them, and they knew that they had gotten off cheaply. In a discussion of the agreement at the executive committee of the Association of German Iron and Steel Industrialists on

14 November 1918, Privy Councilor Hilger led his colleagues along the road to Damascus:

> Gentlemen, I stand before you today a Saul transformed into a Paul. Today we cannot get on without negotiations with the unions. Yes, gentlemen, we should be happy that the unions still find themselves ready to deal with us in the manner in which they have, for only through negotiations with the unions, through our agreement with the unions, can we prevent – call it what you will – anarchy, Bolshevism, rule of the Spartacists, or chaos.

He considered the agreement a 'colossal achievement', which was 'far more favorable' than he had ever expected. In a similar vein Stinnes warned his colleagues not to take the talk of nationalizing key industries seriously: 'I would advise you to pay as little attention as possible to these things, but rather to settle the matter here, for if it is settled here, then the other alternative will disappear of itself.'

It would be a mistake, however, to confuse a change of tactics with a spiritual conversion. When it came to assessing the reasons for Germany's failure, Hilger was as much of a Saul as ever:

> This is neither the time nor the place to discuss the question of guilt, but we want to establish that those who from the very beginning did not oppose the revolutionary movements in the interior of the Fatherland with the necessary energy and vigor are guilty of complicity in the entire collapse.... I have warned many times and stood alone in doing so. I remind you of the negotiations concerning the Auxiliary Service Law, where I fought alone with Stinnes.

If industrialists like Rathenau, Borsig, Sorge and Rieppel were inclined to take a more positive view of collaboration with the unions and regard such collaboration as desirable in itself, the leadership of heavy industry persisted in taking a purely instrumental approach to the entire matter. Less than a month after the conclusion of the Stinnes–Legien Agreement on 15 November 1918, Stinnes was beginning to pay a different kind of 'social insurance premium against insurrections' by giving financial support to the demagogue Eduard Stadtler, who was calling for the establishment of a 'national socialist' dictatorship.[8] The lesson is perfectly clear. German heavy industry would accept help from wherever it came, be it from Legien and Stadtler or, twelve years later, from Hitler.

The question of whether union support of the workers councils and union encouragement of powerful and effective factory councils would have provided more viable alternatives to the alliance with industry lies beyond the scope of this study. What can be established here is that the trade union leadership did not really try to find viable alternatives to their policy. Instead they stuck fast to the unpolitical craft union orientation of the pre-war period. The war, however, had done much to accelerate the growth of industrial unionism. The wartime and immediate post-war growth of the Free Trade Unions was based, by and large, upon the influx of women, youths, and unskilled workers from the large urban factories into the movement. These workers had little sympathy for the old traditions of the craft unions and were hostile to traditional authorities. Embittered by the war and politicized by the Revolution, they were prone to join hands with the old vanguard of industrial unionism, the metalworkers, in an attack on the rule of both the factory owner and the union secretary. In rejecting the demands of these workers for a major transformation of authority relationships within the factory, the trade union leaders were expressing not only their feeling of dependence upon the employers but also their anxiety concerning the threat to their leadership of the working class.[9]

The evidence does suggest, however, that the unions could have done more to restrict the authority of management. Hilger's satisfaction with the Stinnes–Legien Agreement and his surprise over its 'favorable' nature clearly demonstrate that the industrialists expected and might have accepted worse. Most important was the extent to which the union leaders were willing to commit themselves to a standing alliance with the industrialists. It was one thing to enter into a temporary agreement for the purpose of securing an orderly demobilization, another to enter into a 'social partnership' which indicated a commitment to maintain capitalistic institutions and authority relationships without serious modification.

The entire spirit of the 'social partnership' was expressed by an industrialist in December 1919: 'Gentlemen, we Germans have never had any talent for politics. Now, therefore, after the bankruptcy of our political order, it behooves us to harness our economic forces for maximum production.'[10] Maximum production for what and for whose benefit? After four years of economic and human waste, this problem deserved consideration. The union leaders always used the dangerous condition of the German economy and the need to revive production as an excuse for their cautious policy. Yet it was precisely the fact that Germany's economic rate of growth had been seriously set back by the war and the fact that her economic revival would require extensive industrial rationalization that made it necessary to insure that labor would not bear all the sacrifices of the reconstruction. The problem was a political one, and it could never be solved by right-wing Socialist efforts to implement the corporatist schemes of Wichard von Moellendorff, a man so caught up in his technocratic mode of thought that he had expected to use the Hindenburg Program to realize his brave new world.[11]

If General Groener's hope that an alliance of army, industry, and labor would save the monarchy was disappointed, his expectation that it would save what could be saved of the old order was not. Groener was, indeed, the ideal man to replace Ludendorff on 27 October 1918. As Ebert told him, the labor leaders 'would always remember our collaboration with you during the war with pleasure.'[12] He had the confidence of the labor leaders and the intellectual competence and willingness to accept reality to save the officer corps. As might be expected, he fought harder than the industrialists to save the monarchy, but when the monarchy could no longer be saved, he, like the industrialists, gave preference to the interest he represented and saved the officer corps.

As the Stinnes–Legien Agreement bound the industrialists to recognize the unions in return for union protection of employer interests, so the Ebert–Groener alliance bound the army to support the Republic in return for the Republic's support of order. The initial purpose of the latter alliance, like the former, was to secure an orderly demobilization. Here again, however, the labor leaders drifted into a more permanent alliance because they feared the workers and because they were unable or unwilling to use their imaginations and find another alternative.[13]

This failure of leadership not only destroyed the Revolution's chances of success, but also seriously damaged the capacity of the Social Democratic Party and the trade unions to preserve and defend the Weimar Republic. As during the war, so after its conclusion, their alliance with the forces of the old regime, and failure to find a new and imaginative policy, produced discord and rebellion within the ranks of the labor movement. If their timidity prevented them from getting the upper hand over the army and industry, their failure to do so subjected them to such pressure from below that they were compelled to antagonize their erstwhile allies. The army drifted into isolation as a 'state within the state', anachronistic in its social composition and psychologically disoriented because of its inability to find a focus of loyalty and because of its constant conspiratorial activity. As the state, because of the dissatisfaction of the workers, took an increasingly active and, from the standpoint of the industrialists, excessively expensive role in social and economic affairs, the social partnership decayed, and the union leaders and industrialists retreated into their old slogans and attitudes. It was, however, on the basis of the truce between labor and management that the Weimar Republic had been founded, and the Republic could not survive long without it. The final blow came in March 1930 when labor–management disagreement brought down the Great Coalition and began the disintegration of the Republic.

It was then that the groups hardest hit by the war and the inflation, the groups which had been permitted to drift in a limbo of resentment against both capital and labor had their day and joined the ranks of National Socialism. Through their wartime and revolutionary experience, the army and industry had learned that the workers could not be controlled unless they were organized and that their goals could not be attained without the aid of mass movements. It is interesting to note that after Hitler's seizure of power the industrialists gave serious consideration to the resurrection of the 'social partnership' of 1918.[14] Hitler, however, gave the industrialists more than they had bargained for in the form of an organized and disciplined Labor Front which would not demand even Legien's price. Similarly, the army finally accepted a 'drummer', who would rally the nation behind rearmament and aggression. Groener's policy, to be sure, had breathed a last gasp when his protégé, General von Schleicher, vainly had sought to revive the old wartime collaboration between the army and the trade unions in 1932. The army's incompetence as an agency for the organization and control of the masses, however, had been revealed fourteen years earlier. Ludendorff's dream came true, and the army had a 'strong man' in Berlin who was prepared to realize the frustrated militaristic dream of total mobilization in a new and even more insane Hindenburg Program, the Four-Year Plan. The tactical alliances the army and industry concluded with Hitler, however, produced unanticipated results. This time the effort to combine authoritarianism with corporate independence failed, not because, as in the First World War, the interest groups made effective executive action impossible, but rather because, unlike Ebert and Legien, Hitler understood that his revolution could not succeed unless he destroyed the independent power of the army and industry.

Appendix: The Auxiliary Service Law of 5 December 1916[15]

I. Every male German between the ages of seventeen and sixty who is not serving in the armed forces is obligated to perform Patriotic Auxiliary Service during the war.

II. All persons will be considered to be rendering Patriotic Auxiliary Service who are employed in government agencies, in official institutions, in war industry, in agriculture and forestry, in caring for the sick, in war economic organizations of any kind, or in other occupations or trades which directly or indirectly are important for war administration of national supplies, so far as the number of these persons does not exceed the need.

Those who before 1 August 1916 were engaged in agriculture or forestry need not be taken from this occupation to be transferred to another form of Patriotic Auxiliary Service.

III. The administration of the Patriotic Auxiliary Service will be carried on by the War Office established in the Royal Prussian War Ministry.

IV. The question whether and to what extent the number of persons employed by a government agency exceeds the need will be determined by the Imperial or state authorities in collaboration with the War Office. The question of what is to be regarded as an official institution as well as whether and to what extent the number of persons employed by such exceeds the need will be decided by the War Office in collaboration with the Imperial or state authorities.

For the rest, the question of whether an occupation or trade is important in the sense of Section II, as well as of whether and to what extent the number of persons engaged in an occupation, organization, or trade exceeds the need, will be decided by committees that will be formed for the district of every Deputy Commanding General or for parts of the district.

V. Every committee (Section IV, Clause 2) shall consist of an officer as chairman, two high state officials, one of whom must belong to the Factory Inspectorate, and two representatives each from the employers and the employees. The officer and the representatives of capital and labor shall be appointed by the War Office, or in Bavaria, Saxony, and Württemberg by the War Ministry, which in these states is responsible for executing the law in agreement with the War Office. The higher state officials are appointed by the state authorities or by an authority appointed by them. If the district of a Deputy Commanding General extends over the territory of several federal states, the officials shall be appointed by the authorities of these states; in the decisions of the committee the officials of the state in whose territory the business concerned lies will take part.

VI. Complaint against the decisions of the committee (Section IV, Clause 2) shall be made to the central agency established by the War Office, consisting of two officers of the War Office, one of whom shall be chairman, two officials nominated by the central authority of that state to which the business, organization, or person following the occupation belongs, and one representative each from the employers and the employees. These representatives will be appointed as in Section V, Clause 2. If maritime interests are affected, one of the officers shall be appointed from the Imperial Naval Office. In complaints against decisions of Bavarian, Saxon, or Württemberg committees, one of the officers is to be appointed by the War Ministry of the state concerned.

VII. Men liable to Auxiliary Service who are not employed in the sense of Section II may at any time be compelled to serve in some form of Patriotic Auxiliary Service.

The calling up will be as a rule through an announcement issued by the War Office or an authority to be appointed by the state central authorities calling on men to report themselves voluntarily. If there is not sufficient response to this appeal, then an individual summons shall be sent out in writing by a committee to be formed, as a rule, for each district of a Recruiting Commission, which shall consist of an officer as chairman, a high official, and two representatives each from the employers and the employees. When the voting is equal the chairman shall have the casting vote. The officer and the representatives of the employers and the employees shall be appointed as in Section V, Clause 2. The official shall be appointed by the state central authorites, or an authority appointed by them.

Everyone who receives the special written summons must seek employment in one of the branches mentioned in Section II. If employment on the terms of the summons is not obtained in two weeks, the committee will assign the man to an occupation.

Appeals against the committee's decision will be decided by the committee formed by the Deputy Commanding General (Section IV, Clause 2). Appeals will not postpone the obligation to serve.

VIII. In making assignments, due regard will be given as far as possible to age, family conditions, place of residence, and health, as well as to previous occupation. Also the question whether the prospective pay will be sufficient to support the employed and to provide for his dependents shall be investigated.

IX. No one may take into his employ a man liable to Patriotic Auxiliary Service who is employed in a position denoted in Section II or who has been employed during the previous two weeks unless the applicant produces a certificate from his late employer that he has agreed to the man's leaving his service.

Should the employer refuse to give a certificate, complaint may be made to a committee to be appointed, as a rule, for every district of a Recruiting Commission and to consist of a representative of the War Office as chairman and three representatives each from the employers and the employees. Two each of these representatives are permanent; the others are to be taken from the same occupation as the man concerned. If the committee acknowledges, after investigating the case, that there are good reasons for leaving the employment, then it shall issue a certificate which will serve instead of the employer's certificate.

A suitable improvement of working conditions in the Auxiliary Service shall be considered a particularly good reason.

X. The War Office shall issue instructions for the procedure of the committees mentioned in Section IV, Clause 2; Section VII, Clause 2; and Section IX, Clause 2.

Nomination lists from the economic organizations of the employers and the employees are to be gathered in connection with the appointment of representatives of the employers and the workers to the committees (Sections V, VI, VII, Clause 2; Section IX, Clause 2) by the War Office.

Insofar as there already exist committees (war boards, etc.) similar to those charged with carrying out the duties of the committees specified in Section IX, Clause 2, they can, with the permission of the War Office, act in place of the latter committees.

XI. In all businesses engaged in Patriotic Auxiliary Service which fall under Section VII of the Industrial Ordinance and in which as a rule at least fifty workers are employed, there shall be standing workers committees.

If standing workers committees according to Paragraph 134 h of the Industrial Ordinance, or according to the Mine Laws, do not exist for such businesses, they are to be established. The members of these workers committees shall be chosen by workers of full age employed in the business, or in a branch of the business, from among themselves, by direct and secret voting on the principle of proportionate representation. Details shall be fixed by the central authorities of the states.

In businesses employing more than fifty white-collar workers there shall be formed white-collar workers committees having the same powers as the workers committees and formed in the same manner as the standing workers committees in Clause 1 above.

XII. It is the duty of the workers committees to promote a good understanding among the workers and between the workers and their employers. It must bring to the employer's notice all suggestions, wishes, and complaints of the workers referring to the organization of the business, the wages, and the other matters concerning the workers and their welfare, and must give its opinion on them.

If at least one-fourth of the members of the workers committee desire it, a meeting must be held, and the subject to be discussed must be placed upon the order of the day.

XIII. If in a business of the nature denoted in Section XI disputes arise over wages or other conditions of labor, and no agreement can be arrived at between the employer and the workers committee, then, unless both parties appeal to an Industrial Court or a Miners Court or a Mercantile Court as a court of arbitration, the committee referred to in Section IX, Clause 2, shall be called upon by each party to mediate. In this case Sections 66 and 68–73 of the Industrial Courts Law shall be made use of with the regulation that an award is to be given if one of the two parties does not appeal or does not plead, also that persons concerned in any particular dispute, whether as employer or as member of the workers committee, shall have no voice in making the award.

If in any business engaged in Patriotic Auxiliary Service to which Regulation 7 of the Industrial Ordinance is applicable there is no standing workers committee according to the Industrial Ordinance or the Mining Law, or according to Section XI, Clause 2 or Clause 3, of this law, then in disputes between workers and employers over wages or other labor conditions, the committee of Section IX, Clause 2, shall be called in as mediator. The same applies to agricultural enterprises. The provisions of Clause 1, Sentence 2, are also applicable.

If the employer does not submit to the award, then the workers shall receive, if they desire, the certificate (Section IX) entitling them to leave their employment. If the workers do not submit to the award, then the certificate will not be given to them for the cause on which the award has been made.

XIV. The use of their present legal right to unite and meet shall not be restricted for persons engaged in Patriotic Auxiliary Service.

XV. For industrial concerns of the army and navy administrations, regulations shall be made by the proper superior authorities in the meaning of Sections XI and XIII.

XVI. Industrial workers appointed under this law to agricultural labor are not subject to regulations of the legislation concerning agricultural laborers.

XVII. Information concerning questions of employment and labor, as well as concerning wages and business conditions, when demanded by public notice or by direct questioning of the War Office, must be imparted. The War Office is empowered to inspect the business through its representative.

XVIII. Imprisonment not exceeding one year and a fine not exceeding 10,000 marks, or either of these penalties, or detention, shall be the penalty for (1) anyone refusing employment assigned to him on the basis of Section VII, Clause 3, or without urgent reasons delaying the performance of such work; (2) anyone employing a worker contrary to the regulation in Section IX, Clause 1; (3) anyone not imparting within the appointed time the information provided for in Section XV or willfully making false or incomplete statements in giving his information.

XIX. The Bundesrat issues the necessary instructions for carrying out this law. General regulations need the consent of a committee of fifteen members appointed by the Reichstag out of its own members.

The War Office is bound to keep the committee well informed on all important events, to give it any desired information, to accept its resolutions, and to obtain its opinion before issuing important orders of a general nature.

The committee is empowered to meet during the prorogation of the Reichstag.

The Bundesrat can punish neglect to carry out its instructions with imprisonment not exceeding one year and a fine not exceeding 10,000 marks, or with either of these penalties, or with detention.

XX. The law comes into operation on the day of publication. The Bundesrat will fix the time when it shall be abrogated. If the Bundesrat makes no use of this power within one month after the conclusion of peace with the European Powers, then the law is annulled.

Notes

1 Karl Mannheim, *Man and Society in an Age of Reconstruction*, New York, 1954, pp. 53ff. Substantial rationality is to be distinguished from functional rationality, i.e. '(a) Functional organization with reference to a definite goal; and (b) a consquent calculability when viewed from the standpoint of an observer or a third person seeking to adjust himself to it.' The relations between the War Ministry and the industrialists during the first part of the war are a good example of two functionally rational groups acting in a manner that is functionally irrational from the standpoint of one another. In a manner quite relevant to this study, Mannheim suggests that the development of a functionally rationalized society may lead to a loss of the capacity for substantial rationality and a growing tendency to 'appeal to the leader' to solve the problems thereby created.

2 Hans von Raumer, 'Unternehmer und Gewerkschaften in der Weimarer Zeit', *Deutsche Rundschau*, 80, April 1954, pp.428–9. For Legien's claim that the industrialists' acceptance of the social partnership preceded the revolution, see his speech in the 'Niederschrift der konstituierenden Sitzung des Zentralausschusses der Zentralarbeitsgemeinschaft der industriellen und gewerblichen Arbeitgeber und Arbeitnehmer Deutschlands (12. December 1919)', DZA Merseburg, Rep. 120BB, VII, Fach 1, Nr. 3ᵃ, Bd. I.

3 Speech by Dr Reichert of the VdESI, quoted in Richter, *Gewerkschaften*, p. 203. See *ibid.*, pp. 203ff, for a description of the negotiations.

4 See Wolfgang Sauer's interpretation in his forthcoming *Bündnis Ebert-Groener*.

5 Erich Matthias and Rudolf Morsey, *Die Regierung des Prinzen Max von Baden*, Düsseldorf, 1962, p. 569.

6 See Legien's speech and description in the 'Niederschrift', DZA Merseburg, Rep. 120BB, VII, Fach 1, Nr. 3ᵃ, Bd. I.

7 Unless otherwise indicated, the discussion and quotations below are based upon the protocol of the VdESI Executive meeting of 14 November 1918, BA, R 131/152.

8 G.W.F. Hallgarten, *Hitler, Reichswehr und Industrie*, Frankfurt a.M., 1955, p. 92.

9 On this problem, see Eberhard Kolb, *Die Arbeiterräte in der deutschen Innenpolitik 1918–1919*, Düsseldorf, 1962, and Peter von Oertzen, *Betriebsräte in der Novemberrevolution*, pp. 271ff.

10 'Niederschrift', DZA Merseburg, Rep. 120BB, VII, Fach 1, Nr. 3ᵃ, Bd. I.

11 Bowen, *Corporative State*, pp. 195ff.

12 Matthias and Morsey, *Regierung des Prinzen Max von Baden*, p. 561.

13 Sauer, *Bundnis Ebert-Groener*.

14 Karl Dietrich Bracher, Wolfgang Sauer, and Gerhard Schulz, *Die national-sozialistische Machtergreifung*, Köln and Opladen, 1962, p. 232.

15 This translation relies heavily upon 'The Civilian Service Bill of December 5, 1916', in R.H. Lutz (ed.) *Fall of the German Empire*, 2 vols, Stanford, Calif., Stanford University Press, 1932, II, pp. 99–103. In certain cases, however, terminology and wording have been changed for purposes of consistency with the terminology used in this study. I am grateful to the Stanford University Press for their permission to use this material.

7

Recasting Bourgeois Europe

Charles Maier

From bourgeois to corporatist Europe

In an era of upheaval, it is continuity and stability that need explanation. The premise of this study is that European social hierarchies in the twentieth century have proved strikingly tenacious when men often expected otherwise. Violence is not always a midwife of history: despite world wars and domestic conflict much of Europe's institutional and class structure has showed itself tough and durable; the forces of continuity and conservatism have held their own. Real changes have certainly taken place – growing enrichment, loosening family structures, broader educational opportunities. But these have occurred more as a product of the last quarter century's stability than of prior social turmoil, and they have not dispossessed the privileged groups. The Fiats and Renaults of the workers may now push to the campgrounds of the Riviera, but the Mercedes and Jaguars still convey their masters to Cap d'Antibes or Santa Margherita. Industrialists now, as after World War I can still lament the intrusion of labor unions upon their prerogatives; the respectable press can still denounce public service strikes; Ruhr managers command awe in Germany; the nation-state persists. This is not to claim that the relative social stability of the last quarter century may not finally disintegrate under new pressures. But it is to call attention to the persistence of social hegemonies that a half century ago seemed precarious if not doomed.

This study examines a critical period in the disciplining of change, in the survival and adaptation of political and economic elites, and in the twentieth-century capitalist order they dominated. The years after World War I are especially instructive, because security was apparently wrested from profound disorder and turbulence. If in the turmoil of 1918–19 a new European world seemed to be in birth by the late 1920s much of the pre-war order appeared to have been substantially restored. Both perspectives were skewed: the transformations of 1918 had been in good part superficial, and so was the stability of the 1920s. None the less, despite the limits of the restoration, the decade rewarded conservative efforts with striking success.

The process by which this occurred is the subject of this study. In retrospect, it is easy to note that the forces actively pressing for major social or political changes constituted a minority, and a badly divided one at that. But this response is not very revealing; it discourages investigation of how so great a degree of hierarchical social ordering was preserved when mass parties, 'total war', and economic dislocation made some social leveling inevitable. And if the weakness and divisions of the attackers are well known, the strategies of social and political defense remain unexplored. Political and economic institutions served as the outworks of a fortress – so Tocqueville had described them while waiting for the assault on private property he feared as the revolution of 1848 approached.[1] How in the decade after 1917 were the fortifications challenged? How were they defended? The strategy and the ultimate stakes were not always apparent. Partisans of order and partisans of change, besieged and besiegers, too often served as Tolstoyan commanders, mapping delusory tactics for misconceived battles. Noisy clashes were not always significant ones. The spectacular conflicts of the era were not always the important ones in shaking or re-establishing the structures of power. For every March on Rome, Kapp Putsch, or general strike, there were equally determinative disputes over factory council prerogatives, taxes, coal prices, and iron tariffs. These were quieter but still decisive struggles.

In the wake of World War I, these confrontations formed part of an overarching development. That long and grueling combat imposed parallel social and political strains upon the states of Europe, and for years after dictated a common rhythm of radicalism and reaction. All Western nations experienced new restiveness on the left after the Russian Revolutions of 1917 and continuing radical turmoil from the 1918 Armistice through the spring of 1919. The 'forces of order' had to make their peace either with political overturn, as in Germany, or, at the least, new attacks on capitalism. Yet, by 1920–1 they had recovered the upper hand and pushed the 'forces of movement' on to the defensive. By 1922–3 a new wave of nationalist, sometimes authoritarian, remedies replaced the earlier surge of leftist efforts. Right-wing schemes, however, could not durably settle the economic and social dislocations the war had left. By the mid-1920s each country had to find a new and precarious equilibrium, based less on the revival of traditional ideological prescriptions than upon new interest-group compromises or new forms of coercion. Despite their many differences, France, Germany and Italy all participated in this post-war political cycle.

This common tidal flow of politics virtually calls for comparative examination. In a more general work, post-World War I developments could be set in an even wider context of conservative reaction or liberal crisis. Other countries, Austria and Spain, and from some perspectives Britain and the United States, might also have been included. (*Recasting Bourgeois Europe*] sacrifices a broader range through space and time for intensive examination of three countries during one critical decade.

The three countries, moreover, do form a coherent unit for political and social analysis, despite the fact that Italy ended up under fascism, the German Republic as of the mid-1920s remained vulnerable to authoritarian pressures, while France maintained parliamentary institutions until its military defeat in 1940. Despite major differences, the three nations all had traditions of sharp ideological dispute and fragmentation, concepts of liberalism and labels for class distinction that set them apart from Britain or the United States. France, Italy and Germany certainly do not provide the only matrix for comparison, but they do offer a logical one.

In the last analysis, there can be no *a priori* validity or lack of validity in historical comparison. The researcher can group together any range of phenomena under some common rubric. The issue is whether the exercise suggests relationships that would otherwise remain unilluminated. Some comparative approaches are more fruitful than others. Comparative history remains superficial if it merely plucks out elites in different societies – or working-class organizations, or party systems, or revolutionary disturbances. Flower arranging is not botany. A bouquet of historic parallels provides little knowledge about society unless we dissect and analyze the component parts. What is important to learn is what functions were served by supposedly comparable historical phenomena in establishing and contesting power and values. Organized parties, for instance, were critical in Germany but less so in Italy and France, so to follow parties alone would distort historical perspective. Issues deemed vital at one moment often lose the symbolic importance with which they were originally charged. Nationalization of the French railroads was bitterly contested in 1920, yet it meant little when it was finally accomplished in 1937. Issues and associations, therefore, must be scrutinized not according to their external form, but according to the changing roles they played in revealing the stress lines of European society. For this reason, comparative analysis starts here, from the disputes wherein the basic distributions of power were contested or at least exposed.

The analytical description needed here is complicated because what the contestants themselves described as the stakes of conflict was often misleading. The defenders envisioned their struggle in terms of the clashes they knew from before the war. They entered the interwar years with an inherited imagery of social and political conflict. Borrowing their terminology, this study uses the term *bourgeois* to denote the arrangements which conservatives felt they were defending. In many instances

the imagery of bourgeois defense was inadequate for understanding
the new institutional realities that were emerging. To describe these
new realities we cannot borrow from the terminology of the era, but
must impose our own unifying concept. I have chosen the notion of
corporatism. Each of these terms oversimplifies – distorting, on the
one hand, conservative aspirations, and, on the other, the emerging
institutional reality. Taken together, however, they force us to keep in
mind the tension between aspiration and achievement.

What conservatives naturally aimed at was a stability and status associated with pre-war Europe. 'Bourgeois' was the most general term of
orientation they invoked; they employed it as a shorthand for all they
felt was threatened by war, mass politics and economic difficulty – in
short, as the common denominator of social anxiety and political
defense. For an observer suddenly transplanted from Restoration France
or Germany before 1848, the conservative connotations of 'bourgeois
Europe' might have been startling. In those earlier eras the bourgeoisie
had spearheaded the liberalization of economy and politics against the
prescriptive claims of dynasties and agrarian traditionalists. But during
the course of the nineteenth century, bourgeois spokesmen achieved the
civil rights and, at least partially, the access to power they desired.
Increasingly, in Western Europe they formed long-term associations
with the old elite. Universities, government bureaucracies, boards of
directors and marriage beds could not produce a complete fusion of
classes, but they did offer new chances to combine the assets of land,
capital, public service and education.

Bourgeois reformers, moreover, had always had potential enemies to
the left: democrats, artisans, spokesmen for working-class grievances.
Except in periods of crisis, cooperation with these volatile forces was
short-lived, even during the era of bourgeois reform. From the advent
of mass suffrage in the 1860s and after, the left became even more
threatening, especially as it advocated major changes in property
relationships. Under this pressure, too, members of the old elites
perceived the same dangers as did bourgeois leaders. Tory radicalism,
or the effort to outflank bourgeois elites with working-class alliances,
yielded meager results and was never popular for very long among
conservative constituencies. By the twentieth century most of the old
elites had formed a conservative cartel with bourgeois political representatives. They identified the same enemies and defended the same
prerogatives. As the most preoccupying enemy, social democrats set
the terms of attack for the defenders of the social order as well as
for themselves. More consistently than any other group, the socialists
challenged existing property and power relationships as the foundation
of a bourgeois society that rested upon economic exploitation, sacrificed
democracy to elitism, and created suicidal international conflicts to pre-

serve its internal structure. Under the pressure of growing social-democratic strength, both sides focused upon bourgeois society as the ultimate stake of political and economic conflict.

Yet in what sense was 'bourgeois' a meaningful class category by 1918; or had it already been bled of all sociological precision? In the mid-1920s, Croce, for one, complained of the careless usage that 'bourgeois' was receiving as a historical term.[2] He argued that it had really come to mean little more than modern and secular. Similar reservations could be made of its widespread use by social commentators. But its broad use also suggests that 'bourgeois' really did evoke the basic social divisions of a market economy and industrial social order. Frequent recourse to the term revealed a nagging preoccupation with inequality and class antagonism. Conservatives liked to claim that class conflict as Marxists portrayed it was merely conjured up by agitators and demagogues. And yet they devoted major efforts to shoring up the very institutions that anchored class domination in the eyes of the left: they extolled the nation-state, fretted about nationalization of coal mines or railroads, praised property and entrepreneurship. As men of the 1920s employed the term, 'bourgeois' invoked fundamental questions of social hierarchy and power. It remained the code word for a matrix of relationships defined in opposition to what socialists suggested as alternatives.[3] For the elites of the 1920s, bourgeois Europe was both elegiac and compelling: the image of an *ancien régime* that was still salvageable and whose rescue became the broadest common purpose of post-war politics.

This is not to claim that bourgeois defense was the stake of all political conflict in the 1920s. Disputes between Catholics and anti-clerical liberals remained deep enough to influence party organization in each country and to cut across the issues of social defense. Italian fascists or German right-radicals would also have rejected any claim that they sought to strengthen bourgeois Europe, for they fundamentally despised its parliamentary institutions. Even before the war a 'new' European right had moved beyond the conservatism of agrarian, business and bureaucratic elites to embrace a strident chauvinism, anti-Semitism and antiparliamentarism. This new right comprised distressed farmers, retired officers, intellectuals and university youth, clerical employees and hard-pressed small businessmen and shopkeepers. Yet ironically, this rag-tag right-radical constituency could also contribute to the defense of bourgeois Europe. By the 1920s both the old and new right were attacking Marxist socialism (and communism) as an evil incubated by liberal democracy. The gains of socialism testified to a bourgeois failure of nerve; they made counteraction urgent and sanctioned a violent assault on liberalism itself. Thus, even as the radical right rhetorically lashed out against the parasites of finance or corrupt party politics, it moved with violence against the major organized opposition to bourgeois institutions. Disillusioned liberals, traditionalist conservatives, nationalists, and new right-radicals converged in their hostility to socialism and the democracy that permitted it to thrive.[4]

None the less, [this book] focuses neither on the old nor the new right *per se*, but upon the process of stabilizing institutions under attack. It must, in fact, explore positions that were never considered to be on the right at all, in the militant sense usually given to that word. The right incorporated only one of two possible approaches to protecting the social order. While the right accepted a clear clash of ideologies and aimed at repressing changes, moderate and democratic leaders dreaded Armageddon and hoped to disarm the attackers by reformist initiatives. Both strategies come under study here in so far as both envisaged a social order according to bourgeois criteria. To reconsolidate that social order was the overriding aim of conservative thought and action after 1918. It was the essential effort for the old right, often catalytic for the emergence of the radical new right, and a preoccupation as well for many progressives not on the right at all. To anticipate our conclusions, it was an effort that was largely successful, even if the victory required significant institutional transformation.

For there was no simple restoration. While Europeans sought stability in the image of a pre-war bourgeois society, they were creating new institutional arrangements and distributions of power. What began to evolve was a political economy that I have chosen to call corporatist.[5] This involved the displacement of power from elected representatives or a career bureaucracy to the major organized forces of European society and economy, sometimes bargaining directly among themselves, some-times exerting influence through a weakened parliament, and occa-sionally seeking advantages through new executive authority. In each case corporatism meant the growth of private power and the twilight of sovereignty.

Most conspicuously, this evolution toward corporatism involved a decay of parliamentary influence. Already effaced during World War I, parliaments proved incapable of recovering a decisive position of power. Even in Germany, where the Reichstag had always been subordinate, the Weimar Republic's parliament proved a reflection and not a source of effective power. In part, parliamentary incapacity was a consequence of the harsher political tasks imposed by the 1920s. Not the fruits of growth but the costs of war had to be distributed: parliaments faced dilemmas of economic reallocation and relative deprivation that strained older party alignments and precluded coherent majorities. Ultimately, the weakening of parliaments also meant the undermining of older notions of a common good and a traditionally conceived citizenry of free individuals.[6]

In the liberal polity, decisions demanded periodic ratification by a supposedly atomized electorate. The new corporatism, however, sought consensus less through the occasional approval of a mass public than through continued bargaining among organized interests. Consequently, policy depended less upon the aggregation of individual preferences than upon averting or overcoming the vetoes that interest groups could impose at the center. Consensus became hostage to the cooperation of each major interest. If industry, agriculture, labor, or in some cases the military, resisted government policy, they could make its costs unacceptable.

The leverage that each major interest could exert had further institutional consequences. It tended to dissolve the old line between parliament and the marketplace – between state and society – that continental liberals had claimed to defend. The political veto power of an interest group came to depend upon its strength in the economic arena. Conversely, viability in the marketplace required a voice in determining the political ground rules for economic competition, such as tariffs and taxes or the rights of collective bargaining.[7]

Consequently, too, the locus of policy–making changed. Parliamentary assemblies grew too unwieldy for the continuing brokerage of interests. Bargaining moved outside the chamber to unofficial party or coalition caucuses, and to government ministries that tended to identify with major economic groupings, such as the Weimar Republic's Ministry of Labor.

Even the modalities of exerting influence altered. The liberal polity had always sanctioned discreet compacts between powerful individuals and ministers or parliamentary delegates. Influence was also transmitted less directly but just as pervasively in the clubs, lodges, schools, and regiments that formed the social milieu of the government elites. But in the emerging corporatist system, new social elements had to be consulted, above all labor leaders who had earlier been outside the system. Domestic policy no longer emerged intact from the foyers of the ruling class, no longer represented just the shared premises of the era's 'best and the brightest'. Policy formation required formal confrontation in offices and ministries between old social antagonists. Political stability demanded a more bureaucratic and centralized bargaining. If Marx, in short, dictated the preoccupations of bourgeois society, Weber discerned its emerging structures of power.

It would be wrong to exaggerate the suddenness of this transformation, which began before World War I and is really still underway. Labor and tariff disputes spurred the organization of modern pressure groups in the late nineteenth century. Cartelization further signaled the consolidation of economic power. Observers of the same era noted the growing affiliation of political parties with economic interest groups; and they discussed how party competition was changing from a clubby and whiggish rivalry into a professional mobilization of opinion through electoral machines. These developments quietly altered the nature of representative government.[8]

But they did not create a corporatist polity. Two further significant developments emerged only with the massive economic mobilization of

World War I. The first was the integration of organized labor into a bargaining system supervised by the state. This accreditation of labor also had been underway, but the urgency of war production accelerated the process. Adding labor to the interest groups bargaining around the table suggested that a new division between those producer groups which could organize effectively and the fragmented components of the middle classes might become more politically significant than the older class cleavage between bourgeois and worker.

A second decisive impulse was the wartime erosion of the distinction between private and public sectors. As the state claimed important new powers to control prices, the movement of labor, and the allocation of raw materials, it turned over this new regulatory authority to delegates of business, labor, or agriculture, not merely through informal consultation but also through official supervisory boards and committees. A new commonwealth that dissolved the old distinction between state and economy seemed at hand; and some of its beneficiaries looked forward to extending wartime organization as the basis, in Rathenau's phrase, of a 'new economy'.

Advocates for this parceling out of sovereignty spoke out from different points along the political spectrum. Men of the left, right, and center noted the new tendencies at the turn of the century: the growing web of interest groups and cartels, the obsolescence of the market economy, the interpenetration of government and industry. But they hoped to rationalize and order what they saw taking place as an unplanned evolution before 1914 and as an emergency response during the war. Rather than just a new centralization of interest-group bargaining, they wanted to leave brokerage behind entirely and create a planned and harmonious productive system based upon technological or moral imperatives. On the moderate left, guild socialists, Marxist revisionists, and some democratic liberals envisioned a gradual dissolution of central state authority and the growth of works councils and industrial self-government. Their premise was that if normally antagonistic groups, such as the workers and entrepreneurs of a given industry, could be seated at the same table of hammer out common policy, the result must be impartial enough to guarantee the public interest as a whole. Their concept of decentralization sometimes borrowed from French and Italian syndicalism, but the syndicalists envisaged a more radical elimination of the entrepreneurs.

There were also spokesmen for an older corporatism on the right, represented by writers from La Tour du Pin in the 1870s to Othmar Spann a half-century later. These theorists felt that they could undo the social ravages of an atomistic liberalism by creating an estatist representation. This vision differed in an important respect from the new corporatism that was actually emerging, because it envisioned not merely a *de facto* representation of economic forces, but a society of legal orders. As on the left, the corporatism invoked by conservatives was designed to secure a social harmony that transcended mere pressure-group bargaining. The new corporatism, however, did not eliminate class transactions but merely centralized them.

Finally, a technocratic vision of a new industrial order emerged from the ranks of professional engineers and progressive businessmen. American enthusiasts joined Europeans in blueprinting the future industrial commonwealth. Herbert Hoover's crusade for an orderly community of abundance and Walther Rathenau's more mystical revery of a postcompetitive industrial order both drew on the promises of technology and organization. Both men envisaged moving beyond an often wasteful *laissez-faire* economy, subject to cycles of boom and bust and to overproduction in some sectors and shortages in others. Horizontal association among producers would eliminate wasteful competition. Vertical association between industry and labor would ultimately rest upon technological determination of how to share the rewards of productivity.[9]

Each of these groups rejected the Manchesterite, bourgeois state, but their final visions remained different. Socialist and syndicalist theorists, who eschewed the term 'corporative' because of its reactionary overtones, hoped to move beyond state authority to a less coercive and more egalitarian economy. Corporatists of the right, however, sought to re-create earlier hierarchies. The old ladders of subordination and domination, deference and largesse, reflected an ethical universal ordering that liberalism and the commercial spirit had shattered. Technocratic spokesmen denied class objectives in favor of a new efficiency, enhanced productivity, and a society of abundance.

History was to play tricks on each group; for the new corporatism encouraged restriction of output as much as abundance, and it led neither to radical liberation nor to recovery of an estatist social order. Instead it brought enhanced control for the very elites that had come to prominence under parliamentary auspices. Nor could any far-seeing statesman oversee the transformation: there was no Bismarck for the bourgeoisie as there had been for the Junkers. Rather, corporatist stability arose out of new pressures and false starts: as noted, wartime demands upon industry and labor for massive industrial production with a minimum of conflict; the accompanying wartime inflation, which permitted big business and the unions to reward themselves jointly – or at least to lose less than the other, less organized sectors of the economy; thereafter, the failure of liberal parliamentary leaders to solve post-war economic and social problems by traditional coalition compromises; finally, the terms of American economic intervention and of stabilization in the mid-1920s. It was this sequence of events that helped to consolidate the new relationships between private and public power, the development of which is presented below.

It is not claimed here that the trend was uniform throughout Europe. By the mid-1920s the thrust toward corporatism was clear in Germany, emerging under authoritarian auspices in Italy, but only embryonic in France. Corporatist trends in the Weimar Republic could build upon estatist patterns of authority and economic organization that had survived the nineteenth century in Germany. In Italy the traditional elites were more isolated and less protected by guild-like economic organization or by vigorous local self-government. A corporatist defense could not emerge from the fragmented pattern of business groupings and antiquated bourgeois parties. It had to be imposed by political coercion. In France, corporatist developments were even more retarded. Estatist patterns had been pulverized by prerevolutionary and postrevolutionary regimes, while a gentler pace of industrialization than Germany's lessened the scope and impact of powerful pressure groups. Less buffeted by radicalism, too, the French could preserve a bourgeois society through the parliamentary institutions of the Third Republic. Yet even in France the incapacities of the parliamentary regime pointed the way toward corporatist development.

The notion of corporatism is applied to all three countries, in any case, not as a simple description but rather as an ideal type. As such, it helps us to make sense of French tendencies as well as German ones and to forecast the structure of stability throughout Europe. The decade after World War I was a decisive era in this regrouping of conservative forces. The legacy of war precluded any simple return to the model of the liberal polity; and the role of the United States – a society marked by a new cooperation of government and business in the wake of wartime mobilization – helped advance the transformation in Europe.[10] The Depression, World War II, and subsequent American aid in reconstruction would thrust the evolution of corporatism even further along. After 1945, it would no longer be necessary or even comforting for conservatives to imagine the restoration of a bourgeois society as the endpoint of their efforts. The corporatist structure that was emerging in the 1920s as the instrument of social reconsolidation became a goal in its own right by the end of World War II. To re-establish the given hierarchies in western Europe by the late 1940s, it was sufficient to assure the independence of private industry and interest groups. Conservative goals were less Utopian than they were after 1918, less fraught with nostalgia for a deferential and stable bourgeois order. After 1945 bourgeois Europe neither existed nor ceased to exist: an ideological construct, it faded from concern. Stratification, inequality and corporatist power remained, but few had sought to abolish them.

Bourgeois society, considered in retrospect, amounted to a conservative Utopia.[11] It incorporated a collection of images, ideas and memories about desirable ranking in a tensely divided industrial Europe. As a Utopia it spurred conservative, and ultimately corporatist strategies, once simple restoration proved beyond reach. These corporatist arrangements not only helped re-entrench pre-war elites, but also rewarded labor leadership and injured the less organized middle classes. The history of stabilization after World War I thus involved, not a political freeze or simple reaction, but a decade of capitalist restructuring and renovation. The tension between bourgeois Utopia and corporatist outcome – part of history's constant dialectic between men's intentions and their collective realization – provides the interpretive structure for what was a key era of conservative transformation.

The structure and limits of stability

Stability is a relative term. Even the briefest glance at politics, labor relations, and the international economy reveals that no bright sunlit years separated Dawes plan from Depression. How can one write of meaningful stabilization, some might object, in view of the Nazi takeover and the violence and war that lay ahead? I would disagree. A discernible equilibrium among economic interests, classes and nations finally emerged after many false starts. A combination of coercion, payoffs and exhaustion produced a broad political settlement. The equilibrium was certainly hostage to continuing American prosperity and the control of German national resentments. But the collapse of the structure does not mean that we must abandon study of the plans and foundation. They could serve for less rickety edifices.

It would also be foolish to deny the conservative political achievement of the late 1920s. After mid-decade – with the return of Poincaré, the election of President Hindenburg, Britain's return to gold and easy weathering of the General Strike, the silence of suppression in Italy – the passions of domestic conflict abated. Conferences between nations began to yield agreements and not merely endless wrangling. Locarno, Geneva and The Hague produced only transient results, yet the public read in them a spirit different from the constant disputes before 1924. Statesmen now argued over incremental issues of more or less: would occupied German territory be evacuated sooner or later? How quickly would reparations be scaled down? How much of Europe's debt would Washington write off? Exhaustion and frustration attended such bargaining, but cataclysm was not invoked. A Western economy linchpinned upon American participation was functioning again. Savings were reconstituted, even though the great squandering of 1914 – 18 cost at least a decade of development. For those who wrote or performed, a new republic of letters seemed at hand. Harry Kessler chatted at cafes about Proust and Valéry, flitting among the celebrities of a culture that embraced Berlin and Paris. When in October 1929 he noted the death of Stresemann, he also recalled that Diaghilev and Hofmannsthal had been taken in that same year: 1929 . . . '*wahrhaftig eine année terrible*' [truly a terrible year].[12]

Throughout [*Recasting Bourgeois Europe*] our task has been to understand how the reconstruction of a conservative, 'bourgeois' equilibrium was achieved across the unparalleled violence, costs and passions occasioned by World War I. This has sometimes meant departing from the events that were most conspicuous to stress conflicts that were more prosaic but often more decisive. Elections, for instance, usually made less difference than contemporaries, or historians, thought they did; the Ruhr invasion may have changed little that would not have otherwise occurred; such brief explosions as the Kapp Putsch or the Occupation of the Factories altered even less. It would be grossly inaccurate to say that these events signified nothing, for they signified a great deal in the sense of making manifest underlying tension and conflict. But they altered little, demolished few arrangements that were not already undermined. Their institutional legacy was slight.

This is not to claim that nothing had changed or that life in the late 1920s recreated *la belle époque*. In fact, just restoring the façade of stability required significant institutional changes. It is worth mustering them in summary review.

1. Whether under liberal or authoritarian auspices, group conflict was being resolved by what – with some reluctance – we have termed corporatist approaches. In other words, social priorities were increasingly decided not by traditional elites nor by the aggregation of voters' preferences. Elections resolved less than the day-to-day bargaining between industry and labor or among different business, agricultural, and party interests. If these groups failed to negotiate coherently or did not set clear priorities – the French situation in the mid-1920s – policy was becalmed in a Sargasso of ineffective parliamentarism.

The key to consensus or mere civic peace was either forcible suppression or constant brokerage. Any major organized interest could disrupt a modern economy or imperil social order, and hence had to be silenced by duress or granted a minimum of demands. The need for brokerage switched the fulcrum of decision making from the legislature as such to ministries or new bureaucracies. During the war, ministries of munitions had developed into economic planning agencies. Under men of ambition and energy such as Rathenau, Loucheur, and Lloyd George, they extensively regulated the labor market and the allocation of scarce raw materials. They coopted private business in this task, sharing public powers to increase the scope of regulation.[13] Although wartime controls were not retained, the 1920s did not simply revert to the degree of market freedom prevailing before 1914. The Weimar Interparty Committee and Ministry of Labor, the Fascist Grand Council and Ministry of Corporations, in a lesser way the French Coal Agency and Ministry of Commerce (and if Herbert Hoover had had his way, the US Department of Commerce) took on new political tasks. Parliamentary decision making never recovered fully from the eclipse into which it had fallen during the war. By 1925 governments collected and spent perhaps 20 to 25 per cent of national income, in contrast to about half that share before the war. Parliaments did not work well in deciding how to levy this new burden. They worked even less well in trying to adjust the internal burdens of currency depreciation and revaluation. Traditional parties had taken form around earlier issues, and they proved too divided internally for this invidious allocation.

2. From 1918 until about 1924 the chief *political* objective for most bourgeois forces, parties or interest groups, amounted to exclusion of the socialists from any decisive influence on the state. Bourgeois resistance outran opposition to specific social democratic programs, which were generally moderate and reformist. Rather, the working-class parties represented a threat to what was seen as good order just by their new prominence and potential power. Later in the 1920s coalitions with social democrats did become acceptable, but only when social democracy acquiesced in the economic conceptions of its bourgeois partners. If the socialist left seriously presented its own economic objectives on the national level, alarmed conservatives fought back. They resorted either to decentralized but simultaneous boycotts of government bonds and money (as in France), or to concerted political opposition to taxation within the terms of coalition politics (as in Germany), or to extralegal coercion (as in Italy). In the face of such opposition, social democratic forces could not maintain positions of leadership or even parity at the national level. As Engels had foreseen shortly before his death in the 1890s, the socialists had wagered on legality while their opponents were prepared to indulge in violence. Turati recalled the prediction when his party majority foreswore reformism.[14] What more touching tribute to the nineteenth-century liberal belief in the *Rectsstaat* [state based on legal rights] than that European social democrats should have been its most tenacious defenders!

3. A defining characteristic of the corporatist system that we have sought to analyze was the blurring of the distinction between political and economic power. Clout in the marketplace – especially the potential to paralyze an industrial economy – made for political influence. Consequently, economic bargaining became too crucial to be left to the private market, and state agencies stepped in as active mediators. Not surprisingly, labor questions became some of the most crucial tests of political stability. The economic issues were grave in their own right, but they also represented political disputes. The trade-union movements, more precisely the non-Catholic federations, represented the arm of social democracy in the marketplace and were combated as such. If the union federations contributed to the political influence of social democracy, however, they also increased its liabilities during a period of economic recession and unemployment. Working-class forces that were defeated in the marketplace were usually administered blows in the political arena as well.

a. The first major setback after the war was the limitation of factory representation, such as was embodied in works councils. The council movement had promised a restructuring of capitalism from the work-place outward. Even after its messianic transformation failed to materialize in 1918–19, factory representation still beckoned the working class. Factory representation was elective; it was responsive to immediate grievances; it offered a foothold on issues of management. But the 1920s brought one defeat after another for plant representation. In France the movement hardly got started; in Germany the councils were legally restricted in scope; in Italy they were conceded by Giolitti as a diversionary measure and were eliminated by Fascist union leaders – who could not capture their majorities – in concert with industrialists. Fascist union leaders in Italy and later in Germany did not abandon the idea of entrenching their own agents in the factory. But Mussolini (and later Hitler) had no more reason to sanction powerful plant delegates than had earlier leaders.

The last major phase of the Italian controversy developed during the spring of 1929 as Fascist union leaders, who had been set back by the 'unblocking' of their confederation the previous fall, initiated a new campaign to install factory trustees. Only the trustees, claimed the labor leaders, could prevent industrial managers from abusing the legislation that protected workers. Their campaign culminated in a syndicalist congress at Milan's Lyric Theatre at the end of June and early July, after which Mussolini intervened to restore discipline. In a series of extensive 'Intersyndical' conferences from July 6 to 12, the union leaders accused the industrialists of hostility to fascism and evading collective contracts. Mussolini recognized the validity of the charges, but refused to install the factory trustees. Instead he talked about the need for rationalization and technical improvements. Over a summer of debate the union leaders were forced to retreat, abandoning the claims to plant representation and becoming more receptive to schemes for rationalization that they had earlier characterized as exploitative. By its September meeting the Intersyndical Committee unanimously rejected the principle of factory delegates.[15]

b. The upshot was characteristic of the capitalist economies in general and not just the fascist system. If the 1920s began with the left pressing for democratization of the factory, it ended with the right calling for rationalization, Americanism, Fordism, the Bedeaux plan, or equivalent nostrums. All these systems claimed that labor could be utilized as another form of capital, subject to efficient analysis and organization. The trade conditions of the late 1920s, which impelled export competition and cost cutting, made these schemes attractive. But the right also seized upon scientific management as a political weapon. Invocations of 'the organization of labor' really became appeals to factory autocracy in the name of industrial efficiency. Europeans of the left and right gave excess credit to scientific management as the motor of American prosperity and social harmony, because it fitted their respective ideological premises. The left decried a more subtle means of exploitation; businessmen on the right celebrated its efficiency. European industrialists in particular sought a system of labor control that did not entail just an outdated reassertion of factory paternalism. They could not resurrect the *Herr im Hause* [resident owner] but the impartial engineer and technician of management could provide the same authority.[16]

c. While the right defeated worker delegation in the factory, it had to accept certain transformations as irreversible. Entrepreneurs in fascist Italy and Weimar Germany had to come to terms with some continuing trade-union organization and accept collective bargaining. No matter how hollow the forms of labor representation might become under fascism, businessmen could not simply eliminate them entirely. Of the three countries considered here, France alone lagged in the obligation to recognize collective bargaining, as did the United States outside Europe. Both nations, though, would enforce union contracts by the mid-1930s. The Matignon agreements and the Wagner Act imposed requirements on French and American enterpreneurs similar to those of the Stinnes–Legien and Palazzo Vidoni agreements. The reader will rightly object that only the external forms were alike, but that the thrust of democratic and fascist regulation was antithetical. Still, the form was important, for it signified that fascist as well as democratic regimes had to negotiate collective settlements and group bargains. Fascist labor delegates might be spurious representatives for Turin's metalworkers or the *braccianti* [landless farm labourers] of Emilia, but they still retained some influence as a bureaucratic interest group in a political system that claimed to subsume and resolve all social conflict.

Nonfascist societies had to purchase the cooperation of the working class as well as compel it. The left won peripheral rewards in the rearrangement of power in the 1920s. Social democrats retained important political control at the municipal and state level. They won important extensions of social insurance from conservative governments in Britain, France and Germany. These countries also accepted foreign policies aimed at softening the outcome of 1918: a goal that the left had sought since the Armistice. The achievement was largely symbolic – the spirit of Geneva – but important none the less.

4. In the long run the major possibility for social consensus derived from a slow transformation of the principles of class division. Class consciousness was undergoing a double evolution. In the world of work, identification as proletarian or bourgeois was becoming less compelling than interest-group affiliation, less a principle of common action in the economic arena. Yet the world of production was only one reference point for social stratification and political loyalties, and one of diminishing importance throughout the twentieth century. While European socialism appealed to man as worker from its origins, the European right sought to make social roles outside the sphere of production the major determinants of political allegiance. In so far as party competition followed divisions in industry and commerce, the right could not outbid the traditional left. On the other hand, the right could

appeal to man in so far as he was concerned as consumer or as saver about the value of money, as a newspaper reader about the prestige of his nation-state, or even as a commuter about his rights to uninterrupted tram service. Work experiences did not become more unified; a few still commanded, many still followed orders. But mass transit, the cinema, radio, vacations, less formal dress made work-place identity less encompassing and facilitated new collective consciousness.

It was ironic that fascism should encourage this development. For fascism boasted that it had superseded the empty liberal abstractions of citizenship to regroup men as producers. Syndicalism and corporatism supposedly followed from the priority of *homo faber* [man as worker]. In fact, fascism and the right in general increasingly appealed to men outside the work-place. Fascist culture, political rallies, collective gymnastics, and Blackshirts were calculated to build a new unity. Whereas the left celebrated man's liberation and rationality in the world of work, the right appealed to audience-man. As the concept of the 'proletariat' had once replaced 'mob' or 'rabble', so now, for social theorists, 'masses' replaced proletariat. By the latter 1920s, former socialists who had become discouraged at the attrition of their support discovered the same appeal to 'instinctual' rather than rational loyalties in a neosocialism that verged toward fascism.[17]

In retrospect, the left's stress on plant representation and works councils can be interpreted as a last effort to reinstall a producer's consciousness among the old working class. It was rebuffed, and the centrality of work experience as a political rallying point failed with it. It was fitting that observers pointed to Mussolini's *dopolavoro* [afterwork, i.e. leisure programme] and Hitler's *Kraft durch Freude* [strength through joy, an organized leisure programme] as characteristic contributions of fascist labor policy. Both were regimentations of leisure. Bureaucratically, the *dopolavoro* served as one more organization to pit against the fascist labor unions. But it also amounted to a major attempt to alter class perceptions and experiences.

By the end of World War II democratic parties, too, would sense the recasting of class identification and appeal to men in their roles outside the work-place. But committed to work as the defining human experience, social democrats resisted coming to terms with the new principles of group identification in the 1920s, while the right exploited the change. The factory hierarchy defended by Antonio Benni or Albert Vögler could remain intact if outside the plant gates new common experiences eroded old class identities. Bourgeois society was preserved by creating new stakes in continuity, providing access to a community of consumption or sentiment if not of production. The left denigrated these common experiences as spurious, but for better or worse they proved integrating and persuasive.

Two major sorts of tension arose to imperil and then undermine the equilibrium of the 1920s. The very corporatism that facilitated political stability simultaneously imposed fundamental dilemmas. One was the difficulty of reconciling the conflicting priorities of the international economy and domestic needs. The other involved the fate of those who were battered by the very corporate restructuring around them.

1. While the issues of inflation and revaluation encouraged corporatist organization, they also imposed limits to the degree of stability that might ultimately be achieved. Equilibrium remained hostage to the discrepancy between the demands of an international economy and the pressures for compromise between groups at home.

a. The politics of revaluation was an international phenomenon. Each country's debates took place in an overarching context of deflationary pressure that accompanied establishment of the gold-exchange standard. Only in Britain and in Italy did the forces desiring high revaluation triumph: in Italy because a fascist policy of prestige, self-sufficiency, and political hegemony over industry dictated elevating the lira; in Britain because the country had accepted sufficient taxation and deflation to make restoration of the gold standard appear feasible at $4.86 per pound as the City advocated. In both countries the price of high stabilization was unemployment and recession.[18] And while Germany was no longer saddled with major internal debt, Berlin had to meet Dawes annuities. Although foreign loans more than covered this burden, they also made independent monetary policy difficult, and Reichsbank President Schacht sought to recover control and insulate Germany from the vicissitudes of capital flows by restrictive credit measures. The quest for autonomy thus led to deflationary policies in Germany as well.[19]

The overriding thrust toward monetary stabilization came in part from across the Atlantic. The economic trends of the second half of the 1920s reflected American conditions for alleviating the balance-of-payments difficulties that impeded capitalist stability. Since Woodrow Wilson's intervention of 1917, the United States had sought to secure a liberal democratic and capitalist comity of nations. Former Wilsonians, New York bankers, and members of the Republican administrations of the 1920s now defined an international dimension to American and European economic health. As they saw it, the interests of both continents converged in the need for stability, the absence of political rancor, and a favorable climate for entrepreneurial initiative. It was apparent that the United States had become the guarantor of such a political economy.[20]

Before 1914, growing international trade had depended upon shared rules of exchange summarized by the international gold standard. Minor jiggling of internal prices and employment levels permitted international equilibrium. Domestic adjustments were facilitated because investment abroad returned income flows that eliminated any need for radical austerity measures to balance international accounts. Mismanagement and failure occurred, but not really in any pursuit of a positive balance of payments. The war, however, forced massive liquidation of European assets abroad, made the United States Europe's creditor, and dislocated trade flows within Europe and between Europe and her markets elsewhere. By 1922 – to take the date when American financiers and leaders sought to step in again – it was clear that some restoration of pre-war trade and capital flows was needed, to rebuild not merely currency balances but the old equilibrium of social classes. The alternative was envisioned as economic chaos: the immiseration of the middle classes, the bolshevization of labor, a threat not merely of revolution but of gratuitous waste and suffering.

In theory there were several options for America's role in restoring financial and with it social equilibrium: cancellation of war debts, increased purchases abroad, investment in Europe. Politics at home militated against the simple cancellation of debts. Southern Democrats and Western Republicans, including old Progressives, resented the Versailles settlement, suspected 'Eastern' bankers, and feared that their depressed farm constituents would face higher taxation. State and Treasury Department leaders remained cautious after the Senate's rejection of Versailles and the establishment of the Congressionally dominated World War Foreign Debt Commission. Americans who had interests in international trade and remained sensitive to European business needs did work to minimize the Old World's debts through interest reductions and extension of payment. The write-off amounted to perhaps 43 per cent of the total burden, but it still left an unsettling obligation in existence. Massive imports were also precluded, in part because of the protectionist policy pursued through the 1920s, but also because Europe manufactured or grew little that Americans could not provide more cheaply for themselves. This left investment abroad – especially in Germany, where capital scarcity and high productivity promised special rewards. The only prerequisite to this capital flood was regulation of the reparations issue, which Americans helped to supervise from 1924 on.[21]

In the range of alternatives for the Atlantic economy, the American relationship with England was critical. London had been the world financial center and remained a major force for international stabilization. This relationship included elements of cooperation and rivalry. The central bankers in New York and London, Benjamin Strong and Montagu Norman, shared a deep commitment to restoration of the gold standard or gold-exchange standard in which pound and dollar would together serve as reserve currencies. Some conflicts of interest existed: London could gain from interallied debt forgiveness, the United States could not. Strong also feared that Norman's proposals of 1922 might commit the United States to inflationary policies and easy money in order to ease Britain's and other countries' revaluation. Americans resisted again when Norman's financing of Schacht's Gold Discount Bank threatened to cut the dollar out of Eastern and Central Europe. But US representatives on the Committee of Experts won a compromise with the German promise of an early return to a gold currency and full convertibility. American and British aspirations came back into alignment, especially because of London's need for continued support from

New York upon the return to gold in 1925. Hewing to the high rate of $4.86 required the Federal Reserve Bank's continuing cooperation in preventing the draining of gold across the Atlantic. For about three years the priorities of the two monetary systems coincided, and this masked the true extent of British weakness and dependence. Strong and Norman overlooked until 1927 that the gold-exchange standard made greater demands on domestic economic policies than its pre-war counterpart. It required more austerity in Britain and militated for a low-interest policy in New York, which contributed to superheated stock speculation. In short, the effort of convertibility really required a joint Anglo-American monetary policy when the two countries had different domestic requirements. Yet until the end of the 1920s, both partners felt that the banking leadership, commercial advantages, and the general facility of international exchange justified the adverse effects at home. Prosperity masked the inner stresses of the system, and indeed appeared to follow from it.[22]

No monetary system, however, can be free of the social-class relationships within which it is designed. Naturally enough, this one enhanced the influence and prestige of the central bankers and the representatives of the great private houses such as J.P. Morgan or Lazard Frères. As Strong repeatedly lectured, it depended upon bankers keeping their independence from national treasuries that might be tempted into inflation or exchange controls. Central bank sovereignty indicated that a country was a safe haven for stabilization loans and long-term foreign investment. But the gold-exchange standard had broader social repercussions as well. It remained America's price for remitting capital back to Europe. While it endured it required Europeans to maintain a permanent deflationary pressure at home. Such vigilance entailed clear social and political consequences: a downward pressure on employment, hence a restraint upon working-class bargaining power; an impulse to cartelization, 'rationalization', and the subjection of small producers to large ones throughout Europe. American concepts of a stable international financial order – 'the old fashioned religion which our firm has been sending to successive governments for the last three years', to use Thomas Lamont's phrase[23] – thus tended to reinforce a corporatist and bourgeois social settlement.

b. Yet if the international economic system exerted deflationary pressure, the requirements of *domestic* equilibrium would work the other way in the long run. Within each country the growing corporatist organization of interests made a recourse to long-term creeping inflation ever more likely. The avoidance of conflict demanded that no significant pressure group felt so aggrieved in the 'allocation of burdens' that it might try to disrupt the economic or political system. So long as real national income kept approximate pace with the aggregate claims of different interests, the allocation of costs and benefits presented relatively little difficulty. But as had been demonstrated during World

War I inflation was available as a tempting if spurious way to purchase social peace. The easiest way for harried ministries or divided coalitions to arbitrate struggles between powerful interests was to pay off each one's claims in paper values without resistance. The real worth of the income shares would then work itself out subsequently. So long as aggregate income claims increased faster than real growth, the corporatist bargaining system entailed creeping inflation.[24]

Happily, the later 1920s enjoyed enough real expansion to offset inflationary pressures. The pressure that currency stabilization also exerted on domestic economies also counteracted the new institutional causes of inflation. The underlying bargaining mechanisms that made for inflation between 1914 and 1924 did not disappear, however. They were revealed no longer by the ravages of currency depreciation but by the limits that labor and industry jointly set upon appreciation or evaluation. Even while international performance demanded rigorous scrutiny of domestic price levels, long-term inflation lurked as a natural peril of corporatist bargaining in times of prosperity.

True, if any of the social partners accepted restraint, or if substantial unemployment weakened labor's bargaining power, the premises were altered. When the Depression struck, European governments tried ever more desperately to follow the deflationary priorities of the international system, then had to abandon this catastrophic competition to rescue employment and stability at home. After World War II the corporatist impulse to inflation reappeared as an affliction of prosperity. Yet the tensions that exist today between corporatist inflation and the priorities of international competition were first signaled as acute in the 1920s. Business rhetoric in that interval of expansion testified to the new antagonisms and anxieties that have remained inherent in corporatist prosperity.

2. The inflationary decade from 1914 to 1924 had brought together strong unions and big business in a price-wage spiral at the expense of the middle strata of society. Unfortunately, the deflationary *Konjunktur* [economic trend] thereafter did not reassure the middle strata. Income streams might be reconstituted, but the 80 per cent write-off in currency values on the Continent was confirmed and not recovered. The movement toward the concentration of enterprises and the growth of large firms also struck at middle-class independence. The number of independent proprietors declined. Even if income for these beleaguered middle-class groups remained steady, their sense of independence and patrimony must have been eroded.

Ultimately, the unorganized losers – whether old middle-class artisans, shopkeepers, small producers, marginal farmers burdened with debts, or the new middle class of clerical workers and office employees – felt the need for defense. Losers both in inflation and revaluation, their reaction was to attack the corporatist collaboration of labor and industry. Unable to organize in a cohesive economic phalanx, for they faced diverse markets, they could still organize politically. The results would combine hostility to liberalism and organized labor with a vague rhetorical anticapitalism. Weimar Germany could not survive this new strain; France could – among other reasons, because the less developed corporatist organization of her society evoked a less intense right-radical response. The Radical Socialist constituency avoided fascism in the 1930s for the same reason that it had endured economic confusion in the 1920s: the continuing viability of economically archaic modes of livelihood. French democracy was to remain buffered by the society's proverbial reluctance to organize.[25]

If National Socialism is viewed in the perspective of Weimar's corporatism, it becomes evident how different it remained from Italian fascism. The difference takes us to the heart of the developments underway in the 1920s. At the beginning of the decade Italian fascism emerged as a new, coercive way of re-establishing a scaffolding for elites once the old one had corroded with mass suffrage and the war. It involved a coalition between traditional leadership groups and new middle-class allies as well as a young, urban bourgeois cadre mobilized since Intervention. Nazism grouped some of the same elements, but the mix was different, as were the reasons for its success. Before the seizure of power the role of traditional elites may well have been smaller in Nazism, the middle-class objectives more predominant. In the absence of more than a few local studies, estimates of social composition must remain risky. But statements about function are possible. In Italy fascism remedied a defective organization of middle-class and elite elements. If Italy had earlier developed a liberal corporatism to replace her antique parliamentary and party structure, fascism might well have appeared unnecessary for bourgeois defense. On the other hand, if Germany had not passed through the crucible of capitalist corporatism, Nazism might have seemed unnecessary for middle-class viability. Italian fascism substituted for prior organization in the political arena or marketplace; German Nazism arose in resentment against the organization that seemed to dominate.[26]

Nazism thus testified to the success of restoration in the 1920s. The elites of industry and land succeeded too well in the Weimar Republic: by engineering their restoration within a corporatist framework, they provoked a grass-roots rebellion against the capitalist marketplace – against all its liberal rules of the game as well as its economic outcomes. While Italian fascism testified to the preindustrial formation of the Italian elite, Nazism reflected what was simultaneously most retrograde and most modern: retrograde, because in Germany the guild usages of the pre-Napoleonic era – the stress on municipal independence, estatist divisions, elaborate self-enclosed associations – were carried forward to clutter up the twentieth-century sociopolitical landscape; modern, because corporate capitalism and corporatist pluralism have increasingly prevailed as forms of social organization since the 1920s in all western societies. Nazism tried to build off preindustrial corporatism and annul the more recent. It ended by destroying the first and leaving the second largely unscathed.

At the end, the history of the 1920s besets us with its contradictions: Nazism as the revolt against the corporatist state; French democracy tenable because of its relative backwardness in terms of corporatist organization; the utility of international deflation to consolidate a social order that would tend ultimately to purchase stability by continuous doses of inflation.

These paradoxes testify to the discrepancy between change and its perception. The history of the 1920s is marked by the inadequacy of its contemporary ideologies to analyze true social transformation. The categories implicit in political activity – the explanatory approximations embedded in left vs. right, bourgeois vs. socialist – overlapped with the realities of conflict but obscured some of the true stakes. The slogans of the 1920s – the electoral efforts to form bourgeois blocks or 'unions' against a factious left, to unite the tenacious holders of small property with socialists against 'reaction' – encouraged conceptions of a polarized society that were increasingly irrelevant. Only when basic ideological outcomes became the central stake of struggle again in the 1930s did the model of polarization temporarily reconverge with the real struggle underway. Meanwhile, party labels and contests revealed little of social tensions and transformation.

Each side offered its own distortions. Conservatives were successful in restoring to the 1920s the appearance of happier days, but they insisted on a concept of bourgeois society as their supposed goal. Their model was archaic: it implied that conservatives wanted a sharp separation of state and society, public and private sectors, and furthermore that stability was to be rescued from a militant proletariat. These images of society were not adequate to comprehend reality as the 1920s continued the restless push toward corporate organization that World War I had generated. Organization was sensed to be the prerequisite of group survival, the basis for holding on to a secure percentage of national income or a stable share of votes, power, and prestige. Devolution of authority on interest groups had advanced between 1914 and 1918 and now continued in the 1920s. Either by dialectical tricks or cudgeling opponents into submission, supporters tried to claim that this development was actually enhancing public authority. Undoubtedly feudalism had also been presented as a prop to kingship. Bourgeois victory was briefly secured, but only by resorting to the corporatist settlements that undermined the basic anchoring conceptions of the bourgeoisie. Rescuing bourgeois Europe meant recasting bourgeois Europe: dealing with unions (or creating pseudounions as in Italy), giving state agencies control over the market, building interest-group spokesmen into the structure of the state.

An analogous structure of stability arose and endured after World War II, based on agreement between chastened social democrats and moderates either to share or to alternate power and to exclude more extreme alternatives of right and left; upon a western internationalism hinged on coal and steel exchanges and exclusion of Russia; upon US resolution of a balance-of-payments crisis and similar demands for convertibility; upon the interpenetration of state and economy within each national unit. The system after World War II thus retained the old liabilities – the prolongation of Cold War rigidity, confinement of much of the working class to a political ghetto, and an end to criticism of the authority relations in an industrial economy in return for increased welfare. To what degree alternatives were practical cannot be discussed here.

Presumably the system bought sufficient acquiescence to continue through the 1960s. Institutions no longer trembled under the blows of the old challengers or the issues of income distribution that vexed the 1920s. Instead, decolonization agonies or old ethnic antagonisms proved debilitating at times; while the very success of corporatist equilibrium brought its own brief rebellion at the end of the 1960s against the bureaucratic, rationalist terms of stability. Finally, the pressures toward corporatist inflation immanent within the system seem to have emerged as a basic affliction – aggravated today by a rise in primary product prices that the 1920s never faced. This does not mean that internal contradictions must overwhelm the stability attained. Some of the tensions today are reminiscent of those of the late 1920s, but the popular base of prosperity is broader; the reorientation of men as consumers and audience has proceeded further. But neither are all crises to be surmounted without deep change. Distributions of power and privilege can alter swiftly; at the very least they evolve inexorably. In the wake of the catastrophes that followed, historians perceived the 1920s as the often congenial, yet darkening twilight of the liberal era. But if a twilight decade, the 1920s was one of morning as well as dusk, slowly bringing into focus the transformations that carried capitalist societies through a half-century transit. The upheavals that have intervened, or those still to come, should not obscure that conservative achievement.

Notes

1 *The Recollections of Alexis de Tocqueville*, trans. Alexander Teixera de Mattos, J.P. Mayer (ed), Cleveland and New York, 1959, p. 10.
2 Benedetto Croce, 'Di un equivoco concetto storico: la "Borghesia"', *Atti della Academia di Scienze Morali e Politiche della Società Reale di Napoli*, LI, 1927; reprinted in *Etica e politica*, Bari, 1967, p. 275. Although valid as a cross-national designation, the term 'bourgeois' still suggested different qualities from country to country: 'civic' in Germany, a ruling elite in Italy, and refined, perhaps smug upper-middle-class leisure in France.
3 For the generation of class division: cf. Stanislaw Ossowski, *Class Structure*

in the Social Consciousness, trans. Sheila Patterson, London, 1963, pp. 72–3, 133; Ralf Dahrendorf, *Class and Class Conflict in Industrial Society*, Stanford, Calif., 1959, pp. 162–79, 201–5; useful surveys of the literature are in T.B. Bottomore, *Elites in Society*, Baltimore, Md, 1966, and *Classes in Modern Society*, New York, 1968. Cf. also the essays in André Béteille (ed.) *Social Inequality*, Baltimore, Md, 1969.

4 For an introduction to concepts of the right: Hans Rogger and Eugen Weber (eds), *The European Right*, Berkeley and Los Angeles, 1965; René Rémond, *The Right Wing in France from 1815 to de Gaulle*, trans. James M. Laux, Philadelphia, 1966; Ernst Nolte, *Three Faces of Fascism*, trans. Leila Vennewitz, New York, 1966, pp. 29ff, 429ff; Armin Mohler, *Die konservative Revolution in Deutschland, 1918–1932*, Stuttgart, 1950; Karl Mannheim, 'Das konservative Denken. Soziologische Beiträge zum Werden des politisch-historischen Denkens in Deutschland', *Archiv für Sozialwissenschaft und Sozialpolitik*, 57, 1 and 2 1927, 68–142, 470–95.

5 Like an emergency paper currency, the concept of a 'corporatist' Europe is assigned a given value for internal use within the argumentation of this book. I make no claim that the term has a universal value. In fact, it is chosen hesitantly since it generally suggests 'estatist' or a society of legally defined 'orders'. Political scientists might prefer 'pluralist', but this notion usually suggests a free competition among social forces. And while I have resorted to the term 'corporative pluralism' elsewhere it is inappropriate to deal with fascist Italy as pluralist. The Germans have tried 'organized capitalism', but I wish to emphasize the political more than economic transition; hence 'corporatist' as a provisional description of social bargaining under fascism and democratic conditions alike. On the general theme see my own and others' essays in Heinrich August Winkler (ed.) *Organisierter Kapitalismus, Voraussetzungen und Anfänge*, Göttingen, 1974. For discussions of analogous developments within the United States, cf. Grant Mc-Connell, *Private Power and American Democracy*, New York, 1966; Theodore J. Lowi, *The End of Liberalism: Ideology, Policy, and the Crisis of Public Authority*, New York, 1969. Samuel Beer, *British Politics in the Collectivist Age*, New York, 1967, also introduces comparable concepts.

6 On this problem: Brian M. Barry, *Political Argument*, London, 1965, pp. 187–291; 'The Public Interest', *Proceedings of the Aristotelian Society*, suppl. vol. 38, 1964, pp. 1–18. Cf. Jürgen Habermas, *Strukturwandel der Öffentlichkeit*, Neuwied, 1965, for the loss of the idea of the public in liberal society.

7 Cf. Rudolf Hilferding's analysis of 'organized capitalism' as it developed between 1915 and 1927, esp. 'Probleme der Zeit', *Die Gesellschaft*, 1, 1924, 1–13; 'Die Aufgaben der Sozialdemokratie in der Republik', Sozialdemokratischer Parteitag 1927 in Kiel, *Protokoll*, Berlin, 1927, pp. 166–170; also Wilfried Gottschalch, *Strukturveränderungen der Gesellschaft und politisches Handeln in der Lehre von Rudolf Hilferding*, Berlin, 1962, pp. 190–3, 207; and Heinrich August Winkler, 'Einleitende Bermerkungen zu Hilferdings Theorie des Organisierten Kapilatismus', Winkler (ed.) *Organisierter Kapitalismus*, pp. 9–18.

8 Michael Ostrogorsky, *La Démocratie et l'organisation des partis politiques*, 2 vols, Paris, 1903; Max Weber, 'Politics as a Vocation', and 'Class, Status, Party', in Hans Gerth and C. Wright Mills (eds)., *From Max Weber*, New York, 1958, pp. 99–112, 194–5; Robert Michels, *Political Parties, A Social Study of the*

Oligarchical Tendencies of Modern Democracy, trans. Eden and Cedar Paul, New York, 1915; Vilfredo Pareto, *Les Systèmes socialistes* [1902]; Geneva, 1965. On interest-group development: Hans-Jürgen Puhle, 'Parlament, Parteien und Interessenverbände 1890–1914', in Michael Stürmer (ed.) *Das kaiserliche Deutschland*, Düsseldorf, 1970, pp. 340–77; Thomas Nipperdey, 'Interessenverbände und Parteien in Deutschland vor dem Ersten Weltkrieg', now in Hans-Ulrich Wehler (ed.) *Moderne deutsche Sozialgeschichte*, Cologne-Berlin, 1970, pp. 369–78; Heinrich A. Winkler, *Pluralismus oder Protektionismus. Verfassungspolitische Probleme des Verbandswesens im deutschen Kaiserreich*, Wiesbaden, 1972; Etienne Villey, *L'organisation professionnelle des employeurs dans l'industrie française*, Paris, 1923; Mario Abrate, *La lotta sindacale nella industrializzazione in Italia* 1906–1926, Turin, 1967, pp. 31–61.

9 For corporatism on the right: Ralph Bowen, *German Theories of the Corporative State: With Special Reference to the Period 1870–1919*, New York, 1947; Matthew Elbow, *French Corporative Theory, 1789–1948*, New York, 1953; Herman Lebovics, *Social Conservatism and the Middle Classes in Germany, 1914–1933*, Princeton, NJ, 1969, pp. 109–38; on the left, cf. M. Beer, *A History of British Socialism* [1919] 2 vols, London, 1953, II, pp. 363–72; G.D.H. Cole, *Self-Government in Industry*, London, 1917.

10 For diverse perspectives on trends in the United States: Gabriel Kolko, *Railroads and Regulation, 1877–1916*, Princeton, NJ, 1965 and *The Triumph of Conservatism: A Reinterpretation of American History, 1900–1916*, New York, 1963; Robert Wiebe, *Businessmen and Reform, A Study of the Progressive Movement*, Cambridge, Mass., 1962; Wiebe, *The Search for Order, 1877–1920*, New York, 1967; Paul A.C. Koistinen, 'The "Industrial-Military Complex" in Historical Perspective: World War I', *Business History Review*, XLI, 4, 1967, 378–403; Ellis W. Hawley, *The New Deal and the Problem of Monopoly*, Princeton, NJ, 1966, 8–13, 36–42; and Hawley's essay in *Herbert Hoover and the Crisis of American Capitalism*, Cambridge, Mass., 1973.

11 Cf. Karl Mannheim, *Ideology and Utopia*, London, 1960, pp. 206–11.

12 Harry Graf Kessler, *Aus den Tagebüchern 1918–1937*, Munich, 1965, p. 288.

13 See Paul A.C. Koistinen, 'The "Industrial Military Complex" in Historical Perspective: World War I', *Business History*, 41, 1967, 378–403; E.M.H. Lloyd, *Experiments in State Control at the War Office and the Ministry of Food*, London, 1924, pp. 18–26, 259ff; W. Oualid and Charles Picquenard, *Salaries et tarifes, conventions collectives et grèves: La politique du Ministère de l'Armament et du Ministère du travail*, Paris, 1928; Gerd Hardach, 'Französische Rüstungspolitik 1914–1918', in Heinrich August Winkler (ed.) *Organisierter Kapitalismus. Voraussetzungen und Anfänge*, Göttingen, 1974, pp. 101–16; Alberto Caracciolo, 'La crescita e la trasformazione della grande industria durante la prima guerra mondiale', in Giorgio Fuà (ed.) *Lo sviluppo economico in Italia*, Milan, 1969, pp. 197–212; Luigi Einaudi, *La condotta economica e gli effetti sociali della guerra italiana*, Bari, 1933, pp. 99–178.

14 Friedrich Engels, 'Introduction' [1985], to Karl Marx, *The Class Struggles in France, 1846 to 1850*, Karl Marx and Friedrich Engels, *Selected Works*, 2 vols, Moscow, 1958, I, p. 136; Turati's quote to the Socialist Congress of Bologna in October 1919, cited in Angelo Tasca, *Nascita e avvento del fascismo*, 2 vols, Bari, 1965, I. p. 274, n. 81.

15 Sessions of the Comitato Centrale Intersindacale in ACS, Rome: Carte Cianetti, B. 4; controversy followed in Piero Melograni, *Gli industriali e*

Mussolini. Rapporti tra Confindustria e fascismo dal 1919 al 1929, Milan, 1972, pp. 276–311.

16 For the European industrialists' exploitation of scientific management, see Charles Maier, 'Between Taylorism and Technocracy: European Ideologies and the Vision of Industrial Productivity in the 1920s', *Journal of Contemporary History*, v, 2, 1970, 54–59, including further citations; also André Philip, *Le problème ouvrier aux états unis*, Paris, 1927, pp. 39–87, for a social democratic evaluation; cf. Dzherman M. Gvishiani, *Organization and Management: A Sociological Analysis of Western Theories*, Moscow, 1972, pp. 174ff, for the latest specimen of a Russian interest beginning with Lenin. On the roots of Nazi labor policy in Weimar's entrepreneurial attitudes, see T.W. Mason, 'Zur Entstehung des Gesetzes zur Ordnung der nationalen Arbeit, vom 20. Januar 1934', Bochum Symposium paper, June 1973.

17 For a major statement, Hendrik De Man, *Zur Psychologie des Sozialismus*, Jena, 1926, pp. 137–57. Cf. Robert Michels, 'Der Aufstieg des Faschismus in Italien', *Archiv für Sozialwissenschaft und Sozialpolitik*, 52, 1, 1924, p. 71: 'For the psychologists of the masses the history of fascism offers a field of observation of huge dimensions'. Michels' major essay, 'Psychologie der antikapitalistischen Massenbewegungen', *Grundriss der Sozialökonomik*, IX/I, Tübingen, 1926, 241–359, amplifies the theme, mostly with reference to socialist movements, however, and provides a major bibliography. Recent approaches to the problem in Edward R. Tannenbaum, *The Fascist Experience: Italian Society and Culture*, New York, 1972; Gino Germani, 'Fascism and Class', in Stuart J. Woolf (ed.) *The Nature of Fascism*, New York, 1969, pp. 65–96; Renzo De Felice, *Le interpretazioni del fascismo*, Bari, 1972, pp. 113–44, who summarizes the work of Fromm, Adorno, *et al.*

18 For monetary stabilization, see Stephen V.O. Clarke, *Central Bank Coopera- tion, 1924–1931*, New York, 1967, pp. 45–107; Hjalmar Schacht, *The Stabilization of the Mark*, London, 1927; Karl Elster, *Von der Mark zur Reichsmark*, Jena, 1928, pp. 215ff; W.A. Brown, jr., *England and the New Gold Standard 1919–1926*, New Haven, Conn., 1929, pp. 181–233; D.E. Mog- gridge, *The Return to Gold, 1925: The Formulation of Economic Policy and Its Critics*, Cambridge, 1969.

19 R. Stücken, *Deutsche Geld- und Kreditpolitik 1914–1963*, Tübingen, 1953, pp. 69–76; Rolf E. Lüke, *Von der Stabilisierung zur Krise*, Zurich, 1958, pp. 232–9; Gerd Hardach, 'Die beiden Reichsbanken: Internationales Währungssystem und nationale Währungspolitik 1924–1931', Bochum Symposium paper, June 1973.

20 Joan Hoff Wilson, *American Business and Foreign Policy 1920–1933*, Boston, Mass., 1973; Carl P. Parrini, *Heir to Empire: United States Economic Diplomacy, 1916–1923*, Pittsburgh, 1969; N. Gordon Levin, jr., *Woodrow Wilson and World Politics: America's Response to War and Revolution*, New York, 1968.

21 Wilson, *American Business and Foreign Policy*, pp. 124–36; Benjamin D. Rhodes, 'Reassessing "Uncle Shylock": The United States and the French War Debt, 1917–1929', *Journal of American History*, LV, 4, 1969, 787–803; Ellen W. Schrecker, 'The French Debt to the United States, 1917–1929', Diss., Cambridge, Mass., 1973; Melvyn Leffler, 'The origins of Republican debt policy, 1921–1923', *Journal of American History*, LIX, 4, 1972, 585–601; Harold G. Moulton and Leo Pasvolsky, *War Debts and World Prosperity*, Washington, DC, 1932, pp. 396–415. For an emphasis on structural

European difficulties in producing for the American market, see M.E. Falkus, 'United States Economic Policy and the "Dollar Gap" of the 1920's', *Economic History Review*, 2nd series, XXIV, 4, 1971, 599–623.

22 Clarke, *Central Bank Cooperation*, pp. 34–40, 124ff.; Milton Friedman and Anna J. Schwartz, *A Monetary History of the United States, 1867–1960*, Princeton, NJ, 1971, pp. 283–92; Lester V. Chandler, *Benjamin Strong, Central Banker* Washington, DC, 1958, pp. 316–31, 438–59; D. Williams, 'London and the 1931 Financial Crisis', *Economic History Review*, 2nd series, XV, 3, 1962–3, 513–28; W.A. Brown, jr., *The International Gold Standard Reinterpreted, 1914–1934*, 2 vols, New York, 1940, II, 799–806. For the 1924 German issue, see Werner Link, *Die amerikanische Stabilisierungspolitik in Deutschland 1921–32*, Düsseldorf, 1970, pp. 223–40. For the 1924 controversy over Reichsmark convertibility see the extensive letter from Princeton economist and Dawes plan expert, Edward Kemmerer to Charles Evans Hughes, 24 June 1924 in US Department of State Decimal Series 426.00R296/386. From Kemmerer's viewpoint the USA had championed an impartial and efficient gold exchange standard, while the British sought to work Germany into a sterling trade area.

23 Lamont to Russell C. Leffingwell, 28 April 1925, Baker Library, TWL, 103–11.

24 The concept of cost-push inflation is relevant but tends to emphasize labor aspirations one-sidedly. See Fritz Machlup, 'Another view of cost-push and demand-pull inflation', *Review of Economics and Statistics*, vol. 42, 1960; P. Streeten, 'Wages, prices, and productivity', *Kyklos*, XV, 1962; F.W. Paish, 'The limits of incomes policies', in Paish and J. Hennessy, *Policy for Incomes*, 1968, all reprinted in R.J. Ball and Peter Doyle (eds), *Inflation*, Harmondsworth, England and Baltimore, Md, 1969, pp. 149 85, 219–54.

25 Heinrich August Winkler, *Mittelstand, Demokratie und Nationalsozialismus*, Cologne, 1972, and Winkler, 'Extremismus der Mitte? Sozialgeschichtliche Aspekte der nationalsozialistischen Machtergreifung', *Vierteljahreshefte für Zeitgeschichte*, XX, 2, 1972, 175–91, for the best recent syntheses of the huge literature on Nazism and middle-class resentment. For a prediction that the French middle classes in the 1930s must provide a reservoir for fascism, see Leon Trotsky's *Whither France?* [1936], New York, 1968, pp. 12–24.

26 Cf. De Felice, *Le interpretazioni del fascismo*, pp. 256–66, for an emphasis on German–Italian parallels in mobilizing the resentments of the *ceti medi*. For a résumé of what studies exist on social composition of the Italian Fascist Party (which became more 'respectable' and upper-echelon between 1925 and 1928), see Renzo De Felice, *Mussolini il fascista*, vol. II, *L'organizzazione dello stato fascista, 1925–1929*, Turin, 1968, pp. 188–92; and Adrian Lyttelton, *The Seizure of Power: Fascism in Italy 1919–1929*, London, 1973, pp. 54–71, 303–5; the most recent study on Germany is Jeremy Noakes, *The Nazi Party in Lower Saxony 1921–1933*, London, 1971. Cf. William S. Allen, *The Nazi Seizure of Power: The Experience of a Small German Town*, Chicago, 1965, and the review of earlier literature in Seymour Martin Lipset, *Political Man*, New York, 1963, pp. 127–51. Cf. Charles S. Maier, 'Strukturen kapitalistischer Stabilität in den zwanziger Jahren: Errungenschaften und Defekte', in Winkler (ed.) *Organisierter Kapitalismus*, pp. 206–8.

8

Conquest, Foreign and Domestic, in Fascist Italy and Nazi Germany

MacGregor Knox

> between Germany and Italy there exists a community of destiny. . . .
> [Germany and Italy] are congruent cases.
>
> (Benito Mussolini, 1936)
>
> The brown shirt might perhaps not have arisen without the black shirt.
>
> (Adolf Hitler, 1942)

Fascism, Generic and Historic

Mussolini and Hitler have not been alone in emphasizing the common origins, features and destinies of Fascism and National Socialism. Theories of 'fascism' – that elusive generic phenomenon with a small f – have proliferated with abandon ever since the 1920s.[1] Definitions have ranged from the Third International's 'open terroristic dictatorship of the most reactionary, chauvinistic, and imperialistic elements of finance capital' through Ernst Nolte's militant anti-Marxism, to the modernization theorists' 'mass-mobilizing developmental dictatorships under single-party auspices'. Voices of caution have occasionally sounded, urging the 'deflation' of a concept that 'exists in faith and is pursued by reason', or suggesting that fascism fails to encompass adequately the ultimate evil of National Socialist Germany.[2]

But the notion is still with us, even if no two theories of fascism coincide. [. . .] After sixty years of debate, the scene resembles a desert battlefield littered with the burnt-out, rusting hulks of failed theories. What alternatives exist? One largely unexplored possibility, which combines both breadth and reasonable closeness to the evidence, is comparative history. [. . .] Inevitably, the obvious candidates for comparative treatment are the two principal 'historic fascist' regimes of Italy and Germany. Both arose in relatively advanced societies – northern Italy was different from Bavaria, but no more backward economically. Both were in part responses to affronts to the self-esteem of nations that were relative latecomers to unification and industrialization, and that suffered from deep social, regional, and, in Germany, religious cleavages. Finally, both were the creation of leaders who combined conspicuous talents as agitators, political tacticians, and ideological visionaries.

This last quality inevitably implies a collision between vision and reality. Comparison of those visions and of their respective collisions with reality may offer new insight into the nature of both movements and regimes, and into possible distinctions between them and other varieties of political evil. But any attempt to analyze Fascist and National Socialist ideologies and final goals raises several questions. Did the movements have ideologies worthy of the name? If they did, whose pronouncements are authoritative sources, and which of those pronouncements are irrelevant, which are tactical, and which are fundamental? Attempts to answer the first question have frequently fallen into two pitfalls: 'mirror-imaging' and radical skepticism. Victims of the first pitfall have unreflectively applied conventional categories of liberal and Marxist social thought to phenomena that liberalism and Marxism are ill-equipped to explain. They have attempted to understand Fascist and National Socialist ideologies as social ideologies expressing the attitudes of particular classes, and addressing the problems those classes faced in adapting to industrial society.

Unfortunately for this approach, Fascist and National Socialist ideologies were not expressions of particular classes and groups, but – like Marxism – above all the creation of individuals: Mussolini and Hitler. Despite Rosenbergs and Gentiles, Feders and Himmlers and Bottais, the two dictators were the sole unimpeachable creators and interpreters of the doctrines of their movements. The dictators were the doctrine, the word made flesh, and understanding the success of their ideologies requires both appreciation of the role of charismatic leadership in hammering doctrine home, and analysis of the context in which they flourished. No pat social interpretation ('the revolt of the petite bourgeoisie') can help explain extreme nationalist political religions, the first principle of which was the denial of class, and which appealed to all classes, although in varying degrees.

Nor has the widespread assumption that an ideology must be social encouraged fruitful enquiry. Commentators have seized on whatever scraps of doctrine fit their assumptions about what an ideology must contain, especially Mussolini's 'Doctrine of Fascism' essay, written in collaboration with Giovanni Gentile. But that pompous exercise had less to do with Fascist ideology than with Mussolini's intermittent tactical attempts to achieve intellectual respectability. And even the Mussolini-

Gentile essay proclaimed that the true test of manhood and nationhood was war – a curiously antisocial social ideology.[3] As for Fascist corporativism, which the regime itself touted as the answer to the social needs of the age, it remained a sickly plant in which Mussolini himself took little interest. In the German case, nothing even resembling a conventional answer to the social problems of industrial society ever emerged. Only recently have scholars begun to take Hitler's 'status revolution' seriously, although without relating it adequately to his wider ambitions.

Discarding the assumption that an ideology must be a variety of conventional social thought makes it possible to examine Fascist and Nazi ideology and goals in their own terms. But any such attempt inevitably comes up against the second pitfall: the temptation to dismiss everything as propaganda. In the Italian case, radical skepticism has been especially fashionable. [. . .] In the German case, scholars have tended to take Hitler's ideological efforts more seriously. The man did, after all, write a book. But some historians have gamely continued to deny that Hitler had ideas, or to argue that whatever ideas he had were irrelevant to his political course.[4]

The case of the radical skeptics would be stronger if Hitler and Mussolini had displayed the sort of erratic behavior consonant with the absence of ideology and the nihilistic pursuit of power. But in both cases the dictators expressed at the beginning of their careers coherent ideologies that were not necessarily entirely popular or plausible, and continued to profess those ideas both publicly and privately throughout. The steady radicalization of their policies suggests an attempt to bring practice into line with theory, and implies that their increasingly rare moderation was tactical, and their extremism genuine. In the end, both provoked catastrophe by persisting, against steadily increasing risks, in their attempts to bend the world to fit the idea. If that was opportunism and nihilism, it was clearly a strangely elaborate and consistent variety.

From mission to program

The Italian case is admittedly the more ambiguous of the two. Mussolini's pilgrimage from socialism to Fascism, and his apparently sincere although private criticisms of Hitler as a doctrinaire, imply an unwillingness to take principles seriously.[5] [. . .] Both as socialist and Fascist, [Mussolini] had a world view that rested on one underlying assumption, and two political myths. The fixity of these ideas suggests that they were not simply Nietzschean conceits or expressions of a nihilist will to power, but ideas in which he actually believed. What Mussolini did not do was to assemble his ideas into an all-embracing intellectual system or a monocausal, teleological philosophy of history. He may have been a visionary, but unlike Hitler he was not a doctrinaire.

The later Duce's underlying assumption [...] was that life was struggle. History was an endless succession of conflicts between elites, states and tribes. In each epoch a particular elite or state set the tone. By definition, dominant elites or states were the fittest, a conception Mussolini took not as rationalization for resignation, but as a call to battle.[6]

Mussolini's two myths, revolution and the nation, determined the nature of that battle. The first was inevitably that of revolution.[7] This was the myth of Mussolini's childhood and youth in the red Romagna, a myth that a career as a socialist journalist-agitator, and reading Marx and Sorel, reinforced. Not that Mussolini was the most orthodox of Marxists. The Marx he preferred was Marx the revolutionary; for Marx the philosopher of history, the economic theorist, the historian, the German patriot or the heir of the Enlightenment, Mussolini had little use. These latter Marxes he identified with the unadventurous stodginess of the reformist socialists. What Mussolini instead proclaimed was Sorel's 'barbarous notion of socialism', a revolution by an elite of primitives to inaugurate a 'new civilization' of joyous paganism.[8] This was precisely what Mussolini later attempted as a Fascist. Even the terminology, the goal of a new civilization, remained the same, as did most of Mussolini's enemies: the reformist socialists, the bourgeois establishment, the monarchy, the military hierarchy, and the Church.

Mussolini's second fixed idea was that of the nation and the national mission, an idea also acquired in his socialist youth. Revolutionary expectations and adaptation to prevailing socialist dogma prompted occasional antinational outbursts, such as his famous 1910 exhortation to plant the Italian flag in a dunghill, or his neutralist September 1914 party manifesto. But behind protestations that the proletariat had no fatherland lurked the convictions of a radical nationalist. The Socialist Mussolini displayed an unsocialist reverence for Mazzini, as well as public approval of Giuseppe Prezzolini and his circle of quasi-nationalist litterateurs. [...] Finally, from 1909 if not earlier, Mussolini was an 'assiduous and devoted reader' of the eccentric nationalist philosopher-historian Alfredo Oriani. Oriani was a bloodthirsty recluse ('blood will always be the best warm rain for great ideas') who insisted that only war could make post-Risorgimento Italy whole, and demanded that the nation take up Rome's historic mission in Africa and the Mediterranean. This last enthusiasm did not possess Mussolini until the war years, but he could scarcely have called himself *un orianista*, as he did in 1909, without sharing much of Oriani's world view.[9]

It was the shock of European war in 1914 that removed the theoretical opposition between the myths of revolution and the nation. Mussolini greeted the collapse of the Socialist International with something approaching relief. When his attempt to lead the Socialists into support of a 'revolutionary war' failed, his last speech to his comrades before they expelled him from the party in November 1914 was pure Oriani:

> If Italy remains absent, it will be once more the land of the dead, the land of cowards. I tell you that the duty of socialism is to shake this Italy of priests, pro-Austrians, and monarchists.... Despite all your howls of protest, the war will flatten the lot of you [vi travolgerà tutti].

In the following months, the myths of revolution and of the nation fused. War, and war alone could undermine the old Italy of priests, kings, and fainthearted Socialists, assuage the national inferiority complex, and make the nation whole. 'A nation old with fifty centuries of history and young with fifty years of national life' could not behave like 'a nation of rabbits'. War must destroy 'the ignoble legend that Italians do not fight, it must wipe out the shame of Lissa and Custoza, it must show the world that Italy can fight a war, a great war; I say again: *a great war'*. No longer would foreigners see Italy as a land 'of travelling storytellers, of peddlers of statuettes, of Calabrian *banditi'*. And war could also be a kind of revolution. The day Italian bayonets crossed the Ringstrasse in Vienna, 'the Vatican's death knell [would] sound'.[10]

Under the sign of perpetual struggle, internal and foreign policy, revolution and war merged. The barbaric new man of Mussolini the socialist became the 'impatient and generous youth', the 'young rebels' of *interventismo*.[11] And despite stalemate and Caporetto, the war, as Mussolini put it in early 1918, had proved that this 'small, despised people', this 'army of mandolin players', could fight. Combat, and the fact that Italy had willed it by deliberately entering the war, in turn confirmed the nation's historic mission and claim to 'higher destinies'. And it was the myth of Rome that shaped Mussolini's conception of those destinies. In December 1918, while proclaiming Italy's right to expansion, he insisted that Rome would 'once again become the beacon of civilization for the world'.[12] Italy might of course choose to become an 'archaeological bordello or an Anglo-Saxon colony'. But the example of Rome, which had 'laid out roads and drawn boundaries and given the world the eternal laws of its legal codes' placed modern Italians under 'another universal duty'.[13] No one, in Theodor Mommsen's words, could 'remain at Rome without a universal idea'. Rome must again become 'the leading city of the civilization of all of Western Europe', and Italy 'the leading nation of world history'.[14]

The political content of this 'new civilization' was clear from very early in Mussolini's career as a Fascist. The world, Mussolini announced in 1921 and 1922, was moving towards the right; as for Fascism, it was 'scarcely at the beginnings of its mission'.[15] By mid-1925, Mussolini had taken to characterizing Fascism as 'one of the few creative ideas of this tormented historical period'. In early 1926 he described Italy, the last of the great powers to achieve maturity, as the first to construct a truly modern state. Like the French Revolution, the Fascist revolution would have world-wide influence and epochal significance. By late 1926, the

Duce had become self-assured enough to claim that his movement was the bearer of a 'new type of civilization'. The twentieth century would not merely be the 'century of Italian power', it would also be the century of universal Fascism.[16]

If Mussolini's fundamental ideas were not entirely unsystematic, Hitler's 'rock-hard convictions' amounted to a genuine philosophy of history, an all-embracing, all-explanatory system of belief. Its first principle, from which Hitler never wavered after his first recorded enunciation of it in 1919, was pseudo-biological racism, the 'anti-Semitism of reason'.[17] Race, he claimed in January 1921, was 'the driving force of world history'; later, in *Mein Kampf*, he described it as 'the key not only to world history, but to all human culture'. History was the history of race struggle. National Socialism was ultimately a science.[18]

[. . .] Hitler's ideas were at least as systematic as those of the Marx who asserted that history was the history of class struggle. Both Marxism and Hitler's ideology were millenarian religions of world salvation: salvation for man as a species reborn from the proletariat in one case, salvation for the reborn Aryan species of man in the other.[19] Both required the pitiless elimination of groups: the class enemy for Marxism, the racial enemy for Nazism. [. . .]

But despite its fixity and coherence, even Hitler's system did not spring suddenly from the aspirant Führer's brow, although scholars have sometimes overestimated the length of time Hitler took to weld his ideas together.[20] Much later, Hitler conceded to his entourage that 'in the early days of the movement I found myself compelled to act from intuition'. Only during his post-Putsch imprisonment in 1924, he maintained, did he have the time to 'confirm his ideas by the study of natural history [den Gedanken naturgeschichtlich zu begründen].'[21] Hitler's early speeches suggest it required roughly three years, from the fall of 1919 to the winter of 1922, for the 'anti-Semitism of reason' to harden into a genuine world-system, complete with a visionary program for action, of which more later.

Hitler's starting-point was the 'recognition' (English cannot do justice to the force of the German *Erkenntnis*) that the 'race-tuberculosis of nations', the Jews, were responsible for the 1918 revolution and thus for Germany's defeat in the Great War. By the late spring of 1920 [. . .] Hitler began to enunciate an all-embracing interpretation of world history. He now recognized the Jews from Moses to Lenin, or 'from Joseph to Rathenau', as the essence of triumphant evil from the Bronze Age to the Weimar Republic. Jewish 'robber nomads', the 'most national race of all the ages', lived by parasitically corrupting other peoples while seeking world mastery for themselves. Only Germany stood in the way: 'Jewry . . . knew well that its domination could only be broken by a national force as strong as itself, and that would be the German *Volk*.' Hitler's solution, as early as April 1920, was simple and drastic: he proclaimed 'the inexorable resolve to strike the evil at its root and exterminate it root and branch'.[22] That this was at least potentially a project on a world scale was clear from the insistence with which Hitler spoke of the Jews' own 'world power plans' and 'eternal Jewish goal – world domination'. His remarks about German aims widened correspondingly, from the conventional nationalist (and Party program) demand for the unification of all Germans in one state 'from Memel to Pressburg, from Königsberg to Strassburg', to the more grandiose if vaguer project of creating a 'germanic empire of the German nation'.[23]

By March 1921 he had gone far beyond merely pointing out that Germany was the main obstacle to alleged Jewish plans. His aim was no longer defense, but offense: it was Germany's mission to 'heal' a sick world.[24] In the spring of 1922, Hitler began to make this claim a major element in his speeches. Only two alternatives existed: 'either victory of the Aryan side or its annihilation and victory of the Jews'. Germanic blood was gradually becoming exhausted, and the future of the world was grim unless Germany 'made itself free'. The nation's 'greatest deed' lay ahead of it: 'to be leader [Führer] in the coming battle of the Aryans against the Jewish world peril'. Germany, he insisted in the next months, must be 'the foundation of an Aryan world order'. This was Germany's 'historic mission'.[25]

Implicitly, Hitler's 'Aryan world order' would mean an end to history in the conventional sense. In *Mein Kampf* he made this implication explicit:

> And so the folkish philosophy of life corresponds to the innermost will of Nature, since it restores that free play of forces which must lead to a continuous mutual higher breeding, until at last the best of humanity, having achieved possession of this earth, will have a free path for activity in domains which will lie partly above it and partly outside it.

Even the iron law of struggle might fall into abeyance: the pacifistic-humane idea is perfectly all right perhaps when the highest type of man has previously conquered and subjected the world'.[26] Mankind would achieve biological apotheosis. Hitler had fused pseudo-Darwinist anti-Semitism and German nationalism into a religion of world redemption. All that remained was to work out the practical details.

On a fundamental level, the beliefs of Hitler and Mussolini were thus different in kind. Mussolini's assumption that struggle was the father of all things, and his revolutionary and national myths, were scarcely cut from the same cloth as Hitler's political religion. Mussolini did not propose to rescue the world for good – but merely to establish the new Rome's dominant place in it. Nevertheless, the political and geopolitical programs the two leaders drew from their ideologies were rather more similar than the beliefs themselves.

By 1925–6, Mussolini's program was set in all essential details.

Internally, he proposed to create a fanatical following for the national myth, while creating a new sort of Italian and consolidating his own unchallenged power as dictator. If Italy were to fulfil its destiny, Mussolini repeatedly insisted as early as 1919 and 1920, the national will had to be 'directed towards a common objective'. The war had undoubtedly accelerated the 'process of consolidation of the national consciousness', but given Italy's fragile traditions and short existence, *italianità* remained a 'privilege limited to a relatively small minority'.[27] Only a new elite could enforce the unity and discipline necessary for external self-assertion. Here the war itself was a help. It had divided the fittest nations, including Italy, from the unfit, and had divided the Italians themselves into those who 'had been there', and those who had not. The former, the 'lords of the trenches [*trincerocrazia*]', would rule. But this vision soon proved a disappointment; the returning veterans were relatively democratic in their convictions, and disinclined to destroy the liberal system.[28] As for the early Fascists, Mussolini ruefully concluded in 1919 that 'their utter lack of respect for authority [*strafottanza*] and dynamism make it hard for them to form a bloc even with themselves', By mid-1922, Mussolini had apparently concluded that the creation of national unity and of a new elite would take time; it would require 'future Fascist universities and' . . . Fascist schools' to rear the new imperial Italy. But Fascism would yet accomplish the task at which the Risorgimento had failed, the task of 'making Italians'.[29]

The full urgency of this task did not apparently dawn on Mussolini until the summer 1924 crisis following the murder of the Socialist deputy Giacomo Matteotti. The spontaneous revulsion of much of Italian opinion showed that whatever conversion to Fascism had so far taken place had been superficial. After he struck down the opposition in January 1925, Mussolini proclaimed his goal with a new openness. Fascism's 'totalitarian will' was 'to fascistize the nation, so that to-morrow Italian and Fascist, more or less like Italian and Catholic, will be the same thing'. That would give Fascism the right to call itself a revolution [. . .]

[. . .]

By the fall of 1925 Mussolini announced himself satisfied that dictatorship had overcome the old 'image of the Italian people, repeated abroad, . . . of a small nation, disorderly, noisy, and fidgety'. But what Mussolini described as 'the weaknesses of the Italian character: . . . shallowness, fecklessness, the belief that everything will go well', yet remained. These 'traditional defects' must give way to 'tenacity, perseverance, and methodical work'. The regime would create a 'new Italian', a 'Fascist Italian', out of the generations that had fought the war, and above all from the new legions under training in the Party youth organizations.[30] The regime must sweep away 'the sediments deposited in those awful centuries of political, military, and moral decadence that r[an] from 1600 to the rise of Napoleon', and complete the Risorgimento, which was 'only the beginning, the work of a tiny minority'. The final goal, as Mussolini put it in 1934, was an Italian who knew (like Caligula) that being loved was second best: 'the most important thing [was] to be feared'. It was time to smash the old clichés Italians still labored under: 'No more mandolin players; [instead,] grenade throwers; no more exquisite manners; [instead,] the fist'. It was the eve of Italy's unprovoked attack on Ethiopia.[31]

The fist was also in store for the old elites and institutions at home. [...] He made no secret of his conviction that parliamentary democracy was a miserable nineteenth-century relic; this belief was yet another link between Mussolini the socialist and Mussolini the Fascist.[32] He openly proclaimed that he and his Party would entrench themselves 'and defend themselves against all comers'. And in the spring of 1924 he described the new Chamber of Deputies, despite its Fascist majority, as 'the last parliamentary experiment Italy [would] make'.[33]

Nor was he afraid to pronounce the word *dictatorship* with approval as early as November 1921. [...] The new regime was to be no mere personal dictatorship, but the inauguration of a new age in government.[34] Implicitly, the Duce's 'ferocious totalitarian will'[35] required the taming and ultimate removal of monarchy and papacy, as the political struggles of the 1930s were to show.

The method Mussolini chose was entirely consonant with the tradition of Oriani and of other post-Risorgimento yearners for a Great War to make Italy whole. Mussolini had already called in 1914–15 for war as a kind of revolution. All revolutions, he remarked in 1920, apropos of events in Russia, were 'fated to be imperialist'. War and revolution, he insisted in the same 1925 speech in which he celebrated the creation of the new generations in the laboratory, were 'almost always linked. Either war produces revolution or revolution leads to war'.[36] His regime, although he was careful not to alarm his conservative allies with the thought, sought to fuse the two.

In foreign policy, Mussolini's 1914 discovery of the nation and its mission led him naturally to celebration of its imperial destinies in terms familiar to readers of Oriani and of the nationalist leader Enrico Corradini. But Mussolini was more systematic than either in his synthesis of demographic expansionism and rudimentary geopolitics. His starting-point was inevitably the war, which even before its end had made Italy an 'imperial' nation, fully entitled to the Adriatic victory Slavs and Allies sought to deny. Italy also had the right to expansion in the Mediterranean, 'the sea of Rome'; the Italian people was 'prolific and hard-working'. Imperialism, Mussolini insisted unseasonably on the first day of January 1919, in the midst of his countrymen's Wilsonian enthusiasms, was 'an eternal and immutable law of life'.[37] At the March 1919 inaugural meeting of the *Fasci di Combattimento*, Mussolini proclaimed with statistics in hand that Italy's narrow, mountainous land and rapidly multiplying 40 millions entitled it to a greater share of the earth. Should the Allies of 1915–18 cheat Italy at the peace table, Mussolini threatened in the following weeks, Italy should join the Germans. From its position athwart Britain's Mediterranean communications it should shatter the British Empire in Africa and Asia.[38]

Mussolini took up with a vengeance Corradini's myth of the international class war. Italy should challenge the 'quintessentially plutocratic and bourgeois' alliance of French, British and Americans. The French, at least, were demographically exhausted. Italy would follow the Spain of Charles V and the France of Louis XIV and Napoleon as the 'dominant nation of the entire Latin world', thanks to its demographic dynamism and the 'virtues of our race [stirpe]'.[39] Versailles was transitory. Demographic equilibria were shifting. The 'immense wave' of Slavdom would wipe away the small states of central Europe, while the 70 or 80 million Germans would move west into France to rectify that decadent nation's regrettable 'imbalance between territory and population'. As for Italy, it was after Russia and Germany the 'most compact and homogeneous national bloc' in Europe. By 1950 it would have 60 million inhabitants, of which 15 or 20 million would be around the shores of the Mediterranean and across the Atlantic. Italy, 'to be free', must throw off its economic dependence on the Anglo-Saxons by achieving self-sufficiency in grain and energy. It could then 'become the dominating nation of the Mediterranean basin and discharge on the African shores of that sea the majority of its population and energies'. The areas Italy was destined to conquer were 'extraordinarily thinly settled' – an insight that would have come as a surprise to their inhabitants. But some 'overflowings of human masses [*straripamenti di masse umane*]' were 'inevitable and necessary', the 'fertilizing reversals of history'.[40]

Demography continued to furnish a major argument for expansion. But by the mid-1920s Mussolini had turned the argument in a direction unthought of by Corradini and other prophets of the imperialism of the prolific poor. Once in power, Mussolini discovered that pride in the 'riotous development' of Italy's population was misplaced.[41] Some areas of Italy, he recognized as early as mid-1923, were prey to 'demographic decadence', like the despised French. By 1927, after precise statistics had become available, Mussolini had become alarmed. In his marathon Ascension Day speech of May 1927, he surveyed the demographic decline of France and Britain, and insisted that the same decline – in other words, the usual demographic pattern of industrial societies – was a threat to Italy's future as well. Only fools claimed Italians were too numerous. 'Demographic potency' was the fundamental ingredient of national power: 40 million Italians were too few compared to the 40 million French, the 46 million British, the 90 million Germans, the 200 million Slavs, and the 540 million inhabitants of the British and French colonial empires. Italy, 'if it [were] to count for something', must 'approach the threshold of the second half of [the] century with a population no smaller than 60 million inhabitants'. The alternative was renunciation of Italy's mission: 'If we diminish in numbers, gentlemen, we will not found an empire, we will [instead] become a colony'. The tenacious resistance to 'the pernicious currents of contemporary civilization' by Basilicata, one of Italy's most miserably poor and populous regions, was thus an act of foreign policy.[42]

Mussolini's ensuing campaign to 'ruralize Italy, even if it takes billions, and half a century', was no more than a small part of a grand design that stretched far beyond the confines of the Italian state of the 1920s. It was an attempt to create the demographic conditions for Italy's Mediterranean primacy. The 'battle for grain' of 1925 and later years, which many historians have interpreted as a propaganda stunt or as largesse to the landed interests, was a conscious attempt to provide the economic prerequisites of Italy's 'freedom':

> In an Italy entirely reclaimed [bonificata], cultivated, irrigated, and disciplined, in other words a Fascist Italy, there is space for another ten million men. Sixty million Italians will make the weight of their numbers and their power felt in the history of the world.[43]

The geographic and strategic requirements of Italian freedom, and of empire, were as much on Mussolini's mind as the economic and demographic ones. The Great War had resolved the problem of Italy's land frontiers; the future now lay on the waters. Only Italy was a truly Mediterranean nation. French and Spaniards had Atlantic ports. Mediterranean preponderance (*predominio*) was therefore Italy's 'by right of its geographic configuration and the maritime traditions of its race [*stirpe*]'. The inland sea must become an Italian lake, 'expelling those who are ... parasites'. Asserting Italy's rights would require breaking 'the chains of hostility that surround[ed] Italy in the Mediterranean', and might also require 'the demolition of the British Empire'. The British guarded the principal exits from the Mediterranean at Gibraltar and Suez, and thus had a stranglehold over Italy's supplies of food and raw materials.[44] By 1926–7, Mussolini had apparently elevated this insight into a general law of geopolitics:

> A nation that has no free access to the sea cannot be considered a free nation; a nation that has no free access to the oceans cannot be considered a great power. Italy must become a great power.

The 'prisoner of the sea that was Rome's' must break that imprisonment in order to fulfil its historic mission.[45]

Hitler's vision had many similarities with Mussolini's, but was different in three fundamental ways. First, Hitler's unified, monocausal world view allowed him to derive everything from the central tenet of race. Second, the tenet's world-wide implications inevitably pushed any program drawn from it in the direction of world domination and biological Utopia, while Prussia-Germany's tradition of blood and iron and its barely thwarted 'grasp at world power' in 1914–18 made such a program inherently plausible to some Germans. Mussolini's nationalism, by contrast, merely aspired to Mediterranean mastery. [. . .]

From the beginning, Hitler showed greater theoretical rigor than Mussolini. Even the beer-hall agitator of 1920–1 conceived his internal goals, the 'nationalization of the masses', race purification, and creation of a pitiless national dictatorship, as a unified whole.[46] Germany's class, religious, and tribal cleavages must disappear, as they had in the euphoria of August 1914 and the trenches of the Great War. *Klassen- und Standesdünkel* [class and pride of place], religious mistrust, and Prussian-Bavarian enmity all weakened the Germanic Aryan race's struggle against the Jewish world conspiracy. And those internal divisions were themselves the product of racial mixing and Jewish parasitism. Class consciousness was a Jewish disease, a form of false consciousness that the Jews, that 'most national race of all the ages', deliberately and systematically spread, but did not share.[47]

The remedy was simple: a 'revolution of attitudes [Revolution der Gesinnung]' that would sweep away class distinctions and inculcate the 'blind, rock-hard, unshakable *belief* in the irresistible power of the German Volk' and in a better future. 'For this reason, the aim of the National Socialists from 1920 on was *not to become a class organization, but rather a Volk movement*'.[48] And hence Hitler's 'socialism': the term was more than mere demagogy, although Hitler did remark at one point that the movement's title of 'workers' party' was a consequence of the need to 'have the workers behind us'.[49] What Hitler meant by 'socialism' was not a society based on a nineteenth-century theory of political economy, but a new egalitarian style and unprecedented social mobility. The National Socialist revolution would not merely be one of *Gesinnung* [mind] or status.[50] It would liberate those Germans who until now had had no chance to rise. Ossified distinctions of birth, education, and wealth, according to Hitler, profited only the Jewish parasites. 'Make way for talent!' was a corollary of anti-Semitism, the chief social ingredient of National Socialism, and one of its most effective appeals. Hitler, the self-proclaimed and self-evident 'most capable man' of the Party, was simultaneously the prophet of the career open to talent, and its prize exemplar. [. . .]

The career open to talent inevitably had a negative side. By 1923 Hitler had come to the conclusion that those without talent – the requisite pedigree or physical attributes – must vanish. Germany would expel its Jews, if they were lucky, and take measures against the deformed, the mentally ill, syphilitics, and drunkards: 'The preservation of a nation is more important than the preservation of its unfortunates.' The *völkisch* state would see to it that 'only the healthy beget children'. By 1923–4, in connection with the evolution of his foreign-policy ideas, Hitler had also come to the conclusion that the healthiest of the healthy were the peasantry: 'The slums of the cities were responsible for nine-tenths, alcohol for one-tenth, of all human depravity.' The countryside, not the cities, had provided the 'healthier section of the Volk' that had crushed the 1919 red terror in Munich.[51] [. . .]

The final ingredient in Hitler's internal vision was of course a political revolution to accompany the revolution of attitudes, the career open to talent, and the repudiation of the last shreds of Judaeo-Christian morality. Germany, Hitler proclaimed as early as April 1920, needed 'neither monarchy nor republic, but the form of state that is the best for the [German] people. We need a dictator who is a genius.' He demanded 'a [man with an] iron skull, with muddy boots, perhaps, but with a clear conscience and a steel fist, who will end the blathering of these [Reichstag] drawing-room heroes, and give the nation a deed'.[52] Once Hitler had received 'dictatorial powers' from his own party, in the summer of 1921, his utterances on this score took on new authority. In a 'Germanic democracy', the best brain decided, not the 'sluggishness of the majority'. Hitler had already cast himself in the part. He might describe himself as a mere 'drummer' when flattering nationalist notables, but he also claimed for his movement the right to provide the 'strong man' Germany needed. As early as February 1922 he insisted the Party would lead Germany 'when the rotten edifice [of the Republic] finally collapse[d]'.[53]

Mussolini's example was a powerful help. Hitler apparently first took public note of the Duce in August 1922, and was soon proclaiming that Mussolini 'had shown what a minority can do, if a holy national will inspires it'. The Fascists had allegedly smashed 'Jewish-Marxist terror' and dragged a lethargic majority with them. The National Socialists, he now repeatedly proclaimed, aspired 'to take the Volk in hand'.[54] In the course of 1923 he sometimes veiled his claim to supreme leadership ('We must forge the sword; the almighty will give us the man for this sword'). But in predicting to the *Daily Mail* in October 1923 that if a German Mussolini came, 'people would fall down on their knees and worship him', Hitler could only have had himself in mind.[55] In his speeches at his trial after the November 1923 Putsch, he openly claimed political leadership of the *völkische* movement and of a nationalist revolution. His later outline in *Mein Kampf* of the constitutional implications of the Führer principle was no more than confirmation of views he had held since 1921–2 at least.[56]

Hitler's early sense of his vocation as Führer was never more apparent than in the foreign policy that accompanied and complemented his internal revolutionary goals. From very early, as with Mussolini, unity and leadership at home were the indispensable prelude to expansion abroad in fulfillment of the nation's mission: 'Nations are only capable of great advances when they have carried through the internal reforms that make it possible to project the entire race towards foreign policy goals.'[57] Still, unlike the 'prisoner of the Mediterranean', German traditions did not foreordain the direction of German expansion. Hitler was set on war from the beginning, and the Party's January 1920 program demanded 'land and soil for the nation', but it took until 1922 to work out whom to conquer.

Hitler had to start somewhere, and he began with the staid Wilhelmine program of naval and economic expansion he later denounced as naive and unworkable [. . .]

But by the end of December 1922, Hitler had developed a coherent vision, one he stuck to thereafter. His increasingly full-throated espousal of a German mission as '*Führer* of the Aryans' brought with it the need for a commensurate foreign policy. Even before the French occupation of the Ruhr in January 1923, which usually passes as the catalyst that impelled him to define his foreign program, Hitler's ideas had set. In a remarkable December 1922 conversation with an emissary of the then Reich Chancellor Cuno, Hitler outlined with only slight reticence his ideas on both internal and foreign policy.[58] Internally he was tactically circumspect, in deference to his audience. The nationalist dictatorship needed to smash the Left could eventually give way to a monarchy; solution of the Jewish question need not involve violence. His other views were less restrained:

> In foreign policy Germany must adjust itself to a purely continental policy, while avoiding the harming of English interests. We should attempt the carving up of Russia with English help. Russia would provide soil enough for German settlers, and a broad field of action for German industry. Then, when [we] settle accounts with France, England would not get in the way.

Hitler also mentioned Italy as a possible ally; even before hearing of Mussolini's movement he had been alive to the chance of exploiting Italy's aspirations to 'predominance in the Mediterranean'. After discovering the Fascists, he had defied German nationalist orthodoxy by proclaiming in November 1922 and thereafter that the Italian alliance required an end to 'empty protests' over the South Tyrol, which Italy had annexed in 1918.[59]

Hitler's December 1922 remarks included all the essential elements of the program he later outlined in the second volume of *Mein Kampf*, written in 1925–6: the forcible re-establishment of domestic unity; expansion at Russia's expense; a settling of accounts with France; England and Italy as allies, and the most un-Wilhelmine conception of isolating enemies and destroying them one by one. The order of the steps in this *Stufenplan* [step-by-step plan] remained problematic, however.[60] What the Ruhr occupation apparently did do for Hitler was to make neutralizing France his highest priority; eastern expansion could come only after that preliminary step. But that was a relatively minor change. The foundations of Hitler's program were in place. His subsequent elaborations of his vision in an essay of April 1924, in *Mein Kampf*, in his unpublished 'second book' of 1928, and in campaign speeches of 1928 and 1930, in which he unambiguously claimed world mastery for Germany, brought only two new elements. The first was Hitler's discovery of America – the recognition that the United States might prove his final adversary. In that contest, Hitler concluded, Germany's greater concentration of Aryan stock would carry it to victory.[61] The second novelty was the recognition, even more explicit than that of Mussolini, that foreign and domestic policy were inextricably linked:

> Domestic policy must secure the inner strength of a people so that it can assert itself in the sphere of foreign policy. Foreign policy must secure the life of a people for its domestic political development. Hence domestic policy and foreign policy are not only most closely linked, but must also mutually complement one another.

Translated into cruder terms, revolution was a prerequisite for expansion, and expansion for revolution. This insight was in its way as important a part of Hitler's program as his external *Stufenplan*.[62]

If the foundations of the world views of Hitler and Mussolini were rather different, the visionary programs the two developed thus had much in common. Internal policy and foreign aggrandizement were intertwined. Both leaders developed a peculiar blend of demography and geopolitics. Both leaders hoped to proceed by stages: consolidation at home, then exploitation of the rivalries of other powers to gain freedom for conquest. But Hitler was relatively rigid in laying down the alliances and stages by which Germany would climb to world mastery. The early Mussolini never went beyond generic predictions that European turmoil would permit Italian expansion. With the partial exception of his tilt towards France in 1935, he remained uncommitted to a specific alliance structure until 1936 – and in this sense, if only in this sense, was more of a 'realist' than Hitler.
[. . .]

Unholy war

Mussolini's transition to active expansionism aroused less resistance than Hitler's; the Duce's chosen victims seemed less capable of defending themselves. Nevertheless, the decision to attack Ethiopia has found a variety of interpretations. Determinists have argued that the Depression and consequent need to reflate the economy prompted expansion. Another popular claim is that Mussolini sought to 'relaunch' a flagging regime and cement the loyalty of the younger generation by foreign adventure.[63] Renzo De Felice, while rejecting the economic argument and demonstrating convincingly that the regime was at the height of its popularity, has suggested that failure in transforming society at home impelled Mussolini into previously unsought imperial adventure. The decision for war, in all these views, was a choice for second best, and Ethiopia no more than a target of opportunity that

German revival impelled the frightened French to offer Mussolini. Finally, Jens Petersen has argued that what happened between 1932 and 1935 was that international alignments at last permitted Mussolini to implement a long-held expansionist program. German rearmament and French fear (to which one must add the Depression's severing of financial dependence on Washington) at last gave Mussolini his chance.[64]

Mussolini's repeated, almost monotonous references to the goal of empire from 1918 on support the last interpretation. But it was more than a foreign policy program that moved him to action. War, Mussolini insisted both as Socialist and as Fascist, was linked to revolution. Only war, whose uncivilizing effects he well remembered, could help break the old society's resistance to the new paganism, make Italy the 'militarist' nation he demanded,[65] and further undermine monarchy and Church. Foreign adventure was also internal forward policy, not the mere 'social-imperialist' defense of order at home characteristic of more staid authoritarian regimes.

The choice of Ethiopia was long overdetermined. Fascism, as part of its historic mission, had to avenge Adua, the humiliating defeat of its great precursor Crispi. Mussolini's interest in 'profiting from an eventual dissolution of the Ethiopian empire' dated from at least 1925, and concrete planning began in November 1932.[66] Once it had conquered East Africa, the 'prisoner of the Mediterranean' might hope to lever the British out of the Sudan and Egypt.[67] Finally and most importantly, Ethiopia was the one enemy Mussolini's flankers and the European powers would reluctantly permit him to conquer. The flankers also felt the shame of Adua, and assumed that the Italy that had stood up to Austria-Hungary could defeat a land-locked, half-tribal, half-feudal kingdom with perhaps a quarter of Italy's population. And the other powers were ultimately disposed to tolerate an Italian aggression outside Europe that did not directly touch their own possessions.

Mussolini nevertheless faced and overcame major obstacles in launching his Fascist imperial war. Internally, he had to sap the tenacious resistance of the army. That hierarchy remained wedded to its Alpine priorities and dubious of the advantages of empire; the Austrian crisis of July 1934 emphasized the need to keep Italy's guard up in Europe. Both Marshal Pietro Badoglio, the chief of the vestigial interservice general staff, and General Federico Baistrocchi, the dynamic army chief of staff and undersecretary for war, were initially hostile to the project, which originated in the colonial ministry under Mussolini's aegis.[68] Once he had converted Baistrocchi and partially neutralized Badoglio by mobilizing navy and air force support, Mussolini still faced the king and a conservative Establishment that abhorred risk. The Duce complained in 1936 that the monarch bore no responsibility for victory: '*He* didn't want to go – I had to force him.' First-hand evidence of the king's attitude is lacking, but Mussolini's June 1935 complaint to his field commander in East Africa about 'grumblers and defeatists – more on high than below' suggests that king and Establishment were indeed recalcitrant.[69] Even Fascists wavered. The ex-secretary of the Party, Giovanni Giuriati, allegedly told the king that Mussolini's policy would lead to 'national disaster'. And Britain's apparent intention of fighting Mussolini in the Mediterranean if he went ahead produced warnings from Badoglio and the military of 'a disaster that would reduce us to a Balkan level'.[70] Even the Duce's son-in-law and future foreign minister, Galeazzo Ciano, temporarily gave way to despair after the League imposed sanctions.[71] Only the Church, which looked forward to civilizing the heretical Copts, and much of the public, which believed the regime's tales of Ethiopian and British provocations, and of an East African el Dorado, remained stalwart for aggression. Much later, Mussolini complained that many, many important people came to him and said, 'You have already done great things. Now [you should] pull in your oars.'[72]

Mussolini's knowledge of the British fleet's relative unpreparedness – on which he bet too heavily – and Whitehall's craven reluctance to force the issue allowed him to hold his course. But the attack on Ethiopia remained, in the words of overcautious advisors Mussolini later quoted, 'a gamble [*un'avventura*], a great gamble'.[73] The Establishment's reluctance may not have been entirely a consequence of Mussolini's external risk-taking. Defeat at the hands of the British, or stalemate at those of the Ethiopians, would risk far more than Italy's reputation and international position. It would risk the regime and, with it, the advantages the Establishment had secured through its forced compromise with Mussolini. Conversely, victory would excessively reinforce the regime and increase Mussolini's chances of receiving the blind obedience to which he aspired. And Mussolini lost no opportunity to make victory popular and Fascist, rather than military and dynastic. General Emilio De Bono, his original choice as commander in East Africa, was despite loyalty to king and army a man who owed his position to 'Fascist merits'.[74] The Militia mobilized, with army help, to provide specifically Fascist units whose combat performance the propaganda apparatus could then inflate. The new empire, Mussolini proclaimed to frenetic applause on 9 May, 1936, was a Fascist empire that 'bore the indestructible marks of the will and power of the Roman *fasci*'. By implication, it owed nothing to the old order.[75]

Victory indeed had consequences. Mussolini, as 'founder of the Empire', could now impose on his subordinates, without being laughed at, the reverence he aspired to. His subsequent policy – Spanish intervention, the racial laws, the campaign against the bourgeoisie, the annexation of Albania, and the plunge into war in 1940 – was only possible thanks to domestic reinforcement through African victory, and the license for aggression which increasing German preponderance brought. Far from representing a falling off from the famous 'realism' that his propagandists and some historians have ascribed to him, Mussolini's later policies were simply ever more risky attempts to implement his program within his own lifetime. It was his mission to remake 'the character of the Italians through combat'. Revelation of a long-held vision, not the 'involution' of personality and will that some scholars have discerned, presided over Italy's road to the Second World War.[76]

African victory naturally did not remove all obstacles. Mussolini put the League of Nations's sanctions to good use in convincing the great economic interests that autarky – the breaking of Italy's remaining ties to the world market – was the only feasible course. And although autarky proved 'too tight a shirt' for the export industries, the increasing stream of armaments contracts helped ease the pain. Italy's massive dependence on imported energy and strategic raw materials made genuine autarky impractical, but furnished yet another argument for expansion. In both domestic and foreign policy, Mussolini moved with increasing self-confidence. He plunged into Spain apparently without consulting the king; when Baistrocchi objected and Badoglio grumbled, he sacked one and ordered the other to show public approval. Spain, however, provided anything but the expected easy victories, and the disaster at Guadalajara in March 1937 allowed the king to level veiled reproaches at Mussolini.[77] But the humiliation passed with the summer 1937 victories in the Basque country. By early 1938, the German example – Hitler made himself commander-in-chief of the armed forces on 4 February – prompted emulation. The Party, presumably on Mussolini's secret instructions, pushed through Chamber and Senate a bill creating both Duce and king 'First Marshals of the Empire'. This demotion of the monarch to Mussolini's level produced wrath at the Quirinal.[78] Mussolini also promulgated in 1937–8 laws that formally wrote the Party into the constitution, and in January 1939 the Chamber of Deputies became the Chamber of Fasci and Corporations. Only the Senate remained as a relic of the liberal-monarchical past, and it owed its considerable staying power to its life tenure and royal appointment.

Mussolini and his entourage began looking forward with increasing anticipation to the removal of the king, perhaps even as early as the end of the Spanish war. It was only right, the Duce commented cynically in 1936 when exempting the king's foreign assets from the nationalization that League sanctions made necessary, to leave him 'a well-protected nest-egg'. The fate of monarchies was frequently an uncertain one.[79] The Duce's private remarks suggest an ever-growing resolve to smash the internal and foreign-policy restraints the monarchy still imposed.[80]

The military, like the monarchy, also failed to show the necessary enthusiasm for Mussolini's increasing risk-taking. Although he had achieved *de facto* direction of the armed forces during the Ethiopian war, Mussolini remained a prisoner of their institutional structures. Major surgery, such as the 1933 and 1936–7 plans for a tri-service defense ministry that would restrict the services' autonomy, was impossible without disturbing the interservice balance and tampering with the monarchy's prerogatives.[81] Both the rigidity of service promotion procedures and the caste resistance of the senior generals inhibited the injection of fresh and necessarily Fascist blood into the higher reaches of the military. In strategic planning, Mussolini had his way for a while. In 1937 and 1938 the army, under Baistrocchi's successor Pariani, made grandiose plans, with navy cooperation, for an assault on Egypt from Cyrenaica. But after the shock of Munich Badoglio reasserted his prerogatives, and killed the plan. If France were also hostile, Italy was too weak to seize Suez. Badoglio's refusal to permit planning 'that [did] not correspond to the situation' meant that when the situation changed, Italy had no plans. In the event, Mussolini had to trick his generals and admirals into war in 1940 with the assurance that they need not fight.[82]

Less dangerous for Mussolini than the recalcitrance of monarchy and military, but still inconvenient, was the Church. The Vatican, despite its compromise with Mussolini, made difficulties about what Pius XI denounced as 'pagan state idolatry'. Naturally, the Church overwhelmingly supported the Ethiopian campaign and Mussolini's allegedly anti-Bolshevist intervention in Spain. It evinced qualified approval even of the annexation of Albania.[83] But when Mussolini's concern with the 'purity of the race' came home from the colonies, and in deference to the Germans attacked Jews as well as blacks, the Vatican became uneasy. The Church was not averse to religious discrimination, and avant-garde Jesuits urged segregation of the Jews, but the pseudo-biological provisions of the 1938 racial laws included Catholic converts.[84] At the same time, the German alliance and the increasing risk of general war added to the Church's reservations about the regime. War – apart from the predictable loss of life and destruction – would either result in Axis defeat, endangering Italy and the Lateran pacts, or a victory that would bring pagan racist revolution in earnest. Hence the papal protests and peace messages against which Mussolini increasingly railed between 1938 and 1940.

The upper-middle classes, too, began to distance themselves subtly from Mussolini as he moved to implement his vision. It required the shock of defeat to consummate the divorce Italian-style between the regime and what Mussolini described as a bourgeoisie riddled with 'cowardice, laziness, [and] love of the quiet life'. But the origins of that divorce lay in Mussolini's post-Ethiopian activism both at home and abroad. Italy's forced 'non-belligerence' in September 1939 was thus not an example of Mussolini's purported realism, but rather the Establishment's last victory over the regime's expansionism. The pope and Badoglio, Ciano and the diplomats, industrialists and king, all coalesced to hold back Mussolini and the Party enthusiasts. But the victory was a Pyrrhic one. Mussolini remained in control of the machinery of government. Only a coup, which the king briefly contemplated in

March 1940, could remove him. When the king failed to move, the members of the quasi-coalition of 'moderates' remained prisoners of their separate bargains with the Duce, and of their own cautiously expansionist appetites.

The great German victories in the West in May 1940 enabled Mussolini to activate that expansionism with the promise that Italy need not fight. He himself sought instead a swift but decisive conflict that would free Italy from its Mediterranean imprisonment and give him the prestige to crush his flankers. That was why the regime insisted – contrary to common sense, which dictated the mobilization of all strands of Italian nationalism – that this war was *la guerra fascista*. It was a war of internal as well as foreign conquest. And when Italy's independent war ended in the winter of 1940–1 in disaster at Taranto, in the Albanian mountains, and in the sands of Beda Fomm, Mussolini's revolutionary project died with it.[85] The regime survived until the 'moderate' Fascists revolted against Mussolini, and the king and generals overthrew him in July 1943. But the crushing defeats of 1940 and Italy's humiliating new status as first satellite of the Reich had broken the prestige Mussolini needed for internal transformation. In the end, the flankers, emboldened in defeat, repudiated the regime in the name of the same Italian nationalism, and interests, that had once led them to support it.

Hitler fortunately also failed, but his failure was less humiliating and infinitely bloodier than Mussolini's. Hitler had written in *Mein Kampf* that Germany would 'either be a world power, or cease to be'. He almost achieved the first, and barely failed at the second. His starting-point in blending revolution and territorial expansion was his discovery in November 1937 that Germany's growing if foreseeably temporary preponderance in armaments had not convinced Blomberg, Fritsch, and Neurath that Germany could, should, and must fight. Their lamentable lack of faith emerged from the alarmed protestations at the 5 November 1937 Reich Chancellory conference at which Hitler revealed for the first time that he intended to seize Austria and smash Czechoslovakia, situation permitting, as early as 1938. Fritsch and his subordinate Beck did not merely object to the risks involved, but above all to Hitler's implicit claim to be Germany's sole font of strategic leadership. Regrettably, the first civilian since Bismarck to impose on the army both civilian control, and Clausewitz's heretical notion that war was a tool of politics, turned out to be Hitler.

The dictator confirmed his 5 November prediction of war two weeks later in a speech to Party officials: new tasks awaited Germany, 'for the living space of our Volk is too narrow'. And he again stressed the identity of foreign and domestic policy. Just as the National Socialists had 'led the nation upwards' internally, so they would achieve for Germany abroad 'the same rights to existence as other nations'.[86] Two months later, he dismissed both Blomberg and Fritsch, and for good measure, Neurath and the ambassador to Italy, Hassell. [. . .]

In the aftermath of the 4 February coup, many high officers seethed with indignation at the preposterous accusations against Fritsch, but foreign policy came to Hitler's aid. Political developments in Austria allowed him to distract the army with a job to do: the Anschluss. The resulting personal triumph allowed him to brush off Army pressure for Fritsch's reinstatement, while the public, consulted in the first plebiscite since the Rhineland coup, returned an overwhelming vote of confidence. Foreign policy had first demanded domestic upheaval, then blessed it with success.

But obstacles remained. [. . .] Throughout the summer, as preparations to attack Germany's next victim, Czechoslovakia, went forward, Hitler gave vent to a stream of complaints against the generals. Most of them 'had rejected [his leadership], and continued to reject it'. They 'as yet did not understand the meaning of the new age', and were far inferior in élan to his trusty Gauleiters. Delays in the army-supervised construction of the *Westwall* fortifications led him to threaten to turn the job over to Martin Bormann, 'whom he could at least rely on'.[87] Fritz Todt, another Party luminary, actually got the job. And several months later, Hitler apparently intimidated a reluctant Admiral Raeder with the not entirely incredible threat that if further delays slowed the gargantuan naval program, he would turn procurement over to Todt.[88]

The real issue of the summer, however, was what Hitler characterized as '*Angst* and cowardice in the army': the refusal of Beck and the hesitation of other senior officers to accept his strategic leadership and the risks the Czech enterprise would involve. Fortunately for Hitler, Beck was relatively isolated both in his high assessment of the risk of general war and his dogged insistence on the co-responsibility of the army chief of staff for strategic decisions. Nevertheless, Hitler felt obliged to harangue his top commanders twice in mid-August to counteract Beck's influence and steel their nerves for the coming struggle. Conveniently for Hitler, Beck cracked under the strain of isolation and resigned. His successor Halder plotted in secret, but made no attempt at open contradiction.[89] Even more fortunately for Hitler, the West surrendered Czechoslovakia without fighting. Bloodless triumph cut the ground from under doubters and plotters. Munich also raised Hitler higher in the public esteem than ever before – the German people had nationalist triumph without war.[90]

The crisis had other effects besides strengthening Hitler internally. He had passionately sought war against the Czechs, both to steel the young, and to test the newly minted Wehrmacht. Only at the last moment had he accepted a negotiated surrender of the Sudetenland. On the evening of 27 September, Hitler had watched motorized units on their way to the border roll through central Berlin, as he had ordered. The public stood, silent and sullen; no cheers or 'German greetings' honored the Führer's appearance at the Reich Chancellory balcony.[91] The delirious scenes of August 1914 did not repeat themselves. After the euphoria of the Anschluss, this may have come as a shock. The unfeigned enthusiasm of German crowds for Chamberlain added insult to injury.[92] Hence Hitler's post-Munich rage at the British ('we will no longer tolerate the supervision of governesses') and his diatribe to German press representatives on 10 November demanding indoctrination that would 'free the Volk of doubts that make it unhappy' and inculcate '*fanatical* belief' in final victory. The nation must stand like 'formed-up troops' behind his decisions. The 'intellectual strata' – by which he meant those educated Germans, including officers, who still refused to accept him on faith – were unfortunately still necessary: 'otherwise one could exterminate them, or whatever.'[93]

Hitler could have been under no illusion that propaganda alone would consolidate internal unity behind him. As he harangued the press, the SS and police were supervising the cleanup of the debris from synagogues and Jewish shops burned out in the *Kristallnacht* pogrom. Hitler had inspired that action as a hint of things to come and as a salutary release for Party radicalism, but he was too shrewd a judge of public and elite opinion to associate with it openly. Generals were still heard to mutter about hanging 'this swine, Goebbels', who was ostensibly responsible.[94] The time of the Jews was nevertheless coming, Hitler hinted in his 30 January 1939 Reichstag speech. That of the churches, he had said privately the previous August, had not yet come; he still had 'too many other problems'.[95]

Yet as his insistence on his cyclopean building program and his acceleration of the already breakneck pace of naval construction suggest, Hitler had already left the confines of the inter-war German state far behind (symptomatically, Germany proper now became the *Altreich* [old realm]. The immense Nazi eagle with a globe in its claws that Hitler ordered to crown his gigantic Berlin great hall was no mere ideological metaphor. Germany, he told a group of senior officers in early February 1939, was bound for world mastery; the triumphs of 1938 were not the end of the road but the beginning. Germany could best preserve the reputation and prestige acquired since 1933 by 'without letup exploiting every opportunity, however small, to move immediately towards a new success'.[96] He would tolerate no more 'warning memoranda' – an apparent reference to Beck's attempts to thwart him the previous summer. The alleged 'hot-house intellectualism' of the general staff since Schlieffen's day was outdated; he demanded 'believing officers' with 'trust and blind confidence'.[97]

The next major success, Hitler decided shortly after his bloodless absorption of rump Czechoslovakia in mid-March, must come in war against Poland. The origins of that war, which contrary to Hitler's intentions eventually became a world war, have inevitably provoked vast controversy. But until Tim Mason's work on the regime's relationship with the industrial workers, few scholars have had much to say about the internal ramifications of Hitler's decision. Mason has opened the question up by suggesting that Hitler took the plunge largely to escape the economic and political crisis rearmament had created. Conquest was 'an end in itself', an improvised defensive 'flight forward' to escape intolerable domestic problems. The argument is not overly convincing.[98] Hitler had passionately wanted to fight in 1938, before the crisis reached full intensity. Politically, the regime was hardly on its last legs, either in the public or in the official mind. Mason's arguments for social and political crisis echo with the liturgy of the class struggle, but fail to address at least some of the evidence. The Ruhr miners, on whose efforts all of German industry relied, had a lower absentee rate in 1938 than in 1929, and later showed remarkable aptitude for supervising slave labor.[99]

As for the economic crisis, the evidence does not suggest that anyone except a narrow circle recognized it as such. Hitler merely argued, in prodding his generals toward war, that Germany could hold out only 'for a few more years'.[100] This was less a prediction of imminent catastrophe than a ploy to egg the reluctant onward by reminding them of difficulties that they had helped him create. Mason has also claimed in support of his thesis Hitler's remarks in both 1937 and 1939 that Germany faced a choice between expansion and degeneration. But those remarks were Hitler's standard justification, fixed since 1921–2, of the need for *Lebensraum*.[101] The economic strains of 1938–9 were for him no more than confirmation of that insight.

But the foremost difficulty with Mason's theory is that it isolates the events of 1938–9 from those preceding, and thus interprets as cause a phenomenon that is first of all effect. As Jost Dülffer has pointed out, the internal crisis was a consequence of Hitler's ever-increasing demands on the economy for armaments and for the immense building program.[102] Those demands led directly to war, with no need for an intervening *deus ex machina* in the form of internal crisis. Only war could transmute armaments into *Lebensraum* and world mastery. Only war, along with the new Reich's cyclopean monuments and incessant propaganda, could fully nationalize the masses. The 1938–9 crisis was above all a symptom of Hitler's offensive forward thrust towards war and revolution, rather than a driving force behind it.

As for the timing of the attack on Poland, three considerations were decisive. First and least important was the pact with Stalin, which secured Germany's rear and checkmated the remaining doubters among the generals. Second came a broader consideration, which Hitler repeatedly emphasized in his 1939 harangues to his military leaders. Rearmament had created a brief window of opportunity for Germany; after 1941–2 that window would close as the other powers caught up. Finally, of course, came Hitler's ever-growing obsession with the short time left to him personally; as he told his generals 'in all modesty' in November 1939, he alone possessed the nerve (*Entschlusskraft*) to fulfill Germany's mission.[103]

He lost no time putting war to use. Within the Reich, he secretly ordered the killing of the congenitally ill and insane in state institutions. Poland offered an even greater opportunity to implement his internal programs for Germany – using Poles as 'laboratory rabbits'. As Heydrich crudely explained to the army, 'we want to spare the little people, but nobility, clergy, and Jews must be killed'.[104] The generals recoiled in pious horror, then sheepishly yielded responsibility for the occupied territories.

The generals did make a brief stand on the sole issue they could not evade: Hitler's demand, made immediately after Poland's collapse, for an immediate offensive to smash the French and British. The military's resistance, which included yet another hesitant Putsch conspiracy in which Halder again took fleeting interest, was the last twitch of the organized German Establishment. It was short-lived. This time, no one dared openly question Hitler's strategic judgment as Beck had done; instead, the generals took refuge in technical arguments that inevitably lost force as army readiness improved and French ineptitude and demoralization became apparent. Hitler's tirades terrorized Brauchitsch and Halder, and the repeated weather postponements of the attack allowed the generals to prepare it with even more of the thoroughness that was their trademark. The pathetic April 1940 showing of the British and French in Norway did the rest. When army and Luftwaffe crossed the western borders on 10 May, the doubters had long fallen silent or joined the ranks of the converted.

In mid-January, even before the Wehrmacht rolled, Hitler had made clear to some of his associates the internal consequences of victory: 'The war is in this respect, as in many other matters, a favorable opportunity to dispose of it (the church question) root and branch'. In the ancient world entire peoples had been liquidated, and the Soviet Union was setting the example in the present. But the old German 'proclivity for mysticism' still thwarted him:

> If he did nothing now against the rebellious parsons, then it was not least out of concern for the Wehrmacht. There they ran to the field chaplains, and a trooper who was brave with the good Lord was always more useful to him than one who was cowardly without Him. But here the indoctrination of the SS, which was now proving in war that ideologically schooled troops could be brave even without the Lord, would outline the necessary development.[105]

In conversation with Rosenberg, his religion expert, Hitler foresaw the possibility of smashing the churches by force ('ein harter machtpoliti-scher Eingriff') – but this could take place only when Germany was 'fully independent internationally'; 'otherwise the resulting blaze of internal political controversy could cost us our existence'.[106]

The Wehrmacht's crushing victory over France in May–June 1940 did not secure the full measure of freedom Hitler sought, but he now commanded the confidence of the military elite as never before or after.

Symptomatic of that confidence was the pleasurable anticipation with which many senior generals prepared to tackle the next intriguing military problem Hitler set them: the destruction of the Soviet Union and the physical elimination of its 'Jewish-Bolshevik intelligentsia'. [. . .] The public, sullen during the phony war, suddenly went 'berserk with success'; in the words of one jaundiced eyewitness, after the French collapse Germany's cafes were full of 'beer-soaked old pinochle players dividing up continents over their steins'.[107]

Nevertheless, Hitler still lacked the prestige to impose his vision in its entirety inside Germany. The attack on the Soviet Union was thus more than merely a response to Churchill's incomprehensible obduracy and to United States support for Britain, or another momentous step in Hitler's foreign policy *Stufenplan*. It was also a further mighty thrust towards the internal barbarization of Germany itself. *Lebensraum* and foreign policy 'freedom' would enable him at last to crush that 'reptile', the churches.[108] The war of racial annihilation in the East would harden German youth to destroy the old society at home, while the lavish rewards of victory would still whatever unquiet consciences remained.

But even while the Wehrmacht struck deep into Russia, the Bishop of Münster, Count Galen, raised his voice publicly against the euthanasia program, and the regime had to suspend it. Hitler raged in private. This, too, would appear on the churches' final bill. He had, he noted privately in October 1941, also had to put up with the Jews for a long time; now, though he left it unsaid, extermination had begun.[109]

That last foundation of his program was indeed all that remained once the Wehrmacht failed to take Moscow in November–December 1941. In Jodl's words, 'long before anyone else in the world, Hitler suspected or knew that the war was lost', and that suspicion drove him to give the Final Solution an ever higher priority, a priority that soon eclipsed the fighting of the war itself.[110] Internally, SS and Party vied in radicalism, while furtive half-knowledge of Germany's Eastern crimes and of coming retribution bound the public to the regime to the end. What remained of the Establishment had lost in 1938–40 all capacity to put the brakes on Hitler. The final despairing gesture of some of its members, the botched bomb plot of 20 July, 1944, if anything strengthened the regime. Barbarous revenge ended the history of Prussia, while miraculous survival fleetingly refurbished Hitler's defeat-tarnished charisma.[111] Hitler's revolution, unlike that of Mussolini, had at least made itself irreversible from within. And the temporary allies who met across the rubble of Greater Germany could not restore Bismarck's Reich, even had they wished it.

Conclusion

From the perspective of results, Mussolini's claim that Italy and Germany were 'congruent cases' was something of an exaggeration. It also cannot erase the many differences between the societies over which the two regimes arose, and between their myths, traditions and institutions. The degree of freedom of action the regimes achieved was markedly different because of these underlying conditions, and not merely because of the frequently invoked but partly illusory gap in ruthlessness and dynamism between the dictators. The two leaders' visions, despite the differences between their underlying ideologies, were indeed congruent in their mixture of demography and geopolitics, if not in Hitler's racialist teleology. Above all, the relationship between foreign and domestic policy in the two regimes was similar. Foreign policy was internal policy and vice versa; internal consolidation was a precondition of foreign conquest, and foreign conquest was the decisive prerequisite for a revolution at home that would sweep away inherited institutions and values, Piedmontese-Italian and Prusso-German military castes, the churches with their claim to deep popular loyalties and their inconvenient if not always operative Christian values, and, last but not least, the putatively decadent and cowardly upper-middle classes.

In the end it is this identity of foreign and domestic policy that distinguishes these two regimes from the other types of political gangsterism prevalent in this century of war and mass murder. Most twentieth-century revolutionary regimes have sought to destroy either the social order or the international one. Despots that come to power through revolutionary civil war in relatively primitive societies – Lenin, Stalin, Mao, Pol Pot – can have millions shot or starved without need of territorial aggrandizement, though they scarcely despise it. Ideology may dictate expansion, but in practice foreign conquest is a bonus, not the indispensable prerequisite for internal transformation. As for despots who inherit more organized nations, they usually expand partly to defend existing privilege. Brezhnev's troopers did not swoop down on Kabul, or the Argentine navy on the Falklands, to undermine order at home. Only Mussolini and Hitler simultaneously sought to overthrow their societies and their neighbors. In this sense, reason, not faith, unites their two regimes.

Notes

1 I thank the Woodrow Wilson International Center for Scholars and the John Simon Guggenheim Memorial Foundation for generous support during the research and writing of this piece, which attempts to summarize the argument of a book in progress. My thanks also to Hans W. Gatzke, Michael Geyer, Isabel V. Hull, Adrian Lyttelton and Williamson Murray for helpful comments and suggestions. Initial quotations: Strunk minute, 31 January, 1936, US National Archives, microcopy T-454/56/000226; Hitler, *Monologe im Führerhauptquartier 1941–1944*, Hamburg, 1980, p. 43.

2 Nolte, *Three Faces of Fascism*, New York, 1966, pp. 20–1; Gilbert Allardyce, 'What Fascism is not. Notes on the deflation of a concept', *American Historical Review*, 84, 1979, 367–88; see also Berndt Martin, 'Zur Tauglichkeit

eines übergreifenden Faschismus-Begriffs', *Vierteljahrshefte für Zeitgeschichte* (henceforth VfZG) 29, 1981, 48–73.

3 'The doctrine of fascism', p. 47, in Adrian Lyttelton (ed.) *Italian Fascisms from Pareto to Gentile*, New York, 1973.

4 See particularly A.J.P. Taylor, *The Origins of the Second World War*, New York, rev. paperback edn, 1966, pp. 70–2, and Norman Stone, *Hitler*, Boston, Mass., 1980, pp. 16, 67. Hans Mommsen, 'National Socialism', in *Marxism, Communism, and Western Society*, New York, 1973, 6: 67, finds Schumpeter's 'aimless expansion' the best description of National Socialist policy. Gerhard Schulz, *Aufstieg des Nationalsozialismus*, Frankfurt, 1975, p. 218, argues on the basis of a *Mein Kampf* passage (p. 170 of the English edition, trans. Ralph Manheim [New York, 1971] [henceforth MK]), that Hitler was a mere '*Machiavellist*' who did not care whether his ideology was 'true or false' (see also pp. 212–13). But the *Mein Kampf* passage actually establishes only that Hitler thought Marxism 'false'; he viewed his own theoretical task as the establishment of 'absolute truth' (MK, p. 210).

5 See De Felice, *Mussolini il duce*, Turin, 1974, 1, 496.

6 Pareto, elites: *00*, 1: 6–7, 73–5, 128 (1904–08); 3: 26 (1910); Marx and Darwin: 2: 9–10 (1909); Oriani: note 9 below. For Pareto and Marx, see especially Gregor, *The Young Mussolini and the Intellectual Origins of Fascism*, Berkeley, Calif., 1979.

7 I have throughout endeavored to use the term *revolution* in as neutral a fashion as possible, without assuming that revolutions (violent attempts to achieve rapid, fundamental changes in dominant values and myths, political institutions, social structures, leadership and government policies) are of necessity 'progressive'. I have also applied the term to relationships between states, to mean an attempt to achieve violent, fundamental change in power relationships and the distribution of territory. The widespread assumption that only the Left makes revolutions contains a hidden but indefensible teleology, and when applied to the twentieth century falls foul of the obvious confusion between political extremes: was Stalin 'Left' or 'Right'? (See, in general, Eugen Weber, 'Revolution? Counterrevolution? What Revolution?', *Journal of Contemporary History*, 9, 1974, 3–47; Perez Zagorin, 'Theories of revolution in contemporary historiography', *Political Science Quarterly*, 88, 1973, 23–52, and 'Prolegomena to the comparative history of revolution in Early Modern Europe', *Comparative Studies in Society and History*, 18, 1976, 151–74.

8 Barbarous socialism: *00*, 3: 66 (1910); 'I am a primitive', 4: 183 (1912); paganism (Nietzsche): 1: 174ff.; new civilization: 3: 87 (1910); revolutionary elite: 1: 128 (1908), 3: 26 (1910).

9 Nationalism: *00*, 2: 75 (1909); 3: 266–7 (1910); 6: 58–60 (20 January 1920); Oriani: 38: 45–6; 2: 128 (1909). Gentile, *Ideologia*, p. 37, assumes Oriani's nationalism, and hence Mussolini's, was cultural – a charitable interpretation that ignores both ideologues' thirst for blood.

10 *00*, 6: 429 (10 November, 1914); 7: 70 (11 December 1914); 7: 197 (14 February 1915); 7: 418 (24 May 1915); 7: 394 (16 May 1915).

11 ibid., 7: 57 (29 November 1914).

12 The war and Italy's mission: ibid., 11: 86 (19 May 1918); 13: 147 (24 May 1919); 18: 200 (24 May 1922); 21: 443 (4 November 1925); 23: 248 (4 November 1928); beacon of civilization: 12: 77 (20 December 1918); 16: 128 (25 January 1921).

13 ibid., 14: 22 (24 September 1919); also 15: 70, 16: 106, 17: 148; Rome: 15: 217–18 (24 September 1920).
14 ibid., 16: 159 (6 February 1921); 18: 144 (6 April 1922).
15 ibid., 17: 18 (30 June 1921); see also 18: 69, 71; 16: 142 (2 February 1921).
16 ibid., 21: 389 (24 September 1925); 22: 109 (7 April 1926); 22: 187 (early August 1926); 22: 12 (18 November, 1925); 22: 135 (23 May 1926); also, in general, Michael Ledeen, *Universal Fascism*, New York, 1972.
17 Hitler, *Sämtliche Aufzeichnungen 1905–1924*, ed. Eberhard Jäckel and Axel Kuhn, Stuttgart, 1980 (henceforth HSA), p. 89 (16 September 1919); a dearth of sources has so far prevented convincing reconstruction of Hitler's views before 1919.
18 HSA, p. 301 (26 January, 1921); MK, p. 339.
19 On the eschatological core of Marxism, see Robert C. Tucker, *Philosophy and Myth in Karl Marx*, London, 1961, and Leszek Kolakowski, *Main Currents of Marxism*, vol. 1, Oxford, 1978.
20 Common practice is to ascribe canonical status to *Mein Kampf* (1924–26). The early sources in HSA show that all decisive elements in *Mein Kampf* had emerged by the end of 1922.
21 *Monologe*, p. 49 (July 1941); see also p. 262.
22 HSA, pp. 137–8, 145–6, 184–204 (31 May, 11 June, 13 August 1920); HSA, pp. 119–20 (6 April 1920): '... es beseelt uns die unerbittliche Entschlossenheit, das Übel an die Wurzel zu packen und mit Stumpf und Stiel auszurotten (lebhafter Beifall)'.
23 Jewish world domination: HSA pp. 195, 220, 254, 273, 464, etc.; uniting all Germans: pp. 106, 126, 128, 180, 242.
24 HSA, p. 354 (19 March 1921); Hitler borrowed from a nineteenth-century tag: 'und es mag am deutschen Wesen / einmal noch die Welt genesen'.
25 HSA, pp. 620, 623, 631, 698, 779 (12 April 1921; 28 September 1922; 3 January 1923); see also p. 694.
26 MK, pp. 383–4, 288.
27 See particularly 00, 13: 147–8 (24 May 1919); 16; 20 (20 November 1920).
28 ibid., 8: 272, 10: 140 (22 December 1916; 15 December 1917); on the veterans' movement, see Giovanni Sabbatucci, *I combattenti nel primo dopoguerra*, Bari, 1974.
29 00, 14: 71 (18 October 1919); 18: 331 (2 August 1922); 20: 284 (24 May 1924); the Risorgimento as failed revolution was a favorite theme of Mussolini as well as of Gramsci.
30 ibid., 21: 426 (28 October 1925); 22: 23, 100, 117, 246 (5 December 1925; 28 March, 15 April, 28 October 1926); 23: 78–9 (17 December 1927).
31 ibid., 24: 283 (27 October 1930); 44: 91 (29 October 1934): 'Sonatori di mandolino, no; lanciatori di bombe, gente cortese, no. Cazzottatori'.
32 ibid, see 17: 18, 268–9 (30 June, 22 November 1921); 18: 66ff. (25 February 1922).
33 ibid., 19: 196 (March 1923); 20: 295 (27 May 1924).
34 ibid., 17: 268 (22 November 1922); 20: 80 (1 November 1923). De Felice's contention (*Mussolini il fascista*, 1: 537–8 (see also pp. 465, 591, 594, 602, 618, and 2: 9–10, 34–5, 67, 128–9, 342) that Mussolini did not seek a one-party dictatorial regime before late 1925 does not fit the evidence.
35 00, 21: 362 (22 June 1925).
36 ibid., 14: 292, 21: 363 (7 February 1920, 22 June 1925).
37 ibid., 10: 434–5 (7 April 1918); 11: 91–2 (28 May 1918); 12: 77, 101 (20

December 1918, 1 January 1919).

38 ibid., 12: 323 (23 March 1919); 15: 184–5 (5 September 1920); 13: 71, 76 (20, 23 April 1919).

39 ibid., 13: 109, 147–9 (9, 24 May 1919).

40 All from ibid., 16: 105–6 (8 January 1921): 'Per essere liberi'.

41 Demography (among others): ibid., 16: 335, 18: 180, 19: 191, 20: 74, (1921–3) and particularly 21: 97 (4 October 1924); 'decadence' in some areas of Italy: 19: 285 (22 June 1923).

42 French decadence: see especially ibid., 38: 396 (22 June 1923); the rest from 22: 364–7 (26 May 1927) (the 'discorso dell'Ascensione').

43 'Ruralize Italy': ibid., 40: 298 (24 March 1927); the rest from 23: 216 (September 1928). De Felice's assumption that Mussolini's foreign and domestic programs were mutually exclusive alternatives (*Mussolini il fascista*, Turin, 1968, 2: 359–60; *Mussolini il Duce*, 1: 179; *Mussolini il Duce*, Turin, 1978, 2: 155) fits neither Mussolini's words nor the regime's actions.

44 In order: *00*, 13: 143 (22 May 1919); 15: 289–90 (20 August 1920); 16: 300–01 (3 May 1921); 18: 439 (4 October 1923); 15: 37 (15 June 1920) (see also 15: 29, 18: 459); 18: 432 (1 October 1922); 21: 273 (2 April 1925).

45 Block quotation from Emilio Canevari, *La guerra italiana*, Rome, 1948–9, 1: 212 note; 'prisoner': *00*, 24: 234 (17 May 1930); also *I documenti diplomatici italiani*, 7th series (Rome, 1953—), 8, no. 323. For more on this geopolitical vision, see MacGregor Knox, *Mussolini Unleashed, 1939–1941*, Cambridge, 1982, particularly pp. 38–40.

46 For the phrase, MK, p. 336; for some of the background, George L. Mosse, *The Nationalization of the Masses*, New York, 1975.

47 HSA, pp. 136–8, 145–6, 151 (31 May, 11 and 24 June 1920).

48 ibid., pp. 239, 255, 156 (24 September, 26 October, 3 July 1920).

49 ibid., p. 105 (16 January 1920).

50 David Schoenbaum, *Hitler's Social Revolution*, New York, 1966.

51 ibid., pp. 646, 1023, 1026, 1116 (22 June 1922; before October 1923; 28 February 1924); MK, p. 403.

52 HSA, pp. 126, 127 (27 April 1920), also p. 443; 'iron skull': p. 333 (6 March 1921).

53 ibid., p. 438 (14 July 1921); p. 622 (12 April 1922); pp. 643 and 643, note 6; also pp. 753–4 (29 May, 4 December 1922): 'Wir brauchen einen starken Mann, und den werden die Nationalsozialisten bringen'; p. 565 (2 February 1922).

54 ibid., pp. 683, 726, 704, 711 (17 August, 9 and 22 November, 25 October 1922); see also pp. 795 ('heads will roll'), 806, 950. As early as February 1921, Hitler had claimed that the movement's swastika flag was the only appropriate one for a future 'germanic state of the German nation' (p. 323).

55 ibid., pp. 966, 1027.

56 ibid., pp. 1007, 1128, 1188, 1210; MK, pp. 449–50. For a different view, see Albrecht Tyrell, *Vom 'Trommler' zum 'Führer'*, Munich, 1975. Tyrell's stress on the role of Hitler's surroundings and followers in creating the Führer role is well taken. But Tyrell also reads Hitler's comparative modesty between 1919 and 1921–2 as self-doubt, and ignores the more plausible possibility of tactical reticence.

57 HSA, p. 269 (30 November, 1920).

58 Conversation with Eduard Sharrer, ibid., pp. 770–5; for the importance of

the document, see pp. 34ff. of Geoffrey Stoakes, 'The evolution of Hitler's ideas on foreign policy, 1919–1925', in Peter D. Stachura (ed.) *The Shaping of the Nazi State*, New York, 1978.

59 HSA, pp. 118, 122, 168, 728 (29 March, 17 April, 1 August 1920; 14 November 1922); Jens Petersen, *Hitler-Mussolini*, Tübingen, 1973, pp. 65–8.

60 For Hitler's insistence on the need to proceed by stages, see MK, pp. 249–50, and Calic, *Ohne Maske*, pp. 50, 93; for the *Stufenplan* metaphor, Andreas Hillgruber, *Hitlers Strategie*, Frankfurt, 1965; Klaus Hildebrand, *Deutsche Aussenpolitik 1933–1945*, Stuttgart, 1971; and Jost Dülffer, *Weimar, Hitler und die Marine*, Düsseldorf, 1973.

61 For the chain of utterances that links the Hitler of 1924 with that of 1933, Jochen Thies, *Architekt der Weltherrschaft*, Düsseldorf, 1976, pp. 41–61, and Dülffer, *Marine*, pp. 204–20.

62 Adolf Hitler, *Hitler's Second Book*, New York, 1961, p. 34; similarly, pp. 24, 46–7, 79, 210. See also Martin Broszat, 'Betrachtungen zu "Hitlers Zweitem Buch"', VfZG 9, 1961, 422; the only systematic attempt to interpret Hitler's later policies in these terms is Dietrich Orlow, *The History of the Nazi Party*, vol. 2, Pittsburgh, 1973.

63 Franco Catalano, *L'economia italiana di guerra*, Milan, 1969, p. 7; Giorgio Rochat, *Militari e politic nella preparazione della campagna d'Etiopia*, Milan, 1971, pp. 105–7.

64 *Mussolini il fascista*, p. 359; *Mussolini il duce*, 1: 179, 466–7; Petersen, 'Die Aussenpolitik des faschistischen Italien als historiographisches Problem', VfZG, 22, 1974, 417–57.

65 *OO*, 26: 308 (24 August 1934) (the 'discorso del carro armato').

66 See Rochat, *Militari e politici*, pp. 26–33.

67 Pompeo Aloisi, *Journal (25 juillet 1932–14 juin 1936)*, Paris, 1957, p. 382 (8 May 1936).

68 For details, Rochat, *Militari e politici*, chs 1, 2.

69 Luigi Federzoni, *L'Italia di ieri per la storia di domani*, Milan, 1967, p. 233 (also Attilio Tamaro, *Venti anni di storia* [Rome, 1953–54], 3: 217, note 98a); *OO*, 42: 107 (26 June 1935).

70 Badoglio to Mussolini, September 1935, in Rochat, *Militari e politici*, p. 229.

71 Alessandro Lessona, *Memorie*, Florence, 1958, pp. 239–40.

72 *OO*, 44: 325 (17 April 1943).

73 ibid.

74 His replacement in November 1935 by Badoglio was consequently an internal setback for Mussolini – but winning on the battlefield obviously had immediate priority.

75 *OO*, 27: 268–9 (9 May, 1936).

76 Mussolini's words: Galeazzo Ciano, *Diario 1937–1943*, Milan, 1980, 13 November 1937. For the involution thesis, which resembles the folk wisdom of the day ('. . . se dopo l'Etiopia, si fosse fermato. . . .'), De Felice, *Mussolini il duce*, 2, ch. 3.

77 Knox, *Mussolini Unleashed*, p. 30.

78 De Felice, 'Mussolini e Vittorio Emanuele III Primi Marescialli dell'Impero', in Università degli Studi di Messina, *Scritti in onore di Vittorio De Caprariis*, Rome, n.d., pp. 347–68.

79 De Felice, *Mussolini il duce*, 2: 16 (in general, pp. 14–21).

80 See particularly ibid., p. 40, and Giuseppe Bottai, *Diario 1935–1944*,

Giordano Bruno Guerri (ed.), Milan, 1982, entries for 23 June, 12 July and 13 June 1938.

81 Knox, *Mussolini Unleashed*, pp. 17–18.

82 ibid., pp. 18–19, 58, 119–23.

83 ibid., p. 11.

84 See De Felice, *Storia degli ebrei italiani sotto il fascismo*, Turin, rev. edn, 1972, pp. 204–5, 286–87.

85 Knox, *Mussolini Unleashed*, chs 3 and 6, and Conclusion.

86 Domarus, *Hitler*, p. 760 (21 November 1937).

87 Engel, *Heeresadjutant*, pp. 20, 26, 32 (20 April, 25 June, 18 April 1938).

88 Dülffer, *Marine*, pp. 500–1, 512, 541.

89 Müller, *Heer*, chs 7, 8; Williamson Murray, *The Change in the European Balance of Power, 1938–39*, Princeton University Press, forthcoming, chs 5–7.

90 Ian Kershaw, *Der Hitler-Mythos*, Stuttgart, 1980, p. 123.

91 See Telford Taylor, *Munich*, New York, 1979, p. 877.

92 See the editors' remarks in *'Es spricht der Führer'*, pp. 230–1.

93 'Governesses': speech at Saarbrücken, 9 October 1938, Domarus, *Hitler*, p. 956; the rest from *'Es spricht der Führer'*, pp. 283, 281–2.

94 Fedor von Bock, quoted in Müller, *Heer*, p. 385.

95 Domarus, *Hitler*, p. 1058; Engel, *Heeresadjutant*, p. 30 (6 August 1938).

96 All from Thies, *Architekt der Weltherrschaft*, p. 116.

97 Quoted in Müller, *Heer*, p. 383.

98 See Mason, 'Innere Krise und Angriffskrieg 1938/1939', pp. 158–88 in F. Forstmaier and H. E. Volkmann (eds), *Wirtschaft und Rüstung am Vorabend des Zweiten Weltkrieges*, Düsseldorf, 1975; also his *Arbeiterklasse und Volksgemeinschaft*, pp. 119ff. For the criticisms, Jost Dülffer, 'Der Beginn des Krieges 1939: Hitler, die innere Krise, und das Mächtesystem', *Geschichte und Gesellschaft*, 2, 1976, 443–70, and Ludolf Herbst, 'Die Krise des nationalsozialistischen Regimes am Vorabend des Zweiten Weltkrieges und die forcierte Aufrüstung,' *VfZG*, 26, 1978, 347–92 (see particularly pp. 376–82). For public opinion, see Kershaw, *Mythos*, pp. 123–5, which suggests that only fear of war marred the popularity Hitler had achieved through foreign success in 1938–39.

99 John Gillingham, 'Ruhr coal miners and Hitler's war', *Journal of Social History*, summer 1982, 637–53.

100 Hitler speech summary, 22 August 1939 (probably from stenographic notes by Canaris), *Akten zur deutschen auswärtigen Politik*, Serie D, (Baden-Baden, Frankfurt, 1950–) (henceforth ADAP,D) 7: 168. A second version, written that evening by Admiral Boehm, suggests even less urgency: 'perhaps 10–15 years'. Mason prefers the Lochner document (ADAP,D, 7: 171–2 note), which ascribes to Hitler a lament that 'the Four-Year Plan [has] failed and we are finished, without victory in the coming war'. But the Lochner version will not bear much weight; its provenance, its divergences from all other accounts, and its piquant fabricated details (a Goering war-dance on the conference table) mark it as an Abwehr/resistance concoction for Western consumption. (On the sources, see Winfried Baumgart, 'Zur Ansprache Hitlers vor den Führern der Wehrmacht am 22. August 1939', *VfZG* 16 (1968): 120–49).

101 Mason, 'Innere Krise', pp. 182–4.

102 Dülffer, 'Beginn des Krieges', p. 464.

103 ADAP,D, 7: 168 (22 August 1939) and 8: 348 (23 November 1939).

104 Müller, *Heer*, p. 427.

105 All from Engel, *Heeresadjutant*, pp. 71–2 (20 January 1940); see also p. 52 (8 July 1939).

106 Rosenberg, *Tagebuch*, p. 98 (19 January 1940).

107 Friedrich Percyval Reck-Malleczewen, *Diary of a Man in Despair*, New York, 1970, pp. 109, 103.

108 'Reptile': *Monologe.*

109 ibid., p. 108 (25 October 1941). Hitler frequently remarked that the ideal solution would be to let the churches die out naturally (ibid., pp. 40–1, 67, 82–5), but he clearly intended to help them along (see especially ibid., p. 272).

110 Jodl memorandum, October 1946, in Percy Ernst Schramm, *Hitler: The Man and Military Leader*, Chicago, 1971, p. 204; Hillgruber, *Hitlers Strategie*, pp. 551–4 and note 84; Hildebrand, 'Weltmacht oder Niedergang: Hitlers Deutschland 1941–1945', in Oswald Hauser (ed.) *Weltpolitik II 1939–1945*, Göttingen, 1975, pp. 308–13.

111 See Kershaw, *Mythos*, pp. 186–91.

9

Hitler's Foreign Policy

Norman Rich

The very fact that the original volume for which this essay was prepared
was intended to mark the twenty-fifth anniversary of the publication of
A.J.P. Taylor's *The Origins of the Second World War* attests to the impact
of the book on historical thinking and its importance for all subsequent
considerations of the subject. One may disagree with those admirers of
Taylor who regard him as England's greatest living historian, but there
can be no argument that he is one of the most provocative and
controversial. And in none of his many works did he set forth more
provocative ideas than in that book [. . .]

It is a brilliant book, filled with astute observations and insights, with
challenges to conventional wisdom in almost every line. It is also a very
readable book, in part because it is so controversial, for it constantly
prods the assumptions of its readers, stirring up annoyance, argument –
and upon occasion, admiration. It has compelled every student of the
Nazi era to re-examine his or her own views about the subject, and over
the years some of the ideas once considered controversial have become
part of the conventional wisdom.

Taylor professes to be unhappy with his acceptance into the realm of
conventional wisdom. In his memoirs he observes that *Origins* 'despite
its defects, has now become the new orthodoxy, much to my alarm'. He
denies, however, that his book has the qualities I have described above
and which most of his colleagues have attributed to it. 'Where others see
it as original and provocative, I find it simply a careful scholarly work,
surprising only to those who had never been faced with the truth
before.'[1] Taylor's work may be scholarly, but it is not careful, and much
of it remains surprising to other historians, many of them as scholarly as
Taylor and considerably more careful, who have arrived at very different
interpretations of the 'truth'. For, contrary to what Taylor may think,

much of *Origins* has not become part of the new orthodoxy, and the parts of the book which continue to be most vigorously contested are those which aroused most controversy in the first place, namely his theories about the subject of the present essay, Hitler's foreign policy.

In *Origins*, Taylor challenges the interpretation of other historians who based their views about Hitler's foreign policy, at least in part, on documents presented in evidence at the Nuremberg trials. He points out, quite correctly, that these documents were 'loaded' and he maintains, without bothering to prove his point, that scholars who relied on them had found it impossible to escape from the load with which they were charged.[2] Taylor's method of escaping from that load was to ignore these documents altogether, and at the same time he cavalierly disregarded a great deal of other evidence which did not happen to fit with his own theories. Every historian, of course, is compelled to be selective in his use of evidence. The great weakness of Taylor's book, especially his treatment of Hitler's foreign policy, is the perverse nature of his selectivity and his deliberate rejection of much of the thoroughly reliable evidence on which the theories of many of his colleagues are based. An even graver weakness is that Taylor's own theories are frequently inconsistent and contradictory.

He rejects the Nazi claim that the formation of a Hitler government in January 1933 was a seizure of power, but he challenges the views of other historians as to why and how Hitler came to power:

> Whatever ingenious speculators, liberal or Marxist, might say, Hitler was not made Chancellor because he would help the German capitalists to destroy the trade unions, nor because he would give the German generals a great army, still less a great war.... He was not expected to carry through revolutionary changes in either home or foreign affairs. On the contrary the conservative politicians ... who recommended him to Hindenburg kept the key posts for themselves and expected Hitler to be a tame figurehead.

These expectations were confounded, Taylor says, for Hitler proved to be the most radical of revolutionaries. He made himself all-powerful dictator, destroyed political freedom and the rule of law, transformed German economics and finance, abolished the individual German states, and made Germany for the first time a united country.

In one sphere alone, Taylor says, Hitler changed nothing. 'His foreign policy was that of his predecessors, of the professional diplomats at the foreign ministry, and indeed of virtually all Germans. Hitler, too, wanted to free Germany from the restrictions of the [Versailles] peace treaty; to restore a great German army; and then to make Germany the greatest power in Europe from her natural weight.' The only difference between Hitler and 'virtually all Germans' were occasional differences in emphasis. Two paragraphs later, however, Taylor informs us that Hitler's foreign policy did in fact differ from that of at least some of his predecessors, for Hitler did not attempt to revive the 'world policy' which Germany had pursued before 1914, he made no plans for a great German battle fleet, he did not parade a grievance about lost colonies except to embarrass the British, and he was not at all interested in the Middle East. Taylor concludes that 'the primary purpose of his policy, if not the only one' was expansion into eastern Europe.

With that Taylor is saying that the differences between Hitler's foreign policy and that of his predecessors were in fact far more significant than mere matters of emphasis. He then goes on to describe precisely that quality which distinguished Hitler most radically not only from his predecessors but also from all other ordinary statesmen. 'The unique quality in Hitler was the gift of translating commonplace thoughts into action. . . . The driving force in him was a terrifying literalism.' There was nothing new about denunciations of democracy; it took Hitler to create a totalitarian dictatorship. There was nothing new about anti-Semitism; it took Hitler to push anti-Semitism to the gas chambers:

> It was the same with foreign policy. Not many Germans really cared passionately and persistently whether Germany again dominated Europe. But they talked as if they did. Hitler took them at their word. He made the Germans live up to their professions, or down to them – much to their regret.

More careful scholars may deplore Taylor's tendency to assume a knowledge of what 'not many Germans' cared for, and with what intensity, and his own frequent inconsistencies on that subject, but many historians share his views about the importance of Hitler's terrifying literalism and many had drawn attention to this quality long before the appearance of *Origins*. Taylor, however, always unwilling to be thought in agreement with generally accepted opinions, pours scorn on colleagues who have purported to discover in Hitler's writings and policy statements an exposition of the ideas which he proposed to translate into action. *Mein Kampf*, Hitler's table talk, the records of his top-secret conferences with his senior aides and officers in which he described his future plans in minute detail – all these revelations of Hitler's thinking are dismissed by Taylor as irrelevant flights of fancy, not to be taken seriously as indications of his true intentions. Writers of great authority, Taylor says, have seen in Hitler a system-maker who from the first deliberately prepared a great war that would make him master of the world. Taylor rejects such theories with some contempt. In his opinion, statesmen are too absorbed by events to follow a preconceived plan; such plans are in reality the creation of historians, and the systems attributed to Hitler are really those of Trevor-Roper, Elizabeth Wiskemann, and Alan Bullock. Taylor concludes that Hitler did indeed create systems, but these were no more than day-dreams concocted in his spare time.

Taylor attributes much of the success of Hitler's foreign policy to his very lack of preconceptions and prejudices, and cites as examples his willingness to conclude a non-aggression pact with Poland and his disregard of German nationalist sentiment in conceding the South Tyrol to Mussolini to secure Italian friendship. Apart from that, Taylor attributes Hitler's success primarily to his ability to play a waiting game, to take advantage of the offers and opportunities presented to him by his adversaries. Even then Taylor is not sure whether this technique was at first either conscious or deliberate. 'The greatest masters of statecraft are those who do not know what they are doing,' he says, thereby suggesting that Hitler was both a great master of statecraft and that he did not know what he was doing.[3] Yet Taylor has already stated, on the preceding page, that the primary purpose of Hitler's foreign policy was expansion into eastern Europe, and only a few pages later he says that the mainspring of Hitler's immediate policy had been the destruction of the Versailles treaty, although once this objective had been attained he was at a loss as to what to do next. As for any long-range plans, Taylor considers it 'doubtful whether he had any'.[4]

Taylor's inconsistencies continue. Although he states (p. 72) that the primary purpose of Hitler's policy was eastward expansion (which for Hitler meant the acquisition of living space or *Lebensraum*), he then denies (p. 105) that Hitler's desire for *Lebensraum* or economic motives in general were a cause of the Second World War. *Lebensraum* did not drive Germany to war, he says. Rather war, or a warlike policy, produced the demand for *Lebensraum*. Hitler and Mussolini were not driven by economic motives. Like most statesmen, they had an appetite for successes. They differed from others only in that their appetite was greater and that they fed it by more unscrupulous means. *Lebensraum* in its crudest sense meant a demand for empty space where Germans could settle but, Taylor argues, Germany was not over-populated in comparison with most European countries and there was no empty space in Europe. 'When Hitler lamented: "If only we had a Ukraine . . .", he seemed to suppose that there were no Ukrainians. Did he propose to exploit, or to exterminate them? Apparently he never considered the question one way or the other.'[5]

These statements glaringly expose the disastrous consequences of Taylor's refusal to acknowledge the significance of those sources in which Hitler set forth his ideological preconceptions and revealed his long-range plans based upon them. For Hitler *had* considered the question of what to do about the Ukrainians; he *did* propose to exploit or exterminate them – and all other non-Aryan peoples in eastern Europe besides. These plans were set forth in detail in *Mein Kampf*, and Hitler continued to expound them in almost identical terms in subsequent policy statements before and during the war. In rejecting the evidence of such policy statements, Taylor misses the absolutely fundamental point of Hitler's foreign policy – the nature of the literalism which he proposed to translate into practice.

Taylor recognizes that when Germany actually conquered the Ukraine in 1941, Hitler and his henchmen tried both methods, exploitation and extermination, but he comments that neither method brought them any economic advantages.[6] Here again Taylor completely misses the point. Hitler was not primarily concerned with any immediate economic advantage – in 1941 he still thought Russia could be conquered within weeks, and when it became obvious that this would not be possible it was too late to reverse his policies even if he wanted to do so, which he did not. The primary purpose of Hitler's foreign policy and his fundamental aim in the Second World War was the realization of his long-range plan for the acquisition of *Lebensraum* in eastern Europe which was to ensure the security and well-being of the German people for all time. As he specifically declared in *Mein Kampf* and subsequent policy statements, this conquest of territory should not include the conquest of people and the absorption of non-Aryans into the Germanic empire, for such absorption would dilute the purity of Germanic blood and thereby weaken the Germanic peoples. It was for this reason that the non-Aryans would have to be eliminated. This was the policy Hitler and his henchmen actually introduced in Russia after 1941, a policy which, as Taylor correctly says, brought them no economic advantage. On the contrary, the economic consequences of that policy, not to mention the moral, political and military consequences, were disastrous and contributed significantly to Germany's ultimate defeat. This policy, like the extermination of the Jews, cannot be equated with that of other statesmen with a mere appetite for success. It was the policy of a fanatic idealogue who ignored sober calculations of national interest in order to put his manic ideas into practice.

Taylor's belief that Hitler was simply a political opportunist without long-range purposes remains a central theme of his chronicle and analysis of the actual course of Hitler's foreign policy, in which he continues to present us with inconsistencies and contradictions. In his discussion of the annexation of Austria, for example, Taylor concedes that Hitler 'certainly meant to establish control over Austria', but he believes that the way in which this came about was for him a tiresome accident, 'an interruption of his long-term policy' (whereby Taylor seems to admit that there was in fact a long-term policy). At the same time he dismisses as a myth the theory that Hitler's seizure of Austria was a deliberate plot, devised long in advance:

> By the *Anschluss* – or rather by the way in which it was ac-complished – Hitler took the first step in the policy which was to brand him as the greatest of war criminals. Yet he took this step unintentionally. Indeed he did not know that he had taken it.[7]

Taylor is absolutely correct in saying that the *way* the *Anschluss* took place was to a large extent accidental and improvised, and that it was not carried out in accordance with a strategy prepared long in advance.

In the *Anschluss* crisis, Hitler's hand was forced by the actions of others and he took the final step of actually incorporating Austria into the Reich only when the events of the *Anschluss* convinced him he could afford to do so. But to say that he took this step unintentionally, or did not know he had taken it, is nonsense. On the first page of *Mein Kampf* and in numerous subsequent policy statements, Hitler declared that the incorporation of Austria into the Reich was the primary immediate objective of his policy, and the documentary evidence leaves no doubt whatever that the annexation of Austria was indeed a deliberate plot, prepared long in advance, and that it was conceived as the first step in the domination of eastern Europe.

In his analysis of the *Anschluss* and all other episodes in Hitler's foreign policy, Taylor challenges the theory that Hitler was operating according to a carefully prepared blueprint and timetable. Taylor's emphasis on the accidental and improvised quality in Hitler's actual execution of his policies is valid, but in tilting against the blueprint or timetable theories he seems to be setting up straw men in order to knock them down. It is true that some historians have written about blueprints and timetables, but even the most extreme champions of blueprint–timetable theories never suggested that Hitler had precisely conceived plans for every step of his expansionist policy and a precise timetable for carrying them out. Obviously he had to improvise, to take into account the constant fluctuations in the political scene, and to adjust to the moves of his opponents. All the blueprint–timetables people were saying was that Hitler had precisely defined war aims, primarily the conquest of *Lebensraum* in eastern Europe, that he had detailed plans for carrying them out, and that there was an uncanny consistency between the ideas expressed in his pre-war policy statements and the policies he actually put into effect.

When *Origins* was first published, much of the critical wrath directed against the book (and in certain quarters, much of the critical approval it received) was aroused by the belief that Taylor was defending Hitler. Nothing could have been further from the truth. In saying that in foreign policy alone Hitler changed nothing, that his foreign policy was that of his predecessors 'and indeed of virtually all Germans', he is not defending Hitler. Instead he is equating Hitler with 'virtually all Germans', as he makes clear in a later edition of *Origins*:

> Most of all, [Hitler] was the creation of German history and of the German present. He would have counted for nothing without the support and cooperation of the German people.... Hitler was a sounding-board for the German nation. Thousands, many hundred thousand, Germans carried out his evil orders without qualm or question.

And he concludes: 'In international affairs there was nothing wrong with Hitler except that he was a German.'[8]

With that Taylor reverts to the line adopted in his wartime book, *The Course of German History*, which some of his admirers have excused as a regrettable wartime polemic but which Taylor himself stoutly defended in a new preface to that book when it was republished in 1962, the year after the publication of *Origins*. In this preface he explains that his book had proved unacceptable to its original sponsors because it failed to show that Hitler was a bit of bad luck in German history and that all Germans, apart from a few wicked men, were bubbling over with enthusiasm for democracy, Christianity, or some other noble cause which would turn them into acceptable allies once we had liberated them from their tyrants. Not so, says Taylor. The entire course of German history:

> shows that it was no more a mistake for the German people to end up with Hitler than it is an accident when a river flows into the sea.... Nothing, it seems to me, has happened since [i.e. between 1945 and 1962] to disturb the conclusions at which I then arrived.

According to Taylor, the 70–80 million Germans have always feared the Slavs, and this fear underlay the Germans' plans for their conquest and extermination. 'No German of political consequence thought of accepting the Slavs as equals and living at peace with them' – and Taylor believes the Germans have not changed in this respect.[9] The Third Reich, he writes in *The Course of German History*, represented the deepest wishes of the German people. 'Every German desired the achievement which only total war could give. By no other means could the Reich be held together. It had been made by conquest and for conquest; if it ever gave up its career of conquest it would dissolve.' In contrast to the Germans there were the Slavic peoples 'with their deep sense of equality, their love of freedom, and their devotion to humanity', under whose auspices, Taylor believes, conditions in eastern Europe have improved immensely since the dark days of German and Magyar domination.[10]

Taylor continued to adhere to this interpretation of Germany and the Germans. In a discussion of the German problem as it emerged from the First World War, he writes that there has been an almost universal misunderstanding about the nature of that problem, 'a misunderstanding perhaps even shared by Hitler'. The Germans desired equality with the victor states, they wanted to cast off restrictions on their national sovereignty imposed by the Versailles treaty, and many non-Germans sympathized with what they regarded as these perfectly legitimate aspirations. But the inevitable consequences of fulfilling those German desires, Taylor says, was that Germany would become the dominant state in Europe. And what this would have meant for Europe can be seen from the German plans for the rearrangement of Europe if they had won the First World War, plans exposed in detail in 1961 and after in the publications of the German historian Fritz Fischer and his school:

It was a Europe indistinguishable from Hitler's empire at its greatest extent, including even a Poland and a Ukraine cleared of their native inhabitants. Hitler was treading, rather cautiously, in Bethmann's footsteps. There was nothing new or unusual in his aims or outlook.[11]

Taylor thus endorses the most extreme interpretations of Fischer and his followers who, with virtually unrestricted access to German archival records following Germany's defeat in the Second World War, put together a monumental collection of policy statements and speculations about German diplomatic and military goals drawn up by German leaders from every walk of life before and during the First World War.

Taylor and the more extreme representatives of the Fischer school may be right in assuming that a German government victorious in the First World War would have behaved exactly as Hitler did in the Second World War, or worse. The only record we have of a German government's actual treatment of Slavs, however, is that of Prusso-German rule over those segments of Poland taken by Prussia in the eighteenth-century partitions of Poland, at which time, it will be recalled, Slavic Russia took the lion's share. The Prusso-German treatment of the Poles has often been criticized, and with good reason, but during the entire period of German rule over the Poles there was never any suggestion of an attempt to exterminate them. What the Germans were trying to do was to Germanize them, and with notable lack of success.[12] It was Hitler, and only Hitler, who attempted to rectify what he regarded as this mistaken policy of Germanization through extermination – and not at all cautiously, either.

In the years since the Second World War, the United States seems to have replaced Germany as Taylor's principal political bugbear, and although he is not uncritical of the Soviet Union, he has complacently accepted that state's assumption of the role of protector and spokesman of the Slavic peoples and all other nationalities of Eastern Europe. 'I had not the slightest illusion about the tyranny and brutality of Stalin's regime,' Taylor writes in his memoirs:

But I had been convinced throughout the nineteen thirties that Soviet predominance in eastern Europe was the only alternative to Germany's and I preferred the Soviet one. Moreover I believed that East European states, even when under Soviet control, would be preferable to what they had been between the wars, as has proved to be the case. Hence Soviet ascendency of eastern Europe had no perils for me.'

Taylor defends the communist takeover in Czechoslovakia and the Russian suppression of the Hungarian revolution. 'Better a Communist regime supported by Soviet Russia . . . than an anti-Communist regime led by Cardinal Mindszenty. Hence my conscience was not troubled by the Soviet intervention.' Taylor's conscience was similarly untroubled when it was learned that the British art historian Anthony Blunt had spied for the Russians, and he successfully opposed Blunt's expulsion from the British Academy.[13] In notable contrast to this attitude towards the Russians, Taylor has condemned almost every act of American foreign policy. At the time of the Korean war, Taylor, who claims to have been a staunch opponent of appeasement in the 1930s, declared appeasement to be 'the noblest word in the diplomat's language'.[14] 'Even now,' he wrote in 1956, 'which of us on the Left could say, hand on heart, that in a conflict between the United States and the Soviet Union our individual sympathies would be with the United States?'[15]

Such comments aroused consternation among many Americans and their British friends, and they were clearly intended to do so. For in his most recent books, as in *Origins* and indeed all his works, Taylor continues to play the role of gadfly, often striking out wildly and unfairly but often telling us unpalatable truths which other commentators lack the imagination to perceive or the audacity to express. In this essay I have not been sparing of my criticism of Taylor. I find many of his ideas ridiculous and his prejudices downright shameful for a historian, and I am irritated by his persistent efforts to surprise and confound his readers. Yet he has always been and he remains one of the most stimulating and readable of historians, whose great contribution is not his own scholarship but his challenges to the values and assumptions of his audience. In response to critics of *Origins* who accused him, quite mistakenly, of failing to condemn Hitler's criminality with sufficient vigor, Taylor confessed that he himself could not get it out of his head that Hitler was an indescribably wicked man:

> But this is because I belonged to his generation. He was as wicked as he could be. But he was only a beginner. The rulers of the United States and of Soviet Russia are now cheerfully contemplating a hideous death for seventy million people or perhaps a hundred and fifty million people in the first week of the next war. What has Hitler to show in comparison with this? I think we had better leave Hitler's immorality alone as long as we go clanking around with nuclear weapons.[16]

[. . .] The publication of *The Origins of the Second World War* aroused enormous furor in the historical profession and provoked a reconsideration of the policies of all the major powers involved. So far as Hitler's foreign policy was concerned, the principal historical debate set off by Taylor's book was whether, as the Nuremberg prosecution and numerous historians maintained, his policy was dedicated to the achievement of long-range objectives, his strategy and tactics worked out long in advance; or whether, as Taylor contended, Hitler was an opportunist and improviser who took advantage of the accidental shifts in the international situation and the mistakes of his opponents. Taylor says that this debate is now sterile, but in stirring it up in the first place he compelled many historians to revise or modify their views and to recognize how much of Hitler's foreign policy was in fact improvised and opportunistic. Moreover, although the debate as originally formulated may be sterile, it remains central to controversies over Hitler's policies in general, despite changes in the terminology employed, differences in emphasis, and the introduction of new varieties of evidence.

Because of the sheer amount of historical literature dealing with Hitler's foreign policy that has been produced during the past quarter-century, it is manifestly impossible to provide an adequate evaluation of the individual works representing the various schools of thought on the subject in the scope of a brief essay – a mere list of such works would fill a substantial volume. I have therefore confined myself to a short survey of what appear to me to be the principal lines of interpretation and controversy.[17]

Let me dispose at once of the small group of writers who seek to defend Hitler, who represent him as a man of peace who sought only justice and equality for Germany, as the hapless victim of the implacable hostility of Germany's enemies and of Bolshevik-Jewish-capitalist conspiracies. Taylor describes one of these apologies as a 'perfectly plausible book', which it is not.[18] Moreover, all such works are characterized by flagrant misrepresentations or outright falsifications of the evidence and do not deserve to be considered in a discussion of serious historical scholarship.

Apart from the old and neo-Nazis, those writers bearing the heaviest and most obvious ideological burden are the members of the Soviet and East European school of thought, which has been joined by a number of Marxists and other left-wing intellectuals in the west. This group represents Hitler, Nazism and fascism in general as the products and instruments of capitalist-imperialist society, and the Second World War as a western-capitalist conspiracy to destroy the Soviet Union. From this school we hear nothing about the Anglo-French guarantees to Poland in 1939 or the Hitler–Stalin pact, but much about appeasement which is generally interpreted as a diplomatic maneuver to direct Nazi aggression against Russia. Proceeding from these assumptions, the members of this school have no trouble finding and intepreting evidence which proves their case.

Theoretically akin to the East Europeans and their adherents, but on the whole far more honest in their use of evidence and imaginative in the questions they raise, are the members of what might be called the 'fundamental forces' school of thought. These scholars regard Hitler and the Nazi movement as the products of fundamental forces in German political, economic and social life, and of the institutions, modes of thought and behavioral patterns developed in the course of the German historical experience. In their basic assumptions, the members of this school are thus in general agreement with Taylor, especially his *Course of*

German History, but they have gone far beyond his simplistic explanations and generalizations. In their own search for explanations of the Hitler phenomenon, they have produced many profound and original studies of German life and society, and altogether they have enormously enriched our understanding of German history and institutions. There is nevertheless a certain uniformity and even sterility about their work. In proceeding from the assumption that Hitlerism was a product of fundamental forces in German history, they tend to search for and focus on those aspects of the German past which can be interpreted as being precursors of the Nazi movement. In the process they frequently ignore the contemporary circumstances in which those policies were conceived and conducted, or fail to take adequate account of the differences in values and attitudes of earlier epochs. And because their research is dedicated to discovering those qualities in German life that produced Hitler, the lines of their research as well as their conclusions are to a large extent predetermined.

Inseparable from the 'fundamental forces' school, but requiring special mention because of its importance in contemporary German historiography, is the 'continuity' school of German history. The members of this group differ from the 'fundamental forces' scholars in their special emphasis on the consistency in the aims and methods of German leaders, and in their efforts to demonstrate that the policies of Hitler were a continuation of policies already pursued or planned by the rulers of Austria, Prussia, Imperial Germany, and Weimar. They too are thus in basic agreement with the Taylor thesis about German history, and in their research they have discovered an enormous quantity of evidence to substantiate that thesis. But, as in the case of the 'fundamental forces' school, the results of that research are to a large extent predetermined, and as one recent critic has commented, 'with the exercise of a little ingenuity almost anything can be fitted into this concept'.[19]

To be fair to the 'fundamental forces–continuity' historians, they do not all share the view that the Germans are invested with a particularly heavy dose of original sin. A number of them stress the importance of the peculiar nature of the German historical experience, the devastating effects of the Thirty Years' War, and the more lasting effects of the treaties of Westphalia ending that war, which sanctioned permanent French and Swedish interference in German affairs and for over two centuries halted German national development. Others have drawn attention to the importance of geographical factors, the position of the Germans in central Europe between the French in the west and the Slavs in the east, the Germans' lack of readily defensible or even definable frontiers and their consequent emphasis on the need for a strong army.

Opposed to both the 'fundamental forces' and 'continuity' schools are historians who refuse to accept the theory that Hitler was an inevitable product of German history or that his policies were simply the continuation of policies of earlier German leaders. Instead they regard him as a unique phenomenon in the German historical experience, and his regime and its bestial policies as a disastrous deviation from the main lines of German history. Members of this 'discontinuity' school are of course unable to deny the existence of continuity, for all history is a continuous process, but they contend that both Hitler's domestic and foreign policies represented departures from previous German political and diplomatic traditions. This was particularly true of his foreign policy which, unlike all previous German foreign policies, was consciously based on racist ideology, conducted with revolutionary methods and dedicated to the realization of unlimited aims. 'Discontinuity' historians concede that other German leaders and many ordinary Germans were anti-Semitic (as were the leaders and peoples of many other nations), but they insist that only Hitler advocated and actually attempted to carry out the total extermination of the Jews; other German leaders may have desired the acquisition of additional territories in Europe or overseas, but only Hitler conducted a war of conquest which involved the removal or extermination of the indigenous population.

Members of the 'discontinuity' school, with their interpretation of Hitler as a unique phenomenon in German history, have been accused of attempting to exonerate the German people as a whole from blame for the Nazi experience, and the arguments of some of them are certainly intended to achieve this purpose. Whatever their motives, the members of the 'discontinuity' school cannot avoid dealing with the question of how the German people as a whole accepted Hitler, how so many Germans were able to condone his bestial policies, and how so many were willing to put these policies into effect. Their attempts at explanation often bring them close to the 'fundamental forces' school, but with notable differences in emphasis. Whereas the 'fundamental forces' historians regard the Nazi experience as the inevitable product of the German past, their opponents contend that it required the demonic genius of a Hitler to mobilize all the most depraved features of German thought and behavior, that his propaganda successfully deceived the German people about his true intentions (as it deceived foreign governments with far better access to information), and that his totalitarian government successfully repressed all movements of dissent.

Into the controversies among the 'fundamental forces', 'continuity' and 'discontinuity' schools fits the debate over the primacy of foreign politics versus the primacy of domestic politics. Is a country's foreign policy based in large measure on foreign political considerations and conducted quasi-independently of domestic affairs? Or is foreign policy conducted primarily in response to domestic problems and pressures? In dealing with Hitler's foreign policy, scholars who argue in favor of the primacy of foreign policy believe that his domestic program was designed to serve the purposes of his foreign policy; whereas their opponents believe his foreign policy was the product of domestic necessities.

Closely linked with this debate, and more specifically related to the Third Reich, is the controversy between what have been called the 'functionalists' and the 'intentionalists' (terms which seem to me only to add confusion to the argument). The 'functionalists' agree fundamentally with the primacy of domestic politics viewpoint. They contend that Nazi foreign policy was far more the outcome (function) of domestic dynamisms and crises within Hitler's Germany than the result of rational planning, that it was the result of the frantic but completely uncoordinated activity of competing power groups which produced a progressive radicalization of their measures. The 'functionalists' emphasize the polycentric nature of the Nazi government and argue that Hitler, far from being an all-powerful dictator and decision-maker, was on the contrary a weak leader who pursued radical programs to ward off the rivalry of his associates and to escape from the realities of his own weakness. The 'intentionalists', on the other hand, believe that Hitler himself made the major foreign policy decisions of the Nazi state, that he pursued politically intelligible goals, and that the best way to understand the foreign policy of the Third Reich is to understand the personality of Hitler and his ideology.

In their theoretical conceptions at any rate, the 'fundamental forces' school and the 'functionalist' historians deny the importance of the personal qualities of Hitler, and in effect they are saying that if Hitler had not appeared on the German political scene, his place would have been filled by a Müller or a Schmidt. Their arguments are ingenious and they have contributed much to our understanding of the internal dynamics of the Third Reich, but they have obviously not convinced most scholars dealing with the Nazi question, if one is to judge by the volume of research devoted to the background, personality and ideas of Hitler, or by the central position Hitler continues to occupy in virtually all studies of the Nazi state.

What is surprising, in view of the controversy aroused by Taylor's book and the immense amount of research devoted to the Nazi question since its publication, is how little the fundamental lines of interpretation and argument have in fact changed, and to what extent historians are still at a loss to explain the Nazi phenomenon. This situation may be observed in numerous works that have been published analyzing or reviewing interpretations of the Nazi question.[20] The most recent of these is by the German scholar Eberhard Jäckel. His *Hitler in History* summarizes the results of the latest research and comes to conclusions with which I agree on the whole and which I would like to use as a vehicle for conveying my own views.[21]

Jäckel makes the same point as Taylor that Hitler was not the pawn of big business, the Junkers, the army, or other established vested interests in Germany. Representatives of these interests recommended his appointment to Hindenburg in order to make use of the popular support he enjoyed, confident that they could control and manipulate him. Instead Hitler used the power conferred upon him to establish his totalitarian state. Those vested interests that did not seem a threat to his authority and which co-operated with his policies were absorbed into his political and social system, but he disregarded them completely in making all major policy decisions.[22]

It is over the question of Hitler's policies and their implementation that Jäckel, and I believe most historians who have worked through the evidence, would disagree with one of Taylor's most provocative points, namely that Hitler did not know what he was doing and merely took advantage of the opportunities presented to him by his opponents (although as mentioned earlier, Taylor himself is not altogether consistent on this point). Jäckel, who has written one of the most authoritative books on Hitler's ideology, says about this question: 'Perhaps never in history did a ruler write down before he came to power what he was to do afterwards as precisely as did Adolf Hitler. Hitler set himself two goals: a war of conquest and the elimination of the Jews.' Jäckel goes on to review Hitler's war plans, the fundamental points of which he had already formulated in the 1920s, and comments:[23]

> Without knowing his war plans we cannot evaluate how he prepared for, initiated and conducted the war ... Hitler's ultimate goal was the establishment of a greater Germany than had ever existed before in history. The way to this greater Germany was a war of conquest fought mainly at the expense of Soviet Russia. It was in the east of the European continent that the German nation was to gain living space (*Lebensraum*) for generations to come. This expansion would in turn provide the foundation for Germany's renewed position as a world power. Militarily the war would be easy because Germany would be opposed only by a disorganized country of Jewish Bolsheviks and incompetent Slavs.

Before launching his war of conquest in the east, however, Hitler had to meet certain fundamental preconditions. The first was the consolidation of his authority in Germany and rearmament. The second was to put an end to the possibility of a stab in the back in the west while Germany was at war in the east, for a successful attack on the Rhine-Ruhr industrial areas would deal a mortal blow to Germany's ability to wage war of any kind. France was the only power capable of striking such a blow: France, therefore, had to be eliminated as a military power before Germany could launch its campaign in the east. To counter the power of France, Hitler hoped to win alliances with Britain, which was to be offered German support to retain its global empire, and with Italy, which was to be offered supremacy in the Mediterranean and assurances of continued control over the South Tyrol, despite that region's large German population. Hitler gained his alliance with Italy but by 1937 he had despaired of winning an alliance with Britain, although at least until

1941 he continued to hope that such an alliance might yet be possible. 'Even a cursory glance at the diplomatic and military history of the Third Reich demonstrates that this program served as an outline of those German policies that were defined by Hitler himself,' Jäckel says, 'and there is ample documentary evidence to prove that he always kept this outline in mind. It was, of course, not a timetable or even a detailed prospectus, but a definite and structured list of objectives, priorities and conditions.'[24]

Jäckel believes that the controversy between the 'functionalists' and the 'intentionalists' is based on a profound misunderstanding on both sides. 'There is abundant evidence', he says, 'that all major decisions in the Third Reich were made by Hitler, and there is equally abundant evidence that the regime was largely anarchic and can thus be described as a polycracy. The misunderstanding is to suppose that the two observations are contradictory and that only one of them can be true.' Jäckel himself sees no contradiction here. 'The monocrat comes to power on a polycratic basis, supported by conflicting groups that paralyze each other, and he maintains his power by ruling polycratically – that is, by playing the conflicting groups against each other. It is precisely this method that permits him to make the major decisions alone.'[25] The ideas, too, were Hitler's. 'He undoubtedly developed a program of his own, individually and alone', Jäckel says, but he goes on to observe that 'his program must have coincided with the deeper tendencies and ambitions of his country and of his time. We may not be able to explain this, and yet we have to recognize it. Was he an author or an executor, a producer or a product?'[26]

In dealing with this question, Jäckel confesses his inability to provide definite answers, and refuses to take refuge in simplistic explanations. 'What the fact-bound researcher can state and perhaps explain is only that the governments of the Weimar Republic did not seriously prepare for war, whereas Hitler did.'[27] He points out that both the Japanese and Italians preceded the Germans in going to war for imperial reasons in the 1930s, and he might have added that the Poles and Hungarians were happy to join Hitler in the final spoliation of Czechoslovakia in 1939, that the Russians joined in the spoliation of Poland later in that same year and that they went on to take over the Baltic states, Northern Bukovina (at the expense of Romania) and to go to war against Finland. He might have added further that so-called democratic societies have not been altogether pacific in the past, that Britain and France, having acquired the world's largest overseas empires, were hardly in a moral position to point a finger of guilt at peoples (or regimes) which attempted to acquire similar empires, that the Soviet Union continues to control with an iron hand the multitude of national minorities conquered by the regimes of the tsars, and that the United States policy of westward expansion, in the course of which the white man ruthlessly thrust aside the 'inferior' indigenous population, served as the model for Hitler's entire concept of *Lebensraum*.

Jäckel makes no attempt to exonerate the Germans. He stresses that they supported Hitler and carried out his criminal orders, and that their support and obedience was voluntary and not the result of terror and repression. Yet he believes 'this pessimistic view cannot and should not lead to a blanket moral condemnation of the Germans living at that time, for they were as a whole no worse and no better than the generations before and after them. But they were subjected to ordeals and to temptations that others escaped.' Again Jäckel attempts to avoid facile explanations. He is obviously uncomfortable with many of the schools of historical thought discussed earlier in this essay, especially attempts to explain the origins of National Socialism through polemical allusions to one's own political or ideological adversaries. 'Such biased efforts are not only unscholarly but in most cases thoroughly contemptible.' Jäckel believes it is vital to remember that the vast majority of Germans were denied the kind of information that ordinarily builds the foundation of public opinion and that, although we now know that Hitler intended to implement the program presented in such detail in *Mein Kampf*, it is 'beyond doubt that the Germans did not grant him power in order to implement that program'.[28]

But then Jäckel plunges into a simplistic explanation of his own and seems to fall squarely into the 'fundamental forces' school of thought. Hitler's foreign policy followed a rigid plan, he says, but that plan 'was not wholly incongruent with general developments and its realization was therefore ensured'. Later imperialistic territorial conquest was presaged in the development of Germany, just as it was in the development of Japan and Italy. 'Thus Hitler, notwithstanding his own great personal responsibility in shaping events, was no more than the executor of a longstanding tendency.'[29]

Here I part company with Jäckel, with whose views I am in almost complete agreement up to this point. All events, of course, are conditioned by the past, but to say that Hitler was no more than the executor of a longstanding tendency, thereby implying that the man and his policies were an inevitable product of German history, seems to me to place a dangerous emphasis on the principle of historical determinism and suggests that there is nothing an individual or nation can do to escape the fate dictated by its heritage.[30] To me there is something profoundly unhistorical about the 'fundamental forces' school of thought for, by concentrating on problems that apparently foreshadow future developments, the historian may neglect or underestimate the importance of other aspects of a nation's past that may have been far more significant in an earlier age, or at least appeared so to perceptive contemporary observers. Such an approach in effect denies the importance of human beings in history, the role of thinkers, artists, leaders in a people's development, nor does it make sufficient allowance for the many accidents which befall a people (plagues, famines, foreign conquest) which are not necessarily the product of their heritage.

For the study of German history, the inevitability thesis has had the unfortunate result of requiring an emphasis on those features of the German past which seem to have produced the Third Reich and which made Germany different from, and by implication inferior to, more modern, moral and democratic societies. Such an attitude has led to a certain smugness if not to outright racism on the part of many non-Germans (vide Taylor), and to an exaggerated moral self-flagellation on the part of the Germans themselves. It has also contributed to a curiously myopic quality in many works on German history, which by focusing exclusively and obsessively on the problems of Germany and the Germans tend to ignore comparable problems in other societies and fail to take sufficient account of the terrifying universality of the German historical experience. If German history has anything to teach, it is that the veneer of civilization in all societies is perilously thin, and that the qualities we most admire in western societies are in no way guaranteed by western traditions, institutions or national character, but must be safeguarded by eternal vigilance.

Notes

1 A.J.P. Taylor, *A Personal History*, New York, 1983, p. 235.
2 A.J.P. Taylor, *The Origins of the Second World War*, first published in 1961. My references are to the American paperback Premier edition, Greenwich, Conn., 1963, p. 19.
3 ibid., pp. 69–73.
4 ibid., p. 107.
5 ibid., p. 105.
6 ibid., p. 105.
7 ibid., p. 146.
8 Foreword to a new edition of the *Origins*, 'Second thoughts'; Penguin paperback edition, Harmondsworth, 1964, pp. 26–7.
9 A.J.P. Taylor, *The Course of German History*, first published in 1945. My references are to the American paperback Capricorn edition, New York, 1962, pp. 7–8.
10 *Course of German History*, pp. 213–14, 222.
11 A.J.P. Taylor, 'War origins again', reprinted from *Past and Present* (April 1965) in E.M. Robertson (ed.) *The Origins of the Second World War: Historical Interpretations*, London, 1971, pp. 139–40. Bethmann was German chancellor at the beginning of the First World War.
12 Taylor takes it for granted that Habsburg rule was German, but the Habsburgs made no efforts comparable to those of Prussia to Germanize the Slavs, and Hitler certainly never regarded their policies as a model for his own.
13 *Personal History*, pp. 181, 214, 270–1.
14 ibid., p. 182.
15 *New Statesman*, 52, 1956, 523–4, quoted by John W. Boyer, 'A.J.P. Taylor and the art of modern history', *Journal of Modern History*, 49, March 1977, 56.
16 'War origins again', p. 138.
17 All references to schools of thought must be qualified by observing that there

are sharp differences of opinion among scholars who adopt the same general approach to historical problems. For a more detailed survey-analysis of major historical interpretations, see the recent intelligent and level-headed study by John Hiden and John Farquharson, *Explaining Hitler's Germany. Historians and the Third Reich*, Totowa, NJ, 1983.

18 'War origins again', p. 138.
19 Hiden and Farquharson, *Explaining Hitler's Germany*, p. 56.
20 The French scholar Pierre Ayçoberry, for example, concludes: 'One cannot say for certain whether the Third Reich was a radical departure from, or a continuation of preceding regimes. The question remains open, like a gaping hole in the historical consciousness. We still have not settled with the past.' (*The Nazi Question. An Essay on the Interpretations of National Socialism, 1922–1975*), New York, 1981, p. 225.) Anthony Adamthwaite, writing in 1984, takes a parallel line. Many interesting questions remain unanswered he says, 'but in the last analysis Hitler and Nazism can be understood, interpreted, or used as each generation wishes' ('War origins again', *Journal of Modern History*, 56, March 1984, 114).
21 Eberhard Jäckel, *Hitler in History*, Hanover, NH, 1984. My own interpretations may be found in 'Die Deutsche Frage und der nationalsozialistische Imperialismus: Rückblick und Ausblick', in Josef Becker and Andreas Hillgruber (eds), *Die Deutsche Frage im 19. und 20. Jahrhundert*, Munich, 1983, pp. 373–92, and in the introductions and conclusions to my two volumes, *Hitler's War Aims*. vol. 1, *Ideology, the Nazi State and the Course of Expansion*; vol. 2, *The Establishment of the New Order*, New York, 1973–4.
22 Jäckel, *Hitler in History*, ch. 1.
23 ibid., pp. 23–5.
24 ibid., pp. 25–6.
25 ibid., p. 30.
26 ibid., p. 43
27 ibid., p. 40
28 ibid., pp. 90, 94, 96.
29 ibid., p. 104.
30 In an earlier draft of his book, which his publisher kindly sent me for purposes of writing this review article, Jäckel had emphasized the quality of inevitability more specifically. In this draft version he wrote that the realization of Hitler's foreign policy plan was ensured because it 'derived from and conformed to' general developments, and that Hitler 'was no more than the executor of the inevitable' (rather than merely the executor of a long-standing tendency).

10

Hitler's War and the German Economy: A Reinterpretation[1]

R.J. Overy

When the Allied intelligence services at the end of the Second World War examined the performance of the German war economy a paradox was uncovered. Instead of operating at full throttle, the German economy appeared to have been only partially mobilized for war until 1942, despite the fact that Germany had embarked on a programme of European conquest in 1939 for which it was assumed by the Allies that large military and economic resources were necessary. The traditional explanation that this prompted was that the German economy, encumbered with the apparatus of Nazism, performed its tasks inefficiently.[2] This view laid the foundation for an interpretation based on the concept of the *Blitzkrieg*.[3] According to this explanation the German economy was mobilized at a low level because Hitler had intended it to be that way, partly to complement the military concept of the 'lightning war'; partly to take account of the peculiar administrative and political circumstances of the Nazi state; but primarily because he wanted to reduce the burden of war on the German people and thus remove the prospect of an internal upheaval. It was to be 'a system of waging war without reducing civilian consumer standards'.[4] According to these arguments the fear of an internal crisis reached a peak in 1939 and made necessary the launching of the first of those short wars for which the German economy had been specially prepared.[5] This was rearmament in 'width' rather than 'depth'; war in short bursts rather than 'total war'.

Although the military concept of the *Blitzkrieg* has been critically re-examined, the idea of the *Blitzkrieg* economy, and the reasons for it, still remain an orthodoxy. The purpose of this article is twofold: first, to carry out the same critical examination of the concept of *Blitzkrieg* economics to show that in most respects the concept does not fit with the actual facts of German economic life between 1936 and 1942; second, to suggest an alternative interpretation based on a reassessment of Hitler's intentions and the response of the German economy to the demands of war in 1939. It will be argued below that Hitler's plans were large in scale, not limited, and were intended for a major war of conquest to be fought considerably later than 1939. The fact that the large armament failed to materialize was not due to any *Blitzkrieg* conception, but to the fact that economic preparations were out of step with the course of foreign policy; a dislocation that was exacerbated after 1939 by a combination of poor planning, structural constraints within German industry, and weaknesses in the process of constructing and communicating policy. The intention was large-scale mobilization. Hitler's object, in the long run, was European conquest and world hegemony.[6]

I

If the idea of the *Blitzkrieg* economy is to work, it must be shown that Hitler, strongly influenced by short-term economic and political considerations, conceived of, planned and launched a war based on this economic policy in the late summer of 1939.[7] Yet all the evidence – or rather lack of it – suggests that short-term economic and social considerations played only the smallest part in Hitler's foreign policy calculations. If anything, it was the part that he deliberately chose to ignore, since those who understood the intelligence available tried without success, throughout the year leading to war, to demonstrate that the Allies were economically stronger than the Axis and that German economic preparations were inadequate.[8] The reason for this situation is clear enough. Hitler did not think in narrow 'economic' or 'social' terms. He was happy for the economy to perform the political tasks which he set it to do: the creation of employment before 1937, and preparation for war thereafter. But he left Schacht and big business to achieve the first, and, unwisely, expected Goering to achieve the second. His concerns were not primarily with the day-to-day problems of economics, living standards and social peace, as were those of his contemporaries, but with questions of race and foreign policy. What economic views he had were placed in the context of his broader military or social ambitions in a general and uncritical way. Of plans for a *Blitzkrieg* economy before 1939 there is little sign. Hitler provided no detailed analysis of how such an economy might work, no systematic intervention in economic affairs, no plan to switch abruptly from consumer goods to arms and back again, whether in response to raw material shortages or to the monthly reports of his internal security police. Economic questions, when considered at all, were all subsumed into his great plans for the future; the plans for *Lebensraum* and the plan to wage a 'life and death struggle' for the survival of the race.[9]

Indeed the tenor of all Hitler's statements before the outbreak of war pointed towards, not *Blitzkrieg*, but its exact opposite, the prospect of a massive and long-term war of the continents from which Germany would emerge either victorious or destroyed[10] and towards which he believed himself to be progressively restructuring the German economy. For this struggle he announced in May 1939 that 'the government must be prepared for a war of ten to fifteen years' duration' during which the requirements of the army in particular would become a 'bottomless pit'.[11] Most important of all, the lesson he drew from the First World War was not that the hardships of total mobilization should be avoided but, on the contrary, the belief that 'the unrestricted use of all resources is essential'.[12] To the leaders of the Armed Forces to whom Hitler delivered this lecture, the sentiments were unrealistic to say the least. But for the historian it is almost the only evidence available on what Hitler's long-term intentions for the economy were; and it is hardly the language of *Blitzkrieg*. Any review of the projects that Hitler had authorized under the Four-Year Plan and German rearmament confirms this wider intention. The naval programme, the enormous fortifications designed to be completed only in the 1950s, the synthetic oil and rubber programmes, the steel programme of the Reichswerke 'Hermann Goering' were large and expensive projects, launched with Hitler's blessing, but designed for completion only in the long term. Such projects had already begun well before 1939, diverting resources of labour, raw materials and machinery from the consumer sector to the sectors necessary for large-scale war.[13] If it is argued that Hitler's intention had been a limited war fought in 1939 together with the safeguarding of domestic living standards, such preparations did not make sense. But that is not what Hitler intended. Hitler wanted a healthy and expanding economy so that he could convert it to the giant task of European and Asian conquest.

Some of the confusion over Hitler's intentions has been fuelled by his own uncertainty about how an economy worked. He expected much more to be delivered than was actually possible, and had only a very hazy idea of economic time-scale. He wanted a high level of preparation for war and at the same time wanted *Autobahnen* and the *Volkswagen* for the purposes of completing the material structure of the *Volksgemeinschaft* [People's community].[14] He wanted massive building programmes on an unprecedented scale. Speer calculated the cost of 25 milliard marks.[15] Significantly the buildings were scheduled for completion by 1950 to coincide with the achievement of total victory, suggesting that Hitler had already seen his coming war as a long-term struggle of heroic proportions.[16] These many ambitions betrayed Hitler's inability to see the economy as a whole, to grasp that cars and tanks could not be produced at the same time, that fortifications vied for resources with the rebuilding of Berlin. It is this inability that has been mistaken for a positive desire to restrict military production in favour of the civilian sector. This was not so. It was a result of Hitler's curiously compartmentalized view of German affairs which persuaded him that each aim was possible simultaneously. His petulant reaction to all advice during the war to restrict his 'peace-time' projects demonstrated the confusion of his economic thinking.[17]

But, it will be objected, how can the outbreak of war in 1939 be accounted for if not in terms of a short war designed to suit the special economic and social crisis of 1939? Put another way, can it be explained in terms of the large-scale total war-effort which Hitler's plans clearly did express? The answer to both questions lies in the particular circumstances of the Polish crisis. It is necessary to digress a little to examine this explanation because it is on Hitler's intention that so much of the argument rests. The first point to make is that Hitler did not expect a European war to break out in 1939. Of course there was an element of risk as in any act of aggression. But all the evidence shows that from 1938 onwards, and increasingly after March 1939, Hitler had persuaded himself that the western Allies would not take action over Poland and, by implication, over further German action in the east.[18] As late as August 1939 Hitler expressed his conviction to Ciano 'that the conflict will be localized' and that it was 'out of the question that this struggle can begin war'.[19] The head of Hitler's military planning staff was allowed to take leave during August, and even to have it extended until the 18th, so confident were the armed forces that a general crisis would not develop over the Danzig question.[20] When news of the pact with Stalin arrived, Hitler was finally, and it could be argued, sensibly, convinced that the West would not attack.[21] Any hesitation before the invasion of Poland was caused by Italy's panic and the prospect of a second Munich, but on no account did the outbreak of a general war seem any more likely to Hitler in August 1939 than in September 1938 – if anything less so. Indeed, all the intelligence available to the Germans of Allied rearmament and strength confirmed that neither Britain nor France was in a position to risk war with the Axis powers.[22] The general war for which Hitler was preparing was not supposed to break out in 1939, and even when it did, would, according to Hitler, peter out as the Western powers grew tired of their gesture.[23] He did not shirk the war when it came, not because he had any *Blitzkrieg* economic plan prepared, but for the quite different reason that he believed in the long run that the economic and moral resources of the Reich, when stretched to their utmost, would prove greater than those available to the Allies.[24] In other words, even when general war broke out against his expectations in 1939 Hitler immediately thought in terms of the large-scale contest which had coloured so much of his thinking beforehand.

The second point to emphasize is the long-term nature of Hitler's imperial ambitions. The fact that the Polish question led to general war prematurely in 1939 obscured the character of the imperialism, which was designed in two complementary stages.[25] The first was to create a military-economic core for the new German empire comprising

Germany, Austria, Czechoslovakia and parts of Poland, to be achieved without a general war. This core was to be protected by fortifications to east and west and was to provide the resources of the autarkic economy.[26] The achievement of this first stage was to be guaranteed by neutralizing the threat of intervention by concessions to one or other potential enemy, Britain in 1938, Russia in 1939. The second stage involved using this large economic region as the base for launching war against the major powers. It was for this racial struggle that the German economy was to be prepared. Much of the evidence from the pre-war period shows the extent to which Hitler's view of foreign policy was coloured by such irrational biological and geo-political perspectives. France, Russia, Britain and even the United States were the main enemies, a conviction that wavered only with the tactics of diplomacy.[27] This interpretation of Hitler's economic and military ambitions, which required a large rearmament and a continuing militarization of German society, accords much more satisfactorily with the evidence of war preparations, most of which pointed to a war to be fought in the mid-1940s or later. The first stage of the build-up of the Luftwaffe was not to be completed until 1942, and it was to be prepared for a long war only by 1947 or 1950.[28] The naval programme was due for completion only by the mid-1940s.[29] The plans for refurbishing the Reichsbahn laid down in 1939 were to reach fruition in 1944.[30] Hitler himself authorized Keitel to inform the armed forces that they should concentrate on training and internal development until at least 1944 or 1945.[31] And the impression that was given to the Italian leadership throughout 1938 and 1939 was that the war with the major powers, the larger and inevitable conflict, would be postponed until 1942 at the earliest.[32]

Finally, it must be remembered that German strategy was very much dictated by Hitler's personal and fantastic perspectives on world affairs, so different from those of his contemporaries abroad. The *Blitzkrieg* strategy suggests a degree of economic and political realism, and of careful calculation, which the evidence of Hitler's activities does not confirm. Throughout 1938 and 1939 he became more and more pre-occupied with the fulfilment of a German destiny to which he alone claimed the insight, and for which he was quite prepared for the German people to bear the severest consequences. 'War does not frighten me', Hitler told Dahlerus. 'If privation lies ahead of the German people, I shall be the first to starve and set my people a good example. It will spur them to superhuman efforts'.[33] When he told his generals in 1939 that he was the first man since Charlemagne to hold ultimate power in his own hand 'and would know how to use it in a struggle for Germany',[34] he was stating his firmly held belief that the destiny of Germany lay in his hands alone. Hence the reasons which Hitler himself gave for the attack on Poland; that he was growing old and could afford to wait no longer to create the new German empire; and that what counted in foreign policy was will. Lacking the will to restrain Hitler before 1939, the western nations had forfeited their claim to the status of great powers and would not fight.[35]

The fact that Hitler's wider intentions failed to produce the large-scale armament that he wanted was not because he lowered his sights and chose *Blitzkrieg*, but because of the premature outbreak of a general war in 1939 and the difficulties experienced thereafter in mobilizing an economy starved of strategic guidelines and a satisfactory wartime administration.

II

The *Blitzkrieg* economy is just as elusive in the wider context of German war preparations. The restructuring of the economy implied by the Four-Year Plan, and the acceleration of Hitler's diplomacy after 1937, showed what the ultimate purposes of the regime were. If Hitler's precise intentions were not always clear, or were not always taken seriously by the business or military elites, there could be no doubt that the restructuring was taking place.[36] It was a necessary step in preparing for large-scale war and German hegemony. In fact it was precisely because this was a long-term goal that exact details were lacking. The re-orientation of the economy was bound to be a lengthy and clumsy process. The absence of precise economic planning confirmed that the intention was not to wage a short, carefully calculated war in the near future, but a big war at a later date.

It was Hitler's intention that Goering should co-ordinate the efforts to prepare the economy as a whole, using Party agencies and leaders where possible to carry the programme out. Goering's view of the economy was, like Hitler's, concerned with its role in the future conquest of Europe and world war. Like Hitler, he assumed that the scale of preparation should involve the whole economy. His task within the Four-Year Plan was to reorient the total economy to war purposes. That Goering was unsuccessful in doing so by 1939 was an indication not only that he was an inappropriate choice as plenipotentiary, but also that he expected to have much more time to complete his task.[37] Working on a wide range of uncompleted projects, Goering was among the foremost of those who argued against risking war in 1939 and who accepted Hitler's assurances that the crisis in August would be localized.[38] Goering worked on the assumption that any war would be a general and large-scale conflict; hence his anxiety to prevent war until Germany was fully prepared. To the *Gauleiter* in 1938 he spoke of the 'new war' of 'great proportions' to come.[39] To industry in October 1938 he stressed that 'the economy must be completely converted'.[40] A year later he warned industry that 'Today's war is a total war, whose end no one can even approximately foretell'.[41] In December 1939 he wrote to all Reich authorities telling them to 'direct all energies to a lengthy war'.[42] In all this he was merely echoing Hitler's own intention, even though the timing of war had misfired. The picture he presented to the German economy at large, if at times unspecified or unrealistic, was of a future and large-scale conflict for which the complete transformation of the economic structure was required.[43]

The same contingency was prepared for by the armed forces, which were compelled to perform their functions in partial ignorance of the exact nature of Hitler's long-term intentions. The lack of precise information reflected Hitler's own secretiveness and administrative methods. To Halder, the Army Chief-of-Staff, he remarked: 'my true intentions you will never know. Even those in my closest circle who feel quite sure they know my intentions will not know about them'.[44] In this light the armed forces geared preparations to a wide number of major contingencies which they regarded as reasonable. It was widely agreed that all such contingencies required preparations for a total war economy, and the army developed during the 1930s the theory of the *Wehrwirtschaft* – the defence-based economy – to cope with the requirement.[45] General Thomas, head of the army economic office, planned economic mobilization as though any war might mean total war, hoping to avoid the mistakes of 1914. Preparations for this 'armament in depth' existed throughout the 1930s and continued after the outbreak of war in 1939, coinciding with Hitler's view of future warfare.[46]

Thomas himself complained after the war that such preparations had been much less successful than he had expected. Part of the reason for this lay with the administrative confusion surrounding rearmament, what Thomas called 'the war of all against all'.[47] But a major explanation lay in the general unwillingness of much of German industry to co-operate in preparing for total war, the more so as many industrialists regarded a general war as unthinkable in 1939. Industry was faced in 1939 with the prospect of rising trade and a consumer boom based on the continued modernization of the German economy. Instructions from Goering and Thomas were circumvented or ignored.[48] The whole structure of controls and *Wehrwirtschaft* [war economy] preparations was sabotaged by the unwillingness of many industrialists, happy enough to take rearmament orders, to follow the logic through to actual war. The problems with which private industry and banking were concerned were those of markets (including the newly won areas of central Europe) investment, and money supply.[49] This was not, of course, true of all industrialists. The large state sector developed after 1936 was designed to provide the Nazis with war materials which private industry might have been reluctant to provide. There were also sympathizers in private firms, whose board-rooms were penetrated by the Nazis, who were willing to co-operate in the economic restructuring. But the increasing tension between these elements and the rest of the economy, symbolized by the clash over the *Reichswerke* and the *Volkswagen*, placed limits on the pace and extent of the Nazi war-economic programme.[50] The emergence of just such a division showed clearly that the *Blitzkrieg* solution of a small arms sector and protected consumer output was not the option that the Nazis had chosen. The purposes of Nazism and the purposes of German capitalism no longer coincided, as they had appeared to do in 1933. The resistance of business was caused by the crude attempt to force the whole economy after 1936 along the path towards the successful prosecution of a major 'racial struggle'.

III

In the light of this interpretation of Nazi intentions, it is not surprising to find that in most important respects the *Blitzkrieg* economy does not fit with the actual circumstances of German economic life during the period in question. The first problem is the sheer scale of Nazi rearmament. If it is looked at from a pre-war perspective, military expenditure in Germany up to 1940 was very large, much greater than that of any other power, with perhaps the exception of the Soviet Union, and much greater as a proportion of GNP than that of any power.[51] In May 1939 General Thomas boasted that in the following twelve months German rearmament would have almost reached the levels of the First World War.[52] Far from avoiding the total commitment of the previous conflict, the German economy was on the brink of exceeding it. It will be argued later that Hitler did not get value for money, but to contrast German 'limited' mobilization with the 'total' mobilization of the Allies is, before 1941, historically misleading.[53]

More important, however, is the fact that economic mobilization was intended to continue at a high and rising rate. Where the *Blitzkrieg* economy represented the peak of a short-term armaments effort to be used up in a short campaign, the German economy in 1939 was already operating at a high level of military production and was designed to reach even higher levels in the future. Nearly all the plans indicate this. The Navy's 'Z-Plan' required a huge industrial effort which had only just begun when the Polish crisis arose.[54] Such a programme was essential to waging the larger, long-term conflict that Hitler had in mind. Moreover Hitler gave priority to the 'Z-Plan' over every other service programme, even over exports, something which made no sense at all in terms of a *Blitzkrieg* economy.[55] Demands for the air force followed the same course. Germany already possessed a large force of modern aircraft by 1939, if smaller than those of the Allies together.[56] In addition to this, Hitler demanded a five-fold increase in air strength late in 1938, a request that would have needed an annual production of 20,000 aircraft in peacetime and 30,000–40,000 in wartime.[57] Although German aircraft production planners scaled these plans down substantially during 1939, they were almost exactly the sort of plans that Britain was laying down at the same time for 'total' mobilization.[58] Even the Luftwaffe itself, less ambitious than Hitler, planned a much larger output of aircraft than it in fact got from 1939 onwards. The last peacetime programme for the

Luftwaffe planned an output of 14,000 aircraft a year by 1941, nearly three times the output for 1938.[59] The *Wehrmacht* mobilization plans for the air force expected production to rise to over 20,000 aircraft in the first full year of war: actual production was 10,247.[60] All this suggests that Hitler wanted a huge increase in the proportion of the economy devoted to military purposes, even if war had not broken out in 1939.

To carry out such an expansion the Nazi leadership began from 1937–8 onwards to build up a large state-owned and state-operated industrial structure designed to speed up the reorientation of the economy for war. In aircraft production most new investment came from the state and much of it was concentrated in building large-scale production units.[61] In 1938 Goering demanded the construction of three giant aero-engine works capable of producing 1,000 engines a month each, to be followed by plans for a 10,000-a-year bomber factory.[62] In iron and steel Goering pioneered the extraction of low-grade iron-ore, but was also able to use the *Reichswerke* as a convenient cover for large-scale expansion of state involvement in industry, taking over control of Rheinmetall Borsig, almost the whole of the Austrian and Czech iron and machinery industry, and slices of the Thyssen empire.[63] The purpose, as Goering privately admitted, was to construct an industrial empire sensitive to the demands of Hitler's imperialism and on the largest scale.[64] The investments involved were very substantial. The hydrogenation plant at Brüx alone cost 250 million marks, more than all government investment in the aircraft industry in 1939/40.[65] Moreover, the investments were largely long term, making very little sense if the object were to design a *Blitzkrieg* economy. In fact the very scale of all these projects proved to be a drain on productive potential in the early years of war, thus explaining part of the paradox between Hitler's large-scale planning and expenditure and the poor return in the shape of finished armaments. Hitler's intention had been to create this necessary industrial substructure before developing the superstructure of armaments production. War in 1939 interrupted the programme and threw industrial planning into confusion.

The industrial evidence is unhelpful to the *Blitzkrieg* as well. The conversion of industry was planned comprehensively by the armed forces under Thomas, who worked on the 'total war' contingency.[66] The new Volkswagen complex, for example, which Hitler, with his fragmented view of the economy had detailed as a peacetime project, was assigned to the Luftwaffe in the event of war. While its conversion was hopelessly planned, as with so much of the effort to convert, the intention to do so was certainly there.[67] The plan was to draw on the civilian industries to make up for the inadequate provision of factory capacity and to close down inessential consumer production. In February 1940 Goering made it clear that such capacity had to be found 'to a much greater extent in the idle factories, even if in one way or another this does not correspond to all wishes'.[68] The head of the air industry economic group instructed air firms in October 1939 to take over any spare capacity in those sectors that were being closed down or were on short-time.[69] So rapid and wide-ranging was this conversion that the Four-Year Plan Office estimated that the proportion of the work-force employed for military purposes had risen from 20 per cent in 1939 to 60 per cent by early 1941.[70]

Not surprisingly, this led to reductions in civilian goods production. That this did not happen is a crucial part of the *Blitzkrieg* economy. 'There can be little doubt', wrote Professor Milward, 'that the impact of war on the German people over these years was very small'.[71] Consumer spending and civilian output, it is argued, were maintained in the face of the demands of war, while the military budget rose sharply only after the end of the *Blitzkrieg* in 1942. The facts show otherwise. Looking at the German economy as a whole, military spending rose at a consistent rate between 1938/9 and 1943/4. There was no abrupt change in 1942, nor any halt in expenditure in 1940 and 1941, as Table 10.1 shows.

Table 10.1 Military expenditure, state expenditure, and national income in Germany, 1938/9–43/4 (mrd. RM, current prices)

Year	Military expenditure	State expenditure	National income
1938/9	17.2	39.4	98
1939/40	38.0	58.0	109
1940/1	55.9	80.0	120
1941/2	72.3	100.5*	125
1942/3	86.2	124.0*	134
1943/4	99.4	130.0*	130

Source: W. Boelcke, 'Kriegsfinanzierung im internationalen Vergleich' in Forstmeier Volkmann, *Kriegs-wirtschaft und Rüstung*, pp. 55–6: Klein, *Germany's Preparations*, pp. 256–8.
Note: * based on revenue from occupied Europe and the Reich.

In fact the greatest percentage increases in military expenditure were in the years 1939 to 1941. This pattern confirms the fact that German rearmament and war expenditure followed a relatively smooth course of expansion over the period with none of the implied discontinuities of the *Blitzkrieg* economy. As a proportion of National Income and GNP the figures also compare favourably with the performance of the Allied economies.[72] Since military expenditure grew at a faster rate than the German economy as a whole this could only have been at the expense of civilian consumption.

And so in fact it was. Car production, for example, hungry for raw materials and labour, was dramatically cut back from a peak of 276,592 in 1938 to a mere 67,561 in 1940 and to 35,195 in 1941. The military took

42 per cent of the total in 1940, and 77 per cent in 1941.[73] It is the same story for the construction industry. The number of housing units completed fell from 303,000 in 1938 to 117,000 in 1940, and to 80,000 in 1941; again with many of the latter for military use. The volume of construction as a whole fell from 12.8 milliard marks in 1939 to 8.3 milliard in 1940 and to 6.9 milliard in 1941.[74] These were the important areas from which resources could be released into the military economy. Goods whose survival is supposed to demonstrate the maintenance of consumer spending were either those which would be expected to increase under war conditions (such as basic foodstuffs, the output of which increased enormously in Britain as well during the war)[75] or those whose production was divided between military and civilian use, a division disguised by the gross figures. In fact it was the high quality of the equipment that the *Wehrmacht* demanded for its members that swallowed up much of the consumer goods production as well as the increased output of food.[76] For the ordinary civilian consumer much less was available than before the war. By 1943 the armed forces took 44 per cent of all textile production, 43 per cent of all leather goods, and 40 per cent of all paper produced.[77] Of course Hitler kept a propaganda eye on domestic living standards, and the conquest of Europe allowed greater flexibility than might otherwise have been possible, but many of the concessions made were, literally, cosmetic.[78]

The result of this diversion to military purposes was widespread and increasingly comprehensive rationing, some of it before 1939.[79] The Four-Year Plan Office itself openly admitted the need to cut back on consumption. In a speech early in 1941 State Secretary Neumann acknowledged that:

> not only almost all articles of daily use but also practically all other goods have become increasingly scarce in recent years – even prior to the outbreak of war . . . a higher standard of living is the ultimate goal, not the immediate object of the Four Year Plan. Whatever was available by way of labour, materials and machines had to be invested in the production of military-economic importance according to an explicit Führer order. . . The fact that consumer interests had to be put second is regrettable but cannot be helped.[80]

Civilian production as a whole was severely cut back from the outbreak of war, while the bulk of surviving consumer goods production was diverted to the armed forces. The problem facing the German economy was not the release of resources but the ineffective use to which they were then put.

The final question concerns the degree of 'flexibility' in the German economy; the extent to which, under the terms of the *Blitzkrieg* economy, production could be switched within weeks from one weapons group to another or back to civilian production, as strategy dictated.[81] While it is true that priority changed, as would be expected, under the circumstances of war, in practice little substantial shift between weapons groups occurred during the period. The air force, for example, found it impossible to increase production significantly after the Fall of France while enjoying a production priority, but was able to expand output to new levels when the priority was removed and returned to the army.[82] In practice, the production for all the services expanded more or less continuously over the whole period 1939–41, for it was difficult to disrupt production programmes at short notice, and the services jealously guarded their own economic spheres of influence.[83] The same is true of the switch from arms to the civilian economy. Hitler certainly explored the idea of running down arms production in 1940 and again in 1941, not in response to any *Blitzkrieg* conception or preparation, but in reaction to the extraordinary degree of success that his relatively underarmed but well-run forces were able to achieve. But it must be stressed that Hitler did no more than explore the possibility. Success did not blind the Nazi leadership to the fact that enemies remained undefeated, and expenditure on weapons, like overall military expenditure, rose steadily and continuously over the whole period, helped by the expansion of output in the dependent territories in central Europe (see Table 10.2).

Table 10.2 Expenditure on selected weapons in Germany, 1939–41

Weapon	1939*	1940 (1941/2 prices, million marks)	1941
aircraft	1,040.0	4,141.2	4,452.0
ships	41.2	474.0	1,293.6
armour	8.4	171.6	384.0
weapons	180.0	676.8	903.6
explosive	17.6	223.2	338.4
traction vehicles	30.8	154.8	228.0

Source: calculated from Wagenführ, *Deutsche Industrie*, p. 29.
Note: * September–December.

The problem which Hitler faced was not the degree of commitment from what was, after all, a large and heavily industrialized economy, but the fact that, despite such a commitment, the output of finished weapons failed to match the extent of revenue and resources devoted to arms production. This made necessary a significant change in the level of productivity in 1941–2, rather than in the level of aggregate resources.

IV

Why was there such a gap between what Hitler wanted and what was actually produced? The immediate explanation is that the war broke out before the economy could be satisfactorily converted. Both the military and economic leadership were caught in the middle of restructuring the economy, and were compelled to divert energies to the needs of war before the economy was prepared for it. But that is not the whole answer. There were structural problems in the German economy that were not satisfactorily solved by 1939. There were also difficulties that arose from the very nature of German rearmament. This had started late in terms of a war to be fought in 1939, only reaching significant levels by 1937–8. There was little time to build up the plant and resources Hitler's plans warranted.[84] Not only was the question of time crucial, but also there was the fact that so much of the money was spent on refurnishing Germany with a military infrastructure (airfields, barracks, etc.) which had been destroyed or prohibited under the terms of the Versailles Treaty. This was an expensive business made more so by the fact that German weapons were also expensive. The insistence on very high standards of workmanship, and the preference for small-scale over large-scale mass-production contributed to this. So too did the cost-plus system of contracts, which gave no incentive to reduce prices and actually encouraged firms to produce inefficient methods and a high-priced end product.[85] The 50 milliard marks spent on rearmament by 1939 could have been expected, as Hitler no doubt wished, to yield more in terms of military goods than was in fact the case.[86] This situation continued into the war. In 1940 Germany spent an estimated $6 billion on weapons, while Britain spent $3.5 billion. Yet Britain produced over 50 per cent more aircraft, 100 per cent more vehicles and almost as many tanks as Germany in 1940.[87] If German armaments had been less well made and more efficiently produced and paid for, the number of weapons available in 1940 would have been considerably greater.

Another answer lay in Hitler's limited access to accurate information on the performance of the economy. This was partly a product of his style of government. But during the war it was as much a product of self-delusion and misinformation. Having spent large sums on rearmament with the most modern weapons Hitler failed to ensure that they were produced in quantity. He accepted new developments uncritically. He found it difficult to accept the long time-scale involved in developing a weapon or in distinguishing between weapons that were mere prototypes and those that were battle-ready.[88] This element of self-delusion was complemented by a good deal of poor or misleading intelligence. This was very much a product of the regime. Subordinates in the hierarchy hesitated to take initiatives on the economy and preferred to provide only that information which would present an optimistic impression of their achievements.[89] The information that finally reached Hitler was often partial and unrealistic, reflecting the intelligence that it was believed Hitler wanted to hear. Hence Hitler's reproaches to Goering over the failure of aircraft production later in the war; and hence Hitler's bitterness that the range of advanced weapons shown to him in 1939 as virtually ready for combat had failed in every case to materialize by 1942.[90] Hence, too, the persistent underestimation of enemy economic strength provided by German intelligence from 1939 to the invasion of Russia.[91]

One of the main culprits in this process of misrepresentation was Goering. His eagerness to enlarge his political empire through the economy, and his anxiety to present to Hitler the most optimistic picture of his achievement with war production, obscured much of the true state of preparations. Goering was then able to shelter behind the German victories until the poor performance of the economy became more obvious in the course of 1941, after which he was gradually excluded from its direction.[92] Before then, he had taken up all his tasks in the economy with much political enthusiasm, little economic or technical understanding and exceedingly poor relations with sections of heavy industry, the Reichsbank, and the Finance Ministry.[93] He insisted on treating his office as if he were personally responsible for preparing the future war economy, demanding that other agencies should be fused with his to increase the centralization of the economy under his direction.[94] Yet the civilian and military economic leadership did not want to work under Goering, and was able to circumvent his jurisdiction whenever possible. Goering himself was unequal to the tasks of organization that Hitler had set him. The result was that, during the crucial years of build-up towards war and in the early years of conflict, the military economy was not directed in a co-ordinated way.[95] Up to 1938 under Schacht, and after 1942 under Speer, the performance of the German economy came up to expectations. Between those dates came what Speer later saw as an era of 'incompetence, arrogance and egotism'.[96]

The main characteristics of the 'era of incompetence' were the ineffective way in which the resources released for war were taken up, and the general inefficiency and confusion of the military economy. Not that German industry, particularly large-scale industry, was uncompetitive commercially. The problem lay in adopting the same practices in the armament factories. Not only was this slow to happen, but those commercial firms brought into war-work also became infected by the incompetence and inflexibility of the system. One obvious explanation for ineffective mobilization was that industry was caught by surprise by the actual outbreak of war in 1939, and had to divert resources from long-term military projects and from civilian life without a competent central authority for the economy. When war broke out, industry was unprepared for the scale of demands and was anxious, like much of the military leadership, that the war should be over as soon as possible. Moreover, the firms often expressed a marked hostility to a high level of government intervention or military interference and failed to co-operate in achieving high levels of arms output in the way that American or British businessmen did.[97] It is perhaps not surprising that in a situation where not even Hitler's closest subordinates could guess his intentions, business in Germany was unable to comprehend the scope of what was happening in 1940 and 1941, and to prepare accordingly. Moreover, German business was anxious not to lose the prospect of rising profits and expanding trade which had been held out at the end of the 1930s, and the first years of war saw a continuation of the silent struggle over the nature and destination of the German economy.[98] Too much energy was used up in combating excessive state interference on the one hand and in competing for contracts and influence abroad on the other. This, combined with the incomplete nature of preparations for a war in 1939 and the lack of a competent war economic admin- istration, substantially reduced the level of war goods that Hitler had wanted.

There was also the question of industrial constraints. This was not simply a result of a lack of central planning, jurisdictional confusion, and poor co-ordination, or of a shortage of raw materials, the lack of which has been much exaggerated. There were problems within the armaments industry itself. There was too great a reliance on skilled labour in areas of manufacture where increasing automation mght have been expected. The reluctance of the work-force to accept dilution during the 1930s and the early years of war brought many difficulties in introducing mass-production methods and made labour more of a problem than was necessary.[99] So, too, did the conservatism of management faced with the requirements of making the transition from small-scale to large-scale manufacture. This was less of a problem with established firms, such as Krupps. But many of the firms that grew large on government orders in the 1930s were small firms faced with all the strains of making the transition to a different style of management at a vital stage in German war preparations.[100] Only when industrialists from the large commercial firms were brought in to run the war economy in 1942 were some of these difficulties overcome.[101]

One final problem industry could do very little about: the exceptional degree of control exercised over armaments firms by the armed forces. In the absence of a strong civilian economic administration this was perhaps inevitable. But the tight military control over contracts, product selection, and production methods stifled industrial initiatives.[102] The most damaging problem was the extent to which minor technical demands from the armed forces at the front held up the introduction of mass-production methods and encouraged only short and expensive production runs.[103] When the more successful commercial firms were drafted into war production, their productive performance was similarly blighted by contact with the poor planning of the military production authorities.[104] When Todt, Speer and Milch revolutionized production in 1941 and 1942 they did so not by a massive redirecting of resources but simply by using existing resources better. The aircraft industry in 1942 produced 40 per cent more aircraft than in 1941 with only 5 per cent more labour and substantially less aluminium.[105] What produced the low level of mobilization was not a lack of resources but the problem of coping with a premature war in an economy lacking effective central control, dominated by military requirements, and guided by an impulsive strategist whose understanding of the economy was deliberately obscured. Under these circumstances it was possible to produce just enough for the early German campaigns, but not enough for Hitler's 'big war'; not enough, that is, to defeat Britain in 1940 or Russia in 1941.

V

The first conclusion to draw from this interpretation of the German war economy is the inappropriateness of applying a *Blitzkrieg* conception. In terms of economic planning, industrial conversion, consumer goods production, civilian consumption, and strategic 'flexibility', the model breaks down. The ideas that Germany deliberately sought to restrict the economic costs of war, and that German civilian consumption levels were maintained intact over the early war period while the military economy had its resources skilfully switched from one weapon group to another, fit with neither the general strategic picture nor with the details of economic life in Germany between 1939 and 1941.

Hitler's intention was to prepare for a long and total war, using all Germany's resources to achieve a final victory. This perspective explains the nature of the autarkic and rearmament programmes initiated from 1936 onwards, many of them quite redundant for the purposes of a limited and conventional 'short war'. The evidence shows that Hitler expected such a confrontation in the mid-1940s, after an initial period of consolidation in central Europe achieved without a general war, and protected by a series of diplomatic *coups* of which the Nazi-Soviet Pact was the most important. It was this initial stage of preparing a large economic and military bloc in central Europe that backfired in 1939 into a more general war, against Hitler's expectations. That is why the German economy appeared to be prepared for a limited war. It was caught half-way towards the transformation planned by Hitler, with a military base capable of achieving the limited first stage but not the second, more general, one.

It is clear that Hitler, faced with the fact of war in 1939, changed his mind about the time-scale involved in his imperialism, accelerating the move towards the 'big' war which found him in conflict with Britain, Russia and the United States by the end of 1941. That he did so was in part because he believed that the economic time-scale could be speeded up and conversion to the needs of the larger war achieved in the early 1940s instead of later. This expectation was in turn derived from misinformation or lack of information on how the economy was developing. This failure of communication was crucial. It was compounded of Goering's anxiety that the achievements of the Four-Year Plan should be presented in as favourable a light as possible, and Hitler's own predilection for secretiveness and fragmented administration. The failure was helped, too, by Hitler's own poor understanding of production and finance, which led him to expect that military goods could be produced much more quickly and cheaply than was in fact possible. Goering's remark that Hitler was interested only in how many bombers there were, and not in how many engines each had, was symptomatic of this approach.[106]

Most important of all in persuading Hitler that the 'big' war was possible was the remarkable military success enjoyed between September 1939 and June 1940 against enemies whose combined material strength was more than equal to that of Germany. This success was not produced by a *Blitzkrieg* economy. The victories were due, first and foremost, to the staff work, leadership and fighting qualities of the German forces, together with the weaknesses, poor leadership and wrong intelligence on the part of the Allies. Hitler's belief that the 'big' war could now be won still required a huge economic effort based on the large-scale plans laid down, but not yet completed, between 1936 and 1939. It is true that the extent of the military victories, which surprised Hitler as well as the generals, tempted him at times to question the need for a greater economic effort and to rely more on military prowess. But these second thoughts were very much *post hoc*, reflecting the changing circumstances of war, and were not pre-planned; nor, it must be emphasized, did Hitler ever hold back the continued expansion of the arms economy over the whole of the period 1939 to 1942. Moreover, such second thoughts were soon dispelled by the failures against Britain in 1940 and Russia in 1941, which showed the limit of German military potential and the extent to which the German armed forces were under-armed. As it turned out, the German forces were able to perform remarkably in the face of massive material superiority throughout the war. That they were comparatively under-armed was the result of the fact that the German economy could not be converted satisfactorily in 1939–41 to the needs of a large-scale war.

This failure to convert satisfactorily, to adjust to the 'big' war when asked to do so, had many causes. At one level the failure was simply a result of the fact that the war broke out prematurely, while many of the preparations were of a long-term character. Hitler's own uncertainty and impulsive strategy created uncertainty among business leaders and economic planners. The economy was caught between peaceful economic recovery and the programme of war preparations laid down since 1936. This lack of appropriate planning was made more acute by the lack of a satisfactory central economic administration in war time. In the absence of central direction the military had a much greater say in economic affairs, concentrating on matters (such as tactical suitability) that concerned the front line, and not on questions of large-scale industrial production and distribution. When this was added to a reluctance on the part of much of industry to convert for war, and the rapid and unpredictable shifts in strategy, the economy failed to rise to the challenge of a large-scale war as it did in Britain, the United States and Russia. The failure to solve the problem of arms production (disguised by the very good use to which the *Wehrmacht* put what weapons it had) was caused not by a preference for consumer-goods production over armaments, nor by *Blitzkrieg* campaigns deliberately based on a small military economy, but by the fact that Hitler's larger war arrived before preparations for it were complete. The low level of mobilization was not intentional but was a product of this contradiction between economic and diplomatic reality.

Notes

1 I would like to thank Mr B. Bond, Dr W. Deist, Dr Z. Steiner and Professor A. Teichova for advice in the preparation of this article.

2 B.H. Klein, 'Germany's preparation for war; a re-examination', *American Economic Review*, XXXVIII, 1948, pp. 56–77; Klein, *Germany's Economic Preparations for War*, Harvard, Mass., 1959.

3 A.S. Milward, 'Der Einfluss ökonomischer und nicht-ökonomischer Faktoren auf die Strategie des Blitzkriegs', in F. Forstmeier and H.E. Volkmann (eds), *Wirtschaft und Rüstung am Vorabend des Zweiten Weltkrieges*, Düsseldorf, 1975, pp. 189–201; A.S. Milward, 'The end of the Blitzkrieg', *Economic History Review*, 2nd ser., XVI, 1963/4, 499–518; Milward, *The German Economy at War*, 1965; Milward, 'Hitlers Konzept des Blitzkrieges', in A. Hillgruber (ed.) *Probleme des Zweiten Welkrieges*, Köln, 1967, pp. 19–40.

4 A.S. Milward, 'Could Sweden have stopped the Second World War?', *Scandinavian Economic History Review*, XV, 1967, p. 135.

5 On the question of the internal crisis see T.W. Mason, 'Innere Krise und Angriffskrieg', in Forstmeier and Volkmann, *Wirtschaft und Rüstung*, pp. 158–88; Mason, 'Labour in the Third Reich', *Past & Present*, 33, 1966, pp. 112–41; Mason, 'Some origins of the Second World War', *P. & P.* 23, 1964, pp. 67–87; E. Hennig, 'Industrie, Aufrüstung und Kriegsvorbereitung im deutschen Faschismus', in *Gesellschaft: Beiträge zur Marxschen Theorie 5*, Frankfurt, 1975, pp. 68–148.

6 For criticism of the military *Blitzkrieg* conception see: W. Deist *et al.*, *Das Deutsche Reich und der Zweite Weltkrieg*, I, *Ursachen und Voraussetzungen der deutschen Kriegspolitik*, Stuttgart, 1979; L. Herbst, 'Die Krise des national-sozialistischen Regimes am Vorabend des Zweiten Weltkrieges und die forcierte Aufrüstung', *Vierteljahreshefte für Zeitgeschichte*, XXVI, 1978, pp. 347–92; J. Dülffer, *Weimar, Hitler und die Marine*, Düsseldorf, 1973; and J. Thies, *Architekt der Weltherrschaft. Die Endziele Hitlers*, Düsseldorf, 1976.

7 T.W. Mason, *Sozialpolitik im Dritten Reich*, Opladen, 1977, pp. 305–10; Milward, *German Economy*, pp. 8–14.

8 International Military Tribunal, *Trial of the Major War Criminals* (hereafter IMT), Nuremberg, 1947–9, XXXVI, pp. 493–7, Doc. 419-EC, Finance Minister to Hitler, 1 September 1938; W. Warlimont, *Inside Hitler's Headquarters*, 1964, p. 24; on General Thomas's efforts to convince Hitler of Germany's

poor economic position see H.B. Gisevius, *To the Bitter End*, 1948, pp. 355–7; B.A. Carroll, *Design for Total War*, The Hague, 1968, p. 178.

9 *Nazi Conspiracy and Aggression* (hereafter NCA), Washington, 1946, VII, pp. 847, 850–1; Doc. L-79 report of a conference with Hitler, 23 May 1939. For a general discussion see E. Jäckel, *Hitler's Weltanschauung*, Wesleyan UP, 1972, pp. 27–46; K. Hildebrand, *The Foreign Policy of the Third Reich*, 1973, pp. 91–104; A. Kuhn, *Hitlers aussenpolitisches Programm*, Stuttgart, 1970, pp. 96–140.

10 A. Speer, *Inside the Third Reich*, 1970, p. 166. Speer recorded Hitler's statement to his generals that 'if the war were not won, that would mean that Germany had not stood the test of strength; in that case she would deserve to be and would be doomed'; H. Rauschning, *Hitler Speaks*, 1939, p. 125, 'even if we could not conquer then, we should drag half the world into destruction with us, and leave no-one to triumph over Germany'; also pp. 126–8.

11 NCA, VII, pp. 851–3, Doc. L-79. This conviction is echoed in M. Muggeridge (ed.) *Ciano's Diplomatic Papers*, 1948, p. 284, 'Conversation with the Reich Foreign Minister, 6–7 May 1939', when Ribbentrop assured Ciano that 'preparations are being made to carry on a war of several years' duration'.

12 NCA, VII, p. 851.

13 W. Birkenfeld, *Der synthetische Treibstoff, 1933–1943*, Göttingen, 1963, pp. 112–40; M. Riedel, *Eisen und Kohle für das Dritte Reich*, Göttingen, 1973, pp. 155–232; D. Petzina, *Autarkiepolitik im Dritten Reich*, Stuttgart, 1968; Dülffer, *Hitler und die Marine*, p. 498; Thies, *Architekt*, pp. 151–2, 186–7.

14 R.J. Overy, 'Transportation and rearmament in the Third Reich', *Historical Journal*, XVI, 1973, pp. 389–409.

15 Speer, *Inside the Reich*, p. 176; J. Dülffer, J. Henke and J. Thies (eds) *Hitlers Städte. Baupolitik im Dritten Reich*, Köln, 1978.

16 J. Thies, 'Hitler's European building programme', *Journal of Contemporary History*, XIII, 1978, pp. 423–4; Speer, *Inside the Reich*, p. 174.

17 On the Autobahnen in wartime see K. Lärmer, 'Autobahnenbau und Staatsmono-polistischer Kapitalismus', in L. Zumpe (ed.) *Wirtschaft und Staat im Imperialismus*, Berlin, 1976, pp. 253–81; Speer, *Inside the Reich*, p. 176; Carroll, *Design*, pp. 171, 245. For more details of the economic cost of these projects see J. Dülffer, 'Der Beginn des Krieges 1939; Hitler, die innere Krise und das Mächtesystem', *Geschichte und Gesellschaft*, II, 1976, pp. 457–9.

18 L.E. Hill (ed.) *Die Weizsäcker-Papiere, 1933–1950*, Frankfurt, 1974, pp. 149, 153, 155–6; A. Bullock, 'Hitler and the Origins of the Second World War', *Proceedings of the British Academy*, LIII, 1967, pp. 280–1; E.M. Robertson, *Hitler's Pre-war Policy and Military Plans*, 1963, pp. 160–2; Hildebrand, *Foreign Policy*, pp. 84–90. According to Rauschning, *Hitler Speaks*, pp. 123–4, Hitler had already reached this conclusion in 1934.

19 *Ciano's Papers*, pp. 301–2, 'First Conversation with the Fuehrer, 12 Aug. 1939'; p. 303, 'Second Conversation with the Fuehrer, 13 Aug. 1939'.

20 Nuremberg Trials, Case XI documents, Foreign Office Library (hereafter Case XI), Körner Defence Doc. Book IB, pp. 154–5.

21 Speer, *Inside the Reich*, pp. 161–2; W. Carr, *Arms, Autarky and Aggression*, 1972, p. 123; *Weizsäcker-Papiere*, pp. 159–60; J. Toland, *Adolf Hitler*, New York, 1976, p. 548.

22 E. Homze, *Arming the Luftwaffe*, Nebraska UP, 1976, pp. 244–5; W. Baumbach, *Broken Swastika* 1960, pp. 30–1; *Ciano's Papers*, p. 298, 'Conversation with the Reich Foreign Minister, 11 August, 1939'.

23 *Weizsäcker-Papiere*, p. 164.

24 NCA, VII, p. 854, Doc. L-79; according to B. Bahlerus, *The Last Attempt*, 1948, p. 163, Hitler told him: 'If the enemy can hold out for several years, I, with my power over the German people, can hold out one year longer'.

25 There is considerable debate on how many such 'stages' there were. Since there is general agreement that Hitler's policy involved some kind of primary imperialism to make possible the final war for wider dominion, I have concentrated on this broader strategic intention. It did not seem necessary to enter the discussion about how many minor 'steps' each stage required. See M. Hauner, 'Did Hitler want a world dominion?', *Journal of Contemporary History*, XIII, 1978, 15–31; A. Hillgruber, *Hitlers Strategie. Politik und Kriegführung 1940–41*, Frankfurt, 1965; B. Stegemann, 'Hitlers Ziele im ersten Kriegsjahr 1939/40', *Militärgeschichtliche Mitteilungen*, XXII, 1980, 93–105.

26 Carr, *Arms*, pp. 72–80.

27 ibid. pp. 5–20; K. Hildebrand, 'La programme de Hitler et sa réalisation', *Revue d'histoire de la deuxième Guerre Mondiale*, XXI, 1971, pp. 7–36; F. Zipfel, 'Hitlers Konzept einer Neuordnung Europas', in D. Kurse (ed.) *Aus Theorie und Praxis des Geschichtswissenschaft*, Berlin, 1972, pp. 154–74; Rauschning, *Hitler Speaks*, pp. 126–37; A. Speer, *Spandau. The Secret Diaries*, 1976, p. 70, who recalls Hitler's remark: 'But I'll still have to lead the great clash with the U.S.A. If only I have time enough, there would be nothing finer for me than to stand at the head of my people in that decisive struggle as well'; Thies, *Architekt*, pp. 165–6, 187.

28 Bundesarchiv-Militärarchiv (hereafter BA-MA), RL3 234 'Industrielle Vorplanung bis 1.4.1945', 15 October 1940; IMT, XXXVII, Doc. 043-L 'Organisationstudie 1950' 2 May 1938; IMT, IX, p. 60, Milch cross-examination; R.J. Overy, 'The German pre-war aircraft production plans: Nov. 1936 – April 1939', *English Historical Review*, XC, 1975, pp. 779–83; Homze, *Arming*, pp. 242–50.

29 Hauner, 'World dominion', p. 27; Dülffer, 'Beginn des Krieges', pp. 467–8.

30 NCA, VI, p. 729, Doc. 3787-PS, Second Meeting of the Reich Defense Council, 10 July 1939.

31 Case XI, Körner Defence Doc. Book 1B, p. 140.

32 *Ciano's Papers*, p. 242, 'Conversation between the Duce and the Foreign Minister of the Reich, 28 October 1938'; *Documents on German Foreign Policy* (1956) Ser. D, VI, Doc. 211, 'Unsigned Memorandum, Discussion with Göring, 16 April 1939'.

33 Dahlerus, *Last Attempt*, p. 63: Hauner, 'World dominion', pp. 28–9.

34 Speer, *Inside the Reich*, p. 165.

35 Gisevius, *Bitter End*, pp. 361–2; Rauschning, *Hitler Speaks*, pp. 276–87, for a record of Hitler's increasing morbidity and isolation in 1939.

36 Case XI, Körner Defence Doc. Book 1B, p. 140, Fritsche Affidavit, 29.6.1948; pp. 155–6, Warlimont cross-examination; Gisevius, *Bitter End*, pp. 277–360; according to D. Orlow, *The History of the Nazi Party*, Newton Abbot, 1973, II, p. 263, the party itself had no indication that a general war might break out in 1939 and was taken by surprise.

37 W. Treue, 'Hitlers Denkschrift zum Vierjahresplan', *Vierteljahrshefte für Zeitgeschichte*, III, 1955, 184–210; D. Petzina, 'Vierjahresplan und Rüstungspolitik', in Forstmeier and Volkmann (eds) *Wirtschaft und Rüstung*, pp. 65–80.

38 R. Manvell and H. Fraenkel, *Göring*, pp. 154–65.

39 Case XI, Körner Defence Doc. Book 1B, p. 8, statement of Gauleiter Uiberreither, 27 February 1946; see also IMT, XXXVIII, p. 380, Doc. 140-R, Göring address to aircraft manufacturers, 8 July 1938, in which he called for the achievement of a long-term production of 'a colossal quantity' of aircraft.

40 IMT, XXVII, pp. 161–2, Doc. 1301-PS, 'Besprechung bei Göring, 14 Okt. 1938'.

41 Milch Documents (MD), Imperial War Museum, London, LXV, 7302–3, letter from General Brauchitsch, 6 May 1939.

42 MD, LXV, 7299, letter from Goering to Reich authorities, 7 December 1939.

43 Case XI, Prosecution Doc. Book 112, Doc. NI-090, minutes of meeting of iron industry and Four-Year Plan Office, 17 March 1937; Doc. NI-084, minutes of meeting held by Göring, 16 June 1937; Doc, NI-8590, Report from Loeb to Göring, 30 October 1937, 'Results of work done during the first year of the Four-Year Plan'; *Documents on German Foreign Policy*, Ser. D, IV p. 260, Doc. 211.

44 Case XI, Körner Defence Doc. Book 1B, p. 81, Halder cross-examination. See also Gisevius, *Bitter End*, p. 353; R. J. Overy, 'Hitler and air strategy', *Journal of Contemporary History*, XV, 1980, 407–8; W. Carr, *Hitler: A Study in Personality and Politics*, 1978, pp. 41–5.

45 W. Warlimont, *Inside Hitler's Headquarters*, 1964, pp. 17–23.

46 Carroll, *Design for War*, pp. 192–212.

47 Milward, *German Economy*, p. 23.

48 On the resistance of the car industry, see Overy, 'Transportation', pp. 404–5; on industry as a whole, see A. Schröter, J. Bach, 'Zur Planung der wehrwirtschaftlichen Mobilmachung durch den deutschen faschistischen Imperialismus vor dem Beginn des Zweiten Weltkrieges', *Jahrbuch für Wirtschaftgeschichte*, Part I, 1978, pp. 42–5. By May 1939 only 60 per cent of the mobilization plan could be accounted for by the existing industrial agreements.

49 Christie Papers, Churchill College, Cambridge; 180/125, letter from 'a senior German industrialist' to Christie, 7 July 1939; 'Memo by members of Big Business in Germany 1937', pp. 2–23; 'Rough notes of a recent conversation with a German industrialist, 1 June 1939'.

50 Riedel, *Kohle und Eisen*, pp. 167–78, on the Reichswerke; P. Kluke, 'Hitler und das Volkswagenprojekt', *Vierteljahreshefte für Zeitgeschichte*, VIII, 1960, pp. 376–9.

51 Carroll, *Design for War*, pp. 184–8.

52 IMT, XXXVI, p. 116, Doc. 028-EC, 'Vortrag gehalten vor General-major Thomas am 24 mai 1939 im Auswärtigen Amt'.

53 To some extent this is a statistical illusion. The percentage increase in British military expenditure was much greater than that of Germany in 1939–40 and 1940–1 because it was growing from a much smaller base. It is difficult, too, to compare like with like since the structure of state finances and the definition of military expenditure differed between the two countries.

54 M. Salewski, *Die deutsche Seekriegsleitung 1939–1945*, Frankfurt, 1970, I, pp. 58–65.

55 ibid. 1, p. 59. The order was given on 29 January 1939 and was confirmed in May. See NCA, VII, p. 854.

56 French, British and Polish front-line air strength was marginally greater than German in quantity, though not in quality, in September 1939. See R.J. Overy, *The Air War, 1939–1945*, 1980, p. 23.

57 K-H. Völker, *Dokumente und Dokumentarfolos zur Geschichte der deutschen Luftwaffe*, Stuttgart, 1968, p. 211, 'Festlegung der Planungen zur Bergrösserung der Luftwaffe, 7.11.1938'; NCA, III, p. 901, Doc. 1301-PS, 'Conference at General Field Marshal Goering's, 14 October 1938'; R. Suchenwirth, *Historical Turning Points in the German Air Force War Effort*, New York, 1959, pp. 23–4.

58 M.M. Postan, *British War Production*, 1952, pp. 21, 66–8.

59 BA-MA RL3 159, 'Lieferprogramm Nr. 15, 1.9.1939'.

60 National Archives, Washington (NA) T 177, Roll 31, frame 3719681, 'Nachsuchubzahlen für Luftfahrtgerät, 1.4.1938'; MD, LXV, 7410–11, 'Vortragsunterlagen für den Vortrag vor dem Herrn Generalfeldmarschall, 13 Dez. 1938'.

61 For example the Heinkel works at Oranienberg, the Messerschmitt works at Wiener-Neustadt, and the large new investments in the Junkers aero-engine and aircraft factories. Details on state investment can be found in BA-MA RL3 46, Chart 1 'Investitionen; Zellenbau'; Chart 2, 'Investitionen; Motorenbau'.

62 MD, LXV, 7429 'Besprechung in Berlin, 29.11.1938'; LI, 451, letter from Milch to Göring on the Volkswagen factories, 21 September 1938.

63 K. Lachmann, 'The Hermann Göring Works', *Social Research*, VIII, 1941, pp. 35–8; on Austria see NA T 83, Roll 74, frames 3445159-77, I.G. Farben volkswirtschaftliche Abteilung, 'Konzernaufbau und Entwicklung der Reichswerke AG Hermann Göring', 19 October 1939; on Rheinmetall-Borsig see NA T 83, Roll 74, frames 3445356-60.

64 NA T 83, Roll 75, Frame 3445754, Pleiger to heads of firms in Reichswerke organization, 29 April 1942; frames 3445997-8, Göring to Gritzbach, 23 March 1942; T 83, Roll 74, frames 3445207-10, 'Gründung und Wachsen der Hermann Göring Werke 1937–1942'.

65 Speer Collection, Imperial War Museum, London, Reichswerke documents, FD 264/46 'HGW Konzern-Verzeichnis, 15.8.1944'. The Reichswerke alone cost 400 million marks, 93 per cent from state sources. Although many of the factories were set up outside the old Reich, much of the money had to be found from Reich sources.

66 Carroll, *Design for War*, pp. 162–4; NA T 177, Roll 3, frame 3684363, Thomas to heads of services 'betr. wehrwirtschaftliche Räumung, 29 Sept. 1939'; frame 3684308, Göring to all Reich authorities, 24 September 1939; B. Mueller-Hillebrand, *Die Blitzfeldzüge 1939–4*, Frankfurt, 1956, pp. 23–39 on the work of the army.

67 BA-MA RL3 20, letter from Göring to Ley, 15 Sept. 1939; MD LI, 451, letter from Milch to Göring, 21 September 1938. On the difficulties of establishing production there see BA-MA RL3 247, report of a meeting at Junkers, Dessau, 17 October 1939; Speer Collection FD 969/45, Bayersiche Motorenwerke 'Ablauf der Lieferungen seit Kriegsbeginn', p. 5: On Göring's determination to convert all or any firms see NCA III, pp. 901–4, Doc. 1301-PS.

68 MD LXV, 7285, report of a conference with Göring, 9 February 1940; T. Mason, *Arbeiterklasse und Volksgemeinschaft*, Opladen, 1975, p. 1044, Doc. 174, 'Rede Görings in dem Rheinmetall-Borsig-Werke, Berlin am 9 Sept. 1939', in which he said 'In as far as we don't have the production facilities they will be created through conversion, expansion and new construction'.

69 NA T 83, Roll 5, frame 3745418, letter from Admiral Lahs to all aircraft firms, 10 October 1939.

70 Case XI, Prosecution Doc. Book 112, p. 301, Doc. NID-13844, lecture given by State Secretary Neumann at the Verwaltungsakademie, 29 April 1941.

71 Milward, *German Economy*, p. 29.

72 Carroll, *Design for War*, pp. 264–5.

73 United States Strategic Bombing Survey (USSBS), Report 77 *German Motor Vehicles Industry Report*, p. 8.

74 Number of housing units from R. Wagenführ, *Die Deutsche Industrie im Kriege*, Berlin, 1963, pp. 37, 56; volume of construction from Klein, *German Preparations*, p. 105. By 1942, 80 per cent of all construction was for military or industrial purposes.

75 K.A. Murray, *Agriculture*, 1955, p. 375. British grain production increased from 4.6 million tons in 1939 to 8.2 in 1944; potatoes from 5.2 million tons in 1939 to 9.8 in 1943; vegetables from 2.3 million tons in 1939 to 3.4 in 1943. There seems little remarkable about the German economy, better endowed with agricultural potential than Britain, increasing its domestic food production, much of it destined for the well-fed armed forces. It should be noticed that in those areas where the German agricultural economy was weakest – dairy products, fats, oils – production dropped sharply. Milk output fell by a third between 1938/9 and 1939/40; vegetable oils by the same amount.

76 Case XI, Prosecution Doc. Book 112, pp. 296–7, Neumann lecture; see the discussion in W. Williams, *Riddle of the Reich*, 1941, pp. 10–14.

77 Wagenführ, *Deutsche Industrie*, p. 174.

78 One feature of the 'survival' of consumer goods industries was Hitler's insistence that cosmetics, stockings, etc. should still be produced to keep up home morale. But cigarettes, for which there was a large domestic demand, were heavily restricted and of poor quality. In 1941 a heavy tax was placed on tobacco, and women were restricted to a ration half that of men (1½ cigarettes a day). See L. Lochner, *What about Germany?*, 1943, pp. 144–5.

79 M. Steinert, *Hitler's War and the Germans*, Ohio UP, 1977, pp. 53, 64–5, 92–3; Lochner, *What about Germany?*, pp. 142–5, who wrote that both before and after 1939 'the simplest articles of daily life were lacking... Things made of leather, rubber, metal, wool or cotton were almost non-existent'; NCA VI, p. 723, Doc. 3787-PS, 'Second Meeting of the Reich Defense Council, 10 July 1939', on the intention to take resources away from 'the vital industries which are of importance to the life of the people'.

80 Case XI, Prosecution Document Book 112, pp. 293–4, Doc. NID-13844, Neumann lecture.

81 Milward, *German Economy*, p. 32; Milward, 'Der Einfluss', p. 195.

82 R.J. Overy, 'German aircraft production, 1939–42', unpublished Ph.D. thesis, University of Cambridge, 1978, pp. 23–32.

83 Klein, *German Preparations*, p. 161; Carroll, *Design for War*, pp. 154–5; Warlimont, *Hitler's Headquarters*, pp. 8–9.

84 On rearmament totals see BA R2 21776-81, Reichsfinanzministerium, Abteilung I, 'Entwicklung der Ausgaben in den Rechnungsjahren 1934–9', 17 July 1939. Rearmament from 1933/4 to 1935/6 averaged 3.445 milliard marks per year, including the *Mefowechseln*.

85 On the cost of the fortifications, see Dülffer, 'Beginn des Krieges', p. 457. On German arms finance, see A. Schweitzer, 'Profits under Nazi Planning', *Quarterly Journal of Economics*, LXI, 1946, pp. 9–18.

86 Military expenditure had to cover investment in industry, military installations, airfields, as well as military mobilization preparations over the Rhineland crisis, the Anschluss and the Munich crisis.

87 Wagenführ, *Deutsche Industrie*, p. 34; R.J. Overy, 'Die Mobilisierung der britischen Wirtschaft während des Zweiten Weltkrieges', in F. Forstmeier and H.E. Volkmann (eds) *Kriegswirtschaft und Rüstung im Zweiten Weltkrieg*, Düsseldorf, 1977, p. 289.

88 Overy, 'Air Strategy', pp. 406, 415–16; F.H. Hinsley, *Hitler's Strategy*, Cambridge, 1951, pp. 1–4.

89 D. Kahn, *Hitler's Spies*, 1979, pp. 386–7; on the misrepresentation of the strength of the Luftwaffe, see D. Irving, *The Rise and Fall of the Luftwaffe*, 1973, pp. 65–8; R. Suchenwirth, *Command and Leadership in the German Air Force*, New York, 1969, pp. 75–81.

90 Irving, *Rise and Fall*, pp. 73–4, 155–6.

91 Homze, *Arming*, p. 244; W. Schwabedissen, *The Russian Air Force in the Eyes of German Commanders*, New York, 1960, pp. 48–51.

92 Speer, *Inside the Reich*, pp. 252–66.

93 A.E. Simpson, 'The struggle for control of the German economy, 1936–1937', *Journal of Modern History*, XXI, 1959, pp. 37–45; H. Schacht, *76 Jahre meines Lebens*, Bad Wörishofen, 1953, pp. 461–74.

94 Case XI, Prosecution Doc. Book 112, pp. 283–8, Neumann lecture, MD LXV, 7299, letter from Göring to all Reich Authorities, 7 December 1939.

95 Carroll, *Design for War*, chs vii–viii.

96 Speer, *Diaries*, p. 63.

97 Overy, 'German aircraft production', pp. 170–88.

98 In particular the struggle over the whole question of state ownership. See Christie Papers, 180/1 25, 'Die deutsche Staatswirtschaft'. On the Reichswerke and state ownership see NA T 83, Roll 74, frames 3445207-10, 'Gründung und Wachsen der Hermann Göring Werke 1937–42'; Case XI, Prosecution Doc. Book 112, p. 149, Doc. NID-13797, Körner to Schwerin-Krosigk, 7 October 1940.

99 Overy, 'German aircraft production', pp. 159–61.

100 NA T 177, Roll 14, frames 3698887-916, General Bauer 'Rationalisierung der Luftwaffengerät-Fertigung, 1.6.1941'; Roll 12, frames 3695910-12, General Bauer 'Fertigungsvorbereitung, 1935'; Roll 3, frames 3684551-4, 'Klein- und Mittelbetrieb oder Grossbetrieb', GL Report, 24 April 1939.

101 For aircraft production this process began early in 1941 with the establishment of an *Industrierat*. See MD LIV, 1555; D. Eichholtz (ed.) *Anatomie des Krieges*, Berlin, 1969, p. 331, Doc. 161.

102 Schröter, Bach, 'Zur Planung der Mobilmachung', pp. 45–7; A. Bagel-Bohlan, *Hitlers industrielle Kriegsvorbereitung 1936 bis 1939*, Koblenz, 1975, pp. 137–8.

103 Overy, *Air War*, pp. 179–80.

104 Opel claimed for example that when the firm began military production output per man-hour dropped 40 per cent compared with peace-time output. See British Intelligence Objectives Sub-Committee, Final Report 537, p. 7. On the poor utilization of the car industry as a whole, see USSBS Report 77, pp. 5–11.

105 By contrast in 1941 some 50 per cent more labour was diverted to aircraft production but only a 5 per cent increase in aircraft output was achieved. See USSBS, European Report 4, Chart VI-11; USSBS, Report 20, *Light Metal Industry of Germany* (Part I), p. 17a; Irving, *Rise and Fall*, p. 167; Speer Collection, IWM/FDC9, Zentrale Planung, p. 789.

106 Overy, 'Hitler and air strategy', p. 407.

11

The Effects of World War II on French Society and Politics*

Stanley Hoffmann

The purpose of this [chapter] is to suggest a number of hypotheses concerning the impact of the war on the French body politic. Most of these hypotheses need further study and qualification; their author knows very well that as they are presented here, they might appear to be rather arbitrary and insufficiently demonstrated.

These suggestions must first of all be put into proper historical perspective, for what the war did was to bring to a climax a number of trends which had appeared in the last years of the Third Republic. It is the theme of this article that in the period 1934–44 a political and social system which had gradually emerged during the nineteenth century and which had flourished in the period 1878–1934, was actually liquidated; that from 1934 to 1940, this system, which I call the Republican synthesis, suffered severe shocks; that the events of 1940–4 turned these shocks into death-blows, for a return to the previous equilibrium has been made impossible; and that many of the political, economic and social forces which have carried post-war France increasingly farther from the pre-war pattern have their origins in the war years. What the next equilibrium will be like is hard to say, and France still seems far away from any. But it is in 1934 that movement began in earnest, and by 1946, when a political 'restoration' did in fact take place, the departures from the previous equilibrium were already considerable.

Before we examine the impact of the war years in detail, we must first summarize broadly the main characteristics of the Republican synthesis which serves as our baseline, and second, describe briefly the process which, between 1934 and 1940, led to the subsequent destruction of this synthesis.

I

The equilibrium which France had painfully attained before 1934 can be analyzed as follows: the basis was a certain kind of social and economic balance, which will be referred to here as the 'stalemate society' – a term chosen in order to suggest not a *static* society (for there was considerable social mobility and economic change) but a society in which social mobility and economic evolution toward a more industrialized order were accepted only within sharp limits and along well-defined channels. Economic change was welcome only if new factors (such as industrial techniques) were fitted into pre-existing frameworks, so that the traditional way of life was affected only slowly. Social mobility presented some very special features; a remark of Goblot sums them all up: class barriers could be crossed but not destroyed;[1] when one jumped over such a barrier, one had to leave one's previous way of thinking and living behind, and accept (for oneself and one's family) the values and attitudes one found on the other side of the fence. This society was mainly characterized by three features.

1 A form of economic *équilibre* [equilibrium] which thwarted or diluted industrialization and ensured the predominance of a bourgeoisie composed essentially of *indépendants* (non-wage-earners), backed by huge peasant reserves. This system was maintained in various ways. Its first bulwark was the structure of society itself, in which two passageways for entrance into the bourgeoisie were kept open: the line of wealth, passing through the petite-bourgeoisie of artisans and shopkeepers; the line of prestige, which passed through the civil service; those two *antichambres* were protected by state policy. So was the peasant reservoir (through tariff and tax legislation), by contrast with the proletarian swamp. A second bulwark was to be found in the values of society: the bourgeoisie was the model for and the matrix of the rest of society.[2] It emphasized values largely acceptable by all groups in France – values of stability, harmony, permanence, rather than competition, which means both mobility and elimination. It stressed values and attitudes which were dissolvers of class solidarities, so that society would appear like a collection of individuals psychologically alike, of whom the bourgeois would seem like a perfect average. Among those values and attitudes two were particularly significant: the resistance to the machine age and the emphasis on moderation and equilibrium: France was thus presented and seen as a spiritual as well as physical hexagon.
2 A broad consensus on the maintenance of this kind of economic system. This agreement left out – indeed it pushed out – the industrial proletariat, relegated to a social ghetto. The consensus which included the bourgeoisie, its two preserves and its reserves, was perpetuated through a tight and somewhat cramped solidarity between these varied elements: in business, social considerations prevailed

over economic ones,[3] and the celebrated 'freezing' of the capitalist spirit in France proved to be a prerequisite for the conciliation of the interests of the various groups included in the consensus.[4] As a result, there were severe tensions between the workers and those groups, and there developed a tradition of non-cooperation (a clumsy expression, but a more accurate one than 'revolutionary tradition') among labor unions.

3 Its individualism: it was a society in which interests were barely organized. Pressure groups were more effective on a local than on a regional or national scale. Neither business nor peasant nor middle-class organizations had a large membership or a solid structure. The only exceptions were on the one hand the Church, on the other (but only by comparison with other economic interest groups) the labor unions.

The genius of the Third Republic had been to devise an institutional set-up most effectively adapted to such a society. In conformity with the desire of the 'consensus groups' the role of the state was strictly limited. Economic intervention was justified only when it served to preserve the economic equilibrium described, either through legislation or through piecemeal administrative interventions. Otherwise the state's function was an ideological one: it was a state wedded to the social status quo; it was neither industrial (à la Saint-Simon) nor reformist, but politically doctrinaire and economically beleaguered.

Its organization was such that an effective executive, clear-cut economic or social alternatives and a strong party system simply could not emerge. Parliament was supreme but immobile: its supremacy, under the French doctrine of delegated national sovereignty, freed it from any mass pressures from below; its role was deliberative rather than representative. Law was the product of a compromise between opinions, rather than the result of a weighing of forces. Parties, thanks largely to the electoral system, were primarily parliamentary collections of 'fief-holders'; their function was to occupy power rather than to govern. Political life was close to the model of a pure game of parliamentary politics, i.e. the government of the nation by a Parliament which dictated policy-making, put the life of cabinets constantly at stake, and knew no effective institutional restraints on its powers. This game, which was being played in isolation from the nation-at-large by a self-perpetuating political class, saw to it that the fundamental equilibrium of society would not be changed by the state.

This system rested in turn on the rosy hypothesis of an outside world distant enough to allow the French to care primarily about their private affairs. Pride in the universality of French values combined with a pleasant sense of superiority or distance to keep the number of people concerned with France's demographic decline or economic retardation small. After World War I, victory plus new alliances plastered the cracks opened by the shock of invasion. Indeed, World War I – the one war which has not led to a change of regime – froze French society in many ways. (There are of course areas in which the opposite happened, i.e. forces of change or discontent were turned loose, which finally became hurricanes in the 1930s.)

The challenge of the 1930s, by contrast with previous challenges such as World War I, the Dreyfus case, or Boulangism, undermined all the foundations of the Republican synthesis.

First, the equilibrium of society was shattered by the depression and by the financial policies of the Conservative governments of 1932–6 (the policy of deflation, with its 'mystique' of the sanctity of contracts and its stubborn faith in tax cuts and balanced budgets symbolized beautifully the nature and beliefs of the stalemate society). Not only did workers' grievances and the issue of social reform reach the highest danger level since 1848, but also the workers found allies among the 'consensus groups', in their protest against the situation as it had become during the depression: in particular among peasants, civil servants, small businessmen and shopkeepers. The fact that those allies wanted a return to the *status quo ante*, not a jump to the Grand Soir [literally, Great Evening, in the sense of Grand Chinese], was something else again.

Second, the institutions proved of course too weak to weather such a storm. At a time when executive action was needed, the deep divisions within Parliament condemned cabinets to shorter lives than ever before, and to immobility or incoherence during their brief existence. The impotence of Parliament itself was underlined by the abdication of its legislative powers through decree-laws. The ordinary weaknesses of a multi-party system were aggravated by the splits which appeared within some of the major parties.

Finally, the outside world, whose pressure had been strong, though ignored, ever since Versailles, simply could not be explained away anymore. In a world of motion, indeed revolution (Stalin, Mussolini, Hitler, Scandinavian experiments in socialism, Roosevelt's experiment in muscular liberalism), France and England began to appear, even to the most musty readers of the *Revue des Deux Mondes*, like big logs of dead wood.

II

I want to turn now to the process of destruction of the Republican synthesis. The main feature, in the period 1934–40, was the victory of centrifugal forces everywhere. Until then, the Republic had functioned neatly: most of France's political *and* social forces joined in a broad consensus; the rest (i.e. the political Extreme Right and the proletarian Extreme Left) was kept in its ghettos, and stayed there. Now, suddenly, confusion and flux replaced the tiny, if cramped, order of Alain's *République Radicale*.

Why? Because in a period of major trouble the citizens, and especially those who feel the pinch of a depression, rediscover the function and importance of politics. Such a rediscovery occurred all over the world, and it affected parliamentary government all over the continent of Europe; but we are concerned here only with the way in which it stirred up France. Robert de Jouvenel's famous sentence (politics in France was a luxury, not the condition of men's lives) was true only as long as the bases of the system were not threatened. Now, the return to politics of previously indifferent groups can mean two completely different things. It can mean that the existing political system will be *reactivated* because the discontents have found easy access to power through the political parties and pressure groups available. But when those parties do not fulfill their task and when the pressure groups are able only to increase the weaknesses of the state by milking it at the expense of the common good, the political system will be in danger of *collapse*.

The latter situation is the one which obtained in France. Existing political parties simply did not adjust to the new issues: they locked themselves in the traditional Republican fortress, instead of rebuilding it. A look at their program in 1936 shows the extent of sclerosis on both sides of the political fence. The left prevented constitutional reform, a prerequisite of political reconstruction, and, instead of building a positive alliance for the solution of the new problems enumerated above, it threw together a negative one against the forces which attacked the regime for its incapacity to solve those problems. Anti-Ligues [the Ligues were right-wing organizations] feelings were merely put in the place of former anticlericalism: 1935 was 1899 revisited; the economic program of the Popular Front baptised with the new slogan of 'purchasing power theory' the old practice of promising benefits to a huge quantity of groups.

Consequently people, groups, reviews, etc., who 'came from' the Republican parties originally, and found that they could not get their views across within those parties, became dissenters and started to float away. In the middle of the ocean, they found all those men, movements, journals, etc., of the Right, who had never had much faith in the Republic anyhow and had either attacked it all along from their past ghetto, or made it clear that their support was conditional upon the preservation of the kind of society the regime now seemed unable to save. These people became, on the whole, outspoken enemies. Thus the regular institutions looked more like a façade, with real life – suddenly turned most turbulent – somewhere else.

The Right-wing enemies were a highly interesting mass of people. They felt almost permanently deprived of real access to political power: *la République* was, on the whole, the Left. As long as political power did not matter because the dominance of the middle classes was secure, this insufficient access was not a major nuisance: the fact that left-wing parties were better organized than rightist parliamentary clans, that labor unions were more real than business or peasant groups, was of minor importance as long as the conservatives' Bastilles in society (civil service, industry and banks, the professions, the salons) still stood. With those positions threatened by economic chaos and political 'disorder' (1936), access to power had to be reopened. And such access was to be sought in anti-Republican ways rather than through the organization of new, but Republican, parties and pressure groups, for a variety of reasons, of which the most important was that such an effort would have gone against the grain – for it supposed a total change of heart among people who had supported (or tolerated) the Republic only because the regime required no big organizational work or apparatus from groups which wanted to dominate society *qua* élites, not *qua* political parties or *qua* special interests.[5] Anti-parliamentarism came infinitely more naturally – as had been shown by so many historical precedents.

How did the process of destruction unfold? The participants in the revolt against, or dissent from, the Republican system belonged to many categories, which I cannot enumerate in detail here. On the one hand, there were dissidents from existing political parties, such as the three men, who, ironically enough, were the first to speak of a Popular Front, only to be kept away or to turn away from it later: Doriot (ex-Communist), Déat (neo-Socialist) and Bergery (ex-Radical); Tardieu switched also from being one of the main statesmen of the regime to being one of the chief publicists against it. Those dissidents rubbed elbows with various political figures which had turned anti-parliamentary before 1934: the Maurrassiens, the Jeunesses Patriotes of Taittinger. One can put into the same category, or into a neighboring one, the newspapers which came more and more to support the themes of anti-Republicanism and played such a crucial role in bringing to France the climate of Vichy before Vichy.[6]

On the other hand, the 1930s were marked by the 'politization' of various groups of men who, in happier days, would not have dreamed of singing the *garstig Lied* [awful song] of politics: large quantities of intellectuals, after a period in which intellectuals had been singularly non-political – hence the mushrooming of new reviews and sects with grandiloquent programs and spiritualist verbiage; equally surprising numbers of engineers, especially from the École Polytechnique (cf. the X-Crise movement), where the old Saint-Simonian tradition of illuminism-cum-technology flourished again; students, who built up impressive-sounding youth movements (at a time when the parties also reactivated or created youth sections); veterans' associations, who substituted the jargon of national overhaul for the vocabulary of special financial complaints (the Croix de Feu are of course the biggest example); union leaders and businessmen who turned from their previous attitudes of non-cooperation or of no comment on politics, to studies of general reform and examples from other countries (*Syndicats; Les Nouveaux Cahiers* . . .).

Coming from so many different milieux, counting so many people whose sudden discovery of public affairs had gone to their heads like extra-fine champagne, these groups amounted more to a maelstrom of confused anger than to a coherent onslaught on the Republican synthesis. Indeed, if there is one characteristic of these movements in the period under consideration, it is the bitterness of their own divisions. At first, their quarrels were not more than yelps of dissent among dissenters, although, of course, French yelps can be a mighty strain on any ear. Indeed, after a few months in 1933–4, when all these people fraternized in astonishment at their common feelings and slogans, they immediately began to excommunicate each other and to raise nuances to the dignity of abysses once again. Later, once the regime was abolished, or had rather fainted into the trap the Germans, plus Laval, had opened, the disputes among the former critics of the regime led to a quasi-civil war between Vichy and the Resistance, both being composed essentially of the discontents of the 1930s.

Nevertheless they had common grievances against the Republican synthesis and since these themes announce post-war France, it is important to list them. They all express a revolt against the kind of society and state which was described above.

The most superficial common theme was the critique of French parliamentarism. The most interesting example is probably Tardieu's set of volumes composed between 1934 and 1936. Tardieu's remark that if one wants to be heard by the country it is best not to be a parliamentarian is significant enough. Practically all the dissenters from the Republic argued in favor of a stronger State, one less dependent on the whims of the representatives and less submissive to the individual pressures of the voters on the parliamentarians.

A deeper theme is an attack, not so much on the stalemate society as such, but on its individualistic form. This meant two things.

[First], an attack on the neglect of groups in French 'official' thought and public law. The proliferation of youth movements, the concern for new formulas of organization and representation of interests, the rediscovery of man-as-a-social-being in contemporary 'public philosophy', under the loftily vague name of *personnalisme* (*ésprit, l'ordre nouveau* – [spirit, new order]) were the various aspects of this revival of group thinking, opposed to the doctrine of Alain or of the Jacobin state.

[Second], an attack on French capitalism. Here of course ambiguity was supreme, and misunderstandings were most juicy, for some of those attackers wanted (at least they thought so) to overthrow the private-enterprise economy, whereas others criticized French capitalism only because it had not succeeded in freezing the stalemate society once and for all. Thus the former argued for greater socialization of the economy, for more state intervention and planning. But the latter still feared state dabbling more than anything except communism (but that was about the same in their eyes); therefore, they merely wanted France's economic forces to organize solidly at last, and to coordinate their policies among themselves, in order precisely to prevent the state from using the present lack of organization as a pretext for 'étatisme'. What all nevertheless agreed upon, was that present disorganized (i.e. neither state- nor self-regulated) capitalism was rotten; for it wasted national resources through the excesses of competition (Doriot), it demoralized the nation through its materialism (La Rocque), it encouraged uprooted adventurers and nomadic speculators (Bardoux, *L'Ordre nouveau*)[7], it crushed *'les petits'* and benefited only *'les gros'* (*Frontisme*), it built new 'feudal orders' in France (veterans' movements). There is marvelous irony in the spectacle of so many people denouncing in the fiasco of French 1934–5 capitalism the discomfiture of *'l'économie libérale'*, if one remembers how little free competition and indeed how much self-regulation there was in this most restrictive economy. But it was well-concealed self-regulation, and what the partisans of 'organized professions' wanted was officially proclaimed and sanctioned self-regulation, giving to business groups powers snatched away from the state, or from unions. The 'plan du 9 juillet' (1934) shows in its text and in its list of signatories a fine case of generalized but significant confusion.

In both these attacks, all the groups involved addressed themselves primarily to the French middle classes. This was as true of La Rocque or Doriot as it was of men like Déat, Bergery, Izard, or Belin.

Another theme, which went perhaps even deeper, was a universal lament about the moral climate of France. This was the generation of *péguysme* (poor Péguy!), on whom Mounier had just written a book, and the epoch of activism: Sorel, Proudhon, were the patron saints of many of the new reviews. Malraux was of course a shining hero-witness of the revolt against the climate of mediocrity and immobility. The examples given by other countries were constantly displayed, discussed, and sometimes even studied (cf. the meetings at Pontigny).

The ways in which all these groups participated in the demise of the Republican synthesis and pushed France out of the drydock in which it had been waiting for permanently postponed repairs are far too complicated to be described in detail, but two points are of major interest.

First, the confusing mass of dissenters ultimately split into two blocs (heterogeneous, to be sure). On the one hand, all the people who ended on the side of Vichy, or rather those whom de Gaulle calls 'les amants inconsolables de la défaite et de la collaboration' [the inconsolable lovers of defeat and collaboration]: the Murrassiens – hermetically sealed counter-revolutionaries; the Fascists of occupied Paris (literary types, like Drieu, or gangsters, like Doriot's pals) and of Vichy France (muddleheaded activists like Darnand or schemers like Benoist-Méchin), the much bigger groups of disgruntled conservatives, shaking sheep with wolves' voices, like La Rocque, Pétain's Légionnaires and so many of his civil servants, business or peasant leaders; pacifists whose left-wing origins had been erased by their prolonged fight against communism and for appeasement, like Belin and many of Déat's friends. On the other hand, all those dissenters from the Third Republic who nevertheless hated defeat and Nazism more than a French form of democracy and who became the leaven in the more political Resistance organizations, where they met thousands of intellectuals, journalists, doctors, lawyers, military men, and so on, many of whom had had no previous political activity. Those future '*Résistants*' dissenters belonged largely to two groups: a relatively tight one, the Christian Democrats, whose *personnalisme* was politically liberal, not authoritarian, and whose pluralism was democratic, not élitist; a much more loose group, the former *planistes* from business or from the unions.[8] It was only later in the Resistance that the members of the parties of the Third Republic (and, of course, not all of them) joined those former dissenters, gradually submerged them, and turned the Resistance into a second coming of the Popular Front.

Second, if one looks at the direction taken by France after 1934, starting from the equilibrium described in the beginning, one can distinguish, with some exaggeration, two phases. First there was, under Vichy, a movement of contraction: the triumph for a few years of a reactionaries' delirium, which broke with the 'individualistic' society of the Third Republic in order to establish a *société communautaire* whose organized and self-regulating groups were even more Malthusian in economic practice, and more dominated by the anti-industrial, anti-urban ideal than the Republic had ever been. Then, after 1944, movement went in the opposite direction: economic expansion, a loosening up of society instead of the tight and petrified moral order of Vichy.

III

We now have to establish a balance sheet of the effects which the process we have just sketchily described brought about during World War II. The central fact is that the two movements – constriction and renovation – converged on a number of very important points. This strange dialectic can be explained without any recourse to the invisible hand of history: the participants in the two revolutions of Vichy and the Resistance had some common (if often negative) ideas, and since many of Vichy's dreams were beyond realization – 'ce qui est exagéré ne compte pas' [that which is exaggerated does not count] – many of Vichy's reforms inevitably turned into directions Vichy neither expected nor desired, or even produced effects contrary to those which the authors of these reforms had hoped to obtain.

If we look at changes in society at the end of the war, we see both major innovations and a few sharp limits. As for the innovations, the most significant is largely due to Vichy's impact. A number of groups in society emerged from pre-war chaos or confusion with the kind of organization which made of them possible levers for economic and social change. Alain's individualistic society has indeed been left behind. Vichy's motives in setting up these bodies were mixed: corporatist ideology (the 'restitution' to organized groups in society of powers which the Republican state had supposedly usurped) was strengthened by the need to set up bodies which could administer the restrictions forced upon the French economy by defeat and occupation. Furthermore, some of Vichy's authorities wanted to prevent the Germans from controlling the French economy, as they could otherwise have done, either by benefiting from its lack of organization or by setting up a German-directed organization.[9] The result was, in business, the creation of 'organization committees' which became the mold of the post-war Conseil National du Patronat Français.[10] Vichy's Peasant Corporation provided first its structure for the Confédération Générale Agricole instituted at the Liberation in reaction against the Corporation's ideology and leaders, and later many of its former key men for the Fédération Nationale des Syndicats d'Exploitants Agricoles which grew out of the ill-starred CGA. The leaders which the Resistance teams had put in charge of the CGA were gradually ousted as the peasants moved politically back toward the right, and the 'men of Vichy' were returned to the jobs from which M. Tanguy-Prigent, the Socialist Minister of Agriculture of 1945, had expelled them.[11] Embryonic organizations of *cadres* created within the Labor Charter of Vichy have flourished, since. The professions' orders (lawyers, doctors, etc.), established between 1940 and 1944, have been preserved and consolidated.

Continuity here has been most striking. In spite of their revulsion against Vichy corporatism, the Resistance movements did not propose a return to pre-war 'individualism'. The shortages of the Liberation made a continuation of the Vichy-created bodies inevitable anyhow (under different names). But, more significantly, the programs of the main Resistance movements and parties contained, in addition to ritual attacks on *féodalités économiques* [feudal economics] and 'corporative dictatorship' a plea for a new economic system in which the economy would be directed by the state after consultation with the representatives of economic interests.[12] The pluralism advocated by the MRP in particular contributed to remove any tinge of illegitimacy from the organized groups which had survived the Vichy period. Vichy certainly did not create these bodies for purposes of industrialization, economic modernization, or education toward a less fragmented society. But after having been the transmission belts for Vichy's philistine propaganda or for the German war machine, such institutions could serve as the relays of the Monnet plan.[13] Indeed, the sense of shame or embarrassment which many of the leaders of business felt after the Liberation, at a time when the business community was widely accused of having collaborated wholesale with the Germans, probably contributed to making these men almost eager to prove their patriotism by cooperating with the new regime for economic reconstruction and expansion.

A second phenomenon was also initiated by Vichy. The business and peasant organizations set up in these years were put under the direction of men far less reluctant to break away from economic Malthusianism than the spokesmen for 'organized' business and farmers before the war – the Gignoux or the CGPF [Confederation of Businessmen] or the Pesquidoux of the Société des Agriculteurs. In the business committees, delegates of big business, not of small enterprises, were put in charge; furthermore, these men were managers rather than owners. Indeed, spokesmen for small business and representatives of certain traditional, patriarchal family enterprises expressed considerable hostility toward the Committees;[14] they realized that in these bodies men with bolder ideas, who were far from scared by the thought of planning and of economic cooperation with the government, were entrusted with more means of action than the leading businessmen had ever had in France's predominantly non-organized economy before the war. The solidarity between small and large business – the latter protecting the former, the former accepting in return the leadership of the latter in trade associations – was severely tried by the circumstances of 1940–4; under German pressure, but with less resistance from some of the Committee's leaders than from some of Vichy's officials, measures of concentration of enterprises were put into effect.[15]

In the Peasant Corporation, the men in control were neither small peasants representing the more backward areas of rural France, nor big old-fashioned landowners – members of the aristocracy whose farms were really in the hands of tenants – but commercially minded men more concerned with markets and remuneration than with status, or rather, aware of the fact that the traditional *économie familiale* of French peasants could be preserved best through technical improvements, professional education, the regrouping of excessively divided lands, extended credit facilities, and a better organization of markets.[16]

Thus the more dynamic elements of the economy were given effective positions, instead of remaining dispersed or submerged. The ideas of groups such as the *Jeunes Patrons* or the pre-war *Nouveaux Cahiers* received, in these institutions, a kind of official blessing they had never had before. Needless to say, these men were still primarily interested in obtaining advantages for their respective groups; as the post-war record of continued milking of the state by pressure groups shows, an old history of state intervention designed to preserve the status quo and to give privileges to all had not ended by 1945.[17] Nevertheless, one major change of outlook had taken place: the 'new men' had a less parochial and less compartmentalized view of the economic problems of their profession and of the nation than their predecessors. Here as in other areas, one of the paradoxical results of a period which saw France divided into more administrative zones and separate realms than at any time since the Revolution – in part because of the restrictions on, and later the breakdown of, communications – was to inject a greater awareness of the nation-wide scope of economic problems. Consequently, the need for attacking these problems at least from within the framework of a whole profession, rather than through reliance on individual and local pressures, also became understood. The physical fragmentation of 1940–4 dealt a heavy blow to the economic and social fragmentation of pre-war France.

This became apparent in another way as well. Because of the defeat and later in reaction against Vichy there occurred a kind of rediscovery of France and of the French by the French. Common sufferings did a great deal to submerge, if not to close, some of the fissures which the social fabric of France had suffered before the war. This rediscovery took many forms. One of the most paradoxical at first sight was the celebration of Péguy by Vichy as well as by the Resistance; but wasn't Péguy a symbol of love for *la France charnelle* [physical France] independently of political ideologies or philosophical abstractions? It is important to remember that after the orgy of self-lacerations and doubts which had marked the 1930s, both the Resistance forces and the non-Fascist elements of Vichy fostered what I would call a nationalist revival. Much of it may have been Boy-Scoutish, but it was Boy-Scoutism nationalized. The kind of civic education, the *veillées* [evenings] at which Barrès or Péguy were read, the cult of Joan of Arc, which Vichy's youth camps and youth movements offered to their members, the intense, generous and somewhat confused social nationalism of the École des Cadres at Uriage,[18] pointed in the same direction as the Jacobin nationalism of much of the Resistance. Finally, when Vichy became a shrunken, isolated and Fascist-dominated little clique, common opposition to the occupants and the collaborators brought together people and groups who had remained separated both in pre-war France and in the period of Vichy which preceded Laval's return to power. The collaborators played in 1944–5 the sad but useful role of scapegoats, and the shrillest of their enemies were often men who had first put their faith in Pétain and shared in Vichy's integral nationalism of 1940–1. The myth which the Resistance men gladly endorsed – that almost all of France was *résistante* in 1944 – contributed to healing some of the wounds which the clash between Vichy's forces and the Resistance had opened. If Vichy was a well-localized cancer, and the rest of the body of France was healthy, then a reunion in nationalism was possible for all except the black sheep. The extraordinary nationalist fervor of the Communists in the Resistance and Liberation days[19] was far more than a tactical shift. It constituted in many cases a genuine emotional wave of relief after (or should I say expiation for) the somber period 1939–41, when Communist opposition to the war had pushed the Party's members and sympathizers outside of the national community – or out of the Party. The executions of collaborators in the summer and fall of the Liberation were examples of ritual murders far more than evidence of civil war.

Another aspect of this rediscovery of France as a community was the growth of Catholic influence. Again, both political forces contributed to it. Most of the youth organizations created by Vichy were fiascos almost from the start, in the sense that they never succeeded either in attracting the bulk of the nation's youth, or in bringing their members to endorse Vichy's brand of ideology.[20] But Catholic action groups and Catholic youth movements benefited greatly from the encouragements received during the war years: Vichy-created movements, in search of *cadres*, turned to men obligingly placed at their disposal by Catholic movements. The Catholic Association of French Youth thus became a link between the movements operating in France during the Vichy period, and post-war French youth organizations.[21] The role of Catholics in the Resistance needs hardly to be stressed: whereas the Catholic element in the making of France had been more and more minimized by official political leaders, textbook writers, and Sorbonne representatives of the pre-war Republic, the Resistance movements reversed the trend. 'Celui qui croyait au ciel, celui qui n'y croyait pas' [He who believes in heaven, he who does not believe]: Aragon's famous poem testifies to the reconciliation which had taken place thanks to Christian Democracy.

This reconciliation took on more concrete aspects as well. Just as economic groups were encouraged to organize, other associations were launched in order to bring the French closer together: roving companies of young comedians, groups of young music lovers were supposed to bring art back to non-Parisians and to shake the French out of their individualism.[22] The emphasis so heavily put on youth and on the family by Vichy was intended to contribute to the rebirth of a sense of community. The Resistance did nothing to reverse the movement – were not its organizations dominated by young men who acceded to responsibilities which French youth had been deprived of since the days of the Revolution? As for the emphasis on the importance of family life, the Christian-Democrats saw to it that it would not disappear with the Vichy regime.

The revival of community was obviously far from complete or final, and it is impossible to measure the degree of community in a nation. But I would maintain that it has been much higher after 1944 than in the 1930s, despite the return of the Communists into their ghetto, and such phenomena as Poujadism; the tone of public arguments has been much milder; the hysteria so characteristic of debates in the 1930s has been limited to lunatic fringes. France as a *political* community may have been almost as pathetic after 1946 as before 1939. But there are other levels or forms of community as well, and those, which had been badly damaged in the 1930s, were in much better shape after the Liberation.

However, two obvious limitations must be mentioned:

[First], relations between workers and other social groups were not permanently improved. Indeed, they did not improve at all under Vichy, where the policy practiced both by the state and by business organizations was one of reaction and repression. The legislation which the Popular Front had made in order to bring classes closer together had failed almost completely.[23] The bitter denunciations of business attitudes toward labor in most Resistance platforms indicate how deep this fissure had become. The bad memories left, on the workers' side, by the Labor Charter and the rump unions sponsored by Vichy or by Paris collaborators, and, on the management side, by the reforms of the Liberation, were going to doom legislative attempts such as the Comités d'Entreprises (needless to say, Communist domination of the labor movement contributed to the failure). Nationalization has not noticeably contributed to the 'reintegration of the proletariat into the nation' which the Resistance wanted to achieve and which Socialists saw as one of the main advantages of public ownership. What Michel Crozier calls 'l'horreur du face à face' [the horrors of meeting face-to-face][24] has remained a basic obstacle.

[Second], one group has emerged from World War II both split and largely alienated from the rest of the national community: the army. The breach between elements which remained faithful to Pétain and those which followed De Gaulle was never completely repaired. If the Vichy armed forces found themselves increasingly unpopular in a country which was at first put under quasi-military control by a defeated army and navy, the Gaullist military leaders, who fought outside of France (and often against other Frenchmen) found it difficult to adjust to the political and moral climate of France after the war ended. Their dream of a France *pure et dure* had been cruelly shattered, and the famous clash of December 1945 between the Constituent Assembly and General de Gaulle indicated that in the new regime, once De Gaulle was eliminated, the army would not have a *'place de choix'*. In a way, both the misuse of its armed forces by Vichy, and the predominantly civilian character of the Resistance contributed to discredit the army, despite De Gaulle's attempts at an *amalgame* between Resistance, Free French, and formerly Vichyite forces.[25]

The changes on the political front have been more contradictory than those in society, but many nevertheless deserve to be discussed.

The following innovations have drastically transformed the political system as it had developed before:

[First], power fell into the hands of the previous 'minorities' – of those groups of men who, for one reason or another, did not belong to, or had become separated from, *'la République des Camarades'*. The fall of France was the 'divine surprise' of many of the dissenters or enemies whom we have mentioned before; metropolitan France became the battlefield between the factions into which those groups split – corporatists against *belinistes*, pro-Pétain Christian-Democrats against Maurrassiens, and of course Fascists against conservatives or technocrats – or against other Fascists. Those dissenters who either refused to support Vichy or abandoned Vichy after a few months of hesitation (as did many Catholics, who were first taken in by institutions such as the Uriage school or youth camps)[26] became, as we know, the backbone of the early

Resistance. One of the paradoxes of the restoration of 1945–6 is that although it brought back many of the parties discredited in 1940, and political institutions close to those which had collapsed on 10 July, the political personnel of the Third Republic never succeeded in coming back in toto. Of course there was Queuille and Schuman; but the latter had hardly been a star before the war: he had belonged to a party which never fitted the system of the Third Republic. Neither these two men, nor Herriot – more a monument now than a leader – ever gave its tone to the Fourth Republic. In the old parties which re-emerged, purges liquidated many of the pre-war leaders. Thus in the Socialist Party, new men like Mollet, Daniel Mayer, and the syndicalists (Lacoste, Pineau) took over from the generation of Blum and Paul Faure.

[Second], a second and major change was the acceptance of an interventionist state – at last. Vichy's philosophy was, to start with, diametrically opposed to it; Vichy's dream was the 'absolute but limited' state, so dear to counter-revolutionaries ever since Bonald. But despite its theory of decentralization and of corporations running the economy under a distant and discreet check from the state, Pétain's regime was unable to practice what it preached. In the business organizations Vichy set up, civil servants and managers learned to run the show together. Here, Bichelonne's influence was considerable. One of his associates calls him the father of professional statistics in France;[27] his all-encompassing activity as minister of industry marked a break with the past tradition of a civil service whose interventions in economic affairs were largely limited to measures protecting vested interests, defending them against competition but never challenging their privately decided policies. Bichelonne's selection of the bosses of the business committees contributed mightily to replacement of those businessmen for whom the state could only be either an enemy or a servant with managers for whom the state could be a guide. Thus Bichelonne's administration initiated practices of cooperation which the Monnet Plan later institutionalized.

Indeed, on the other side of the political fence, the need for a more active state had become one of the main planks of Resistance platforms: planning by the state, nationalization, by public investments, 'economic and social democracy', state control over cartels, prices or capital movements, all these suggestions showed that the revulsion against the lopsided 'economic liberalism' of pre-war times had become irresistible. The measures taken in 1944–6 in order to put these proposals into effect are well known. None of the 'conquests of the Liberation' has been seriously threatened since; the attacks against 'dirigisme' by Radicals and Conservatives were successful only when they were aimed at price controls and at those measures of intervention into the affairs of rural France which the peasant organizations had not requested themselves.

[Third], a change in public issues resulted. Already before 1939, a subtle shift had occurred. On the one hand the key ideological issue of the Third Republic had begun to fade away, for official hostility to the Church had weakened ever since the Popular Front.[28] Except for the years 1945–51, private schools have received help from the state since 1941. [...]

On the other hand, the state began to promote measures of income redistribution which went far beyond what the theory of the stalemate society allowed, or showed concern for social welfare on a scale unknown before. The *politique de la famille* [politics of the family] has been followed by every regime since Daladier's decrees of July 1939. Vichy gave tremendous publicity to its main contribution to social insurances: the old age pensions for retired workers. Resistance platforms emphasized the need for extending protection against social risks, and the social security system of the Liberation was built by a man who had been one of the main drafters of the law of August 1940 setting up Vichy's business committees.[29] The participation of workers' delegates in at least some of the activities of the firm became the subject of various laws, from the Popular Front's shop stewards to Vichy's *comités sociaux* and the Liberation's *comités d'entreprises*. Thus, economic and social issues tended to replace the old ideological ones, and this shift contributed to the 'nationalization' of opinion and issues which proportional representation accelerated. The fragmentation of the political scene into 'fiefs' and local issues began to fade just as economic fragmentation did. [...]

A few words should be said about the changes in the French image of France in the world; this is a subject which is very difficult to treat, for there is little evidence to back one's statements, and which deserves much further study.

On the one hand, the need to readjust France to a changed world was felt by many, both in Vichy and in the Resistance; even though the battle between those two groups of forces was fought largely because of their different views of the world and of France's role, there were again at least two points on which the antagonism was far from complete.

The need to put an end to the alarming economic retardation of France in order to restore or preserve France's position in the world was understood by a large number of the dissenters from the Third Republic. Many of the civil servants who joined in Resistance movements, or even served throughout in the Vichy regime, were in close touch with the formidable German war economy and came to realize how strong the link between industrial organization and political power was.[30] Many of the business leaders and engineers of Vichy were also thrown into contact – often collaboration – with Germany's extraordinary dynamism; they negotiated with German business leaders and officials, and many of them visited German plants and business offices. As a consequence, these men became far more aware of the need for organization, concentration, higher productivity, an improved statistical equipment, better industrial relations and more cooperation between the business community and the state. In the last period of the war and in the months which followed its end, the contact with America's own war machine, industrial economy and bureaucratic efficiency provided the same groups of Frenchmen with another compelling display of the pre-requisites of influence in the modern world.

Civil servants and businessmen had also realized – often under duress – during the occupation the amount of interdependence of Western European economies and the possibilities of cooperation across borders. This point, like the preceding one, had been made by small cliques of 'dissenters' before the war: the men of *Les Nouveaux Cahiers* or X-Crise, Déat and his *planistes*. Now it became a matter of daily life. Second, within a different context, post-war European unity became also a theme of many Resistance movements, who were either looking forward to a European holy alliance of the peoples against trusts and munition makers, or dreaming of a powerful Europe playing once again a major role in world affairs. Despite this more ideological or political approach, Resistance 'European' feelings buttressed the practical concern of the more technocratic Vichyites; indeed it is thanks to such Resistance dreams that the idea of European unity survived its exploitation by Nazi propaganda. Third, General de Gaulle also looked forward to a European political force playing its own part in world affairs.[31] Of course, the officials and businessmen of Vichy thought primarily in terms of Franco-German cooperation, whereas the Resistance and De Gaulle thought in terms of the links forged between the victims of Germany by Nazi domination. But the two conceptions were not mutually exclusive. After the war, when the Fourth Republic decided to scrap its policy of revenge and to replace it with a Franco-German partnership, although the new approach met with numerous protectionist objections from French businessmen, it did not encounter much opposition (outside of the Communist Party) to its basic idea of the need for reconciliation and cooperation between the two former enemies. Many Resistance platforms and De Gaulle himself had mentioned such a need for after the war and denazification. In a way, Laval's statement that, whatever the result of the war, France and Germany would remain neighbors and would therefore have to find a *modus vivendi* was more universally understood than one realized at first, and the contacts which had been established between 'élites' of the two countries during the occupation period, especially in the business world, were probably far from wasted. Within the *Festung Europa* [Fortress Europe] which waited for its liberation from the outside, occupied peoples and temporary masters discovered that they might be enemies, but that they also had a lot in common, which distinguished them from the outsiders.

The separation between Nazi-dominated Europe and the outside world however had some far less constructive effects, which were probably more important at least in the immediate post-war period.

The main factor here could be described as follows: at the same time as many Frenchmen came to understand that a deep economic transformation was needed in order to preserve France's importance in the world, the trauma of the war years blinded them to changes which made France's restoration to the status of a world power highly problematic, even in case of domestic economic overhaul. They overlooked the forces which were turning into an obsolescent delusion the old French image of a world responsive to the universality of French values and the vision of a map in which French colors would occupy almost as much space as England's. Here again, many elements contributed to the same result – Vichy's fantasy of neutral France mediating in the war;[32] the lack of concern for foreign affairs displayed by the Resistance; the inevitable reaction of bitter and almost desperate pride which the humiliation of submission to the occupant was bound to provoke; the tremendous effort by De Gaulle in 1944–5 to restore French self-respect by emphasizing France's contribution to the Allied victory; the huge quantities of war prisoners who spent the war *hors jeu* in German camps. On the colonial front in particular, the curtain which cut off France from the world outside of Europe prevented both the Vichy élites and the future leaders of the Fourth Republic who were in the metropolitan Resistance from realizing how deep the revolt against a simple restoration of pre-war colonial rule, or even against half-hearted liberal measures, had become in the former Empire.

The force which, because of its very humiliations, internal splits and traditions, was least likely to adjust to the change in the international position of France was of course the army. Those elements which remained on the side of Vichy were both submitted to, and willing partners in, constant xenophobic propaganda; those elements which joined De Gaulle or re-entered the war after the Giraud detour, primarily wanted to erase the memory of the defeat of 1940 and to restore France to an uncontested position of eminence. Many of the post-war aspects of *le malaise de l'armée* – the tendency to see a plot against France behind every incident, the readiness to see defeatism in every concession – have their roots in World War II.

IV

By way of a summary and instead of a conclusion, here are a few paradoxes for our meditation.

First, the Resistance and Vichy, which fought one another so bloodily, cooperated in many ways without wanting or knowing it, and thus carried the nation to the threshold of a new social order. It can be said that the two groups which gained most from the war years were business and the Catholic Church – a far cry from the France of 1936. Vichy brought into existence social institutions which could become the channels for state action, and gave a considerable boost to the descendants of the Saint-Simoniens, men who were willing to serve as agents of the Count's old dream – organization, production, industrialism. The Resistance brought to power teams of engineers, civil servants and politicians determined to use these agents and these channels for economic and consequently for social change. Had those teams not arrived, it is quite possible that the social institutions erected by Vichy would have withered away just as the consortiums of World War I had vanished after 1919. But without readily available transmission belts and without the shock of discovery produced on French economic élites by sudden and brutal contact with foreign economies, post-war planning might have failed. The transformation of the French economy and society since 1952 is due to the combination of the wills of a statist De Gaulle – and a Saint-Simonien Monnet – who used instruments prepared by Vichy and strengthened them by adding quite a few of their own (nationalizations, the Planning Commission, a reform of the civil service, etc.). The meekness of the *patronat* [business owners], unwilling to oppose the government of the Liberation, and the big production drive of the Communists in 1944–7 which contrasted with labor's pre-war attitude, both contributed to the initial success of the movement. The process is far from completed, and no transformation of French political life has resulted from it so far. But World War II had on French society effects opposite from those of World War I.

Second, the continuity between Vichy and its successor, which we have noted when we mentioned the economy, family protection, the 'rediscovery' of youth and the revival of Catholicism, appears also, in more ironic fashion, in a number of failures. The hope of reconciling the workers and the employers has not been fulfilled. Neither the paternalistic solutions of the Vichy Labor Charter nor the social measures of the Liberation have succeeded in overcoming a long tradition of mutual suspicion. In the future, perhaps new attitudes among businessmen concerned with 'human relations', and the increasing hierarchy and specialization within the working class – all resulting from economic change – might gradually overcome old antagonisms. Both Vichy and the Resistance movements emphasized the need to preserve, in agriculture, the traditional family units; their post-war decline has been spectacular, and no amount of protection from the state has been able to suspend it. Indeed, mechanization of the farms has often contributed to this process, for it increases the financial difficulties of farmers whose products sell at prices which remain at a lower level than the cost of the machines, as well as the plight of peasants whose land is too small for efficient production. Both regimes have failed to preserve the morale, the unity and the strength of the army. Finally, both have failed to stabilize the French political system. The new society of France still awaits a political synthesis comparable to the early Third Republic; all it presently has is a respite.

Third, both regimes provide us with choice examples of serendipity. Vichy, which wanted to coax the French back to the land and back to rule by traditional notables, consolidated instead the business community and demonstrated conclusively that the elites of 'static' France could not provide leadership any more. Vichy also wanted to restore old provincial customs and dialects and peculiarities – instead of which it put into motion powerful forces of further economic and social unification. The Resistance, which wanted to purify French political life and was prone to proclaim the death of the bourgeoisie, ended as a political fiasco, but was the lever of an economic modernization which has certainly not meant the demise of the bourgeoisie. Indeed, those of the dissenters from the Third Republic who turned against it because they wanted to save the stalemate society which the Republic seemed unable to defend, an order based on the preponderance of the middle classes, could remark today that French society is still dominated by these classes. The proportion of industrial workers has barely increased.

However, French society is no longer the same. The division between proletarians and *indépendants* has been largely replaced by a less original hierarchy of functional groups in which many of the workers partake of middle-class characteristics and in which managers, *cadres* and employees are increasingly numerous. The village is less important as an economic unit; the family is a less tightly closed one; the attitude toward savings and credit has been reversed; there is less distance between ranks and statuses in society; businessmen, peasants and shopkeepers alike are more dependent on the national economy than on a mere segment of it; the economy is far more planned (or at least *concertée* [organized]), and the market is at last seen as growing instead of frozen. In other words, a more dynamic society has replaced the tight stalemate society of the past. Between 1934 and today, the transition from *la France bourgeoise* to *la France des classes moyennes*, from the *Revue des Deux Mondes* to *Réalités* has been crossed.

The double consensus on which the Third Republic had lived (with increasing discomfort) has consequently been transformed. The political consensus included all the groups which accepted the tenets of the Revolution; it left out only the Extreme Right, and it had its center of gravity on the left. But this formula has been affected by the divison and deterioration of the left after the Liberation, as well as by the quasi-liquidation of the Extreme Right. Hence the weight has shifted to the right, and the relevance of the old issues has diminished. The social consensus encompassed all the groups which accepted the stalemate society; it excluded only the proletariat, and had its center of gravity on the conservative side, but this formula has been affected by industrialization, which tends to reintegrate the working class into the enterprises and the nation, and to make the business community less economically and socially conservative. [. . .]

Notes

1 Edmond Goblot, *La barrière et le niveau*, (Paris 1925), p. 6.
2 See Sartre's definition of the bourgeois: 'le moyen terme élevé à la toute-puissance', [the middle way raised to omnipotence] in 'Qu'est-ce que la littérature', *Situations*, II, Paris, 1948, p. 157.
3 See the analyses by David Landes and John Sawyer in E. Earle (ed.) *Modern France*, Princeton, NJ, 1950, and Jesse R. Pitts, 'The Bourgeois Family and French Economic Retardation', Harvard Ph.D. thesis, unpublished, 1957.
4 For instance: within the business world, between big firms and small firms thus protected against cut-throat competition; in the relations between the business world and the landed notables, both groups indulging in joint investments in land ... or in protectionism; in the relations between business and the civil servants, with highly developed practices of *connubium, convivium,* and 'pantouflage'.
5 See for further elaboration, my article 'Aspects du Régime de Vichy', *Revue française de science politique*, January–March, 1956, pp. 44–69.
6 See C. Micaud, *The French Right and Nazi Germany*, Durham, 1943.
7 See his book, *L'Ordre nouveau face au communisme et au racisme*, Paris, 1939.
8 Cf. the Resistance movements *Libération-Sud* and especially the *OCM*.
9 See on this point René Belin's statement in *La vie de la France sous l'occupation*, Paris, 1957, I, 145.
10 See Henry Ehrmann, *Organized Business in France*, Princeton, NJ, 1957, chs II–III.
11 See Adolphe Pointier's embattled testimony in *La vie de la France sous l'occupation*, I, 275 ff, and H. Mendras and J. Fauvet (eds) *Les paysans et la politique*, Paris, 1958, *passim*.
12 See for instance the famous program of the Conseil National de la Résistance in B. Mirkine-Guetzévitch and H. Michel (eds) *Les Idées politiques et sociales de la Résistance*, Paris, 1954, pp. 215 ff. [Reprinted, in translation in *War, Peace and Social Change: Documents* 2, Milton Keynes, 1989]
13 Continuity is well demonstrated by the case of Aimé Lepercq, who was the head of one of Vichy's main business committees (coal mines) and later De Gaulle's Finance Minister.
14 See for instance Belin's reference to a letter of M. de Peyerimhoff, the head of the Comité des Houillères, *La Vie de la France*, I, 150. Pierre Nicolle's book, *Cinquante mois d'armistice*, Paris, 1947, is a perfect record of all the campaigns waged by small business against Vichy's Business Committees.
15 See *La Vie de la France*, vol. I, pp. 14ff.
16 See the interesting collection of *Syndicats Paysans*, for 1940–2 (the paper of Jacques Leroy-Ladurie and Louis Salleron).
17 See for instance the story of such measures in post-war France in Warren C. Baum's rather one-sided book, *The French Economy and the State*, Princeton, NJ, 1958.
18 See the study of the School by Janine Bourdin, in the *Revue française de science politique*, IX, 4, Sept.–Dec. 1959.
19 Remember Aragon's poems ('mon parti m'a rendu les couleurs de la France ...') [Reprinted in translation in *War, Peace and Social Change: Documents* 2, Milton Keynes, 1989]

20 The most edifying story is that of the movement of *Les Compagnons de France*: see issue 27 (1943) of *Métier de Chef*, which tells most of it.

21 See *Positions d'ACJF, 7 ans d'histoire au service de la jeunesse de France*, Paris, 1946.

22 The artistic association *Jeune France,* sponsored by Vichy, became a breeding ground for numerous talents that were to become famous in post-war France. The *Jeunesses Musicals Françaises* dates from the war years also.

23 See Val R. Lorwin, *The French Labor Movement*, Cambridge, 1954, pp. 78–9.

24 In his article, 'La France, terre de commandement' in *Esprit,* December 1957, pp. 779–97.

25 On these points, there are many interesting remarks, in vol. III of De Gaulle's Memoirs, *Le Salut*, Paris, 1959.

26 The very swift evolution of *Esprit* in the latter half of 1940 is particularly interesting; so is that of the Uriage school, whose last class joined the Maquis.

27 See M. de Calan's testimony in *La Vie de la France*, I, 31ff.

28 See for instance the article by Father Renaud in *Revue des Deux Mondes* of 1 June 1939.

29 On Pierre Laroque's role in August 1940, see Belin in *La Vie de la France*, I, 146.

30 The testimonies in *La Vie de la France,* vol. 1, show how extensive the contacts between French civil servants in charge of the economy, and their German civilian or military counterparts had been.

31 See *Le Salut*, pp. 221ff.

32 See for instance Thierry-Maulnier, *La France, la guerre et la paix*, Paris, 1942.

* This article was presented as a paper in April, 1960 at the meeting of the Society for French Historical Studies in Rochester.

12

The 'Levelling of Class'

Penny Summerfield

Many historians subscribe to the idea that the Second World War was a 'leveller of classes'. Above all, Arthur Marwick depicted the war as a time when the gulf between classes narrowed. He attributed the change to the opportunities for participation in areas of work, politics and social life usually reserved for members of a single class which arose as a result of the labour shortage and political pressure associated with the war.[1]

This interpretation is influenced by the earlier writings of Stanislas Andrzejewski[2] and of R.M. Titmuss, who wrote, 'Mass war, involving a high proportion of the total population tends to a levelling in social class differences'.[3] Marwick argued that the 'relative changes' were greatest for the 'working class', which experienced a significant reduction in class differences *vis-à-vis* the 'middle class', even though the position of the 'upper class' was not much altered. He supported his argument with evidence of changes in the political position of the working class due to such things as the participation of trade union leaders and Labour politicians in government and with examples of new working-class self-images in wartime. Though indicative of change, however, this evidence does not represent a complete substantiation of the contention that a 'levelling of class' specifically benefiting the working class was achieved during the war. Discussion of the issue requires, first and foremost, clarification of the concept 'class'.

The definition of 'class' is itself a contentious issue.[4] But an omission from Marwick's account which is common ground in other discussions of class is a serious attempt to grapple with class as an economic relationship, whether in terms of income, occupation or ownership of capital. There is, of course, more to class than 'stratification' according to these criteria, notably 'consciousness of the nature and distribution of power in society' and 'sensations of collective identity of interest among individuals' which give rise to class consciousness and political and industrial organization and action.[5] A full investigation of 'the levelling of class' in the Second World War would embrace changes in both social stratification and class consciousness and activity, and if the hypothesis that wartime participation led to 'levelling' is right, one would expect to find both a reduction in the degree of stratification and a weakening of the political identity of separate social classes.

My intention here is to address only the first part of the hypothesis. This does not mean that I attribute exclusive importance to 'objective' economic indicators of class rather than to 'subjective' experiential ones relating to perception, consciousness and political expression, but it seemed important to tackle the issue of economic stratification in order to redress the balance of previous writing, and the matter became so complex and intriguing that I decided to devote this chapter to it.

The question of changes in social stratification before, during and after the war has been discussed, particularly in the 1950s and 1960s, by historians and sociologists interested in the course of social change during the twentieth century. They can be divided into three camps: those who believed that levelling took place in the Second World War and was permanent; those who argued that by some criteria levelling can be seen to have taken place but that it was not necessarily permanent; and those who concluded that no levelling took place at all.

D.C. Marsh's book *The Changing Social Structure of England and Wales* presents a case for permanent levelling over the period in which the Second World War occurred. Writing in 1958, Marsh concluded from his survey of income data based on tax returns that 'the gap between the very rich and the very poor is much smaller than it was even thirty years ago, and in money terms the inequalities in the distribution of income are less marked'.[6] Two and a half times as many incomes came within the tax ranges in 1950 as in 1920, embracing half the adult population, compared with about a quarter in 1919–20. A larger proportion came into the higher range of incomes over £500 (8 per cent compared with 2 per cent), and a smaller number declared themselves to be in the highest tax bracket, of incomes over £20,000. As far as accumulated wealth was concerned, in both 1930 and 1950 the vast majority of estates assessed for death duties were in the lower ranges, under £5,000, and only a small number were in the highest ranges over £100,000. The main change was in the range between these two figures, in which more than twice the number of estates were left in 1950 compared with 1930.[7] This apparent evidence of expansion of numbers in the middle income brackets and improvement in the position of those at the bottom gave rise to both optimism and alarm in the late 1940s and 1950s. The optimism was voiced by those who saw the war and, particularly, post-war reconstruction as ushering in a period of rising affluence and social stability.[8] The alarm was expressed by those such as Roy Lewis and Angus Maude who feared that the lowest income groups were making gains at the expense of 'the middle classes', whose drive and initiative were being fatally weakened as a result.[9]

In fact, of course, analyses of money incomes based on tax returns have well-known imperfections. Tax returns tell us nothing about the incomes of those below taxable levels, who constituted half of income-earners even in 1950, and, as many critics have pointed out, returns may not be accurate and will almost certainly not reflect 'hidden' income such as occupational perquisites most likely to benefit the higher-income earners.[10] Further, tax returns are taken to represent individually earned and consumed incomes, and it is rare for any attempt to be made to assess how many individuals in fact contributed to and lived on each income: wives (whether earning or not) and dependants such as children are invisible. Finally, the usefulness of tax returns for comparisons of income over time is severely limited by the changing value of money. G.D.H. Cole argued in 1955 that the fact that the value of money diminished in the period 1930 to 1950 by a factor of between two and three, while tax thresholds remained the same, 'accounts for a large part of the increase in the total number of incomes over £250, and also for a large part of the shift from lower to higher income grades'.[11] Thus Marsh's failure to take account of *real* incomes greatly exaggerates the 'levelling up' of incomes over the period of the war.

Work on income changes by Dudley Seers in the late 1940s came to more qualified conclusions. Seers made a crude division of income-earners into 'working-class', i.e. all wage-earners and non-manual workers with salaries of less than £250 per annum, and 'middle-class', i.e. all other salaried non-manual employees, and then used technically complex methods of attaching correct weightings to class-specific indices of pay and prices in order to assess changes in the real incomes of these two classes.[12] Seers claimed that after the war (1947) wages took up a larger proportion of the national income than salaries, which, coupled with the faster rise in the middle-class than in the working-class cost-of-living index, meant that the gap between the real net incomes of the two classes had narrowed. Comparing aggregates, Seers concluded that the real net incomes of the working class had risen by over 9 per cent, and those of the middle class had fallen by 7 per cent, between 1938 and 1947.[13] As far as causes were concerned, Seers explained the improved working-class share partly as a result of the rise in the national product during the war, and partly as a result of fiscal changes, including subsidies, which gave the working class 59 per cent of post-tax incomes in 1947 compared with 55 per cent in 1938. This led Seers to point out that the wartime redistribution of income could be 'largely reversed by fiscal means (e.g. by lowering the standard rate of income tax, reducing food subsidies, etc.)'. He suggested that such changes were already beginning with tax changes in 1947, the reduction of subsidies and the government policy of 'wage stabilization'.[14]

The upshot of Seers's arguments was that the future of the wartime redistribution of income was dependent on State action, a conclusion at which others arrived by different routes. For example, after observing that higher income groups retained less of their income than they had pre-war, G.D.H. Cole argued in 1955 that 'the effect of taxation on the distribution of real incomes has clearly been very substantial',[15] and later writers such as Westergaard and Resler noted that the more progressive direct taxation of the 1940s indeed reduced the share of top and middle incomes in the post-tax total between 1938 and 1949, while government controls over the cost of necessities – notably food, housing and fuel – during the war 'favoured those on low and moderate incomes'. These authors argued that the removal of controls after the war led to disproportionate increases in the price of these necessities, and that the reduction of the share of the richest 20 per cent in post-tax income was slight after 1949: 'The effect of this reversal of trends is to sharpen the contrast between the equalising tendencies of the decade of war and post-war "social reconstruction", and the stability or accentuation of income inequality from around 1950.'[16]

Thus the conclusion of these authors, led by Seers, on the subject of the levelling of class in the Second World War, differed from that of Marsh. The examination of real, post-tax incomes produced a more convincing case for levelling during the war than that which Marsh presented, but the stress on fiscal policy suggested that wartime levelling was not permanent, but was being reversed in the 1950s by government action. On the other hand, two aspects of this body of work may have led to overstatement of the degree of levelling during the war. First, the data used were aggregates rather than *per capita* incomes. The relative growth of the group earning either wages or salaries under £250, compared to that earning larger salaries, may have been important in pushing up the proportion of national income going to wages as opposed to salaries.[17] Second, this division of the recipients of income into wage- and salary-earners, manual and non-manual workers, members of the working and of the middle classes, is arbitrary and may have obscured both overlap between the two groups and stratification within them. We shall return to these points later in the discussion of levelling.

Of course, levelling of earned income is not all there is to levelling of social strata, let alone of social classes. Several authors have seen the situation with regard to property as ultimately more decisive. Thus T.B. Bottomore wrote, 'the inequality of incomes depends very largely upon the unequal distribution of property through inheritance, and not primarily upon the differences in earned income'.[18] For the class position of wage-earners to change,then, does not require simply enlargement of earnings, but the kind of consistent saving which would allow them to acquire and pass on property. 'Levelling', by this argument, is meaningful only if it is seen as a change in the distribution of property owners in society.

Most authors agree that the belief held by some public figures, particularly Liberal spokesmen, in the 1930s, that there was a widespread distribution of small savings and property in the working class, was erroneous.[19] However, the shift from high levels of unemployment and underemployment in the 1930s to full employment, overtime work and rising wage rates during the war caused some investigators to ask whether this situation was transformed between 1939 and 1945. Notably, Charles Madge, a sociologist, undertook to discover the truth about working-class accumulation during the war. He expected to find widespread and extensive working-class saving caused by the pressure, on the one hand, of improved earnings coupled with a limited supply of consumer goods due to shortages and rationing, and, on the other, of the official wartime campaign to promote savings as a counter to inflation. He therefore thought he would find a process of 'levelling up' within the social structure as more members of relatively low-income groups joined the ranks of small property holders.[20]

Madge reported that 'a great campaign' had been launched since 1939, to persuade people to save in three principal ways, through Trustee Saving Banks, by buying National Savings Certificates through the Post Office and through Savings Groups, which were usually based in the work-place, where a fixed deduction from the member's pay was made each week. The government had spent £834,100 on this campaign by June 1941. Madge found that the campaign had been successful in increasing the number of savers. There was considerable regional variation, but in the towns which Madge looked at, between 10 per cent and 30 per cent more families were saving by the new methods in 1942 than had been before the war, and they included those usually outside 'the orbit of national savings', such as 'families at low income levels and secondary earners'. This wartime saving was in addition to traditional methods of working-class saving, such as contributions to industrial assurance, pension funds, trade union subscriptions and voluntary health insurance, which Madge said were 'relatively unaffected by the war', and which would not lead to a change in the class position of the saver.[21]

Nevertheless, although there was an absolute increase in the number of working-class savers, Madge concluded from his survey of a large sample of households in Glasgow, Leeds and Bristol that the new savers represented a tiny proportion of the working class as a whole. Madge concluded that 'a large proportion of wage-earners' savings are due to a small proportion of wage-earners'; to be precise, among Leeds wage-earners 31 per cent of national saving came from 3 per cent of families. Forty-four per cent of families had no savings at all, and the majority of the rest (38 per cent of the total) saved less than 5s a week. The median weekly amount saved was 3s 4d, while the most popular single figure was 1s.[22]

Madge found that patterns of saving were in some respects not surprising. National saving behaved as a luxury – that is the proportion saved rose rapidly as income increased, whereas the proportion saved in the form of insurance behaved as a necessity, decreasing slightly as income rose. But beyond this the relation between income and saving was less straightforward. Madge did not look simply at the income of the 'chief wage-earner' of a household, but took account of the entire income and outgoings of each housekeeping unit, from which he calculated its 'excess income', that is the money beyond that necessary to satisfy its basic needs in terms of housing, food, fuel and clothing. He found, at both low and high levels of 'excess income', only a weak relation between excess income and national saving; for example, just seven out of seventy-one Leeds families with excess incomes below £1 5s did 57 per cent of the saving at this level. 'Heavy' saving of over 13s a week, likely to lead to significant capital accumulation on average began with a gross family income of more than £6 10s, but even here 'not all the heavy savers have so much as £2 10s in excess income. Neither are all those who have £2 10s excess income heavy savers'.[23] Even in this subgroup, savers were a minority. Madge commented, 'National saving is much more strongly concentrated than insurance saving, mainly because saving, apart from for a definite security purpose, is a new thing for the majority of wage-earners'.[24] He concluded (in 1943) that this meant that even 'if real incomes continue to rise and there is a progressive redistribution of incomes, the wage-earning class will not advance as a class towards middle-class standards'.[25] Rather, the small group of *'rentier* proletarians', whose growth the war had stimulated, would continue the process of accumulation and try to assimilate with the middle class. Madge thought that the principal methods of doing this were by acquiring property or a small business (such as a shop), or investing in education for children with a view to their joining the ranks of the black-coated or professional salariat.

Even within the minority group of savers, however, such upward social mobility was not the universally held objective. The interviews conducted in the course of his inquiry led Madge to conclude that most savers were motivated first by the fact that large consumables (like furniture or motor cycles) were not available in wartime but might be afterwards, and second by the not unconnected 'fear that present earning capacity may not last'.[26] Many of Madge's respondents expected and dreaded a post-war slump, but their desire to 'put something by' to meet such an emergency did not represent an urge to change their class position, nor did the amounts they typically saved warrant such as a result.

Madge thought that wartime unpredictabilities themselves encouraged 'mild hoarding', but questioning in Glasgow suggested that not more than a quarter of manual and black-coated workers kept reserves at home, typically behind the clock or in a jar on the mantlepiece, and the amounts put by were usually under £2. Madge was adamant that the apparently numerous 'suitcases full of ancient crumpled notes' deposited by workers in the Glasgow Savings Bank when the town was blitzed were 'exceptional'.[27] In this context it is worth noting that Madge's own methodology would tend to exaggerate rather than diminish the proportion of savers in his samples. He based his findings on budgets voluntarily kept by his respondents, and, as Seers pointed out, 'only the more literate and more careful would keep budgets, and there is reason to expect a correlation between ability to keep budgets and care in arranging outlay'.[28] The fact that only a tiny proportion of these budget-keepers were amassing war savings which might permanently alter their class position is therefore the more remarkable.

Madge's investigation of working-class patterns of saving and spending tends to make Seers's presentation of the improved aggregate share of the working class in national income as a form of 'levelling' look somewhat misleading. Madge showed that, as far as working-class experience was concerned, its rising share of the national income did not signify a trend towards economic equivalence in terms of property ownership. Indeed, the achievement of social mobility through the accumulation of savings appeared extremely limited. In addition, Madge's work emphasized that there were many divisions within the class of manual workers. It is relevant to our discussion to consider whether a 'levelling' process occurred as between these different groups within the working class during the war, or whether pre-war subgroups continued to exist and new ones were created.

Looking first at the overall picture, the numbers of those in paid employment rose during the war, from 19,473,000 in 1938 to a peak of 22,285,000 in 1943, composed of 15,032,000 men and 7,253,000 women (compared with 14,476,000 men and 4,997,000 women in 1938).[29] This expansion of the labour force obviously meant an improvement in living standards for the nearly 3 million people who in 1938 had been outside paid employment (e.g. housewives, schoolchildren and those unemployed). Average earnings rose, according to official figures, by 80 per cent (from 53s 3d in October 1938 to 96s 1d in July 1945).[30] On the other hand, hours worked also went up – from an average of 46.5 per week in 1938 to 50 in 1943, falling to 47.4 in July 1945 – and so too did the cost of living. The official figure for the rise in the working-class cost of living index was 31 per cent between 1939 and 1945,[31] although Seers criticizes this for underweighting some items of working-class expenditure, notably alcohol and tobacco, and put the increase between 1938 and 1947 at 61–62 per cent.[32] Either way, these averages suggest that full employment made manual workers better off than they had been pre-war.

However, they are no more than averages. Earnings during the war varied greatly between men and women, and between different industries, as they had done before it. If there was any 'levelling' of the differences between men and women it was very moderate. Women's average weekly earnings in manual work were 47 per cent of those of men in 1938 and 52 per cent in 1945.[33] As this suggests, few women received equal pay with men, in spite of the 'dilution agreements' which were supposed to guarantee women on 'men's work' the full male rate after a certain length of time. Both private employers and government ministries were loath to give women '100 per cent' and exploited clauses in the agreements stating that, to qualify, women must do the work 'without additional supervision or assistance'.[34] However, by far the most important means by which the gender differential was maintained was the classification of work as either 'men's' or 'women's'. Employers endeavoured to place any jobs women did in the 'women's work' category, where lower wage rates applied, and the trade unions pressed for as much work as possible to be labelled 'men's work', in which case it would be paid at men's rates and the women doing it would be regarded as temporary.[35] According to the official historian, in September 1942 three-quarters of women in munitions 'came under the women's schedule as performing women's work'.[36] This did not only mean that the economic position of male and female wage-earners remained sharply differentiated; it also meant that there could be wide differences in what women earned within a single factory, according to whether they were paid at men's or women's rates.[37] Age made a difference, too. The average earnings of girls under 18 were the lowest of any group throughout the war. In addition, women's earnings in different industries diverged increasingly. In 1938 women's average weekly earnings in six industrial groups were within 3s 3d of each other, the lowest being textiles at 31s 9d and the highest, transport, at 34s 11d. By 1945 the differential was 26s, with women transport workers' average earnings standing at 81s 7d and clothing workers' at 55s 7d.[38]

To some extent this is accounted for by differences in union bargaining power in the different industries, since women's hourly pay, bonuses and piece rates were mostly fixed at a proportion of those of men. Like women, male workers in textiles, clothing and food, drink and tobacco received lower earnings than workers in other industries in 1938, and the differential widened during the war. However, the top male earners in 1945 were in metals, engineering and shipbuilding. Their average earnings of 133s exceeded those of male workers in chemicals by 10s 2d and in transport by 20s 2d. In contrast, the earnings of women transport workers exceeded those of women engineering workers by 12s 6d. The tendency among employers to confine women to 'women's work' in engineering and metals, together with divisions in policy towards women between the unions involved (notably the craft and the general unions), may go some way to explaining why, in contrast to the situation for men, engineering and metals were not the industries in which women's average earnings were greatest by the end of the war.

Far from industrial workers' earnings levelling during the war, differentials widened. To put a figure on this in the case of men, the gap between the highest and the lowest average earnings had been 12s in 1938 whereas in 1945 it was 28s 5d[39] (over twice the amount Madge thought necessary for significant saving). Further, within the 'best paying' industries – engineering and metals – earnings varied very greatly, and union efforts to maintain differentials were, if anything, more successful than counter-pressures to reduce them.

Earnings varied not only between grades and skill categories of men, but also between districts, mainly owing to factors like local union strength, the level of organization among employers, the degree of technological change in the particular branch of the industry and the position with regard to labour supply.[40] For example, earnings in Midland aircraft and engineering factories were relatively high before the war, and in the context of labour shortage arising during rearmament and the rapid expansion of production during the first years of the war, unions succeeded in pushing them up higher.[41] Much engineering work was organized as piece work, the rates for which were settled job by job. Some skilled craftsmen on time rates, such as tool-room workers, were given guarantees that their earnings would not be allowed to fall below those of the most productive piece workers. In addition, in both the engineering and the aircraft industries, there was a system of bonus payments. Before the war these bonuses were typically 25–30 per cent of time rates; by spring 1940 they had risen to 40–50 per cent in the north-west region, while in the Midlands they were as much as 100 per cent and by 1942 one Coventry motor factory was reported to be paying an average bonus of 324 per cent, with a top figure of 581 per cent. Not suprisingly, Coventry engineering workers rejected the employers' offer to fix the bonus at 100 per cent![42]

The particularly high earnings of men in the Midland engineering and aircraft factories gave rise to national concern. It came not so much from employers, whose anxiety to limit the size of their wage bills was less pressing in wartime because they could pass on their labour costs to the government, but more from various government departments dealing with the control of labour. For example, the Ministry of Labour was concerned about the difficulties of transferring skilled men from the Midlands to new factories in other districts where rates were lower, the Ministry of Supply was worried about the impact of high engineering wages in private firms on the expectations of its workers in Royal Ordnance Factories, and the Select Committee on National Expenditure was worried about the negative effects on productivity of very high earnings.[43] Its suggestion that £12 to £15 a week constituted a threshold beyond which a man lost interest in increasing his efficiency underlines the great divergence of earnings among manual workers in wartime.[44] Expressed in shillings, these sums are 240*s* and 300*s*, compared with average male earnings in engineering in 1941 of 112*s* 2*d*, average female earnings in engineering of 48*s* 1*d*, average male earnings throughout manufacturing of 99*s* 5*d* and equivalent female earnings of 43*s* 11*d*.[45]

Whether this small minority of men with exceptionally high wartime earnings should be regarded as having 'levelled up' to the middle class is another matter. Most of the social surveys of the 1940s used an income of £250 a year, or £5 (i.e. 100s) a week as the approximate dividing line between the working and middle classes, by which criterion such men would qualify as 'middle-class'. However, Madge believed that skilled men earning spectacularly large amounts in new industries tended not to be regular savers, but enjoyed the 'windfall' while it lasted, especially if they came from a background of unemployment in the 1930s.[46] They therefore did not, in general, accumulate capital which could have assisted their assimilation into the middle class.

Further, in the debate of the 1950s and 1960s on the class position of manual workers with high incomes, numerous sociologists argued against seeing working-class affluence alone as sufficient to close the gap between classes. For example, W.G. Runciman pointed out that the conditions under which a manual worker earned a relatively high income differed sharply from those of a non-manual worker at the same level of income, in terms of the overtime and piece-work components, the meals, furnishings and sanitation available in the work-place, rights to holidays and pensions, chances of promotion and the degree of security in the employment.[47]

It would be fascinating to draw up a balance sheet of these aspects of manual and non-manual work in wartime. In the absence of the kind of research which would permit such precision, it can be said that there was improvement in some of these areas for some manual workers, while some non-manual workers, evacuated to temporary office accommodation, for example, may have been worse off than pre-war. Most obviously, the number of work-place canteens expanded from about 1,500 pre-war to 11,800 in 1944 under a requirement in the Essential Work Order, and the Ministry of Labour also urged employers to improve lavatory facilities and to employ a works doctor or nurse. The occurrence of change was patchy, however. For example, the increase in the number of work-places with canteens by over 10,000 must be set against the total of 67,400 undertakings covered by Essential Work Orders in 1944, and against the fact that in no industry did more than half the workers use the canteens. Married women workers in particular missed out because of the tendency to use the lunch hour for shopping.[48]

Any improvements in work-place conditions need to be seen in the context of the increasing organization of manual work on a piece-work basis (which brought with it greater pressure), the long hours expected and infrequent holidays.[49] The chances of promotion for a male manual worker (e.g. from machinist to setter, setter to chargehand and so to overseer, foreman and manager) may have been slightly greater in wartime, with the expansion of work-forces and introduction of new processes, though the same may have been true for salaried workers (moving, for example, from clerical to administrative or managerial grades). But security of employment for manual workers lasted for only as long as the war effort required a particular type of production, as the transfers and lay-offs from engineering and Royal Ordnance factories in 1944–5 demonstrated.[50]

Thus I am arguing here that widening differentials in wartime both caused the working class to become more heterogeneous, and did not automatically lead to the 'levelling up' of the best-paid manual workers.

Undoubtedly government departments would have liked there to have been a levelling of income among manual workers, and pressed for it when they could, as in the case of the Royal Ordnance Factories, where the Ministry of Supply did achieve some degree of standardization between districts, if not between grades of worker. The upward movement of earnings stabilized in the Midlands during the war, though not because of government intervention. Rather, the explanation lies in the fact that the pace of technological change slowed somewhat, so there was no longer a constant process of fixing new prices, and communist shop stewards tended to work against disruption in the shops after the entry of Russia to the war in June 1941, while in other districts growing militancy and a mounting propensity to strike in 1943–4 may have made earnings less stable.[51]

But differentials between grades of workers and between districts continued throughout the war and after it. The official historian wrote, 'In June 1953 weekly earnings in the Coventry district averaged more than 43s 0d above those in any other district even though hours worked there were comparatively short'.[52] In other branches of the munition industries the regional pattern of differentials was different; for instance, in shipbuilding, earnings were particularly high in London and Southampton, and the best-paying Royal Ordnance Factories (ROFs) were in London and South Wales. Although greater geographical uniformity was achieved in these industries than in the case of the motor and aircraft branches of engineering, differences remained between the earnings of time and piece workers (particularly between those of machine setters on time rates and dilutees on piece rates in ROFs), between the rates of adults and apprentices, and between those of men and women, and frequently caused contention.[53]

To sum up, the division of industries into 'essential' and 'non-essential' and the combination in the former of labour shortage, 'dilution', the premium on 'skill', and growing union strength, coupled with the government's fear of strikes, in the context of major local differences dating from before the war, ensured that the war had the opposite effect on manual workers' earnings to 'levelling'.

Another aspect of the distribution of income within the working class is its allocation between and within households. It is possible that the overall rise in working-class earnings during the war led to 'levelling' in this respect. Madge's data on working-class spending patterns provide a basis for discussion of this question.

Commenting on expenditure trends since 1904, Madge wrote, 'The most striking change in the pattern of demand is the great decline in the proportion allotted to food, and the corresponding increase in the proportion allotted to "other items"'.[54] The war accelerated, though it obviously had not initiated, this trend. 'Other items', which were mainly 'non-essentials' like alcohol, tobacco and entertainment, rose from 30 per cent of working-class budgets in 1938 to 34 per cent in 1942, and the proportion spent on food fell by 3 per cent (from 40 per cent to 37 per cent),[55] even though (in spite of relatively heavy subsidies, price control and rationing) food had risen by 22 per cent in the working-class cost-of-living index between 1939 and 1941.[56]

Authors of social surveys agree that a major factor explaining the declining proportion of working-class expenditure on food was the reduction in family size during the twentieth century. The war made a special contribution to this, with particularly low birth-rates 1939–41, though during 1942–5 there was something of a recovery.[57]

However, there were of course wide variations in family size, as there had been pre-war. In wartime, as before, an increase in the number of children heralded the decline of the family's standard of living, a point graphically illustrated by the finding of the Wartime Social Survey in 1942 that the heaviest users of credit facilities were families with three or more children under 14.[58] It follows that the majority of three-child families (75 per cent) had no National Savings.[59] Madge observed that working-class families with five or six non-earning children were almost invariably in relative poverty, regardless of the skill status of the main wage-earner. He wrote, 'If one arranges a random sample of wage-earning families in order of effective wealth, skilled, well-paid workers with children will come lower down than unskilled, low-paid workers without any children'.[60]

A survey of 'The British Household' in 1947 found that in fact a higher proportion of households of the middle-income group of 'better-paid unskilled operatives', 'lower-paid skilled operatives' and 'lower-paid clerical workers', with a basic weekly wage rate of £4 to £5 10s, had children under 15 than any other income group. Twenty-four per cent had two or more children, compared with 15 per cent in the group of lower-paid unskilled operatives immediately below them and 20 per cent in the group of better-paid skilled and clerical workers, and lower-paid managerial and professional workers, above them. The households of the middle group were also more overcrowded than those of the other groups: 33 per cent had more than one person per habitable room, compared with 24 per cent in the group below, 17 per cent in the group above, and 4 per cent in the top income group.[61] The larger than average family size of the middle group, then, limited the potential for 'levelling up' offered by its improved wartime earnings.

The uneven distribution of income per head of the working-class population due to family size was further intensified by uneven distribution within families. Madge noticed that wage-earning husbands quite frequently did not share the rise in their incomes with their wives and children. In none of the seven towns he looked at did a majority of husbands hand over all their weekly earnings to their wives, and in most only a small proportion (under 15 per cent) did so. The dominant pattern was for husbands to give wives a fixed sum as a result of an 'actual or implicit bargain ... driven at intervals', and in some towns, notably Glasgow, a majority of husbands kept their wives in the dark about the wartime increase in their earnings. It was here that Madge 'came across evidence of revolt against the whole system' of housekeeping 'allowances'.[62] Madge wrote, 'fortunately the deceptions occurred mainly at the higher income levels', meaning by the word 'fortunately' that actual undernourishment of wives and children due to the husband's contribution of too low a figure to meet the rising cost of living was limited to a minority.[63] But his findings nevertheless suggest that in the majority of families in Glasgow, and possibly elsewhere, the husband neither declared his income accurately nor passed on a rising proportion of his rising earnings to his wife.[64] Thus, far from there being any 'levelling' in the household distribution of income, the economic gulf between husbands and wives actually widened.

The households in which the wife was most likely to share the benefit of her husband's wartime earnings were those in which incomes were pooled and then distributed according to need. Though nowhere universal, Madge found that this pattern was most prevalent in Leeds and Blackburn, where 24 per cent and 49 per cent of families pooled their incomes. The benefits to wives and children are reflected in the proportions of family income allocated to housekeeping and husband's pocket money, which were 65 per cent and 17 per cent in Leeds, in contrast to 58 per cent and 27 per cent in Glasgow, where only 14 per cent of families pooled their earnings.[65]

The extent of pooling appears to have been a very local matter, only partly determined by the degree to which it was customary for women, including wives, to do paid work. Madge noticed that in Bradford only 15 per cent of families pooled their incomes, in contrast to the high figure of 49 per cent in Blackburn, even though there was a high female participation rate in both towns. In spite of the rising numbers of married women in war work (43 per cent of women workers were married in 1943, compared with 16 per cent in 1931),[66] Madge did not observe an increase in the habit of pooling, and was emphatic that the wife's economic position remained highly inequitable.[67]

Having said this, there is no doubt that women's earnings made a significant contribution to family incomes in wartime. It could be that the rising share of total personal allocated income going to the lower income groups in the 1940s, which Seers depicted, was a result less of 'redistribution' (which, as we have seen, was how it was interpreted) than of the greater extent of paid employment among the wives of lower-income than higher-income husbands during and after the war. It would, of course, be difficult to determine this accurately.[68]

The idea of extensive social mixing among women workers, much vaunted in wartime progaganda, is a confusing factor when considering which class benefited more from women's work. It is usually suggested that women from upper and middle-class families took wartime jobs beneath their social status for the duration.[69] The Wartime Social Survey report *Women at Work* contains evidence that 28 per cent of women who had worked pre-war in the white-collar category 'professional, administrative and clerical' took manual jobs of various types. However, they formed no more than 7½ per cent of the total number of women manual workers of all types of the sample, and the report commented that most of these ex-white-collar women had been clerks,[70] whose class position was in any case somewhat intermediate, especially after a decade in which opportunities for the daughters of manual workers to obtain their first job in white-collar work had increased rapidly.[71] This evidence, plus information on the educational backgrounds of women factory workers, strongly suggests that social mixing among women war workers, and the social levelling implied by it, has been exaggerated.[72]

The most compelling evidence against social mixing, however, is the attempt by the Wartime Social Survey to classify women workers in wartime industries by the income of the 'chief wage-earner' in the woman's household, which revealed that a higher proportion of women war workers were in households in which the 'chief wage-earner' received up to £5 a week than the proportion of such households in the population as a whole (87 per cent, compared with 75 per cent). The WSS concluded that 'Women in the higher income groups have gone into other forms of National Service and that the group from which the greatest proportion of working women has been drawn is that of the semi-skilled and skilled workers with wage rates of £3 12s 0d to £5 0s 0d'.[73] In view of the evidence which we have already reviewed about the large family size of precisely this middle group and its tendency towards financial shortfall, it makes good sense that wives and daughters from such households filled the factories in greater proportion than they occurred in the community at large.

The WSS evidence also lends substance to the view that women's wartime paid employment contributed more to the increase in the share of the working class in national income than to that of the middle class. The forms of National Service chosen by the majority of women whose husbands or fathers were in the middle-class income groups were either relatively low-paying, as in the case of the women's auxiliary services and the Women's Land Army, or entirely voluntary, like the Red Cross and the Women's Voluntary Service. Participation of this sort in the war effort would have added little to middle-class aggregate income, and thus would have assisted 'levelling' – ironically, in view of the resentment which middle-class women's preference for exemption from paid work and for involvement in voluntary work provoked among some working women, who saw it as a sign of 'inequality of sacrifice'.[74]

However, it is difficult to assess the extent of working-class women's contribution, either in terms of the financial effects on individual families, or in terms of the proportion of families affected in each working-class income group, given the invisibility in survey data of working women's earnings.[75] One can only return to the WSS statement that the majority of working women came from homes classified as belonging to the middle-income bracket of the working class, and official evidence that the overall average earnings of women workers were 64s in 1944.

Whether the addition of this average sum to the budget of working-class homes either did no more than pull a family out of debt or succeeded in pushing it into the narrow ranks of upwardly mobile savers must have depended on how many mouths there were to feed in the household, the extent of additional expenditure on nurseries, laundries and other facilities for the domestic work which the wife was no longer doing unpaid, and the proportion of the couple's joint income which they chose to spend on those 'other items' to which, as we have seen, the working class had been devoting an increasing proportion of its expenditure since 1904, a trend which the war intensified.

Madge repeatedly stated that, after they had given their wives an allowance or paid for their board and lodging if they were single, men spent the surplus of their increased wartime earnings on such 'non-essential' items of consumption. Though critical when such spending was at the expense of the well-being of wives and children, he was mainly concerned to show that alcohol and tobacco were more important to the vast majority of working men than were savings: 'National savings is . . . considered more of a luxury than tobacco and alcohol in that, when there are more mouths to feed, it is the former and not the latter which are dispensed with.'[76]

Women were, of course, not immune to these pleasures, and many started smoking cigarettes for the first time during the war, but Madge said that 'the great bulk of the spending on tobacco and alcohol is contributed by husbands and other male earners'.[77] In contrast, 'most of the spending on "Entertainment" comes from female earners'. Madge thought the reasons for increased spending on these items were primarily social and narcotic, though he hinted that for men there was an element of compensation for 'giving up' the bulk of their income for housekeeping.[78] One may add that, for both men and women, beer, cigarettes and cinemas offered some solace in the face of the immeasurably discomforting aspects of war: the blackout, bombardment, long hours of work, the difficulties of travel and the anxiety of separation.

Such reasons for spending a rising proportion of income on 'non-essentials' evidently outweighed the relatively rapid rise in cost. The price of tobacco doubled between 1939 and 1942, and the price of beer went up steeply, unchecked by the government (and underweighted in the government's calculation of the working-class cost-of-living index) because of its value as a source of revenue.[79]

Of course, the working class was not alone in its consumption of tobacco and alcohol, nor in its need for consolation. But according to Seers it devoted a larger proportion of its total expenditure to these things than did the population as a whole: 5 per cent on tobacco and 7 per cent on alcohol, compared with a global figure of just over 4 per cent on each. A more direct comparison with middle-class spending shows that nearly half working-class expenditure on 'other items' went on drink and tobacco, compared with under a fifth of middle-class expenditure.[80] It is almost irresistible to conclude (with Madge) that most male members of the working class were drinking and smoking their wartime 'excess incomes' rather than using them as a means by which to 'level up' socially, because for the majority such a shift in class position had very little meaning.[81]

We have established, I hope, that there was a great deal of variety in the economic circumstances of working-class families during the war. Whether both husband and wife were earning, the occupations and industries in which they worked, the region in which they lived, the number of dependants and the method by which income was allocated in the household were important determinants of the capacity of a family to generate 'excess income'. But, even when all these circumstances were favourable, spending rather than accumulation was the norm, even (or especially) in the face of wartime shortages.

Individuals living outside family households tended to be particularly disadvantaged, in economic terms. Pensioners had been a relatively poor subgroup before the war which, because of its dependence upon a fixed income at a time of rising cost of living, became worse off during the war, in spite of a patchily applied Exchequer supplement to old age pensions on a 'household needs' basis after January 1940.[82] Nevertheless, Madge showed that 'single' pensioners were falling into heavier debt during the war than those living in 'mixed pensioner families'.[83]

The same contrast occurred in the economic circumstances of servicemen's wives. A private soldier's wife with two children received a total allowance of 32s in 1939, which rose to 33s in 1940, 38s in 1941 and 43s in 1942.[84] But Madge discovered a sharp contrast in standard of living between the 20 per cent of service wives in his sample with no children, living with their parents and working, who were saving heavily (to the tune of 27s a week), and the 20 per cent of service wives at the other extreme, who did not live with other adults, were not doing paid work and had children to support, who were falling heavily into debt (to the tune of 15s 6d per week).[85]

A large proportion of service wives were dependent on credit buying (nearly 53 per cent compared with 38 per cent of a sample of working-class women), though it is not surprising that the Wartime Social Survey found that they were the main group to which shopkeepers were reluctant to give credit and landlords loath to let rooms.[86] Nor is it surprising that servicemen's wives were keen to find paid work and were often given priority for places in wartime nurseries.[87] As 'the new poor' of the war, whose plight was caused by their husbands' service in defence of the country, they commanded considerable sympathy from members of the public who did not stand in a direct financial relationship with them. Public pressure resulted in a 'rise' to an allowance of 60s for the service wife with two children.[88] Though an improvement, this was still below the woman's average wage of 64s.

Servicemen and women themselves (whatever their class) were, of course, a relatively low-paid group. They had little chance of amassing savings during their period in the forces, even though part of a pay rise in January 1942 took the form of a post-war credit of 6d a day.[89] Madge would not have considered this a high saving. It represented 3s 6d a week, and about £9 a year. However, there were opportunities in the forces for men and women to 'level up' in non-financial ways, for instance raising their status by becoming non-commissioned or commissioned officers, and acquiring skills ranging from clerical and administrative to technical, which may have opened up new job prospects in the postwar world. The financially disadvantaged position of the private soldier also applied to the officer, who received more pay and allowances but was still at an income level well below a middling white-collar salary. There was much complaint in 1941–2 that officers' pay was so inadequate that it needed supplementing with a private income simply to cover mess bills, uniform and other essentials.[90] Officers' wives received larger allowances than privates', but their incomes were still relatively low in the wartime context.[91] Much the same stratification must have existed where officers' wives were concerned as Madge depicted for servicemen's wives, the best-off being those without children who were living with relatives, and the worst-off those struggling to make ends meet on their own with children.

Servicemen of all ranks and their wives may have experienced quite considerable 'levelling', in the sense of sharing a similar economic position, depressed in comparison to their civilian pre-war peers. Ironically the service hierarchy, which was apparently maintained as energetically among service wives as within the services themselves, countered with sharp status differentiation this economic levelling.

Up to this point in the discussion the 'middle class' has been largely neglected, because interest has focused on the question of whether the rise in the working-class share of the national income meant for that class (or a substantial part of it) a process of permanent 'levelling up', either as between the working class and the middle class or within the ranks of the working class. It has not been possible to be definitive, but the suggestion here is that permanent levelling up affected only a tiny group of self-denying savers, and that the war may have increased differentials between groups of workers and between husbands and wives, rather than diminishing them. It is now time to examine the other side of the coin of Seers's findings on the working-class aggregate income. Did the relative fall in the middle-class share of national income mean that the middle class (defined as non-manual workers with an income over £250 p.a.) experienced permanent 'levelling down'?

To recap, Seers wrote that between 1938 and 1947 the salary bill had 'risen by only just over fifty per cent, compared with a near doubling of most other forms of income'. When taxes and the cost of living were taken into account, this meant that 'the real net incomes of the working class had risen over nine per cent, and those of the middle class had fallen over seven per cent'.[92] Seers stated that outside these aggregates there were wide differences in the income position of different groups within the middle class, but though he presented evidence about differences in the middle-class cost of living he omitted evidence about income differences.

Guy Routh, however, looked at trends in average earnings in the various occupational classes used in the census, over a longer period than that of the war itself. He found that 'the only really big changes' between 1910 and 1960 were the declining differentials of three occupational classes – professionals, clerks and foremen – between 1935 and 1955. The income of all three groups had been 'levelled down' towards the average for men and women in all occupational classes, although the extent of the fall varied and in some cases the differential was still extensive. For instance, 'higher professionals' enjoyed incomes nearly three times the average, even though this represented a fall of 26 per cent compared with their position in 1935–6. The relative drop had been particularly severe for men and women in the 'lower professional' group, though clerks of both sexes were the non-manual group with the lowest earnings. The occupational group 'managers and administrators', in contrast, improved its position.[93] Thus, as in the working class, so in the middle class, the picture was not one of overall levelling, but of differing fortunes for different groups.

Of course, it may be misleading to look at change over the period 1935–55, since by then the effects of war may have been overtaken by subsequent developments. But Routh provided some details on the relative movement of average manual earnings and the salaries of various classes of civil servants, which show the period 1938–40 to have marked the beginning of the fall of non-manual pay in relation to manual earnings and 1944 to have marked its nadir.[94]

Undoubtedly, the shortage of manual labour in the munition industries and the improved leverage of the trade unions immediately before and during the war had much to do with the overall narrowing of differentials between non-manual and manual occupations. However, Routh stated that changes in the averages of occupational groups were only partly caused by changes in the pay of individual occupations, and were also caused 'by changes in the numbers occupied in occupations at different levels of pay'.[95] Elsewhere he suggested that the apparent reduction in the average pay of the non-manual industrial employee population in 1938–40 'could have been brought about by the substitution of female for male labour'.[96] In other words, because of the influx of women at low rates of pay, and the outflow of men, the earnings averages of various non-manual occupational groups were depressed. Routh unfortunately did not subject this suggestion to careful scrutiny, and the necessary research is a larger project than can be undertaken here. It is made particularly difficult by the absence of an occupational census for the war. However, using the rather unsatisfactory Industrial Classification some suggestions can be made.

Workers in national government can be taken as primarily 'non-manual'. The wartime influx of women into this group was extreme. The total in 1945 was 1,214 per cent what it was in 1939, whereas the number of men was 174 per cent of the 1939 figure, making the proportion of women rise from 14 to 54 per cent of the total number of workers in national government. By comparison, the total number of insured women in industry in 1945 was 128 per cent of the number in 1939, and the proportion rose from 28 to 39 per cent.[97]

It does look possible, then, as Routh suggested, that the extensive substitution for men in white-collar work of women, employed by custom in different grades from men and at lower rates of pay, made a significant contribution to the reduction of the differential between civil service non-manual salaries and average manual earnings.

Earlier, however, we suggested that the wartime earnings of women in manual work may have made a significant contribution to aggregate working-class income, even though women's average manual earnings were only just over half those of men. Why did the increased number of white-collar women not augment middle-class earnings in the same way? The issue hinges on where low-paid non-manual workers, especially women, are placed in terms of class. Routh simply compared all civil service salary-earners with wage-earners, but Seers took as his criterion for membership of the middle class 1938–47 non-manual workers with incomes of £250 or above. This would disqualify numerous male clerks, whose average pay in 1938 was £192 p.a. (rising to approximately £224 in 1942), almost all women clerks, whose average was £99 (rising to approximately £115), and many women in the lower professions, whose average was £211 (rising to approximately £246).[98] By his own declaration Seers cannot have included the salaries of low-paid white-collar workers, particularly those of the numerous women entering this section during the war, in his estimate of the middle-class share of national income, but subsumed them in aggregate 'working-class' income.[99] In Seers's work, then, the wartime influx of women to white-collar work assisted the levelling up of the working class, whereas in Routh's work the low salaries of such women contributed to the levelling down of the salariat.

All this points to the difficulty of using income and occupational criteria of 'class', as well as to the particular problem of locating white-collar women workers in the class structure.[100] It also supports the idea of the growth of a 'cross-class' group of low salary-earners and better-paid manual workers, which George Orwell described as an 'intermediate stratum at which the older class distinctions are beginning to break down',[101] and which excited both him and G.D.H. Cole, who thought it would swell the ranks of Labour voters.[102] However, harmonious assimiliation within the 'intermediate class' after the war was not guaranteed, notably when it came to housing. Referring to the feelings of manual and low-paid non-manual groups, a Middlesbrough planner wrote in 1948, 'there is a good deal of evidence that mixing of social classes and other groups ... creates social friction', and he recommended separate housing provision.[103]

Let us look, finally and very briefly, at the extent to which the middle class was accumulating savings during the war. Though unfortunately we do not have details of middle-class patterns of saving of the kind Madge collected from the working class, both he and Seers made some suggestive comments.

They both argued that during the war the middle class (or, as Madge emphasized, its wealthier sections) saved money which would normally have been spent on 'other items', notably motor cars, education and domestic help.[104] Certainly expenditure on large 'luxury' items dried up during the war. For example, that on 'cars and motor cycles' fell from £152 million in 1938 to nil in 1943.[105] In addition Seers noted that shortages, subsidies and rationing meant that the goods which members of the middle class bought during the war were cheaper than the sort of things they had bought pre-war. Further, they stood to benefit from the 'undistributed profits' of wartime, which enforced the saving of dividends and increased the value of shares.[106]

Madge viewed wealthier middle-class families as 'pertinacious savers' by dint of both their 'high excess incomes' and their 'outlook and upbringing', and attributed to them the bulk of the money raised by National Savings and the sale of Defence Bonds.[107] If indeed they were saving heavily in wartime, they would have increased the property differential between themselves and other middle-class as well as working-class groups. In a 'hidden', or at any rate individualized and private way, then, the narrowing of income differentials such as those of 'higher professionals' may have been offset by wartime savings, and the improvement in the position of 'managers and administrators' may have been even greater than it appeared. This is ironic in that levelling of consumption during the war was a major component of the popular impression of the 'levelling of class'.[108]

What can we conclude from this review of surveys and accounts pertinent to the issue of the 'levelling of class'? I should like to end by drawing together three main points.

First, permanent 'levelling up' of the working class, as depicted by both defenders of middle-class status and advocates of a 'classless' society in the 1940s and 1950s, is thrown in doubt by the absence of any guarantee of the permanence of relatively enlarged working-class incomes and by the beginnings in the late 1940s of the reversal of fiscal policies which had favoured the working class during the war.

Second, on the other hand, there were certainly wartime changes in social stratification, and there is no doubt that some groups of manual workers improved their pay position markedly, relative both to other groups of manual workers and to some groups of salaried workers. In addition, it seems that working-class women undertook paid work to a greater extent (and at higher levels of pay) than women of the middle class, apart from those in the latter group who entered low-salary white-collar jobs, whose class position is one of the unresolved problems of stratification theory. All the same, there were wide variations in the income levels of different working-class groups – for example, aircraft workers and servicemen's wives – and little sign of any 'levelling' within the working-class household. Likewise, some middle-class groups, such as 'managers and administrators', fared better than others, such as 'professionals'.

Third, evidence of differences in saving patterns within and between classes suggests that when class is seen in relation to property, rather than income, the war gave rise to very little movement out of the working class via accumulation, and it may even have encouraged the widening of property differentials, both within the middle class and between it and the working class.

Finally, it must be emphasized that much of the above is, of necessity in view of the available data, tentative. It is intended as an antidote to a focus entirely upon images and attitudes, and indeed has at some points suggested that popular contemporary ideas of the way levelling would be achieved in wartime (e.g. by drawing women of all classes into paid industrial work and by establishing equality of consumption) may have been quite mistaken, in terms of underlying economic tendencies conducive to levelling, as opposed to appearances of equality. This chapter, then, is offered as a challenge to previous interpretations and it is hoped that it will both provoke debate and stimulate further research.

Notes

1 Arthur Marwick, *Class, Image and Reality in Britain, France and the U.S.A. since 1930*, London, Collins, 1980, ch. 11.
2 Stanislas Andrzejewski, *Military Organisation and Society*, London, Routledge, 1954.
3 R.M. Titmuss, 'War and social policy', in *Essays on 'The Welfare State'*, London, Allen & Unwin, 1963, p. 86.
4 For a stimulating discussion of the way recent historians have used 'class' see R.S. Neale, *Class in English History, 1680–1850*, Oxford, Blackwell, 1981.
5 Neal, *Class*, p. 132.
6 D.C. Marsh, *The Changing Social Structure of England and Wales, 1871–1951*,

London, Routledge, 1958, p. 220.

7 Marsh, *Changing Social Structure*, pp. 218 and 223.

8 See discussion in J. Westergaard and H. Resler, *Class in a Capitalist Society: a Study of Contemporary Britain*, London, Heinemann, 1975, p. 32.

9 Roy Lewis and Angus Maude, *The English Middle Classes*, London, Phoenix House, 1949. See also discussion in W.G. Runciman, *Relative Deprivation and Social Justice: a Study of Attitudes to Social Inequality in Twentieth-century England*, Harmondsworth, Penguin, 1972, p. 94.

10 See for example, Richard M. Titmuss, *Income Distribution and Social Change: A Study in Criticism*, London, Allen & Unwin, 1962, chs 3 and 8.

11 G.D.H. Cole, *Studies in Class Structure*, London, Routledge, 1955, p. 75. Cole's reservations are supported in A.H. Halsey (ed.) *Trends in British Society since 1900: a Guide to the Changing Social Structure of Britain*, London, Macmillan, 1972, p. 75.

12 Dudley Seers, *Changes in the Cost-of-living and the Distribution of Income since 1938*, Oxford University Institute of Statistics, Oxford, Blackwell, 1949, pp. 5 and 8. Westergaard and Resler refer to Seers's work as 'probably the most comprehensive examination of the 1940s shift' in incomes, *Class*, p. 55.

13 Seers, *Changes*, p. 65.

14 ibid.

15 Cole, *Studies*, p. 76. See also Halsey, *Trends*, table 3.15, p. 95.

16 Westegaard and Resler, *Class*, pp. 54–5, and tables 1 and 2, pp. 39–40. T.B. Bottomore also believed this to be so. See *Classes in Modern Society*, London, Allen & Unwin, 1965, p. 34: 'between 1939 and 1949 redistribution may have transferred some ten per cent of the national income from property owners to wage earners; but . . . since 1949 there has again been growing inequality'.

17 Seers is explicit on how he arrived at figures for the total wage and salary bills (see *Changes*, pp. 59–65), but surprisingly silent on the issue of the calculation of the size of the two groups. In the absence of an occupational census for the war period, and in view of the presentation of all employment data using industrial classifications, it seems that there is no obvious way in which it could be done.

18 Bottomore, *Classes*, p. 16.

19 See discussion in Runciman, *Relative Deprivation*, p. 90, and John Hilton, *Rich Man, Poor Man*, London, Allen & Unwin, 1944, pp. 60 and 68–9. He found that 70 per cent of savings in Post Office accounts were under £25, and 90 per cent of those earning less than £200 rented their accommodation.

20 Charles Madge, *War-time Patterns of Saving and Spending*, National Institute of Economic and Social Research Occasional Papers, IV, Cambridge University Press, 1943, pp. 1, 4, 7, 9.

21 Madge, *War-time Patterns*, pp. 41–9.

22 ibid., pp. 1 and 50.

23 ibid., p. 69.

24 ibid., p. 67.

25 ibid., p. 82.

26 ibid., p. 73.

27 ibid., pp. 47–8.

28 Seers, *Changes*, p. 6.

29 Central Statistical Office, *Statistical Digest of the War*, London, HMSO, 1951, table 9, p. 8.

30 Central Statistical Office, *Digest*, table 187, p. 204.
31 ibid., table 188, p. 204, and table 190, p. 205.
32 Seers, *Changes*, pp. 22–3.
33 Penny Summerfield, *Women Workers in the Second World War: Production and Patriarchy in Conflict*, London, Croom Helm, 1984, p. 200.
34 The official historian wrote that the practice was 'that the 100 per cent concession should be limited to individual cases', P. Inman, *Labour in the Munition Industries*, London, HMSO, 1957, p. 357.
35 Summerfield, *Women Workers*, ch. 7.
36 Inman, *Labour*, p. 354.
37 Summerfield, *Women Workers*, p. 170.
38 Central Statistical Office, *Digest*, table 189, p. 205.
39 ibid.
40 Richard Croucher, 'Communist politics and shop stewards in engineering, 1935–46', unpublished Ph.D. thesis, University of Warwick, 1978, ch. 1.
41 Inman, *Labour*, pp. 319–20.
42 ibid., pp. 320–5.
43 ibid., pp. 323, 338, 355.
44 Select Committee on National Expenditure, *Fifteenth Report*, Session 1940–1, section 7.
45 Central Statistical Office, *Digest*, pp. 204–5.
46 Madge, *War-time Patterns*, p. 15. See also W.K. Hancock and M.M. Gowing, *British War Economy*, London, HMSO, 1949, p. 330, who corroborate this.
47 Runciman, *Relative Deprivation*, pp. 98–100.
48 Summerfield, *Women Workers*, pp. 19, 100–1.
49 Inman, *Labour*, pp. 396–7; PRO, Lab. 10/281, 'Causes of Industrial Unrest, 1943'.
50 Richard Croucher, *Engineers at War, 1939–1945*, London, Merlin, 1982, pp. 297–9; Summerfield, *Women Workers*, pp. 160–1.
51 Croucher, *Engineers*, ch. 3, particularly p. 168.
52 Inman, *Labour*, p. 327, n. 2.
53 ibid., pp. 329–30, 340–6, 334; Croucher, *Engineers*, pp. 197–244; Summerfield, *Women Workers*, ch. 7.
54 Madge, *War-time Patterns*, p. 70.
55 ibid., table XLIV, p. 70.
56 Central Statistical Office, *Digest*, table 190, p. 205. On food subsidies, etc., see Hancock and Gowing, *War Economy*, pp. 167, 333–4, 501–2. Clothes consumed more of working-class expenditure in 1942 than 1938, not surprisingly in view of their steep rise in the working-class cost-of-living index (92 per cent in 1939–42), though clothes rationing (1941) and the Utility clothing scheme (1942) brought clothes' prices down thereafter. There was a small decline in the proportion spent on rent, probably due to rent control under the Rent and Mortgage Interest Restrictions Act, 1939, which held rents to an (official) rise of only 1 per cent in 1939–42. See Hancock and Gowing, *War Economy*, pp. 502–3 and 166.
57 Central Statistical Office, *Digest*, table 7, p. 5.
58 Central Office of Information, Wartime Social Survey, Report no. 23, New Series, 42, *Credit Buying*, July, 1942.
59 Madge, *War-time patterns*, p. 62.
60 ibid., p. 16.

61 Central Office of Information, Social Survey, *The British Household*, by P.G. Gray, based on an inquiry carried out in 1947 (1949), table 5, p. 7, and table 33, p. 24.

62 Madge, *War-time Patterns*, p. 54.

63 ibid., p. 53.

64 ibid., pp. 53, 58–9.

65 ibid., table XXVIII, p. 54.

66 Central Office of Information, Wartime Social Survey, *Women at Work*, by Geoffrey Thomas, June 1944, p. 1; Census of England and Wales, 1931, *Occupational Tables*, I, 1934.

67 Madge, *War-time Patterns*, p. 55.

68 As Westergaard and Resler point out when making a similar point, *Class*, p. 41.

69 Summerfield, *Women Workers*, pp. 55–7.

70 Central Office of Information, Wartime Social Survey, *Women at Work*, table 14, p. 9.

71 E. Gamarnikow *et al.*, *Gender, Class and Work*, London, Heinemann, 1983, ch. 5, 'Trends in female social mobility', by Geoff Payne, Judy Payne and Tony Chapman.

72 Ninety-four per cent of women on assembly and unskilled repetitive work and 96 per cent of machinists and hand-tool operators had received no secondary education, compared with a total of 80 per cent of the age group who had received such education in 1938. Central Office of Information, Wartime Social Survey, *Women at Work*, p. 6; Board of Education, *Report of the Consultative Committee on Secondary Education*, London, HMSO, 1938, table I, p. 88.

73 Central Office of Information, Wartime Social Survey, *Women at Work*, p. 7. The actual proportions given were as follows:

Weekly wage of chief wage-earner	%
Up to £3 12s	29
£3 12s–£5	58
£5–£10	11
Over £10	3 (as in original)

74 Ian McLaine, *Ministry of Morale: Home Front Morale and the Ministry of Information in World War II*, London, Allen & Unwin, 1979, pp. 176–7. Middle-class women showed a preference for the Women's Royal Naval Service and the Women's Auxiliary Air Force rather than the Auxiliary Territorial Service, where the gulf between working-class privates and upper-class officers was thought to present a problem for recruitment. See PRO, Lab. 26/63, Women's Services (Welfare and Amenities) Committee, 'Recruiting of Womanpower', and Central Office of Information, Wartime Social Survey, *An Investigation of the Attitudes of Women, the General Public and A.T.S. Personnel to the Auxiliary Territorial Service*, October 1941.

75 The convention (followed by the Wartime Social Survey) was (and remained) to classify families by the income of the 'chief' wage earner, defined as male. Even Madge, who did attempt to assess complete family incomes, did not record the separate contribution made by wives, and actually blurred it in his breakdown of Glasgow family incomes into hus-

bands, 62 per cent; 'other earners over twenty-one', 26 per cent; and juvenile earners, 12 per cent. Madge, *War-time Patterns*, p. 53.

76 ibid., p. 62.
77 ibid., p. 32. A comparison of the spending of a male and female lodger-earner in Leeds showed that the man spent 8s 6d on tobacco, compared with the woman's 2s 6d, 5s 1d on alcohol compared with 3d, and 2s 8d on entertainment, compared with 2s 3d. See table XII, p. 33.
78 ibid., p. 73.
79 ibid.; Seers, *Changes*, p. 23; Hancock and Gowing, *War Economy*, pp. 170, 327, 330.
80 Seers, *Changes*, pp. 22 and 8.
81 See especially appendix II of Madge's book, in which many negative working-class opinions about saving are quoted, e.g. a man whose family generated a considerable 'excess income' but who drank and smoked more than the average, said, 'the average man, if he does himself and his family justice, has nothing to save', and a riveter said, 'some people will starve their weans to put money in the bank'.
82 Hancock and Gowing, *War Economy*, p. 169.
83 Madge, *War-time Patterns*, p. 40.
84 Hancock and Gowing, *War Economy*, p. 169, n 5; R.M. Titmuss, *Problems of Social Policy*, London, HMSO, 1950, p. 162.
85 Madge, *War-time Patterns*, pp. 17 and 39.
86 Central Office of Information, Wartime Social Survey, *Credit Buying*, p. 3. Middlesbrough service wives reciprocated the negativity of landlords by being 'the group most dissatisfied' with their social environment. See Central Office of Information, Social Survey, *Middlesbrough: A Social Survey*, 1948, Part IV, p. 4.
87 Titmuss, *Problems*, p. 414, n. 2; Summerfield, *Women Workers*, pp. 83–4.
88 Hancock and Gowing, *War Economy*, pp. 505–6.
89 ibid., pp. 325, 340, n. 4. p. 505. It was alleged by the government that a private's total pay and allowances, including payments in kind and income tax relief, were close to average industrial earnings, but this argument was apparently rather unconvincing to privates themselves.
90 Mass-Observation Archive, Topic Collection: Armed Forces, box 4, file E. Cuttings from *Sunday Express*, 13 April 1941, and other newspapers. An officer's pay at this time was said to be £3 17s per week, whereas a male clerk's pay (relatively low down on the salary scale) was about £4 15s.
91 The differential provoked adverse comment. For example, a 'teacher and housewife' wrote in her diary in September 1942, 'I can't see why a soldier's child should have 1s 0d per week increase, but an officer's 1s 0d per day'. Mass-Observation Archive, Topic Collection: Armed Forces, box 4, file E.
92 Seers, *Changes*, pp. 62 and 65.
93 Guy Routh, *Occupation and Pay in Great Britain, 1906–1960*, Cambridge University Press, 1965, p. 106, and table 48, p. 107. Men in the lower professions earned 115 per cent of the average in 1955/56, a fall of 40 per cent since 1935/36, and women in this group earned 82 per cent, a fall of 37 per cent. Male clerks earned 98 per cent of the average, a fall of 18 per cent, and women clerks earned 60 per cent, a fall of 2 per cent. Male managers improved their position by 3 per cent, earning 279 per cent of average earnings, female managers earned 151 per cent, an improvement of 45 per cent.

94 Routh, *Occupation and Pay*, p. 124. Manual earnings increased by 30 per cent in 1938–40, whereas the increase for all employees was 14 per cent, and by 1944 manual earnings stood at 182 per cent of the 1938 level, compared with an average of 117 per cent for white-collar civil servants.

95 ibid., p. 106.

96 ibid., p. 125, n. 1.

97 Ministry of Labour and National Service, *Tables Relating to Employment and Unemployment in Great Britain, 1939, 1945 and 1946*, London, HMSO, 1947, pp. 4–5. In another relatively 'white-collar' industrial category, 'commerce, banking, insurance and finance', the number of men had actually fallen by 1945 to 38 per cent of the 1939 number, whereas the number of women rose to 149 per cent of what it had been, changing the proportion of women from 31 per cent to 63 per cent.

98 Routh, *Occupation and Pay*, pp. 104 and 124.

99 Seers, *Changes*, p. 64.

100 The first jobs of around 35 per cent of the daughters of working-class fathers entering the Scottish labour market between 1939 and 1945 were non-manual. See Gamarnikow, *Gender*, pp. 65–6, especially fig. 5.1. Other authors in the same collection suggest that a high proportion of women in low-paid non-manual work marry men in manual occupations. If this was occurring in the 1930s and 1940s it would again have caused the group of women white-collar workers to straddle the conventional class boundaries. See Gamarnikow, *Gender*, p. 60.

101 George Orwell, 'England, your England', 1941, quoted by Runciman, *Relative Deprivation*, p. 130.

102 Cole, *Studies*, p. 77.

103 Central Office of Information, Social Survey, *Middlesbrough*, Part IV, p. 3. See also H. Orlans, *Stevenage: a Sociological Study of a New Town*, London, Greenwood, 1971, pp. 160–3.

104 Madge, *War-time Patterns*, p. 74; Seers, *Changes*, pp. 41–2.

105 Halsey, *Trends*, table 3.5, p. 87.

106 Seers, *Changes*, pp. 41, 59.

107 Madge, *War-time Patterns*, pp. 74, 50. Both the National Savings scheme and the sale of Defence Bonds were introduced as a form of government borrowing in November 1939. See Hancock and Gowing, *War Economy*, p. 171.

108 McLaine, *Ministry of Morale*, pp. 177–8. 'Home Intelligence' reported in 1941–2 that apparent 'unfairness' in the distribution of consumer goods due to the greater purchasing power of better-off groups 'seemed to rankle increasingly', but McLaine comments, 'As long as the government appeared to be doing its best to impose the burdens of war equally upon all sections of the community, expressions of discontent did not threaten to coalesce into a serious danger to morale and national unity'.

13
The Impact of World War II on Leningrad

Edward Bubis and Blair A. Ruble

The brutality and destruction unleashed by the Second World War were perhaps nowhere more intensely revealed than in Leningrad, the scene of the longest and most devastating siege of a major urban center in the history of modern warfare. To place the Leningrad Blockade in comparative perspective, more than ten times the number of people died in Leningrad between August 1941 and January 1944, than died in Hiroshima following the atomic blast of August 1945. By March 1943, the once vibrant city of 3.2 million souls had been reduced to a militarized encampment of just 639,000 inhabitants.[1] Moreover, German bombardment obliterated much of the city's physical plant. In addition to the loss of countless architectural and artistic treasures, the Germans destroyed 25 per cent of Leningrad's capital stock, 16 per cent of the city's housing stock, plus scores of miles of streets, sewer lines and water lines.[2]

Beyond physical destruction and loss of life, Leningrad sustained far less tangible but perhaps ultimately more significant losses. Anthropologist Clifford Geertz has written of the importance of charismatic active centers in the social order: the points at which a society's leading actors, ideas, and institutions come together.[3] Prerevolutionary St Petersburg was such a center. However, as early as the 1890s, a national rail system, focused on Moscow and central Russia, began to diminish St Petersburg's importance as a port of entry for Imperial Russia. Moreover, the city's peripheral location and lack of a large, wealthy and populous hinterland further eroded the city's importance as an industrial center, at least in relation to Moscow. Postrevolutionary Leningrad continued to function as an active center in Soviet society despite a ruinous series of corrosive events: the transfer of the Soviet capital from the city to Moscow in 1918; the end of massive importation of industrial raw materials to be processed at ports of entry; the dispatch of the Academy of Sciences from Leningrad to Moscow in 1934; and the decimation in 1934 of the local political elite during the purges following the assassination of Leningrad Party First Secretary Sergei Kirov. After the Second World War, Moscow emerged as the sole charismatic active center remaining in the Soviet Union. Meanwhile, Leningrad rebuilt after the war so that, by the 1950s, prewar population levels had been achieved and economic production levels surpassed. None the less, the city's once pre-eminent (and, after 1918, coequal) status in comparison to that of Moscow was lost, seemingly forever. In this final sense, then, the war's impact on Leningrad has probably been permanent and most certainly has been negative. To better understand how this situation developed, it is necessary to look beyond aggregate growth rates to examine the evolving composition of the Leningrad work-force, political life and economic and scientific bases.

The transformation of the city's work-force

Unfortunately, the available data are not sufficient to identify the social composition of the city's post-war population with any certainty. All one can do is try to make a reasonable and reasoned attempt to reconstruct what occurred on the basis of very scattered and incomplete data. In making such an assessment, it appears that the high level of population turnover that took place in Leningrad during the first half of the 1940s resulted in the replacement of one of the most educated and skilled urban populations in the Soviet Union by one that was relatively unskilled and undisciplined. Such characteristics were shared by the populations of other urban centers across the Soviet Union so that Leningrad came to resemble other typical Soviet provincial centers more than it resembled the country's major charismatic center, Moscow.

Of Leningrad's pre-war metropolitan population of 3.2 million, nearly 1.4 million are not accounted for by official statistics on wartime population losses.[4] Such statistical lacunae probably result from the scores of more pressing concerns burdening the local wartime leadership rather than the problem of data collection. In addition, population shifts throughout the war were probably taking place too quickly to be recorded accurately. We know, for example, that between March 1943 and September 1945 the city's population doubled from 639,000 to over 1.2 million.[5] It appears unlikely that Leningraders, spread halfway to Vladivostok, would have been able to make the necessary hundred- and thousand-mile treks across a war-torn Soviet Union back to their native city in sufficient numbers to account for this increase. The characteristics of the new population suggest that much of the city's post-war population may have been drawn from rural areas rather than from among returning wartime evacuees.[6] If this is the case, Leningrad experienced a qualitative decline in its population in the sense that the new Leningraders were not well suited to the needs of the specialized industrial and scientific enterprises that had dominated the city's economy prior to the war. This qualitative decline occurred despite the quantitative recovery of pre-war personnel and population reserves.

Leningrad was a traditionally male city, yet by April 1945, 76 per cent of all Leningraders employed in industry were now female, a figure suggesting that women were the predominant sex in the city's population as a whole.[7] Post-war in-migration increased the city's male population, as might be expected in a period of demobilization. Still, the city remained predominately female throughout the post-war period at a rate slightly higher than those of the USSR and RSFSR general and urban populations as a whole.[8] This feminization of Leningrad can be attributed to several factors, not the least of which is the high participation levels and losses of Leningrad males at the front or in support positions both during the Winter War with Finland and the blockade. The process may also have been augmented by a significant immigration from already female-dominated rural areas.

Local officials criticized the relatively undisciplined nature of the post-war Leningrad population during the first months of post-blockade reconstruction.[9] This general social indiscipline, which apparently was pronounced in the city's industrial establishments, might be another symptom of extensive rural flight and in-migration to Leningrad. In December 1946, Petr Sergeevich Popkov, the wartime chairman of the Leningrad City Soviet, who had recently become first secretary of the Leningrad City and Regional Party Committees, reported to the Leningrad City Party Committee that labor turnover had soared to 58.6 per cent in the city's factories, a situation that necessitated inordinately high levels of overtime work.[10]

Once again, the data are far from complete and one must infer more from the available sources than is perhaps advisable. Still, commentaries by local Leningrad political and economic elites point to behavior that could be expected of large numbers of demobilized soldiers, of rural immigrants to the city's industrial plants, or both.[11] At a minimum, the image offered of the Leningrad proletariat during the period is not that of a highly skilled, long-employed labor elite. Rather, it suggests a workforce consisting of fairly substantial numbers of low-skilled peasant workers, be they former soldiers or new migrants directly from the collective farm.

The immediate post-war period, then, was one of considerable instability and change in the city's population and work-force. By the time of the 1959 census, the city's metropolitan population barely surpassed its pre-war level of 3.2 million residents. Yet, these 3.2 million-plus inhabitants were qualitatively different from the 3.2 million who had inhabited the city prior to the Second World War. Leningrad's population was now more rural and less skilled than before. Although

Table 13.1   Membership in Leningrad city Party organization, 1939–1954 (on January 1)

Date	Full Members	Candidate Members	Total Membership
1939	100,610	29,972	130,582
1940	114,591	36,737	151,328
1941	117,745	34,048	151,793
1942	61,842	12,386	74,228
1943	30,305	13,588	43,893
1944	35,363	14,280	49,643
1945	56,982	14,269	71,251
1946	95,217	16,452	111,669
1947	156,047	23,100	179,147
1948	176,741	22,677	199,418
1949	189,511	17,318	206,829
1950	196,664	13,915	210,579
1951	200,213	14,935	215,148
1952	204,071	16,658	220,729
1953	207,545	15,967	223,512
1954	219,965	8,696	228,661

Source: S.S. Dmitriev et al., Leningradskaia organizatsiia KPSS, 70. See also B. Ruble, The Russian Review, 42, 3, July 1983, 309.

other Soviet cities experienced similar post-war trends, the consequences for Leningrad proved far greater than elsewhere. The highly disciplined and technologically advanced workers of whom Leningrad politicians had been so proud in the past had been swamped by yet another wave of migrants from the countryside. These changes were sufficiently large that they cannot be explained solely by the 632,253 civilian deaths cited in official Soviet publications. More people undoubtedly died during the blockade than Soviet statistical handbooks acknowledge. Moreover, a large percentage of the half-million evacuees probably never returned to live in Leningrad. The city may have survived the war, but not necessarily with its pre-war population intact.

The transformation of the city's political elite

Changes within the city's governing elite were, if anything, even more dramatic than those that were taking place within the population at large. During the first two years of the war, the membership of the Leningrad Party organization dropped by nearly 75 per cent (see Table 13.1). This decline occurred at a time when the national Party membership increased, so that, by the end of World War II only 2 per cent of the All-Union Communist Party (Bolshevik) membership hailed from Leningrad, as opposed to some 10 per cent when Kirov was

Table 13.2   Leningrad Party membership as a percentage of national Party membership, 1917–1971 (selected years)

Year	*(On January 1)* Percentage
1917 [On October 1]	16.6
1927	8.1
1934	10.3
1939	5.7
1941	3.9
1946	2.0
1952	3.3
1956	3.8
1966	3.3
1971	3.1

Source: S. S. Dmitriev *et al.*, *Leningradskaia organizatsiia KPSS, v tsifrakh, 1917–1973 gg.*, Leningrad, Lenizdat, 1974, 70; N.A. Petrovich *et al.*, *Partiinoe stroitel'stvo*, 62. See also B. Ruble, *The Russian Review*, 42, 3, July 1983, 310.

assassinated in 1934 (see Table 13.2). Such developments eroded Leningrad's pre-war political power base, a base that had helped to sustain the city as an active center in Soviet society throughout the 1920s and 1930s.

While the relative weight of Leningrad Party membership within the national Communist Party organization declined, the composition of the Leningrad Party itself also underwent considerable change. For example, 54,000 of the 153,531 Leningrad Party members on 1 July 1941 left for the front almost immediately following the outbreak of hostilities.[12] By January 1943, death rolls contained the names of 13,000 Party members, and Party membership plummeted to 43,893.[13] Between 1943 and 1945, 21,608 new members joined the city's Communist Party.[14] Moreover, many of the 368,416 recruits, who joined the Party on the Leningrad front during the war, remained in the city,[15] so that two-thirds of all the members of the Leningrad city Party organization in 1947 had not been in the Party when fighting broke out.[16]

The makeup of Party leadership councils was altered even more than that of Party membership at large. In September 1952, 663 of 759 delegates elected to the Eleventh Regional Party Conference had been elected to such a gathering for the first time, as had 91 of 99 alternate delegates.[17] Regional Party First Secretary V.M. Andrianov, who had been brought in from Sverdlovsk in 1949 to supervise a massive purge of the Leningrad Party, reported to that gathering that more than 2,000 Party leaders (in addition to another 1,500 state, trade union, and *Komsomol* officials) had advanced in rank during his brief tenure in office.[18] In October 1952, Andrianov told the Nineteenth Party Congress

Table 13.3   Composition of Leningrad City and District Soviets, 1939 and 1947 (percentage)

Category	1939	1947
Educational background		
Higher education	41.0	54.5
Secondary education	30.0	25.2
Primary education	29.0	20.3
Age		
29 or younger	23.2	4.6
30–39	48.7	30.0
40–49	19.9	47.2
50 or older	8.2	18.2

Source: Z.V. Stepanov (ed.) *Ocherki istorii Leningrada*, 38–9. See also B. Ruble, *The Russian Review*, 42, 3, July 1983, 313.

in Moscow that such advancement proved necessary as a result of the previous distortion of ideological work in Leningrad that had led to 'toadyism and servility' in personnel practices.[19] One can assume, then, that the new incumbents had benefited from the involuntary departure of their predecessors.

Municipal government institutions proved no more stable than those of the Party. In May 1944 the Leningrad City Soviet convened for the first time since the war began. Less than one-third of the soviet's deputies attended as 708 of 1,037 council members were either dead or still at the front.[20] When, in 1947, a new city soviet as well as fourteen new district soviets met for the first time, their deputies were, as a group, older and better educated than their pre-war counterparts (see Table 13.3).

Uncertainty within local political institutions accelerated following the death of former Leningrad Party First Secretary, Andrei Zhdanov, in August 1948, as his major rivals, Giorgii Malenkov and Lavrenti Beria, set in motion a large-scale purge of Zhdanov's associates and protégés in Leningrad and beyond. Before the end of March 1949, nearly every senior Leningrad Party official had been removed from his post, never to be seen again. By September 1952, more than one-quarter of all primary Communist Party committees in Leningrad changed secretaries with perhaps as many as 2,000 other officials losing their jobs as well.[21] This purge of local political elites consumed a leadership cohort that had sustained the city's political power base throughout much of the 1920s and 1930s. Subsequent Leningrad leaders may have been present in the city during the late 1940s; for the most part, however, the Leningrad political elite of the 1960s and 1970s did not enter active political life until after these purges, known as the Leningrad Affair, had run their course.

The Leningrad Affair makes a sharp demarcation in the city's political history, one which completed a process of political decline begun with the transfer of the national capital to Moscow in 1918. The discontinuities in the Leningrad population and in the city's political life undermined the remaining vestiges of the city's heritage as an active center in Russian and Soviet cultural and political development. Throughout the 1940s and in large part because of the destruction of the war, Leningrad was coming to resemble other Soviet provincial centers more than it resembled Moscow. This break with the pre-war past becomes ever more evident as one examines changes in the Leningrad economy brought about by the war's destruction.

The transformation of the city's economic base

If, in 1913, 12 per cent of the country's gross industrial output was produced in Leningrad, only 10 per cent was produced in the city in 1940 and merely 7 per cent in 1960.[22] This relative decline occurred despite a steady and, at times, rapid absolute increase in the city's productive capacity (see Table 13.4). By 1969, for example, Leningrad industry would produce as much in one week as local industry had produced in the entire year of 1928.[23] This diminishing relative importance of the Leningrad economy on the national scene was accompanied by perhaps more pernicious phenomena as the once diverse Leningrad industrial complex became ever more specialized. Such specialization constrained opportunities for the spontaneous interaction of diverse social and economic forces, which many urbanists suggest make great cities great.[24] As a result, Leningrad ceased to function as an economic charismatic center and came increasingly to resemble other specialized Soviet provincial economic centers.

In 1945, the Regional Party First Secretary, Aleksei Kuznetsov, reported to the USSR Supreme Soviet that 75 per cent of the city's industrial equipment had been evacuated or destroyed during the war.[25] At the same time, the city's gross industrial output in 1945 fell to just 32 per cent of the 1940 levels.[26] Meanwhile, as discussed previously, the qualifications of local industrial workers declined sharply.[27] In certain key sectors, the reduction of productive capacity was enormous. In 1945, for example, Lenergo (the organization responsible for the city's power supply) was able to generate only 22.9 per cent of its 1940 kilowatt capacity.[28] Remarkably, the city's overall industrial output managed to surpass pre-war levels as early as 1950.[29] From the available data it now appears that this achievement was accomplished through the abandonment of the previous productive capacity in a variety of industrial sectors with an accompanying specialization in a more limited range of economic activity.

The policy of local economic specialization emerged during the Fourth Five-Year Plan period (1946–50) as economic planners emphasized the city's shipbuilding and modern machine-building sectors at the expense of other formerly important local industries. On the positive side,

Table 13.4 Production of selected industrial products, USSR and Leningrad, 1940, 1950, and 1955

Product	1940		1950		1955		Leningrad % of USSR		
	USSR	Leningrad	USSR	Leningrad	USSR	Leningrad	1940	1950	1955
Hydroturbines, thousands of kwt	207.7	200.2	314.9	159.0	1491.9	839.0	96.4	50.5	56.2
Generators for hydroturbines, thousands of kwt	154.6	154.6	258.0	196.9	1413.0	889.0	100.0	76.3	62.9
Spinning frames for cotton, units	1109.0	520.0	1958.0	676.0	1990.0	506.0	46.9	34.5	25.4
Passenger cars, units	1051.0	315.0	912.0	221.0	1751.0	311.0	30.0	24.2	17.8
Cotton cloth, billions of meters	3954.0	129.0	3899.0	156.0	5904.0	234.0	3.3	4.0	4.0
Woollen cloth, billions of meters	119.7	5.3	155.2	7.3	251.0	11.6	4.4	4.7	4.6
Hosiery, millions of pairs	485.4	79.8	472.9	47.0	771.5	62.4	16.4	9.9	8.1
Knitted goods, millions of units	183.0	24.0	197.5	20.8	430.1	36.7	13.1	10.5	8.5
Leather footwear, millions of pairs	211.0	34.6	203.4	27.2	274.5	30.4	16.4	13.4	11.1
Rubber footwear, millions of pairs	69.7	39.9	110.4	50.1	131.1	64.1	57.2	45.4	48.9
Paper, thousands of tons	812.0	57.3	1193.0	73.0	1862.0	81.2	7.1	6.1	4.4
Confectionery goods, thousands of tons	790.0	91.3	993.0	85.1	1382.0	102.0	11.6	8.6	7.4
Soap (40 per cent equivalent)	700.0	97.9	816.0	95.0	1075.0	108.6	10.0	11.6	10.1

Sources: *Narodnoe khoziaistvo SSSR, 1956*, 55–9; *Narodnoe khoziaistvo goroda Leningrada, 1957*, 22–7.

Table 13.5 Relative increase in productivity of selected branches, 1940, 1950, and 1960

Economic branch	1940 (1913 = 1)		1950 (1913 = 1)		1960 (1913 = 1)	
	USSR	Leningrad	USSR	Leningrad	USSR	Leningrad
Gross output of industry	7.7	12.0	1.7	1.3	5.2	3.6
Chemical and petrochemical industry	17.5	7.4	2.0	0.9	7.7	3.1
Machine-construction industry	29.6	22.0	2.1	1.5	9.0	5.6
Light industry	4.7	9.0	1.1	1.0	2.8	2.2
Food industry	3.8	6.8	1.0	0.9	2.3	1.7

Sources: *Narodnoe khoziaistvo SSSR, Iubileinii statisticheskii ezhegodnik*, Moscow Statistika, 1972, 132–3; *Leningrad i Leningradskaia oblast' v tsifrakh. Statisticheskii sbornik*, Leningrad, Lenizdat, 1971, 23.

Table 13.6　Structure of Leningrad industry in 1960 (percentage of total)

Branch	Output	Quantity of workers	Capital funds
Iron and steel industry	2.6	2.5	6.0
Non-ferrous metallurgy	1.2	0.6	0.8
Power plants	0.5	0.5	8.4
Metal-fabricating industries	35.1	49.8	56.3
Chemical industry	8.1	6.2	6.0
Wood-working and paper industry	3.1	4.0	2.7
Building-materials industry	1.6	2.0	3.5
Light industry	24.2	21.5	6.9
Food industry	18.4	5.5	5.5

Source: Ia. A. Lavrikov, E.V. Mazalov, *Leningradskaia promyshlennost' i ee rezervi*, 1960, 15.

Leningrad industry came to specialize in such technologically intensive industries as radio-electronics, radio-technics, optics, precision machine tools, and the like. Indeed, many of the city's oldest, largest and most important industrial establishments such as the famous Kirov, Elektrosil and Metal factories underwent extensive modernization.[30] At the same time, some traditional Leningrad industries developed at a slower rate than they had previously in Leningrad and expanded at a slower rate than the same industry was then growing nationally (see Table 13.5). Gross output in light and food industries in Leningrad in 1940, for example, had been 9 times and 6.8 times above their 1913 levels while the analagous indices for the national light and food industries were only 4.7 times and 3.8 times respectively. In the post-war period the correlation between the rates in Leningrad light and food industries and in the national branches were reversed, so that by 1960 both Leningrad industries were at or below the national average rate of production increase. In the final analysis, the significance of both sectors within the economic structure of Leningrad diminished substantially (see Tables 13.6 and 13.7).[31]

The process of specialization occurred not only among industries but within individual economic sectors as well. In the crucial metalworking industry, Leningrad's production of electric-power equipment, metal-working, machine tools and communication equipment expanded throughout the first fifteen years after the war at a rate nearly two times faster than did the city's production of transportation machinery, hoisting and conveying machinery, and equipment for light industry.[32] Intersector and intrasector specialization combined to simplify the city's economic base and, in so doing, restricted its role in the national economy. This reduction in the scope of local economic activity appears to have been the result of a conscious policy decision, one which may have been beneficial in the short run immediately following the war as it

Table 13.7 Output of selected Leningrad industries, 1956

Industry	1956 as percentage of 1940	1950
All branches	259	203
Machine-construction industry	353	241
Power plants and supply	103	166
Chemical industry	231	240
Rubber industry	195	206
Wood-working and paper industry	194	180
Building-materials industry	575	257
Tailoring industry	164	180
Textile industry	191	184
Leather, footwear and fur industries	142	167
Food industry	141	160

Source: *Narodnoe khoziaistvo goroda Leningrada*, 1957, 18.

·facilitated the return to pre-war aggregate production levels. Over the long run, however, the impact was profoundly negative for the overall health and vitality of the city. During the First and Second Five-Year Plans (1928–37), Leningrad had received approximately 5 per cent of all investment in the Soviet economy. During the postwar Fourth Five-Year Plan (1946–50), the city's share of national economic investment was reduced to 2.5 per cent despite obvious and critical needs for postwar reconstruction funds. Even the 2.5 per cent investment level was not sustained during the 1950s as Leningrad's share of national economic investment fell to 1.9 per cent during the Sixth Five-Year Plan (1956–60) (see Table 13.8). Such policies insured that Leningrad would no longer rival Moscow as an economic center, much as the evolving character of the Leningrad political elite discussed previously guaranteed that the northern capital would no longer challenge Moscow politically. Leningrad – socially, politically and economically – was coming to increasingly resemble other Soviet provincial centers while Moscow emerged as the single charismatic center in Soviet life.

The transformation of the city's scientific base

Any discussion of Leningrad's loss of stature during the first half of the twentieth century would remain incomplete without mention of its lost primacy in science and education. On the eve of the First World War, St Petersburg remained the unchallenged national academic center. Over the course of the next half-century or so, the city's general academic stature eroded as Leningrad became an important, yet profoundly provincial, scientific axis. This relative decline occurred despite signs of

Table 13.8   Investment in the national economy, 1918–1960

Plan period	USSR (billions of rubles)	Leningrad (billions of rubles)	Leningrad as percentage of USSR
1918–August 1928	4.4	0.1	2.3
First Five-Year Plan (September 1928–1932)	8.8	0.4	4.5
Second Five-Year Plan (1933–1937)	19.7	0.9	4.6
Third Five Year-Plan (1938–June, 1941)	20.4	0.6	2.9
War period (July 1941–1945)	20.5	0.4	2.0
Fourth Five-Year Plan (1946–1950)	47.4	1.2	2.5
Fifth Five-Year Plan (1951–1955)	89.8	1.8	2.0
Sixth Five-Year Plan (1956–1960)	168.0	3.2	1.9

Sources: *Narodnoe khoziaistvo SSSR za 60 let*, 1972, 432; *Leningrad i Leningradskaia oblast' v tsifrakh*, 1971, 63.

aggregate growth. The number of scientific research organizations in Leningrad increased from 23 in 1914 to 141 in 1937.[33] Meanwhile, the national scientific and educational capacity was expanding at an even faster rate, so that, for example, Leningrad's educated population came to represent a shrinking percentage of the educated population of the Soviet Union as a whole (see Table 13.9). These trends, already apparent prior to the outbreak of World War Two were accelerated during the post-war period.

The underlying causes of Leningrad's academic demise extend far beyond the impact of the war upon the city's scientific community. The most important single event in an extended process of deterioration most certainly remains the transfer of the USSR Academy of Sciences' headquarters to Moscow in 1934.[34] Even after that transfer, however, Leningrad remained the Soviet Union's most prominent educational and university research center (see Table 13.10). Moreover, Leningrad's loss of stature is attributable in part to the emergence of a genuinely national scientific and educational infrastructure for the first time in Russian (and Soviet) history.[35] In the final analysis, then, Leningrad's academic decline has been as much relative as absolute.

Such developments do not make the impact of the Second World War upon the city's scientific base negligible. The evacuation of educational and scientific research institutions during the blockade was more total

Table 13.9 Numbers of specialists with higher and technical education in national economy, 1913, 1940, and 1955 (without servicemen)

Years	Higher education			Technical education			Total		
	USSR (000s)	Leningrad (000s)	Leningrad as percentage of USSR	USSR (000s)	Leningrad (000s)	Leningrad as percentage of USSR	USSR (000s)	Leningrad (000s)	Leningrad as percentage of USSR
1913	136	22	16.2	54	8	14.8	190	39	15.8
1940	908	75	8.3	1492	47	3.2	2400	122	5.1
1955	2184	114	5.2	2949	85	2.9	5133	199	3.9

Sources: *Leningrad za 50 let, 1967, 77; Narodnoe khoziaistvo SSSR, 1956, 193.*

Table 13.10   Research assignments made by RSFSR People's Commissariat of the Enlightenment, by discipline and location, 1935

| | Percentage | | | |
| | Moscow | Leningrad | Other | Number of assignments |
Discipline				
Mathematics	35	38	27	244
Mechanics	35	53	12	98
Physics	26	37	37	308
Astronomy	42	43	15	209
Chemistry	29	37	34	326
Geography	36	46	18	80
Geology	0	20	80	54
Paleontology	0	65	35	23
Petrography	0	47	53	19
Mineralogy	0	63	37	16
Chrystography	0	100	0	5
Mineral sciences	41	23	36	70
Microbiology	80	15	5	97
Botany	19	14	67	184
Genetics	36	16	48	25
Zoology	38	32	30	241
Histology	43	43	14	37
Physiology	26	70	4	186
Anthropology	100	0	0	18
History	25	75	0	99
Linguistics	0	100	0	90
Psychology	62	38	0	64
Party history	0	100	0	46
Total	31	42	27	2539

Sources: Upravlenie universitetov i nauchno-issledovatel'skikh uchrezhdenii NKP RSFSR; *Svodnyi plan nauchnogo-issledovatel'skii rabot institutov i kafedr universitetov NKP RSFSR na 1935 g.*, in Blair A. Ruble, 'The expansion of Soviet science', 542.

than that of industry. Once the blockade was lifted, most academic establishments were reconstituted in Leningrad, although there is scattered evidence that the new institutions were not necessarily staffed by returning Leningrad scholars.[36] Indeed, it appears that once hostilities had ceased, many prominent and productive researchers either remained at their new institutions in the east or chose to move to the now dominant Moscow academic community (a process which has continued).

Had the diminution of Leningrad's scientific and educational capacity occurred in isolation, its impact upon the city's general well-being need not have been devastating. However, occurring as it did in concert with the other areas of decline discussed above, the reduction of the city's stature as an academic center only contributed to a larger process of disintegration. In this manner, the transformation of the city's scientific base resulting from the war, while far less dramatic than the other spheres of urban life examined here, none the less proved to be profoundly damaging to Leningrad's status among Soviet urban centers.

Conclusion

By the late 1950s, Leningrad appeared to have more than recovered from the impact of the Second World War. The city's population had finally surpassed its pre-war level and the economic output rose far in excess of previous performance records. Yet, Leningrad's visible health obscured deeper, long-term, destructive patterns of urban development which had been either initiated or exacerbated by the city's harrowing experience during the war. Leningrad's vaunted work-force had lost much of its historic competitive edge, created by formerly high skill levels in relation to other Soviet industrial centers. Its previously powerful political machine had been crushed, only to be replaced by a far less potent local Party elite. The city's economic base had lost ground in relation to the rest of the Soviet economy while individual industrial sectors began to experience absolute decline in addition to the general pattern of comparative decrescendo. Finally, Leningrad's academic community relinquished national prominence to Moscow and now found itself in competition in specific disciplines with newer scientific centers developing in Novosibirsk and some of the larger republican capitals. In short, behind the restored neoclassical facades along the Nevskii, the Moika, and the Fontanka emerged an increasingly provincial urban center. The city had little but pretense to compete with against Moscow, which had, by then, emerged as the Soviet Union's sole charismatic center. Leningrad, for its part, became, more simply, second city.

   The war and the immediate post-war period proved to be decisive for the pattern of decline just described. Despite the loss of many important functions to Moscow during the 1920s and 1930s, Leningrad had remained a direct competitor to the Soviet capital in numerous other spheres. Both physically and psychologically, the war destroyed much of the city. Perhaps even more important in the long run, the war's destruction provided an excuse for anti-Leningrad leaders in Moscow (who, after all, emerged as predominant in the wake of the Leningrad Affair) to justify the diminution of Leningrad economic and academic capacity. Leningrad's former preeminence could now be destroyed through simple inaction as opposed to requiring direct force. By not rebuilding secondary economic sectors, for example, central economic planners insured that Leningrad's economic base would diminish in national stature annd significance. The end result has been that, to a considerable degree, Leningrad has never recovered from the impact of World War II.

Notes

1 Leon Goure, *The Siege of Leningrad: August, 1941–January, 1944*, New York, McGraw-Hill, 1964, 239.
2 V.A. Kamenskii and A.I. Naumov, *Leningrad. Gradostroitel'nyi problemy razvitiia*, Leningrad, Stroiizdat, 1977, 144; N.S. Aleshin *et al.*, *Leningrad. Entsiklopedicheskii spravochnik*, Moscow, Bol'shaia Sovetskaia Entsiklopediia, 1957, 134; and E. Bubis, G. Popov and K. Sharligina, *Optimal'noe perspektivnoe planirovanie kapital'nogo remonta i rekonstruktsii zhilishnogo fonda*, Leningrad, Stroiizdat, 1980, 42.
3 Clifford Geertz, 'Centers, kings, charisma: reflections on the symbolics of power', in Joseph Ben-David and Terry Nichols Clark (eds) *Culture and Its Creators*, Chicago, Ill., University of Chicago Press, 1977, 150–71, 309–14.
4 Official data identify a low population of 639,000 in March 1943 as well as 554,000 evacuees and 632,253 civilian deaths. These figures account for approximately 1.8 million persons in a pre-war population of 3.2 million. L. Goure, *The Siege of Leningrad*, 239; Harrison E. Salisbury, *The 900 Days: The Siege of Leningrad*, New York, Harper & Row, 1969, 513–18.
5 L. Goure, *Siege of Leningrad*, 239; 'Iz letopisi sobytii', *Leningradskaia panorama*, 1982, 6, 7.
6 V.A. Ezhov, 'Izmeneniia v chislennosti i sostave rabochikh Leningrada v poslevoennyi period (1945–1950gg.)', *Vestnik Leningradskogo universiteta, seriia istorii, iazyka i literatury*, 2, 1966, 15–21.
7 ibid., 19.
8 G.M. Romanenkova, 'Sotsial'no-ekonomicheskie posledstviia demograficheskogo razvitiia', in N.A. Tolokontsev and G.M. Romanenkova (eds) *Demografiia i ekologiia krupnogo goroda*, Leningrad, Nauka, 1980, 54–5; TsSU SSSR, *Itogi vsesoiuznogo perepisi naseleniia 1970 goda*, Moscow Statistika, 1972, vol. 2, 5–11, tables 1–2.
9 See, for example, N. Shiktorov, 'Ukrepim obshchestvennyi poriadok i bezopasnost' v Leningrade', *Leningradskaia pravda*, 23 October 1945, 2–3.
10 P.S. Popkovo, 'Rech' na plenume Leningradskogo gorkoma VKP (b). 28 dekabriia 1946 goda', *Leningradskaia pravda*, 1 January 1947, 2–3.
11 V.A. Ezhov, 'Izmeneniia v chislennosti i sostave rabochikh', *Vestnik Leningradskogo Universiteta seriia istorii, iazyka i literatury*, 2, 1966, 15–21.
12 S.S. Dmitriev *et al.*, *Leningradskaia organizatsiia KPSS v tsifrakh, 1917–1973 gg.*, Leningrad, Lenizdat, 1974, 39–45.
13 ibid.
14 ibid., 74–5.
15 S.P. Kniazev, 'Kurs na vosstanovlenie posle sniatiia blokady (1944–1945 gg.)', in Institut istorii partii Leningradskogo obkoma KPSS—Filial Instituta Marksizma-Leninizma pri TsK KPSS, *Ocherki istorii Leningradskoi organizatsii KPSS, Chast' II: noiabr' 1917–1945gg.* Leningrad, Lenizdat, 1968, 649.
16 S.S. Dmitriev *et al.*, *Leningradskaia organizatsiia KPSS*, 45–51.

17 N.A. Romanov, 'Doklad predsedatelia mandatnoi komissii', *Leningradskaia pravda*, 25 September 1952, 3.

18 V.M. Andrianov, 'Doklad sekretariia Leningradskogo oblastnogo komiteta VKP (b)', *Leningradskaia pravda*, 28 September 1952, 2–4. Frol' Kozlov repeated the 2,000 person figure in his report to the Nineteenth Party Congress the following month (F.R. Kozlov, 'Rech', *Leningradskaia pravda*, 16 October 1952, 3).

19 V.M Andrianov, 'Rech', *Leningradskaia pravda*, 9 October 1952, 3–4.

20 A.R. Dzeniskevich, V.M. Koval'chuk, G.L. Sobolev, A.N. Tsamutali and V.A. Shishkin, *Nepokrennyi Leningrad*, 2nd edn, Leningrad, Nauka, 1974, 455.

21 In September 1952, City Party Committee Secretary A.I. Alekseev indicated to a city party conference that 1,213 officials had been appointed in recent months to primary party posts. Later, Alekseev noted that there were 4,230 such primary party organizations (A.I. Alekseev, 'Doklad sekretariia Leningradskogo gorodskogo komiteta VKP (b)', *Leningradskaia pravda*, 23 September 1952, 2–3). At the subsequent regional party conference, Regional Party First Secretary V.M. Andrianov referred to 2,000 new officers having been appointed during his brief tenure in Leningrad, a figure repeated by Regional Party Second Secretary Frol' Kozlov at the Nineteenth Party Congress, a month later ('Doklad tov. Andrianova, [28 September 1952] 'Rech' tov. Kozlova', 16 October 1952).

22 Planovaia komissiia ispolkoma Lengorsoveta and Statisticheskoe upravlenie goroda Leningrada. *Leningradskaia promyshlennost' za 50 let*, Leningrad, Lenizdat, 1967, 6; and other estimates calculated on the basis of Soviet data by Edward Bubis. Unfortunately, totally reliable economic data for Leningrad during and following the war are not available. Therefore, one must compare the relatively more reliable data for the 1930s and 1950s to determine how the Leningrad economy might have performed and developed throughout the decade of the 1940s.

23 N.B. Lebedeva *et al.*, *Partiinaia organizatsiia i rabochie Leningrada*, Leningrad, Lenizdat, 1974, 44.

24 See, for example, Jane Jacobs, *The Economy of Cities*, New York, Vintage Books, 1970.

25 A.A. Kuznetsov, 'XI sessiia Verkhovnogo soveta soizuza, 1-ogo sozyva, preniia po dokladu o Gosudarstvennom biudzhete SSSR na 1945 god. Rech', *Leningradskaia pravda*, 28 June 1945, 2.

26 Ia. A. Lavrikov and E.V. Mazalov, *Leningradskaia promyshlennost' i ee reservy*, Leningrad, Lenizdat, 1960, 9.

27 *Leningrad. Entsiklopedicheskii spravochnik*, 134; *Leningradskaia promyshlennost' za 50 let*, 27.

28 *Leningradskaia promyshlennost' za 50 let*, 29.

29 *Leningrad, Entsiklopedicheskii spravochnik*, 135.

30 *Leningradskaia promyshlennost' za 50 let*, 29.

31 For a discussion of subsequent changes in the Leningrad economic structure, see Blair A. Ruble, 'Romanov's Leningrad', *Problems of Communism*, November-December 1983, 36–48.

32 Statisticheskoe upravlenie goroda Leningrada, *Narodnoe khoziaistvo goroda Leningrada. Statisticheskii sbornik*, Moscow Gosstatizdat, 1957, 20.

33 I. Osipov, *Leningrad i Leningradskaia oblast' za XX let Sovetskoi vlasti*, Leningrad, Lenoblizdat, 1973, 37.

34 *Leningrad. Entsiklopedicheskii spravochnik*, 411–412.
35 Blair A. Ruble, 'The expansion of Soviet science', *Knowledge: Creation, Diffusion, Utilization*, 2, 4, June 1981, 529–53.
36 Several regional educational and research institutions east of the Urals, for example, trace their origins to the evacuated academic institutions of the war period; ibid.

References

Alekseev, A.I., 'Doklad sekretariia Leningradskogo gorodskogo komiteta VKP (b)', *Leningradskaia pravda*, 23 September 1952, 2–3.
Aleshin, N.S. *et al.*, *Leningrad. Entsiklopedicheskii spravochnik*, Moscow, Bol'shaia Sovetskaia Entsikopediia, 1957.
Andrianov, V.M., 'Doklad sekretariia Leningradskogo oblastnogo komiteta VKP (b)', *Leningradskaia pravda*, 28 September 1952a, 2–4.
_____ 'Rech', *Leningradskaia pravda*, 9 October, 1952b, 3–4.
Ben-David, Joseph and Terry Nichols Clark (eds) *Culture and Its Creators*, Chicago, Ill., University of Chicago Press, 1977.
Bubis, E., Popov, G. and Sharligina, K. *Optimal'noe perspektivnoe planirovanie kapital'nogo remonta i rekonstruktsii zhilishnogo fonda*, Leningrad, Stroiizdat, 1980.
Dmitriev *et al.*, *Leningradskaia organizatsiia KPSS v tsifrakh, 1917–1973 gg.*, Leningrad, Lenizdat, 1974.
Dzeniskevich, A.R., Koval'chuk, V.M., Sobolev, G.L., Tsamutali A.N., Shishkin, V.A., *Nepokrennyi Leningrad*, 2nd edn, Leningrad, Nauka, 1974.
Ezhov, V.A., 'Izmeneniia v chislennosti i sostave rabochikh Leningrada v poslevoennyi period (1945–1950 gg.)', no. 2, in *Vestnik Leningradskogo universiteta, seriia istorii, iazyka i literatury*, 1966, 15–21.
Goure, Leon, *The Siege of Leningrad: August 1941–January, 1944*, New York, McGraw-Hill, 1964.
Institut istorii partii Leningradskogo obkoma KPSS—Filian Instituta Marksizma-Leninizma pri TsK KPSS, *Ocherki istorii Leningradskoi orgranizatsii KPSS, Chast' II: noiabr' 1917–1945 gg*, Leningrad, Lenizdat, 1968.
'Iz letopisi sobytii', *Leningradskaia panorama*, 6, 1982, 7.
Jacobs, Jane, *The Economy of Cities*, New York, Vintage Books, 1970.
Kamenskii, V.A. and Naumov A.I., *Leningrad. Gradostroitel' nyi problemy razvitiia*, Leningrad, Stroiizdat, 1977.
Kozlov, F.R., 'Rech'', *Leningradskaia pravda*, 16 October 1952, 3.
Kuznetsov, A.A. 'XI sessiia Verkhovnogo soveta soiuza, 1-ogo sozyva, preniia po dokladu o Gosudarstvennom biudzhete SSSR na 1945 god. Rech', *Leningradskaia pravda*, 28 June 1945, 2.
Lavrikov, Ia. A. and Mazalov, E.V., *Leningradskaia promyshlennost'i ee rezervi*, Leningrad, Lenizdat, 1960.
Lebedva, N.B. *et al.*, *Partiinia organizatsiia i rabochie Leningrada*, Leningrad, Lenizdat, 1974.
Petrovich, N.A. *et al.*, *Partiinoe stroitel'stvo*, Moscow, Politizdat, 1976.
Planovaia komissiia ispolkoma Lengorsoveta and Statisticheskoe upravlenie goroda Leningrada, *Leningradskaia promyslennost' za 50 let*, Leningrad, Lenizdat, 1967.
Popkov, P.S., 'Rech'', *Leningradskaia pravda*, 1 January 1947, 2–3.

Romanov, N.A., 'Doklad predsedatelia mandatnoi komissii', *Leningradskaia pravda*, 25 September 1952, 3.

Ruble, Blair A., 'The expansion of Soviet science', *Knowledge: Creation, Diffusion, Utilization*, 2, 4, 1981, 529–53.

_____ 'Romanov's Leningrad', *Problems of Communism*, November-December 1983, 36–48.

Salisbury, Harrison E., *The 900 Days: The Siege of Leningrad*, New York, Harper & Row, 1969.

Shiktorov, N. 'Ukrepim obshchestvennyi poriadok i bezopasnost' v Leningrade', *Leningradskaia pravda*, 23 October 1945, 2–3.

Statisticheskoe upravlenie goroda Leningrada, *Narodnoe khoziaistvo goroda Leningrada*, Moscow, Gosstatizdat, 1957.

_____ *Leningrad i Leningradskaia oblast' v tsifrakh. Statisticheskii sbornik*, Leningrad, Lenizdat, 1971.

Stepanov, Z.V. (ed.) *Ocherki istorii Leningrada*, Leningrad, Nauka, 1970.

Tolokontsev, N.A. and Romanenkova, G.M. (eds) *Demografiia i ekologiia krupnogo goroda*, Leningrad, Nauka, 1980.

Tsentral'noe statisticheskoe upravleniia SSSR. *Narodnoe khoziaistvo SSSR. Statisticheskii sbornik*, Moscow, Gosstatizdat, 1956.

_____ *Itogi vsesoiuznogo perepisi naseleniia 1970 goda*, Moscow, Statistika, 1972a.

_____ *Narodnoe khoziaistvo SSSR za 60 let. Iubileinii statisticheskii sbornik*, Moscow, Statistika, 1972b.

Upravlenie universitetov i nauchno-issledovatel'skikh uchrezhdenii NKP RSFSR *Svodnyi plan nauchnogo-issledovatel'skii rabot institutov i kafedr universitetov*, Moscow, Narkompros RSFSR OGIZ UchPEDIGIZ, 1935.

14

World War II and Social Change in Germany

Mark Roseman

I

At first sight, total war would seem likely to have had a greater impact on Germany between 1939 and 1945 than any war on any other nation. Surely the war waged by Germany was the most total ever? Was it not a German, Josef Goebbels, who, alone of all the statesmen involved in World War II, presented a total war not as a necessary evil but as something heroic and desirable: *'Wollt ihr den totalen Krieg?'* And surely the Germans experienced the destructive capacity of modern war as intensively as any people has ever done? Yet if this is so, it is striking how little of the historical research concerned with social change in Germany has concentrated solely on the war years or on the impact of war. The emphasis has been on the Nazi period as a whole; 'fascism' or 'Nazism', rather than 'total war', have been seen as the transformative experience for German people.[1]

Why is this? One point is, of course, that when democracy re-emerged in West Germany after the war it did so to a society for whom total war was merely one of a series of powerful shocks. Democracy was suspended in Germany not, as in Britain, simply by five or six years of war but twelve years of fascism and a further four of occupation. So to understand the new features of post-war society it will not do to look at the war alone. In addition, many German observers, whether explicitly or implicitly, have seen war and wartime measures essentially as a continuation of the Nazis' pre-war policies. In the German context, therefore, analysis of the impact of total war must be accompanied by at least some investigation of the changes wrought by the Nazis before 1939 and by the Occupying Powers after 1945. This is a truly massive subject, and one on which a lot of the research remains to be done. In the present chapter, which can do little more than touch on some of the most important issues, attention is focused on two aspects of German society. One is social policy in a broad sense. It has been frequently argued that total war irrevocably advances the frontiers of state intervention in society and encourages social reforms and social engineering; the question is to what extent and as a result of what factors this applies to Germany both during and after the war. The other aspect is the position of the working class in West German society. If there is one striking contrast between the Weimar and Bonn republics it is the absence in the latter of the tensions and polarization of the former, the diminution of class-conflict and the disappearance of left- and right-wing radicalism. To what extent – that is the question here – were fascism or war responsible for this change?

II

When the war came to Germany in 1939, its impact on National Socialist policy was rather limited. True, the call-up proceeded relatively quickly and by May 1940 over 4 million men had been called to arms. But in general the outbreak of war did not precipitate major changes in the state's role in society.[2] One reason for this was that many of those features of wartime experience – particularly the mobilization of society and economy – that were novel in, for example, Britain and the USA had already been implemented or at least prefigured by the six years of Nazi rule prior to 1939. Germany had, as it were, already experienced a rather 'total' peace.

Consider the example of industrial relations. In both World Wars, the advanced industrial nations have felt obliged, with greater or lesser degrees of consultation or coercion, to intervene in the relations between capital and labour. The primary motivation has been to prevent strikes that might endanger vital production and to ensure that wage settlements are in alignment with established economic priorities. In Germany, the state had already arrogated the necessary powers to itself in 1933 and 1934. The unions were forcibly dissolved and state commissioners, '*Treuhänder der Arbeit*', appointed to fix wage levels.

Beyond industrial relations, the Four-Year Plan in 1936 created the machinery and procedures to institute widespread controls over the economy. Although, as we now know, there were many limits to the competence and coherence of the Four-Year Plan organization, it is a fact that before war broke out in 1939, Germany's occupational structure, investment activity and raw materials allocation had already undergone substantial modification in preparation for the needs of war.[3] Many analysts speak of a 'peacetime war economy' (*Kriegswirtschaft im Frieden*). Apart from the specific achievements of the Four-Year Plan, there were other signs of a general encroachment of the state economy. Compulsory labour directions were implemented in the 1930s; there was the *Reichsarbeitsdienst* for young men and a compulsory year's work on the land for young women. The result was that the outbreak of war required far fewer new measures than in the democracies – the relationship of state and society had been sufficiently redefined, liberty sufficiently curtailed already.

Many of these changes, particularly the restrictions on group and individual liberty but also, to a certain extent, the organizing of economic life were not designed primarily to meet the needs of a future war. It is not in dispute that the Nazis in general and Hitler personally gave military and economic preparations for a war high priority; the notion of an eternal struggle between nations was central to Hitler's ideology. And what the advance calculation of military requirements certainly did do was to ensure that those anti-modernist elements of the National Socialist programme which initially hindered rearmament – the support given to the small businessman and the farmer, for example – were speedily removed. But elsewhere the role of war preparations is less direct. The increasingly intimate co-operation between the state and leading industrialists in planning and controlling the economy manifested (and encouraged) a grander conception which it was intended should outlast any future conflict. With growing clarity, leading industrialists and Nazis promulgated the notion of a highly centralized and organized economy, an authoritarian corporatism, which it was intended should provide a German rival to American-style capitalism.[4] Similarly, the Nazis' attack on the parties, the unions and political liberties (which, of course, went far beyond what the Western Allies deemed necessary for their war effort) was designed to consolidate the Nazis' power in peacetime and to impose the Führer-Prinzip on both politics and the economy. The Nazis certainly hoped and believed that society thus remodelled would be effective at waging war. Nevertheless, the changes implemented by the Nazis were intended to be permanent, creating a new order in peace as well as war.

It is therefore hard, and perhaps also unnecessary, to determine how far the extension of state activity and the mobilizing of society and economy before 1939 were a sign that war was already asserting itself in peacetime and how far they manifested other National Socialist goals and ideals. Having said that, there is no doubt that from 1936 onwards the direct impact of the rearmament drive became ever more obvious as armaments and autarky projects absorbed ever greater resources and the occupational structure of the labour force shifted towards war production.

The other key reason for the lack of change in 1939 was that, as most historians agree, Germany waged a far from total war, at least until 1942.[5] In the field of economic mobilization, from having been so far ahead in 1939, the Nazis were slow to consolidate their control. If the economy prior to 1939 was the 'peacetime war economy', the economy between 1939 and 1942 was just as much the 'wartime peace economy' (*friedensähnliche Kriegswirtschaft*). For example, it was not until the labour registration law of January 1943 that the Nazis laid the basis for total mobilization of labour – and even then the full potential of the law was never exploited. Similarly, it was not until 1942–3 that the Nazis began to ensure that industry was thoroughly combed for inessential employment. Particularly in the first half of the war (although in fact throughout the war years) Germany harnessed its population to the war effort less effectively than Britain or the USA.[6]

The limits to wartime mobilization can in part be explained by the fact that, for the first two years of the war, Germany pursued a type of campaign brilliantly suited to its state of half-preparedness. The strategy of lightning war was a deliberate attempt to avoid the need for armament in depth. But, as is well known, Germany was not properly prepared even for the *Blitzkrieg*. The three-week campaign against Poland in 1939 completely exhausted the supply of spare parts and key munitions. Germany in 1939 presents the curious picture of a nation in which centralized planning and the reorientation of society and economy to wartime needs was already well advanced and yet one in which basic requirements for sustained military effort were lacking.[7]

Another part of the explanation is that the Nazis were unwilling to impose too many sacrifices on the population. This was already apparent before the outbreak of war when, particularly after 1936, the economy began to overheat and suffered from an ever more acute labour shortage. Despite the absence of trade unions, key labour groups were able, on an individual basis, to exploit their scarcity value and negotiate wage increases, a tendency which the Nazis did not resist, despite the costs involved to the war effort.

Once the war started, the Nazis remained very sensitive to public opinion. During the first two years of the war, a whole series of government measures were attempted which were then withdrawn completely or only very half-heartedly implemented. As late as 1943 moves, for example, to revise piece-work rates in order to stimulate higher productivity were made very half-heartedly.[8] Even when new rates had been determined they were often not implemented. The Nazis' reluctance to upset the established wage structure stemmed from the fear that any change would open a Pandora's box of resentment about existing wage differentials. It is perhaps ironic, but certainly comprehensible, that Germany's fascist leaders felt less assured of their legitimacy and thus less able to mobilize society than were the democratic governments of the Western Allied powers.

In addition to the nervousness of the Nazis, there was also the fact that the confusing proliferation of competing authorities, special plenipotentiaries and powerful interest groups made the regime susceptible to a whole variety of pressures. For example, even before the war, the quest of the DAF (German Labour Front) for power had led it to espouse workers' demands and encourage the drive for higher wages.

Business interests found spokesmen at every level and were often able to oppose mobilization measures. Even when a policy had been decided upon by the body nominally responsible for a particular area, it was perfectly possible for it to be sabotaged by some other organization.[9]

In the case of the mobilization of women, these two factors were joined by a third: the reluctance of important sections of Nazi leadership to involve German women – the mothers of today and tomorrow – in the rigours of war production. The upshot was an amalgam of traditional cosy bourgeois views on women's place at the hearth and a new racist social-eugenic stress on the importance of optimum conditions for reproduction. One result of this ideology was that wives of enlisted men were given a very high income supplement, so that many stayed at home or even left former employment. All later attempts to reduce these supplements so as to encourage female employment failed in the face of ideologically motivated resistance and fear of a deleterious impact on soldiers' morale. As a result the number of German women in the economy actually fell between 1939 and 1941 and in 1942 was still lower than in the pre-war period. Whereas in 1943 almost two-thirds of British women were in employment, the equivalent figure for Germany was only 46 per cent.[10]

The regime's reluctance to extend or intensify social and economic mobilization at home encouraged it to exploit the occupied countries. They were to bear the full brunt of Nazi tyranny in order to protect the German population from the ravages and demands of war. Thanks to the massive confiscation of foodstuffs, manufactured and luxury goods abroad, living standards at home remained remarkably stable until towards the end of the war. After a drop in 1942, rations, for example, did not fall again significantly until the summer of 1944. Even more important than the importation of material resources was the recourse to foreign labour. By August 1944 there were over 7.5 million foreign workers on German soil, making up around one-quarter of all employees. By resorting to conscript labour, the Nazis were able to avoid or defer a whole range of unpleasant measures in relation to the German population such as the diversion of labour from inessential plants, enforced rationalization and retraining, the mobilization of women and so on.

The general point is that, for a variety of reasons, wartime social and economic policy relating to the *German* population was very often simply a continuation or a modest extension of peacetime policies. What the war did bring about, however, was the cessation or suspension of a number of social experiments in which the Nazis had been engaged during the 1930s. Not all of the Nazis' social engineering was sacrificed to the war effort; racial policy, as is well known, became more and more radical and there was also the continued reluctance to mobilize women. But, generally, social political goals were shelved for the duration. During the 1930s there had been, for example, various attempts to integrate the working class into the *Volksgemeinschaft*. Employers had been encouraged, particularly by the Nazi labour organization – the DAF – to improve their social policy provisions. Some employees had been given the chance to become owners of their own homes. Opportunities for upward mobility had been consciously created by the Nazi organizations. The Strength Through Joy movement had given considerable numbers of workers the chance to be tourists for the first time. All sorts of symbolic gestures had been made to indicate that the old class divisions no longer applied in the new Germany, the employers, for example, joining the DAF. But during the war, the DAF, though it continued to suggest possible post-war social reforms, became little more than an adjunct of the Nazis' productivity policy. It was no time for *sozialer Klimbim*.[11]

As the war drew on, the severity and intensity of the measures taken to sustain the war effort increased. The impetus came from the failure of the Russian campaign in the second half of 1941 which galvanized Hitler and the Nazi leadership to take mobilization more seriously. Hitler's directive, 'Armaments 1942', which appeared in January of that year, the appointment of Speer as Armaments Minister in February, and the elevation of the Gauleiter Fritz Sauckel to General Commissioner for Manpower, all indicated and encouraged the change in approach that was taking place. Between May 1941 and 1943, the number of industrial workers called to arms doubled; by mid-1944, 40 per cent of the industrial work-force had been enlisted. By then almost half of all German adult males were in the army or had died in combat. In the reorganization of the economy, the Nazis were much less successful than in the call-up and many of the restraints noted above continued to apply. Nevertheless, such measures as retraining labour for work in the armaments industry met with considerable success. A considerable, although not quantifiable, shift took place in the occupational and qualification structure of the German workforce. From mid-1942 onwards, Sauckel was increasingly effective at preventing undesirable, voluntary labour mobility, while at the same time labour direction increased and in the course of 1942 over a million German workers were transferred to war production. The mobilization of German women, on the other hand, remained half-hearted and brought only limited results.[12]

These policies were augmented and supported by the expansion of the police state as the strains of total war increased the Nazis' anxieties about their position. State terror became an increasing part of everyday life. By 1944, death sentences were being imposed on 14–16-year-olds. Between 1940 and 1943, the annual number of executions increased from 926 to 5,336. The Gestapo also took an ever more active role in enforcing discipline at work. In 1942, 7,311 workers were arrested by the Gestapo for breaches of labour discipline, but by 1944 the figure had risen to 42,505.[13]

The growing use of terror had yet another rationale. For alongside and sometimes in direct opposition to the mobilization of society's energies for the war effort, the Nazis were engaged in increasingly radical racist and imperialist policies. The war encouraged such policies in a number of ways. Wartime occupation provided, for the first time, the opportunity to create the European empire of which Hitler had already dreamt in the 1920s. Industry was quick to exploit the opportunities and comprehensive plans were drawn up in 1940–1 for the creation of a closed European economy, dominated by Germany. In the East, the occupation of vast tracts of Russian and East European territory allowed the Nazis to initiate their Utopian plans for racial resettlement and the subjugation of the Slavic peoples. The war against the Soviet Union exposed and unleashed that hatred of the Russians that was deeply ingrained in substantial sections of the military elite. The war also forced a new solution to what the Nazis regarded as the Jewish problem. It became impossible to get rid of the Jews through emigration and, in addition, the occupation of Poland presented the Germans with millions of additional Jews to dispose of. Under cover of war and unrestrained, as in the 1930s, by the desire to maintain goodwill in the West, competing Nazi agencies tried various means of removing the Jewish element culminating in the extermination camps.[14]

Much of this activity impinged on German society only indirectly, or only on small proportions of it: on those German minorities unlucky enough to be the victims; on the sections of the business, political and administrative elites involved in planning and extending the racial and economic empire; on the SS units charged with dirty work. It is true that most of the millions of German soldiers who at some point or other fought on the Eastern Front had at least some experience or involvement in National-Socialist policies towards Russians citizens, whether prisoners of war or civilians. How could they not? In the three months November and December 1941 and January 1942 alone, for example, *half a million* Russian POWs died in German captivity. A British investigation of German soldiers' wallets discovered that they generally contained three categories of photo: mother and girlfriend, pornographic, and atrocities.[15] Yet such experiences, important, shocking or brutalizing though they may have been, were usually short-lived episodes and had no systematic character.

The one area of Nazi racial policy which did involve the extended participation of a substantial proportion of the German population was the use of conscript labour. In its scope and social impact, this was unquestionably the most significant innovation in domestic wartime policy. At the beginning of the war, substantial sections of the leadership had been hostile to the use of large numbers of foreign workers on German soil. Some had been concerned about the threat to internal security, others about the implications for national hygiene and racial purity. Yet from the early months of the conflict, labour shortages combined with the resistance to total mobilization of the German population made pressing the recruitment of foreign labour. Once this had been acknowledged, all those sections of the Nazi leadership that had viewed the use of foreign labour with suspicion now set to work to create the conditions which would avert the ostensible dangers of employing racially inferior foreigners and would remind the German population of its role and responsibility as the racial elite of Europe. As the number of different nationalities amongst the conscript labour grew, the Nazis developed an ever more complex and comprehensive hierarchy of rules which dosed payment, nutrition, freedom, living standards and severity of punishment according to the racial 'calibre' of the group involved and their status as civilians or POWs. German workers were drawn into a series of complex relationships with the forced labour. It was a deliberate aim of the Nazis to make the workers active participants in the regime's racist and imperialist policy, to practise in *Kleinformat* in the factory that racial imperialism which would be enacted on a grand scale in Europe after the war.[16]

In their forced labour policy as in many other of their wartime measures it is evident that the solutions adopted to the problems posed by the war were influenced as much by pre-existent features of the Nazi regime as by any inherent characteristics of total war. The Nazis' imperialist and racial ideology, their ruthlessness but also their insecurity all left an indelible stamp on wartime policy. And after 1945, when the Nazis had fallen, it was the continuities, the specifically National Socialist elements in wartime policy, which left an abiding impression on German and foreign observers alike.

III

Total defeat, when it came, provided the opportunity to create a new society. The war had so drained Germany's military, social and psychological resources that the way was open for the victorious powers to reshape the nation as they wished. This is clearly manifested by Soviet occupation policy which, in the space of a few years, totally reorganized society and economy within its influence. In the Western Zones, however, the underlying trend was restorative. A capitalist democracy was created on the same lines as Weimar. True, the new constitution was more overtly federalistic, most of the major parties had experienced some change in identity and a change of name, and the economy was subjected to a certain amount of decartelization and reorganization. Yet there was a great deal of institutional and even personal continuity. In politics and the labour movement, the leaders of the Weimar era returned to their former positions. In industry and administration only a few top Nazis were removed, otherwise there was little change.[17]

The war had little positive influence on economic and social policy in the post-war era. In many Western countries, the close involvement of the state in wartime mobilization created a precedent for continued involvement in peacetime economic affairs and for a more managed economy generally. In such cases, wartime not only enlightened the state as to the role it might play in the economy but also increased the 'fiscal capacity' of the nation – i.e. the psychologically acceptable proportion of national income appropriated through taxation. In Germany, war's impact was rather the reverse. With the support of the USA, a school of economic thought became dominant which argued from the experience of Weimar and fascism that both political and economic stability depended on the vigorous removal of all constraints on free market activity. Cartels were to be broken up, all state bureaucracies removed and taxation was not to be used for demand management. For these theorists, wartime experience simply underlined the negative character of a state-run economy. Industrialists too had grown more wary than ever of state intervention as a result of the war; industrial figures who were too closely associated with Albert Speer, for example, found it hard to gain positions in post-war industry. The result was that the post-1948 economy was less cartelized and concentrated than in Weimar years, with far less state intervention.[18]

In most spheres of social policy, too, the war had only limited impact, often serving merely to underline anxiety about an interventionist state. It had, of course, created a number of new, though temporary, problems for the legislators, above all that of integrating and compensating the expellees. But war did not stimulate or promote innovative solutions or responses to established social problems. In health and pensions policy, in housing and in education, the authorities returned to the established practices of the pre-war era. It is well known that in Britain, victory brought considerable pressure for social reform in the aftermath of both World Wars, I and II, but in Germany the idea of making a 'home fit for heroes' hardly applied. The nation was far too concerned to restore the basic features of normal life to attempt major innovations in social policy. In the chaotic conditions of the immediate post-war period, the authorities chose to focus on familiar and established practices. In any case, whatever Germany's politicians and citizens thought in private, it was not possible in the early post-war years to celebrate Germany's soldiers as returning heroes, nor could they harbour any expectations of reward for their military service.[19]

Some innovations from the *pre-war* fascist period survived into the post-war era, particularly when they had themselves built on achievements or developments of Weimar. The promotion of owner-occupied homes in the 1930s, for instance, was considerably extended in the 1950s. The reconstruction of German towns was much facilitated by the extended powers the planners had gained under the Nazis. The 1950s saw a flowering of the type of company social policy so beloved of the DAF. But on the whole, neither fascism nor war left many positive institutional or political legacies in the post-war period.

On the other hand, there is no doubt that the general attitudes towards both democracy and labour on the part of Germany's administrative and managerial elites had been profoundly affected by the experience of fascism. One of the most reactionary elements of Germany's elite, the *Junker*, had been completely eliminated from the political scene by Nazi purges and the Soviet Occupation. And for the rest, the excesses of the fascist state and the proximity of the Soviet threat combined to create a new awareness of the attractiveness of the Western democratic model, of the need to avoid extremes, of the virtues of a representative political system and the desirability of institutionalized collective bargaining. In other words, what was new was not the institutions – they had been largely created in Weimar – but the commitment to these institutions of those whose job it was to run them and work within them.

IV

What was the impact of war on the wider German population and on the working class in particular? We should start by looking at the effects of the Nazis' attempts to control, mobilize and reshape German society during the 1930s.

The first point must be that by 1939 Germany had become a repressive society, full of fear and suspicion. The majority of the population were not overtly subject to direct terror. But everyone knew certain things were best left unsaid, actions best left undone. Through analysis of dreams, through the exaggerated fervour with which Germany's middle classes threw themselves into their private amusements, we can detect the undercurrent of fear that ran through German society. Workers in particular had to be careful, former activists were sent in hundreds of thousands to concentration camps, the individual workers were isolated and political communication became too dangerous in all but the most close-knit of neighbourhoods.[20]

At the same time it was a society that seemed to be working again. That feeling of being on the brink of disaster that had haunted much of the 1920s and early 1930s was replaced by a new confidence in the social order. Criminality seemed to be decreasing. After the war, even left-wingers and liberals felt bound to acknowledge that the Nazis had appeared capable and purposeful, harnessing social energies in a productive way. The Nazis drew respect from almost all sections of the population for the skill and finesse with which they organized public spectacles and for their success in getting the economy to work.[21]

It was also a society in which class relationships were visibly changing. Though changes in class composition were far from dramatic, there is evidence that mobility from manual to white-collar positions increased considerably in the 1930s.[22] Furthermore, quite a number of workers, particularly youngsters in the Hitler Youth, experienced a sort of informal upward mobility outside work by taking on positions of responsibility in Nazi organizations. The status hierarchy had been made more complicated: party ranking offered an alternative status calibration. In addition, the Hitler Youth, sports groups and other organizations were, to a certain extent, able to bring the classes together. Everywhere there was the characteristic and peculiar mixture of Führer-Prinzip and egalitarianism. There are indications that Nazi policy, in conjunction with the spread of mass culture through radio and the cinema, was beginning to change the younger workers' social and self-perceptions. For instance, young miners in the Ruhr abandoned the traditional Sunday dress of an open-necked shirt and cap and opted for the collar and tie. In a small way, they were manifesting the weakening of a working-class subculture and a desire to be citizens in the wider community.[23]

Yet the Nazis were clearly far from winning the loyalty and obedience for which they had hoped. The accelerated rearmaments programme, though it initially benefited from the way the Nazis had disciplined and terrorized the labour movement, actually began to undermine the Nazis' control and integration strategy. The increasing demands placed on the labour force and the awareness of their own power in the tight labour-market led to growing criticism of the regime and a new aggressiveness in wage and other demands. Absenteeism increased and productivity suffered while wages in key economic sectors drifted upwards. By 1939, there were signs that the Nazi labour strategy was crumbling into a familiar pattern of (albeit informal) wage bargaining and material gratification.[24]

These trends and patterns were initially little affected by the outbreak of war. For substantial sections of the population, particularly those not subjected to military call-up, it took a long time for war to make significant changes in their way of life. New features of wartime, such as rationing, had little impact on the general standard of living; real wages held up until 1944. In 1943 there was official opposition to the idea of introducing an evacuation programme for women and children because, it was argued, this would be to disrupt a private sphere hitherto little affected by the war.

For many of those on the home front, it was only in 1942 and 1943 that the war began to bite, partly because of intensified mobilization, but even more because the destructive and disruptive capacity of war began to reach home. German casualties rose steeply in the course of the Russian campaign after two years of relatively bloodless combat. In the beginning of 1942, consumers were shocked by a sudden fall in rations. True, they then revived somewhat and stabilized until the closing months of 1944. But other articles began to run short and everyday life became increasingly dominated by shortages. In the winter of 1942–3, for example, areas outside the coal-producing districts received less than a third of their coal requirement. It was above all the increasingly frequent and intensive air raids that disrupted every aspect of normal life. In 1943 there were three times as many bombs as in 1942, and in 1944 five times as many as in 1943. Travel became difficult and time-consuming after bombs disrupted public transport. Many families became homeless. For all this, there was as in Britain, a determination to go on living as normal a life as possible and it was only in the closing months of 1944 that the normal fabric of social life began to disintegrate.[25]

One important effect of the war was to maintain and indeed increase the comparatively high level of geographical and social mobility of the 1930s. On the home front, while most labour directions did not involve moving home, a considerable number of workers found themselves drafted to new areas. Many women and children in the big cities were evacuated to rural communities. For enlisted men, of course, there was a great deal of travel involved. Many accounts of the first years of the war sound – until they reach the Eastern Front – very much like recollections from an extended holiday, a welter of vivid scenes and impressions from strange and colourful countries; the parallel with tourism extends even to the cheap bargains that were to be had at the exchange rates imposed by the Nazis.[26] To paraphrase Clausewitz: war as the continuation of tourism by other means. Much of this mobility was of a temporary nature, yet it seems to have had some long-term significance for those groups which had previously been rather self-enclosed and isolated: the rural communities and also substantial sections of the working class. The war extended the way in which the Nazis in peacetime had already begun – through the media, tourism and mobilization – to break through the barriers of local consciousness.

At the same time economic mobilization during the war created new job opportunities and the chance of upward mobility. Retraining programmes, for example, enabled a considerable number of unskilled or semi-skilled workers to obtain a new qualification and better rates of pay. The army itself offered considerable opportunities for advancement. Such advances were not always easily transferable to the civil sphere but in practice a good war career proved advantageous at most levels of the post-war job market. For the many workers who became non-comissioned officers and the few who went further, holding positions of authority and responsibility was often a new and important experience which was to inform post-war behaviour.[27]

The influx of foreign forced labour created a form of collective upward mobility for German workers. Since foreigners made up one-quarter of the work-force by the end of the war, many German employees now found themselves elevated to the position of overseers and foremen. In some cases, solidarity developed, particularly where German workers were training their own replacements, as it were, before being sent off to the front. In such cases, the unwilling draftees had an interest in making the training proceed as slowly as possible and needed the foreign trainees' help in doing so. But in general, the Nazis were successful in actively involving an increasing number of German workers in the control and repression of the forced labour. From interviews we know that many workers did perceive their new responsibility as a sort of promotion and, just as for their counterparts in the army, the experience of authority was often a significant and lasting one. These experiences of formal and informal social mobility reinforced those of the pre-war period.[28]

At the same time total war meant the intensification of repression and terror and strengthened the tendency to withdraw into the private sphere and to remain guarded and non-committal in public. The individual was isolated and social groups became fragmented.

Another consequence of the war was that labour's attitude to work and the firm begins to shift. Whereas in the late 1930s discontent manifested itself in climbing rates of absenteeism, the war years see astonishingly stable levels of productivity and absenteeism despite increasingly unfavourable conditions. The more disordered everyday life became, the more attractive was the dependable regularity of the work itself. Even for the conscript labour, the work-place became increasingly a sort of haven and from 1943, the productivity of Russian labour actually rose, amidst deteriorating conditions. For a number of reasons, the interests of labour and employers moved closer together. Both had an interest in protecting plant from call-up and from labour transfers. German labour was given a new role as overseers of the foreign conscripts. And as the employers saw defeat approaching, many were at pains to mend bridges with the labour force.[29]

In general we can say that the war undermined the Nazis' own appeal while reinforcing many of the social changes which they had initiated in the 1930s. It was the increasingly obvious hopelessness of the war that cost the Nazis the last remnants of what limited support they had enjoyed amongst German labour. Yet through isolation and terror, through collective and individual mobility and through the forging of new loyalties and solidarities, the war confirmed the Nazis assault on class traditions.

As the conflict approached its conclusion, all these changes paled increasingly in relation to the fight to survive. From the autumn of 1944 gas and electricity supplies were often missing for large stretches of time in the major cities. In the following spring rations fell below starvation levels. Sybil Bannister wrote in her book, *I Lived under Hitler*, that 'Within a few months, with the Allies advancing on all sides, town-dwellers were reduced from a finely organised community to primitive cave-dwellers'. And for the troops, the initially comfortable war on the Western Front and in Africa had been replaced on all sides by an increasingly hopeless and bitter struggle.

In August 1944 the Red Army entered German territory for the first time and from December onwards the mass exodus of refugees from the East began. By the end of the war two-fifths of the German population were on the move – soldiers, evacuees, refugees, 'displaced persons' (d.p.'s), former Nazis and so on. Thus the major consequence of the war in the immediate post-war period was the hardship and dislocation that resulted from the destruction of the cities, from economic collapse and from the massive population mobility. The destruction itself was unbelievable. Over 50 per cent of housing in the big cities had been destroyed. Production fell to almost zero in April 1945. In 1946, production in the Western Zones still had not exceeded 25 per cent of pre-war figures. Rations remained little above starvation levels until 1948. For three years after the end of the war, life was one long struggle for the ordinary citizen.[30]

Though they dominated the immediate post-war period, the hardship and the disruption of normal life were shortlived. Malnutrition disappeared rapidly after 1948. By the mid-1950s unemployment was waning rapidly and living standards exceeded pre-war peaks by a comfortable margin. Enormous strides were made in the housing market. The speed of economic recovery was such as to restore a normal way of life within a few years.

The pace of recovery revealed that, destructive as the war had been, it had left the country's industrial capacity relatively undamaged. Despite bomb-damage and post-war dismantling, the value of industrial plant in 1948 was higher than in 1936. The supply of labour had been harder hit – no less than 25 per cent of the male population in the age range 35–50 had been killed by the war – yet here total war had created its own solution: the refugees and expellees from the East. By 1948 there were getting on for 20 per cent more people available for work in the Western Zones than there had been in 1936.[31]

On the back of economic recovery, the massive number of expellees – by 1950 there were 10,000,000 of them in West Germany – were integrated rapidly. Initially they faced severe problems of adaptation and were particularly hard hit by the high unemployment that followed the currency reform. Yet the tensions between the newcomers and the established community were for the most part temporary and the expellees were quick to find employment. Their party, the BHE, reached its highpoint in the 1953 election with less than 6 per cent of the vote and soon dwindled to insignificance.[32] In other words the destructive and disruptive impact of total war did not present post-war German society with problems it could not solve. Of greater long-term significance for the German working class were the subtler changes to perceptions, behaviour and relationships, above all the weakening of traditional class identities and antipathies which had been wrought by fascism and war.

Yet this is to look into the future. In the immediate post-war period there was good reason to believe that the working class would conform to the Weimar mould. The effect of the capitulation had been to create a power vacuum within Germany and the surviving leaders of the working-class movement were keen to realize that synthesis of parliamentary and economic democracy which had already been outlined by labour theoreticians in the Weimar era. The experience of fascism merely underlined the urgency of introducing such a system. True, the fascist experience also convinced the different political groupings within the trade unions of the need to form a united organization, an innovation which was to be realized in the following years. But otherwise the stage seemed set for a repeat of the political struggles of the post-World War I era. However the Allies saw to it that the goal of economic democracy was largely stifled. Labour was prevented from exploiting the collapse of authority within Germany. Just as important was the fact that it was not the German employers who prevented it from doing so. It was American power, American intentions and the clear dependence on US aid that made most labour leaders accept fairly rapidly that a capitalist restoration was inevitable. Here and elsewhere the effect of the Allies was to prevent the bitter conflicts between labour and capital that had resulted after 1918 and would otherwise probably have resulted after 1945.[33]

Once the Allies had restrained the reforming impulses of the immediate post-war period and helped to undermine the radical element in the working-class movement, it was Germany's labour leaders themselves who (often unwittingly) ensured that the depoliticization of everyday life and the diminution of working-class identity achieved by the National Socialists was sustained and strengthened. Nervous of the Communists, uneasy about recreating a divided society and sensitive to the criticism that as a mass organization they were liable to extremism, labour leaders were at pains to avoid rebuilding a conflict-oriented labour movement. The old workers' cultural organizations were not rebuilt, a concerted effort was made to keep politics out of industrial relations and a co-operative, conciliatory approach towards the employers was adopted. The Social Democrats moved towards the centre and tried to win a middle-class following.

Under these conditions, the integrative, depoliticizing tendencies of the Nazi era were able to survive into the post-war period. What emerged, as we know from many surveys in the 1950s, was a hard-working, consumer-oriented, sceptical and unpolitical working class. A strong suspicion of the bosses coexisted with the feeling that labour's status had collectively improved. The boom economy of the 1930s with its possibilities for individual advancement and the toughening experiences of soldiering and surviving the hardships of the Occupation years had encouraged in many workers a confidence in their ability to stand up to those in authority and to profit from the capitalist system. Such individual experiences and the chaos of the pre-1948 rationing system fostered a resigned acceptance of the capitalist system and a recognition of the need for continual rationalization and modernization of production. The language of class conflict lost much of its appeal and younger workers in particular did not even understand terms such as 'proletariat'. In their dress, leisure habits and taste younger workers differed little from their bourgeois counterparts. Despite large inequalities in wealth, German society was probably more culturally homogeneous than at any time before or since. In short, even before the economic miracle had had its effect, fascism, war and Allied policy had together created in the working class a far more solid social and ideological base for a democratic capitalist system than had existed in Weimar.[34]

V

It is evident that 'total war' is not an independent cause of social change. Its influence on German society was shaped decisively by the nature of the regime which waged it and that of the regime which followed it. It is true that certain features of the war would have impinged on society no matter what regime was in power. Any political system would have faced the need to mobilize all possible reserves of labour, materials and energy for the war effort. No regime could wish away the destructive capability of the enemy's weapons. But the way the Nazis responded to such challenges and opportunities and the way the Allies' post-war policies refracted and channelled the experiences and wishes that were the legacy of war were as important in shaping its impact as any such 'objective' features of war itself. This would be a point of lesser interest in a country where, as in Britain, the only changes in the political system were those brought about by the needs of war. But in Germany, the political discontinuities make it of crucial importance.

Partly because of these discontinuities, total war does not stand out as a revolutionary impulse in the way that it perhaps does in some other countries. Even where it stimulated or impelled the Nazis to introduce quite new policies, it is often the specifically National Socialist flavour of these measures that is striking and that carried the greatest potential for social change. In any case, war was slow to bring any changes at all. Many of the innovations necessary for a nationally co-ordinated and concerted war effort had been carried out already, in some cases in advance calculation of wartime requirements, in others because mobilizing society's energies for the national cause was a central goal of the National Socialists.

Nevertheless, the war did have a specific impact which differed from the preceding period. In the first place, it intensified the Nazi assault on established milieus, the fragmentation of social groups and the isolation of the individual. Second, for the German workers, the experience of destruction and dislocation and of common interests with the employers – *vis-à-vis* the Nazi state and later the Occupying Powers – prepared the way for the pragmatic acceptance of the capitalist system. Thus war was preparing the ground for Western Germany's return to capitalist democracy even before total defeat brought the fall of the Nazi regime.

Notes

1 Footnotes are intended to provide an indicative bibliography only and no attempt at comprehensive or systematic references has been made. For general accounts of social change in this period see David Schoenbaum, *Hitler's Social Revolution: Class and Status in Nazi Germany*, New York, 1966; Detlev Peukert, *Volksgenossen und Gemeinschaftsfremde: Anpassung, Ausmerze und Aufbegehren unter dem Nationalsozialismus*, Cologne, 1982; Werner Conze and M. Rainer Lepsius (eds) *Sozialgeschichte der BRD*, Stuttgart, 1983; R. Dahrendorf, *Society and Democracy in Germany*, London, 1968.
2 On wartime social policy see Marie-Luise Recker, *Nationalsozialistische Sozialpolitik im 2. Weltkrieg*, München, 1985. For labour policy specifically, see Wolfgang Werner, *Bleib übrig: Deutsche Arbeiter in der nationalsozialistischen Kriegswirtschuft*, Düsseldorf, 1983.
3 The most comprehensive account of German mobilization is Ludolf Herbst, *Der Totale Krieg und die Ordnung der Wirtschaft: Die Kriegswirtschaft im Spannungsfeld von Politik, Ideologie und Propaganda 1939–1945*, Stuttgart, 1982.
4 See Volker Berghahn, *The Americanisation of German Industry*, Leamington Spa, 1986, introduction.
5 For a view which places more emphasis on changes in the 1939–41 period, see Richard J. Overy, 'Hitler's war and the German economy: a reinterpretation', *Economic History Review*, XXXV, 2, 1982, 277–91.
6 See Recker, *NS Sozialpolitik* and Werner, *Bleib übrig*.
7 Timothy W. Mason, *Sozialpolitik im Dritten Reich: Arbeiterklasse und Volksgemeinschaft*, Opladen, 1977, passim.
8 Werner, *Bleib übrig*, pp. 220ff.
9 On the competition between the DAF and other elements of the Nazi regime, see for example, Gunther Mai, 'Warum steht der deutsche Arbeiter zu Hitler? Zur Rolle der Deutschen Arbeitsfront im Herrschaftssystem des Dritten Reiches', in *Geschichte und Gesellschaft*, 1986, 12, 2, 212–34.
10 On women in Nazi Germany see Jill Stephenson, *Women in Nazi Society*, London, 1975, and Dörte Winkler, *Frauenarbeit im 'Dritten Reich'*, Hamburg, 1977.
11 On social political initiatives towards labour see Schoenbaum, *Hitler's Social Revolution*, and the essays by Reulecke and others in Detlev Peukert and Jürgen Reulecke (eds) *Die Reihen fast geschlossen. Beiträge zur Geschichte des Alltags unterm Nationalsozialismus*, Wuppertal, 1981. See also Günther Mai, 'Warum steht der deutscher Arbeiter zu Hitler'.
12 Werner, *Bleib übrig*, esp pp. 277ff.
13 Richard Grunberger, *A Social History of the Third Reich*, Harmondsworth, 1971, contains a useful description of the impact of Nazi terror. A systematic account can be found in Hans Buchheim *et al.* (eds) *Anatomie des SS-Staates*, 2 vols, Munich, 1967.
14 See Berghahn, *Americanisation*, introduction; Hans Mommsen, 'Die Realisierung des Utopischen: Die Endlösung der Judenfrage im "Dritten Reich"', in *Geschichte und Gesellschaft*, 9, 1983, 381–420.
15 Grunberger, *A Social History*, p. 63.
16 The standard work on forced labour is now Ulrich Herbert, *Fremdarbeiter: Politik und Praxis des 'Ausländer-Einsatzes' in der Kriegswirtschaft des Dritten Reiches*, Berlin, Bonn, 1985.

17 For a good general discussion of the balance between restorative and innovative elements in the post-war settlement see Jürgen Kocha, '1945: Neubeginn oder Restauration', in Carola Stern and Heinrich August Winkler (eds) *Wendepunkte deutscher Geschichte 1848–1945*, Frankfurt, 1979, pp. 141–68.

18 See here Berghahn, *Americanisation*, passim.

19 See for instance Hans Günther Hockerts, *Sozialpolitische Entscheidungen im Nachkriegsdeutschland 1945–1947*, Stuttgart, 1980.

20 Detlev Peukert, *Volksgenossen und Gemeinschaftsfremde*, passim.

21 See Ian Kershaw, *Der Hitler-Mythos: Volksmeinung und Propaganda im Dritten Reich*, Stuttgart, 1980.

22 See the discussion of mobility in Josef Mooser, *Arbeiterleben in Deutschland 1900–1970*, Frankfurt/M, 1984, pp. 113ff.

23 On class and status, see Schoenbaum, *Hitler's Social Revolution*; Michael Zimmermann, 'Ausbruchshoffnungen: Junge Bergleute in den Dreißiger Jahren', in Lutz Niethammer (ed.) *'Die Jahre weiß man nicht, wo man die heute hinsetzen soll'. Faschismuserfahrungen im Ruhrgebiet* Berlin, Bonn, 1983, pp. 97–132.

24 These trends are well documented in Mason, *Sozialpolitik*.

25 See Werner, *Bleib übrig*, and Lutz Niethammer, 'Heimat und Front. Versuch, zehn Kriegerinnerungen aus der Arbeiterklasse des Ruhrgebietes zu verstehen', in Niethmammer (ed.) *Die Jahre weiß man nicht*, pp. 163–232.

26 See Niethammer, 'Heimat und Front'.

27 There is no satisfactory account of the impact of war-time experience on post-war labour. See Niethammer. 'Heimat und Front', and my Ph.D. thesis, 'New labour in the Ruhr Mines', Warwick University, 1987.

28 In addition to Ulrich Herbert's study referred to above, see also his essay 'Apartheid nebenan. Erinnerungen an die Fremdarbeiter im Ruhrgebiet', in Niethammer (ed.), *Die Jahre weiß man nicht*, pp. 233–66.

29 Both Herbert and Werner draw attention to the factory's role as a refuge. On employers' changing attitudes, see Günther Mai, 'Warum steht der deutsche Arbeiter zu Hitler', esp. p. 232. See also John Gillingham, *Industry and Politics in the Third Reich*, Methuen, 1985.

30 For an introduction to conditions after the war, see Manfred Overesch, *Deutschland 1945–1949: Vorgeschichte und Gründung der Bundesrepublik*, Königsten/Ts, 1979.

31 The standard work on the recovery is Werner Abelshauser, *Wirtschaft in Westdeutschland 1945–1948: Rekonstruktion und Wiederaufbaubedingungen in der amerikanischen und britischen Zonen*, Stuttgart, 1975.

32 For a good survey of recent work on the refugees, see Wolfgang Benz (ed.) *Die Vertreibung der Deutschen aus dem Osten: Ursachen, Ereignisse, Folgen*, Frankfurt/M, 1985.

33 An excellent introduction to the post-war labour movement is to be found in Lutz Niethammer, 'Rekonstruktion und Desintegration: Zum Verständnis der deutschen Arbeiterbewegung zwischen Krieg und kaltem Krieg', in Winkler (ed.) *Politische Weichenstellungen in Nachkriegsdeutschland 1945–1953*, Göttingen, 1979, pp. 26–43.

34 Among many other studies, see H. Popitz and P. Bahrdt, *Das Gesellschaftsbild des Arbeiters*, Tübingen, 1961; H. Schelsky, *Die skeptische Generation*, Düsseldorf, 1963; Helmuth Croon and K. Utermann, *Zeche und Gemeinde: Unter-*

suchungen über den Strukturwandel einer Zechengemeinde im nördlichen Ruhrgebiet, Tübingen, 1958; Frank Deppe, *Das Bewußtsein der Arbeiter: Studien zur politischen Soziologie des Arbeiterbewußsteins*, Köln, 1971. In English, see Angi Rutter, 'Elites, Estate and Strata: Class in West Germany since 1945; in Arthur Marwick (ed.) *Class in the Twentieth Century*, Brighton and New York, 1986, pp. 115–64.

Brief Guide to Further Reading

1 General History; Social Change

Berghahn, V.R., *Modern Germany*, London, 1982; second edition, 1987. (High-quality text book.)

Calvocoressi, Peter and Wint, Guy, *Total War: Causes and Courses of the Second World War*, revised edition, London, 1989. (Particularly useful for the military side.)

Clark, Martin, *Modern Italy 1871–1982*, London, 1984. (Very rich text book, strong on the post-1945 years.)

Dahrendorf, Ralf, *Society and Democracy in Germany*, London, 1986. (Celebrated example of a sociological approach to historical issues: discusses the effects of the 'revolution of modernity' on 'the German question'; adopts a conflict model of society.)

Lichtheim, George, *Europe in the Twentieth Century*, London, 1972. (Lichtheim was one of the leading authorities on Marxism; his generalizations have to be approached with caution, but he is strong on culture and science.)

Macmillan, James F., *Dreyfus to De Gaulle: Politics and Society in France 1898–1969*, London, 1985. (Very sound text book.)

Maier, Charles, 'The two postwar eras and the conditions for stability in twentieth-century Western Europe' together with comments and reply, *American Historical Review*, **86** (2), April 1981, pp. 353–67. (Interesting presentation and discussion of Maier's ideas extended so as to apply to the post-1945 era.)

Middlemas, Keith, *Politics in Industrial Society: the Experience of the British System Since 1911*, London, 1979. (Famous application of the corporatist thesis – associated in this collection with Feldman, and Maier – to Britain.)

Nove, Alec, *An Economic History of the USSR*, London, 1969. (Classic account thoroughly laden, despite the intractability of the sources, with statistical tables.)

Perkin, Harold, *The Rise of Professional Society: England Since 1880*, London, 1989. (The central thesis about the triumph of the professional class is controversial, but the general coverage of social change is excellent as is the attention to the effects of war.)

Roberts, John, *Europe 1880–1945*, revised edition, London, 1988. (The general history selected by the Open University A318 Course Team as being the most thorough and comprehensive for the study of war, peace and social change.)

Schmitt, Bernadotte E., *The World in the Crucible*, New York, 1984. (Slightly old-fashioned but comprehensive study of Europe and the First World War.)

Wright, Gordon, *The Ordeal of Total War 1939–1945*, New York, 1969. (Comprehensive study of Europe and the Second World War with a fair attention to war and social change.)

2 War, Revolution, Internal War

Conquest, Robert, *The Great Terror*, London, 1968. (A detailed study of the Stalin purges.)

Dunn, John, *Modern Revolutions: An Introduction to the Analysis of a Political Phenomenon*, Cambridge, 1972; second edition, 1989. (An important and stimulating introduction to the subject which ranges from Europe to the Third World.)

Ferro, Marc, *The Russian Revolution of February 1917*, London, 1977. *October 1917*, London 1980. (These two volumes constitute a thorough and important study of the Russian Revolution by one of France's leading historians.)

Fest, Joachim C., *The Face of the Third Reich*, London, 1970. (An attempt to understand the organization of a 'totalitarian' state by exploring the lives of its leaders.)

Gross, Jan T., *Revolution from Abroad: The Soviet Conquest of Poland's Western Ukraine and Western Belorussia*, Princeton, N J, 1988. (A very useful addition to the growing literature on Stalin's 'terror', particularly interesting since the lands considered here have been so little explored by historians in this context.)

Kershaw, Ian, *The Nazi Dictatorship*, London, 1985. (Rightly regarded as one of the best studies of an overworked period, it ranges widely over the Nazi control of Germany including popular responses to the regime.)

Leed, Eric J., *No Man's Land: Combat and Identity in World War I*, London, 1979. (Original work on how soldiers were themselves affected by waging war.)

Lincon, W.B., *Passage through Armageddon: The Russians in the War and Revolution*, New York, 1986. (A useful, up-to-date account.)

McInnes, Colin and Sheffield, Y.D. (eds), *Warfare in the Twentieth Century: Theory and Practice*, London, 1988. (Contains other important essays apart from the Beckett one reprinted in this collection.)

Peukert, Detlev J.K., *Inside Nazi Germany: Conformity, Opposition and Racism in Everyday Life*, London, 1989. (An important study of how the Nazi regime affected everyday life in Germany and how the regime itself dealt with those that it considered to be undesirable and/or deviant.)

Ryder, A.J., *The German Revolution of 1918*, Cambridge, 1967. (Still the best single-volume treatment of the German Revolution in English.)

Stone, Norman, *The Eastern Front*, London, 1974. (Classic account of the front too often neglected in British studies.)

Tannenbaum, Edward R., *The Fascist Experience: Italian Society and Culture 1922–1945*, New York, 1972. (Strong on social as well as political history.)

Watt, Richard M., *The Kings Depart. The Tragedy of Germany: Versailles and the German Revolution*, London, 1969. (A popular account, but thorough and highly readable.)

3 The Causes of Wars

Bell, P.M.H., *The Origins of the Second World War in Europe*, London, 1986. (A valuable introduction to, and assessment of, the current debate.)

Berghahn, V.R., *Germany and the Approach of War in 1914*, London, 1973. (One of a series of single-country studies of the origins of the First World War designed for students and providing an introduction to the current literature as well as analysis.)

Fischer, Fritz, *Germany's Aims in the First World War*, London, 1966. *War of Illusions: Germany's Policies from 1911 to 1914*, London, 1975. (These are the two volumes in which Fischer outlines in detail his challenging view of the German responsibility for the First World War.)

Joll, James, *The Origins of the First World War*, London, 1977. (An excellent introduction to the current debates and controversies, in the same series as the book by P.M. Bell.)

Keiger, John, *France and the Origins of the First World War*, London, 1977. (A helpful survey in the same series as Berghahn.)

Koch, H.W. (ed.), *The Origins of the First World War: Great Power Rivalry and German War Aims*, London, 1972. (A useful collection of readings on the Fischer debate.)

Lieven, D.C.B., *Russia and the Origins of the First World War*, London, 1983. (A very readable account of less well-known events, again from the same series as Berghahn.)

Martel, G. (ed.), *The Origins of the Second World War Reconsidered: The A.J.P. Taylor Debate after 25 Years*, London, 1986. (The debate rumbles on.)

Robertson, Esmonde M. (ed.), *The Origins of the Second War*, London, 1971. (Readings making a companion volume to Koch.)

Steiner, Zara S., *Britain and the Origins of the First World War*, London, 1977. (A study of the diplomatic and domestic pressures on Britain in the period immediately before the First World War; again from the same series as Berghahn.)

Taylor, A.J.P., *The Origins of the Second World War*, London, 1961. (A challenging, some would say infuriating, account of Hitler as a diplomat, and why Britain and France finally decided to oppose him over Poland.)

4 The Consequences of Wars

Addison, Paul, *The Road to 1945: British Politics and the Second World War*, London, 1975. (Authoritative study which demonstrates a shift to the left in British politics caused by the experiences of war.)

Becker, Jean-Jacques, *The Great War and the French People*, Leamington Spa, 1986. (Richly documented from the French local archives.)

Cadwallader, Barry, *Crisis of the European Mind*, London, 1981.

Cruickshank, John, *Variations on Catastrophe*, London, 1982. (Both of these books are concerned with the intellectual and cultural impact of the First World War).

Ferro, Marc, *The Great War*, London, 1973. (Particularly strong on the war's effects on attitudes and perceptions.)

Fussell, Paul, *The Great War and Modern Memory*, New York, 1975. (Widely praised study of the effect of the First World War on English literature.)

Hardach, Gerd, *The First World War*, London, 1977. (Marxist account which perceives few social consequences apart from the Russian Revolution.)

Harris, Frederick J., *Encounters with Darkness: French and German Writers on World War II*, New York, 1983. (Extremely useful.)

Kocka, Jürgen, *Facing Total War: German Society 1914 to 1918*, Leamington Spa, 1984. (Written philosophically, though not politically, from a Marxist perspective.)

Lask, Vera, *Women in the Resistance and the Holocaust: The Voice of Emptiness*, West Port, Connecticut, 1983. (One of the most important contributions in the growing literature on women's role in war.)

Marwick, Arthur, *War and Social Change in the Twentieth Century: A Comparative Study of Britain, France, Germany, Russia and the United States*, London, 1974. (A full statement of the ideas about war and social change referred to in Beckett's chapter.)

Marwick, Arthur (ed.), *Total War and Social Change*, London, 1988. (Essays by leading authorities on France, Britain, Germany, and Russia.)

-Milward, Alan, *War, Economy and Society, 1939–1945*, London, 1977. (One of several important studies by a distinguished economic historian.)

Smith, Harold L. (ed.), *War and Social Change: British Society in the Second World War*, Manchester, 1986. (Contains the fruits of much recent research; the editor insists strongly that the war had no effect on British society, but the individual essays do not always seem fully to support this contention.)

Waites, Bernard, *War and a Class Society 1910–1920*, Leamington Spa, 1987. (Authoritative study of changes affecting the working class.)

Wall, Richard, and Winter, J. (eds), *The Upheaval of War: Family, Work and Welfare in Europe, 1914–1918*, Cambridge, 1988. (Indispensable collection of thoroughly researched chapters by individual expert.)

Winter, J.M., *The Great War and the British People*, London, 1986. (Points to wartime improvements in British health and nutrition.

Index